CHERISHING MEN FROM AFAR

TCHIEN-LUNG, EMPEROR OF CHINA
who gave Audience to the British Embafsy in 1793
London Published as the Act directs July 18 1801 by J.Wilkes.

CHERISHING

MEN FROM AFAR

Qing Guest Ritual and the Macartney Embassy of 1793

James L. Hevia

Duke University Press
Durham and London   1995

Frontispiece: An impressionistic portrait of the Qianlong emperor probably taken from the paintings of William Alexander. Note the rendition of the audience ceremony places the emperor and the British ambassador on the same level, presumably asserting sovereign equality between Great Britain and China.

© 1995 Duke University Press
All rights reserved
Printed in the United States of America on acid-free paper ⊗
Typeset in Minion by Tseng Information Systems
Library of Congress Cataloging-in-Publication Data appear on the last printed page of this book.

For my parents and Judith

CONTENTS

Preface xi

1 *Introduction*

1.1 New Patterns in the Study of Imperialism 2

1.2 The Great Transition and China-centered History 7

1.3 The Tribute System and Its Critics 9

1.4 The Problem of Ritual 15

1.5 Beyond Symbolic and Functional Ritual 20

1.6 Considerations in the Organization of This Study 25

2 *A Multitude of Lords: The Qing Empire, Manchu Rulership, and Interdomainal Relations*

2.1 The Qing Empire in the Eighteenth Century 30

2.2 Multiple Centers, Multiple Powers 31

2.3 Qing Inner Asia 37

2.3.1 Manchu Rulership and Tibetan Buddhism 38

2.3.2 Encounters between Emperors and Lamas 42

2.4 The Coastal Frontier 49

2.4.1 East and Southeast Asian Kingdoms 50

2.4.2 West Ocean Kingdoms 52

3 *Planning and Organizing the British Embassy*

3.1 Introduction 57

3.2 The Letter from George III to the Qianlong Emperor 60

3.3 The Public Sphere and the Intellectual World of Lord Macartney 62

3.4 National Character 66

3.5 Discussions of Taste and Images of China 68

3.6 Ceremony, Sovereignty, and Diplomacy   74

3.7 From Diplomatic Ceremony to the Business of Diplomacy   80

3.8 From the Court of St. James to the China Coast   82

4 *King Solomon in All His Glory: The British Embassy in China*

4.1 The Naturalist's Gaze   84

4.2 First Encounters   90

4.3 Field of Play   96

4.4 The Audience Negotiations: Speaking the Public Sphere   97

4.5 The Gifts and British Manufactures   102

4.6 Macartney's Audience with the Qianlong Emperor   105

4.7 On to Business   108

4.8 Events in Peking   110

5 *Guest Ritual and Interdomainal Relations*

5.1 Locating Guest Ritual in Qing Imperial Discourse   118

5.2 The Metaphysics of Rites and Imperial Ritual   121

5.3 Lordship and Guest Ritual   125

5.4 Guest Ritual and the Constitution of Rulership   128

5.5 Ritual as Action   130

6 *Channeling Along a Centering Path: Greeting and Preparation*

6.1 Initial Contact: The Announcement and Request to Enter   134

6.2 Preparation for Reception   138

6.2.1 Mobilization of the Coastal Provinces   139

6.2.2 The Problem of the Investigation Ship   140

6.3 The British Gifts and Imperial Rewards   144

6.3.1 Landing the Embassy and Gifts   144

6.3.2 The Translation of the British Gift List   147

6.3.3 Emerging Concerns about the British Ambassador's Intentions   148

6.3.4 The Decision to Split the Embassy and Gifts   150

6.3.5 The Embassy Roster and Recommendations
about Imperial Bestowals 151

6.3.6 Initial Resolution of the Placement of the Gifts
at the Yuanming Gardens 152

6.4 Preparing the Embassy for Imperial Audience 155

6.4.1 First Meetings and Issues Surrounding Ceremonies in Tianjin 155

6.4.2 Displacement of the Tianjin Ceremony 159

6.5 Crisis in the Rite I: Mismanagement by Imperial Officials 160

6.6 Crisis in the Rite II: Reappraisal of the
British Ambassador's Intentions 163

7 *Convergence: Audience, Instruction, and Bestowal*

7.1 Alterations to Imperial Audience for the British Embassy 170

7.1.1 Adjusting the Ritual Process 170

7.1.2 Precedent and Innovation 170

7.2 Imperial Audience 172

7.2.1 The Guest Ritual Process and Imperial Audience 173

7.2.2 The British Audience 175

7.3 Imperial Intervention I: The Emperor's Poem 177

7.4 Imperial Intervention II: Bestowals 178

7.5 The Period of Grand Assembly and Feasting at Rehe 179

7.6 Crisis in the Rite III: Reevaluating the British Embassy 181

7.6.1 The Continued Inability of the Ambassador
to Understand Relations in the Rite 181

7.7 Imperial Instructions of September 23, 1793 184

7.7.1 The Emperor's Instruction to Officials on the Periphery 184

7.7.2 The Emperor's Instruction to the English Lord 187

7.8 Preparations for Departure and Further Assessments
of British Attributes 189

8 *Bringing Affairs to a Culmination*

8.1 The Emperor's Reply to Macartney's Six Requests   193

8.2 From Peking to Hangzhou: Songyun and Macartney   197

8.3 From Hangzhou to Canton: Changlin and Macartney   202

9 *Guest Ritual and Diplomacy*

9.1 Guest Ritual and the Fashioning of the Qing Imperium   212

9.2 Lord Macartney and Diplomacy   218

9.3 An Engagement   220

10 *From Events to History: The Macartney Embassy in the Historiography of Sino-Western Relations*

10.1 The British Embassy as Qing Precedent   226

10.2 The Macartney Embassy as British Precedent   229

10.3 The Koutou Question in Euro-American Discourse   232

10.4 The Qianlong Letter and the Tribute System Synthesis   238

10.5 From Routines of Empire to the Narrative Histories of the Nation-State   239

10.6 Horizons of History   244

Appendix   249

Glossary of Chinese Characters   253

Abbreviations   259

Bibliography   261

Index   285

PREFACE

The title of this book is taken from a phrase that recurs often in Qing court records. Cherishing men from afar is both a description and an injunction. As the pivot between the Cosmos and the earth, the emperor was morally enjoined to order the world. The sage ruler showed compassion and benevolence to those who were outside his immediate dominion; he cherished those who traveled great distances to come to his court. These notions were at the heart of rituals which organized relations between Qing emperors and other powerful rulers. This study, then, is about Guest Ritual and imperial audience, rites which I will argue were the idiom through which Qing foreign relations were conducted. I focus on an embassy from one such foreign ruler, that of the king of Great Britain, whose ambassador, George Lord Macartney, arrived at the court of the Qianlong emperor in 1793.

This book is a response to three issues related to the way the embassy has been treated in previous scholarship. The first arises from the critique of structural-functional systems theory that emerged in anthropology by the 1970s. This critical analysis of systems theory encouraged a rethinking of classic formulations like the "Chinese world order" and the "tribute system." The question that emerged was this: if the "tribute system" is removed, what does Sino-Western contact from the late eighteenth century forward look like?

The second problem, again stimulated in part by critical anthropology, had to do with the sociological treatment of ritual. I became convinced that the particular way in which ritual was thought about among Euro-American secular intellectuals had constructed Sino-Western conflict as a matter of cultural misunderstanding. The question that I have considered is in two parts: (1) What was the view of culture informing this interpretation? (2) What would conflict look like if it were set aside?

The third issue had to do with my own discomfort with the notions of sinocentrism and a sinocentric world order, particularly when one considered that the founders of the Qing dynasty, the Manchus, were not Chinese. These concerns led me to a third question: Suppose rather than treating European and Asian contact in terms of a dynamic and expansive West versus a stagnant and isolated East, the encounter was recast as one between two expansive imperialisms, the Manchu and British multiethnic imperial formations—what then would Qing and British interaction look like from the Macartney embassy forward? This book and a second now in the works are attempts to address these questions.

At various points in this study, I have separated the Qing and British accounts of the events of the embassy in order to emphasize the different modes of practice and different conceptual frameworks that Qing and British actors brought to the encounter. Following a critical introduction that considers other interpretations of Qing foreign relations, chapter 2 provides an overview of the Qing imperium and an introduction to aspects of Qing rulership, a topic explored with specific reference to Guest Ritual in chapter 5. Chapter 3 discusses the late-eighteenth-century cultural milieu in Great Britain and presents British perceptions of diplomacy, trade, and the understanding of China then current among Britain's intellectual aristocracy. Chapter 4 reexamines Lord Macartney's account of events leading up to and including imperial audience. Chapters 6 and 7 cover similar ground, but do so by considering the Qing record of the embassy through notions of ritual practice and Qing rulership. The Qing and British records of events after Macartney's audience are brought together in chapter 8. After summarizing some conclusions about the encounter in chapter 9, the final section reviews the career of the embassy in the historiography of Sino-Western relations.

This book also grew out of a dissertation project completed at the University of Chicago in 1986. Many intellectual debts were acquired in the years leading up to the completion of that manuscript, debts which for me have special significance because of the unusual graduate experience Chicago provided at the time. Between 1980 and 1985, it was something of a joke and only partly an exaggeration among graduate students in the humanities and social sciences that we taught each other. The unofficial graduate student seminars I attended regularly were held on a daily basis in various coffee shops around campus. Among the participants I most recall were Roger Bradshaw, Jeff Marti, Rafael Sanchez, Fred Chiu, and Naoki Sakai. John Calagione, Dan Nugent, and Ana Alonso appeared from and disappeared into field work, but when present, also taught me much. There were many others who drifted in and out of focus then as now.

During those years, I was also fortunate to meet a friend and colleague whose work has had a profound influence on my own. Angela Zito and I began comparing notes in earnest around 1982, coming to the remarkable discovery that not only were our class, ethnic, and academic backgrounds very similar, but that somehow independently of each other and certainly against the grain of certain trends within the field of Chinese studies, our intellectual projects had developed along similar lines. More importantly, Angela shared with me her broad understanding and extensive research into ritual texts such as the *Comprehensive Rites of the Great Qing* (DQTL), and taught me ways of reading them. To say that I am grateful for her extraordinary generosity is somewhat of an understatement.

While it may have felt as though we were teaching ourselves at Chicago, there were numerous professors pointing and guiding us in new and interesting directions. Before arriving at the university I was extremely fortunate to have been taught by Robert Himmer and E-tu Zen Sun, both of whom provided intellectual stimulation and endless reading lists for me to devour. At Chicago, Michael Dalby, Edward Ch'ien, and Susan Mann deserve special thanks for support, encouragement, and serious critical engagement. Ron Inden and Barney Cohn always found time to read and comment on what I was doing, and continue to do so. I am also grateful to David Roy, Guy Alitto, Tetsuo Najita, Harry Harootunian, Jean and John Comaroff, and Valerio Valeri, all of whom contributed to my intellectual development. Marshall Sahlins shared his interest in the subject of this book, and asked many prickly and stimulating questions. I also recall one or two formative conversations with Masao Miyoshi, whose book about the first Japanese embassy to the United States (*As We Saw Them,* 1979) came at a time when I was beginning to imagine this project.

I am particularly grateful to the History Department of People's University, Peking, especially to professor Ye Fengmei, for their willingness to sponsor me as an independent scholar in 1990–1991. It was through their auspices that I was able to work in the Number One Historical Archive in Peking. The staff at this archive was extremely kind and helpful, especially Yin Shumei, who more than once brought sources to my attention that were not part of the well-cataloged collection on the Macartney embassy. I am also grateful to the staff in the Rare Book collection of the Peking Library.

The staffs of the India Office Library, the British Museum, the Victoria and Albert Museum, the National Maritime Museum, and the Chinese collection of the Cambridge University Library were always gracious and helpful. Aubrey Singer and Frances Wood were kind enough to send me a copy of James Dinwiddie's memoir.

Since I left Chicago, I have met a number of scholars who have been kind enough to share insights and support. They include Greg Blue, Paul Cohen, Pamela Crossley, Arif Dirlik, Michael Hunt, Lionel Jensen, Lloyd Kramer, Susan Naquin, Evelyn Rawski, William Rowe, Nathan Sivin, Margaret Wiener, and John Wills. I owe a special debt of gratitude to Charlotte Furth, who showed an extraordinary degree of faith in me when it was sorely needed.

Tao Feiya and Jia Huanguang were an invaluable help with the finer points of translation. Adam Liu tutored me in Qing sources at the dissertation stage.

While in Peking at People's University in 1990–1991, I met a number of scholars, including Stephan Shutt, Nancy Park, Mark Elliot, Jim Millward, and Mellisa Macauley. Each of them contributed to different portions of this work, while also enriching my stay there.

I also wish to express special gratitude to Bruce Doar, Ann Stewart, Brad Strickland, Cathy Lutz, Donald Lopez, Tomoko Masuzawa, Penny Taylor, Tim Pettyjohn, and Don Nonini, all of whom commented on different portions of this manuscript in various stages of production.

Funding at the dissertation stage of this project was provided by the Humanities Division of the University of Chicago, which allowed me to visit London in 1983. The preparation of this manuscript was supported by a research grant from the Joint Committee on Chinese Studies of the American Council of Learned Societies and the Social Science Research Council with funds provided by the Chiang Ching-kuo Foundation. I also received a China Conference Travel Grant from the Committee on Scholarly Communication with China. The funds allowed me to attend the "Symposium Marking the Bicentenary of the First British Mission to China" in September 1993. To those who wrote letters of support and to the committees which made the final decisions on the grants, I am extremely grateful.

I would also like to thank Timothy Barrett and Liu Taotao for inviting me to London in 1992 for the British Association of Chinese Studies annual meeting held at the School for Oriental and African Studies. I was fortunate to meet a number of scholars with common interests, all of whom commented on my work. They include Peter Marshall, Robert Bickers, Craig Clunas, Pierre-Henri Durand, Roger Derrobers, Sylvie Pasquet, Verity Wilson, Bonnie McDougall, Aubrey Singer, Wang Tseng-tsai, and Zhang Shunhong.

This study exploits previous work, questions it, and occasionally feels uncomfortable using it, but at the same time acknowledges that without John Fairbank, E. H. Pritchard, John Wills, and J. L. Cranmer-Byng, my concerns would have remained ill formed. It is their extraordinary scholarship that I have tried to emulate.

Tani Barlow and Donald Lowe provided intellectual, practical, political, and gustatory comradeship.

Portions of this manuscript appeared in different forms and in slightly altered contexts in published articles. Chapter 3 appeared with some modification in "Oriental Customs and Ideas: The Planning and Execution of the First British Embassy to China," *Chinese Social Science Review,* 1994. Portions of chapters 2, 7, 9, and 10 appeared in the following: "Lamas, Emperors, and Rituals: Political Implications of Qing Imperial Ceremonies," *Journal of the International Association of Buddhist Studies;* "A Multitude of Lords: Qing Court Ritual and the Macartney Embassy of 1793," *Late Imperial China;* and "The Macartney Embassy in the History of Sino-Western Relations," in R. Bickers, ed. *Ritual and Diplomacy: The Macartney Mission to China.* Full citations are given in the bibliography.

Finally, Judith Farquhar tirelessly and enthusiastically read, commented upon, criticized, and labored over each draft of this manuscript. Since the words "thank you" seem only marginally sufficient acknowledgment of her contribution, perhaps the dedication will in some small way make the point for me.

1 INTRODUCTION

On the tenth day of the eighth lunar month in the fifty-eighth year of his reign, Hongli, the Qianlong emperor, received George Lord Macartney, ambassador of Great Britain, in audience at the Qing empire's summer capital in Rehe (present-day Chengde). Dressed in ordinary court audience robes, the emperor took his throne in a tent set up in the Garden of Ten-thousand Trees (Wanshu yuan), an audience site located within a larger complex called the "Mountain Retreat for Avoiding Summer Heat" (Bishu shan zhuang). Eager to demonstrate his regard for "oriental customs and ideas," the British ambassador wore a "rich embroidered velvet" coat, over which he displayed "the mantel of the Order of the Bath, with a collar, a diamond badge and a diamond star." On his head was a hat of enormous white plumes. Macartney approached the throne, and rather than performing the humiliating "genuflexions and prostrations" (later termed kowtow) demanded by the Chinese court, knelt on one knee, bowed his head, and placed directly in the emperor's hand a jewel-encrusted box containing a letter from his sovereign, George III, king of Great Britain, Ireland, and France. As was usual in such circumstances, Hongli handed Macartney a *ruyi*, or jade scepter, which, the ambassador noted, did not "appear in itself to be of any great value." The emperor then inquired after the ambassador's and his king's health. Thus began, at least from the point of view of Lord Macartney, the first formal contact between the two richest and most powerful empires in the world.

This brief account of the audience of September 14, 1793, is taken primarily from Lord Macartney's journal of his embassy, and from drawings made by embassy members of the event.[1] Chinese-language court records

---

1. MD, 122–123. See the pictures in Singer 1992 and Peyrefitte 1992. Additional discussion can be found in chapters 4 and 7.

indicate only that the emperor wrote a poem for the occasion. One purpose of the present study is to reconsider the differing presentations of this historical encounter by Qing and British participants. It is also concerned with the significance of gestures that seem, at first glance, trivial — Hongli's inquiries into King George's health, for example, or Macartney's dismissal of the jade scepter as an object without "great value." Lastly, it is about how this event has been remembered over the past two hundred years.

The Macartney embassy is, of course, not a new subject of research. Since the 1930s Anglo-American historians have written a number of studies based on archival sources in Great Britain and China. More recently, the embassy drew renewed attention as the Qing archives in Peking were reopened to Western scholars and as the bicentennial of the embassy approached. Most previous scholarship has treated the meeting between the Qianlong emperor and Lord Macartney as symbolic of the confrontation between "traditional" and "modern" civilizations at the dawn of modernity (see section 1.2 below).

My concerns are somewhat different. For the purposes of this introduction, two of them are of primary importance. The first has to do with my attempt to reevaluate the encounter between the Qing and British empires in light of recent theoretical and empirical studies of imperialism and colonialism in Asia. These works have raised significant questions not only about interpretation, but perhaps more significantly about the moral ground upon which engagements between present and past are constituted. The second has to do with new research emphases in China studies that have arisen over the last two decades. In particular, there has been a growing imbalance toward endogenous as opposed to exogenous factors in explaining change in late imperial China.[2] In the following sections of this introduction, I will explore each of these topics and, drawing from my critical engagement with them, indicate the ways in which this book takes a different approach.

1.1   New Patterns in the Study of Imperialism

Since the 1970s the study of European imperialism and colonialism has undergone significant changes. Stimulated in part by liberation movements

2. The term "late imperial" itself marks this shift. As a new mode of periodizing Chinese history, it refers to a Ming-Qing continuum covering the period from the mid-fourteenth to the end of the nineteenth centuries.

in Africa and Asia, by social movements of women and people of color in the industrialized world, and by the movement against the Vietnam War, scholars who studied imperialism began to challenge the notion that eco- nomic considerations were the primary and, in some cases, the exclusive explanation for European global expansion. Theoretically, much of this re- thinking was stimulated by new strains of Marxist criticism that flourished in England, France, and Germany. Directed at strict economism and overly mechanistic interpretations of base/superstructure relations, historians and social theorists as diverse as E. P. Thompson, Raymond Williams, Stuart Hall, Michel Foucault, Louis Althusser, Roland Barthes, Jürgen Habermas, and Barry Hindess and Paul Hirst directed attention to the complex pro- cesses of making social worlds within the constraining conditions of indus- trial capitalism and the imperial state.[3] With the exception of Hall and a few writings by Barthes, however, these scholars seldom dealt directly with the question of European colonial domination. Yet the particular theoreti- cal turn they effected enabled others to introduce a host of new subjects of study.

Among these topics have been gender construction in the colonial set- ting, the role of intellectuals and elites in the colonial and postcolonial world, routines and rituals of colonial administration, the part played by imaginative fiction in shaping the subjectivities of colonizers, the mutual implication of race, class, and gender in the construction of bourgeois culture and consciousness, and the modes of producing and deploying knowledge of colonized peoples.[4] In many cases, scholars have sought to defamiliarize objects and products of knowledge, while blurring the con- ventional boundaries between disciplines.[5] Most fruitful in this regard has been the way in which these shifts in emphasis have allowed significant strains of criticism from the former colonial world (and here I think espe-

3. The works of each of these writers are well known and voluminous. Rather than repeat them here, I would direct attention to a few works which help to locate their significance for scholarship: see Brantlinger 1990, Rosenau 1992, G. Turner 1990, and R. Young 1990. Also see P. Burke 1992 for an extended treatment of the relation between history and social theory.

4. See, for example, the collection edited by Dirks (1992), Mani 1985 and 1992, Raphael 1993a and b, and Stoler 1989.

5. Exemplary in this regard have been the writings of Cohn 1987 and the essays col- lected in Hobsbawm and Ranger 1983. Also see the discussion in Hebdige 1988 on post- modernism (181–207).

cially of "third-world" feminism and the Subaltern Studies Group) to enter the study of imperialism and vastly enrich the discussion.[6]

A central element in these new directions of research and writing has been a sensitivity to the place of representation in the imperial projects of North Atlantic nation-states, particularly its crucial role in the production of knowledge about colonial others. Just why representation would become a focal point of colonial studies, however, is far from obvious and requires some elaboration. Consider, for example, how the domains of practice in which many of us routinely operate are founded upon representation. From the national to the local level, the political system of the United States functions in and through representation; so, too, the legal system. The origin myth of the liberal nation-state is ordered around issues of representation, which are welded to the economic through the constantly reiterated phrase, "No Taxation without Representation." The right of representation, defined as the law of inheritance from eldest son to eldest son, serves as a model of Euro-American patriarchy. In a historical social formation that had long privileged the relationship between the individual mind and a stable external object world or fixed reality, representation has simultaneously functioned as the thing observed, as the act of presenting to the eye and mind, and as the product of mind; that is, it might be understood as a clearly conceived idea, concept, or description. In this last sense, representation is thoroughly implicated in what we define as knowledge, as well as in knowledge's philosophic framing discourse, epistemology.[7] Representations can be pictorial, mathematical, or linguistic—and each kind has its own theoretical understanding of how a present figure stands for and refers to an absent reality. If we are personally to function within the social order we inhabit, we must be adept at constructing and recognizing, making and engaging with, representations of ourselves, others, and the world. Moreover, the logic of representation has completely colonized our own world, to say nothing of the worlds of countless others. If something cannot be represented, it is not simply invisible, but, more importantly, not real.

It was precisely the recognition of the hegemonic force of a particular cultural commitment to the logic and practice of representation that helped to

6. See the essays in Barker 1985; Guha and Spivak 1988; the essays in Mohanty, Russo, and Torres 1991; and Spivak 1987 and 1990.

7. For historical and philosophic critiques of representation see Judovitz 1988; Lloyd 1984; Lynch and Woolgar 1990; Rorty 1979:390; and, more recently, Stewart 1994.

revolutionize the study of imperialism and colonialism. Critics from fields as diverse as feminist studies, literary criticism, cultural anthropology, and history began to note that scrutinizing or gazing at other places, peoples, and peoples' artifacts and then re-presenting them in writing or in pictures (first drawing and painting, later photography) was a fundamental way in which knowledge was produced about colonized populations in European empires. Rather than seeing knowledge in all times and places as constructed in this way, some scholars argued that the colonial mode of producing knowledge was an historically specific form of practice, one that gave ontological priority to the ocular faculties as the primary conduit for making things known and knowable.[8]

Exemplary in indicating the political and intellectual significance of representation in the colonial context has been Edward Said, whose *Orientalism* (1978), perhaps more than any other single work, forced the question of representationalism into scholarly consciousness.[9] Focusing attention on images of the "Orient" produced by Euro-American politicians, businessmen, and academics on the one hand, and the political and economic actions of European nation-states in the Orient on the other, Said suggested that knowledge about the Orient was intimately linked to European domination of the Orient. The effect of this link between knowledge production and state projects was to authorize a kind of bird's-eye view of the non-Western world, one that positioned the knowing observer as superior in every respect (more rational, logical, scientific, realistic, and objective) to the object of contemplation. Combining the theoretical insights of Antonio Gramsci, Raymond Williams, Walter Benjamin, and Michel Foucault, as well as those of early postcolonial critics such as Anwar Abdel-Malek (1963), Said's analysis reworked European expansion as a broadly cultural project, while simultaneously opening a new intellectual space for the study of colonialism.

Said's timely analysis had a number of important consequences. It dem-

8. On the centrality of the ocular in European epistemology see Lowe 1982 and Reiss 1982. On the European or Western gaze, see Mitchell 1991 and Lutz and Collins 1991.

9. Many critics have, I believe, misconstrued the nature of Said's argument by making claims about it that are difficult to locate in the work itself. One of the more common ones is to ignore the fact that his focus is primarily on the nineteenth century. To argue, as some have done, that Said is speaking about knowledge in general or about the last four hundred years of Euro-Asian contact is to misunderstand or misrepresent his project. See, for example, Spence 1992:90.

onstrated, for instance, how one might go about launching a critical project designed to take up issues of knowledge, epistemology, and culture as they relate to imperialism. Close readings of orientalist sources, combined with contemporary scholarship in Africa and Asia, helped to destabilize classic orientalist representations. Drawing attention to images of the Orient and Orientals current in Western scholarship also made it possible to discern that in order for orientalism to operate, it had to control what Foucault called the "enunciative function" (1972:88–105). The orientalist's mastery of the Orient was thereby shown to be based on commanding the sites of its representation. Such authority, in turn, excluded native constructions except insofar as they were translated by the orientalist and transported for consumption in imperial metropoles. As a result of this engagement with the forms of knowledge production characteristic of orientalism, Said's work suggested that it might be possible to think different forms of knowledge, knowledges which might operate through other epistemological formations just as powerful as that which provided the foundation for representationalism.

At the same time, Said also suggested that there was no simple way out of the orientalist's discourse,[10] that one could not simply substitute "true" representations of the Orient for "false" ones. This is so because representations are more than simply passive reflections of reality. Rather, they contribute to the production of the real. This has especially been the case in a situation where epistemological issues were conjoined with the physical power and resources at the command of imperial states. As the works of those who followed Said have shown, imperial projects constructed an Orient that mimicked orientalist representations, and these constructs were, in turn, recovered by later generations of Western scholars as proof of the timeless regularities of the East.[11]

Finally, by including theoretical analyses that presented alternative understandings of colonialism in Africa and Asia, Said drew attention to a

10. On the notion of discourse I follow Foucault, especially 1977:199, where he makes the important point that the regularities of discourse are not confined to a single work. Also see H. White 1978:230–260. Belsey provides a useful working definition of discourse as "a domain of language use, a particular way of talking (and writing and thinking) involving certain shared assumptions which appear in the formations that characterize it" (1980:5).

11. See, for example, Chatterjee 1986, Inden 1990, Mitchell 1991, and Viswanathan 1989. Inden also notes native appropriations of such representations and their use against colonialism (1991:38).

pervasive practice among orientalists and their area studies successors—the tendency to apply "objectivist" Western theory, particularly social science models, to non-Western data. In Said's terms, such strategies constructed the relationship between "West" and "East" as one of ontological and epistemological priority of the former over the latter (1978:2–9). After *Orientalism*, it became extremely difficult to sustain a position that purported merely to reflect or passively to report on "non-Western" realities. It was also difficult to ignore the political relationship between first-world scholars and their subjects of study. Rather Said persuasively demonstrated that the relationship between "Occident" and "Orient" was, and to some extent remains, one of "complex hegemony" involving forms of political, economic, and cultural domination.

In the following sections of this introduction, I draw upon Said both to question the usual representations of "China" and the "West," and to challenge the kinds of models or theoretical frameworks that have been brought to bear on the subject. As such, this study is necessarily positioned in dialogue with both postcolonial criticism and China area studies scholarship. Further, throughout the book, I will treat British, American, and some recent Chinese representations—images in words and pictures, the themes and tropes of cross-cultural encounters—of the Macartney embassy as themselves historical events taking place within real conditions, ones which have, moreover, been substantially produced in practices of representation.[12]

1.2   The Great Transition and China-centered History

For most of the postwar period, the historiography on eighteenth- and nineteenth-century China has been dominated by two approaches. The first of these, the sociocultural (Cohen 1984), arranged China's history with reference to the grand narrative of the "Great Transition," the move from traditional to modern society.[13] Scholars usually referred to this pattern of

---

12. On the world-constituting nature of representations, particularly from feminist positions, see Haraway 1989 and Levy 1991, especially 4–15.

13. Scholars globally, whether broadly defined as Marxist or liberal, have taken it as axiomatic that they not only understood the general characteristics or features of the modern and the traditional, but that the latter would inevitably be replaced by the former. For a discussion see Francis, who emphasizes that the very notion of transition was based on ideas of holism and contrast (1987:1).

development under the rubric of "China's Response to the West" (Teng and Fairbank 1954). Positing a stagnant and involuted traditional China, socioculturalists took the Western invasion of the nineteenth century as the necessary stimulus that effected the transition from traditional to modern China. Moreover, since the role of Western influence was a crucial feature of this interpretative framework, China's traditional form of foreign relations and its early relations with the West were a central focus of scholarly inquiry.

By the 1970s, the sociocultural approach came under a variety of assaults. In the general atmosphere of New Left criticism and opposition to the Vietnam War, some charged that practitioners of the approach, especially those who worked on foreign relations, had constructed an elaborate apologetics for Western imperialism in China.[14] Others abandoned the approach altogether and turned to other currents then shaping the Euro-American scholarly world. Under the influence of the *Annales* school and the descriptive structural sociology of G. William Skinner, a new "China-centered history" (Cohen 1984) emerged that discovered a China rich in events and energized by patterns of development with their own internal logics. In addition to providing ready-made bounded entities that did not demand the reference to a Chinese totality, Skinner's micro-regionalism undercut its predecessor in another significant way: it treated culture as epiphenomenal and variable, helping to muddle, perhaps irreversibly, the coherent notion of tradition that the sociocultural approach to China's past had taken as its foundation.[15]

As eighteenth- and nineteenth-century Chinese history became laden with events, scholars also uncovered a rich and dynamic history of social movements, ordinary life, class and gender conflict, intellectual ferment, and political and economic transformation. However, like its European counterpart, this emphasis on social history had the consequence of allowing, perhaps unintentionally, the state and China's relations with maritime Europe and Inner Asia to recede from view. As a consequence, a field once dominated by an interpretation which privileged exogenous factors as the primary cause for the change from traditional to modern China suddenly found little from the outside that was relevant to China's internal develop-

14. See, for example, Peck 1969, Esherick 1972, and M. Young 1973.

15. Parenthetically it is worth noting that many of those who followed Skinner continued to maintain (however anachronistically) notions of tradition and culture that remained firmly embedded in the earlier approach.

ment. As a result, China now has a dynamic internal history, while studies of China's external relations have been neglected for the past twenty-five years.[16] Moreover, most writers who find it necessary to give passing mention to foreign relations in their studies uncritically retain the venerable sociocultural interpretation of those relations known as the "tribute system."[17] Meanwhile, a small number of scholars who still have an interest in historical Chinese foreign relations find it increasingly difficult to support such broad generalizations (e.g., Wills 1988:229). It is to the tribute system and current discussions of its limitations that I now turn.

1.3 The Tribute System and Its Critics

Beginning as early as the 1930s, historians in the United States and China identified the causes of nineteenth-century Sino-Western conflict as more than simply a result of Western imperialism and expansive capitalism, but also as a product of the peculiar nature of traditional Chinese foreign relations. According to this view, isolated from other great centers of civilization and complacent in its own cultural superiority, China developed early in its history a unique method of dealing with foreign powers, one that required the acknowledgment of the supremacy of China's "Son of Heaven" (*Tianzi*) as superior to all other rulers in the world. Foreign princes expressed their acceptance of this proposition in two "symbolic" ways, by presenting ritual tribute (*gong*) to the emperor and performing the "full" *koutou*, kneeling three times, each time bowing their head to the ground thrice. Over the course of the last two thousand years, these symbolic elements of the system were buttressed by ever more sophisticated bureaucratic institutions and regulations. Modern scholars call this institutional and textual complex the "tribute system." As elaborated by John K. Fairbank, this system defined Chinese attitudes and practices in foreign relations from virtually the dawn of Chinese civilization until the confrontation with the West in the nineteenth century.

But why, we might ask, would Chinese imperial courts or foreign princes see the necessity of constructing or participating in such elaborate sym-

---

16. Wills has noted that since the late 1960s the foreign relations field has been "unfashionable and underpopulated" (1988:229).

17. For the "original" formation see Fairbank and Teng 1941. For examples of ongoing use see Naquin and Rawski 1987:27–28 and Elman 1989:385.

bolism? In his seminal essay "Tributary Trade and China's Relations with the West" (1942), Fairbank took up this question by observing that tribute was "not exactly what it seemed." On the one hand, the value of the items presented by foreign rulers were of little benefit to the imperial treasury. On the other, the value of the items given by the Chinese court to missions balanced or outweighed the value of the tribute gifts (1942:129, 135). What, then, did the court gain from this clearly unequal economic transaction? According to Fairbank, the motivation of a succession of dynasties was quite clear when one considered that the emperor claimed the Mandate of Heaven (*Tianming*) to rule all humankind. As he put it, "if the rest of mankind did not acknowledge his rule, how long could he expect China to do so? Tribute had prestige value in the government of China, where prestige was an all-important tool of government" (1942:135). Tribute presented by foreign rulers performed, therefore, the useful function of garnering to the court the prestige it needed to remain in power. In other words, the submission of foreign princes to the emperor *functioned* to legitimize the ruling house. For their part, foreign rulers gladly participated because they desired the valuable imperial objects bestowed by Chinese courts, as well as the opportunity to trade for other kinds of Chinese goods such as tea and silk. In this sense, what sustained the tribute system over long stretches of Chinese history, as Fairbank later elaborated, was that it had become an "ingenious vehicle" for trade (1953:32).[18]

Implicit in Fairbank's argument was another, one that appears heavily influenced by nineteenth- and twentieth-century studies of historical empires, especially that of Rome. In the 1930s, historians of ancient history seem to have understood tribute as an archaic form of political submission and as an arbitrary form of fiscal extraction. Over time, tribute gradually gave way to new definitions of sovereignty and to regularized taxation epitomized in the ever increasing economic rationality of disinterested capitalism.[19] Coterminous with the development of economic rationality was the growth of legal rationality. Here law functioned in two ways: it protected the domain of economic activity within a bounded entity such as a

18. Also see Fairbank's discussion of the tribute system in the many editions of *The United States and China*; there is very little variation, except for a subtle shift from tributary to tribute system; see 1948:130–135, 1958:115–118, 1971:137–40, and 1979:158–161.

19. See, for example, the entry under "tribute" in the ESS. In the most recent edition of the EB (1974), tribute has become synonymous with traditional China.

nation, and established rules of behavior within and between nations, societies, and cultures.

Because of the tribute system (as imagined on the model of the Roman empire), none of this happened in China. Rather, the absence of external challenges was seen to have produced a kind of involution in which law and economic activity collapsed into *culture*. The tribute system, presumably inappropriately, combined "diplomacy" and "trade," while never overtly acknowledging that it was fulfilling either of these quasi-natural functions. This was because within the terms of Chinese culture there could be no true diplomacy (based as it must be on natural equality between sovereign states) and because commerce was not as highly valued as, say, farming.[20] The upshot was that a sinocentric and isolated China developed an entrenched culturalism, as opposed to a more modern nationalism (see Fairbank 1942; Levenson 1968; and Fairbank, Reischauer, and Craig 1989: 177–179), and was, as a result, ill prepared to deal with the Western powers when they arrived in force at China's door in the nineteenth century.

Unwilling or unable to recognize the new international order of state-to-state relations spearheaded by European powers, or to separate diplomatic intercourse from commercial relations, China found that its classic defensive strategy of the tribute system provided little guidance or precedent for responding creatively to demands made by Europeans. The main cause of this blindness was cultural, including the traditional anticommercial and antitechnological biases of China's dominant belief system, Confucianism. Moreover, it was precisely this distinct culturally produced system of rigid forms that Lord Macartney confronted when he arrived in China. Macartney's inability to break through the intellectual and bureaucratic barriers of the tribute system explains why his embassy failed to open China to wider intercourse with the West and why relations between China and the West were so fraught with conflict in the nineteenth century.[21]

Those who have followed Fairbank have generally accepted the useful-

20. To paraphrase Parsons, whose sociological categories Fairbank claims to have employed (1982:326), Chinese culture, while in some aspects providing the basis for rationality, was strongly subject to substantive rather than formal rationalization, and was shot through with particularist themes, all of which served to retard proper development (1966:77).

21. Fairbank 1953:31, Pritchard 1943, Cranmer-Byng 1957–58 and 1963, and, more recently, Peyrefitte 1992. In the final chapter of this work, I will take up the significance of the embassy in the historiography of modern China.

ness of the tribute system and its associated beliefs as an explanation for Sino-Western hostilities from 1839 forward. However, since the late 1960s, some historians of traditional foreign relations have questioned a number of the assertions that make up the tribute system model. For example, Fairbank placed the origin of the system in the Zhou period. Others such as Morris Rossabi favor a Han origin (1975:18–19), while John Wills prefers the Ming period. In the latter case, Wills has built upon the work of Henry Serruys (1960, 1967) to insist that the late imperial tribute system does not predate the fifteenth century. In challenging the usual assumptions, Wills identifies coherent institutional structures, as opposed simply to beliefs or values, as the crucial index of origin (1984:173).

Other scholars have questioned the notion that material benefits flowed only in one direction, from Chinese courts to foreign kingdoms. Studies of Chinese relations with Inner Asia, for example, have moved from a view that these regions were dependent on contact with China to satisfy their needs for certain Chinese commodities to one that sees needs as bi-directional, thus taking issue with the Chinese rhetoric of self-sufficiency.[22] China needed horses, raw materials, and possibly even foodstuffs from the outside, and could provide finished products as well as commodities unique to it (tea stands out in this respect).[23]

Still others have questioned the rigidity and unitary nature of traditional foreign relations that the tribute-system model implies (Rossabi 1983). Among them, Joseph Fletcher found a high degree of flexibility in Qing Inner Asian policy at almost the same moment that the European presence in China had become more pronounced (1968 and 1978a). In noting "an embarrassment of traditions," rather than a single one defining Chinese foreign relations, Michael Hunt juxtaposed the "unshakable sinocentrism" of the tribute system to "more extroverted" and open policies of the Han and Tang eras (1984:6). Following upon Hunt, James Polachek has recently taken issue with transhistorical models and argued that one must look closely at specificities and context in order to understand policy making in the Qing period (1992).

22. The tendency to see economic needs as a primary motive for foreign involvement in the tribute system pervades much of the literature on Chinese relations with peoples of East, Central, and Southeast Asia. Underlying this assumption is a view that levels of development create demand for commodities and luxury goods. See, for example, Moses 1976:64.

23. See, for example, Rossabi 1970, Sinor 1972, and Viraphol 1977.

Both Hunt and Polachek benefited from the revisionism of John Wills, who from the time of his contribution to Fairbank's *The Chinese World Order* (1968) cautioned against overgeneralizing from the tribute system model. I want to deal with Wills's arguments in some detail because in many ways they provide a point of departure for this study. As early as his 1968 essay, Wills noted that relations with Europeans, particularly as they were worked out in the Canton system of trade in the eighteenth century and in the few embassies to China over the preceding two centuries, did not fit the rigors of the tribute-system model. In a number of subsequent writings, he has added that the system as such was primarily relevant in the Qing period to relations with Korea, Vietnam, and Liuqiu. Moreover, he has highlighted a number of differences between Ming and Qing policies on the Inner Asian and coastal frontiers, drawing attention to what might be called a pragmatic approach on the part of Chinese bureaucrats to specific historical challenges.

It is this latter argument in particular that has probably been most damaging to the tribute-system model. In close readings from empirical "case studies" (1988), Wills has identified numerous anomalies that disturb the structural integrity of the "comprehensive-tribute-system" approach. More recently, he has called for and begun to formulate ways for fitting these ✓ China-based case studies into the larger framework of a Euro-Asian history from 1500 forward (1988, 1993). At the same time, Wills has tended to be skeptical of all theoretical positions that are not compatible with a methodology that combines a positivist historiography with elements from the sociological studies of "high" civilizations.[24]

In some ways, the conclusions that Wills has drawn from empirical

24. In 1974, Wills noted that he was skeptical of applying anthropological insights developed in the study of "small-scale non-literate societies" to complex societies or civilizations like China (205–206). More recently and with reference to the work of Foucault and Derrida, he has expressed suspicion of studies which construct European rationalism as "uniquely bent on systematic power over others" (1993:101). I will have more to say on this subject below, but it is worth noting here that nineteenth-century imperialists, colonial administrators, historians of empire and global history, scientists, legislators, businessmen, and missionaries overwhelmingly linked rationalism to empire building. The connection between rationalism and empire was, moreover, held up by contemporaries as that which separated modern from ancient imperialism. See, for example, the writings of James Mill on India and studies of British utilitarianism and India (Stokes 1959 and Iyer 1983), as well as other similar works cited and discussed by Viswanathan 1989. Also see Breckenridge 1989, Mitchell 1991, Richards 1993, and Rydell 1984.

studies are to be expected. Fairbank's tribute system was for all intents and purposes a functional one, and thus shared the weaknesses of classic functional models.[25] As many anthropologists have noted, what appears elegant and logically coherent when frozen in a synchronic dimension breaks down under the strain of time and history (Hevia 1990a). Nevertheless, Wills's revisionism is significant. The sources and topics he has chosen to pursue have allowed him to offer an interpretation of "traditional" foreign relations, especially in the Qing period, which transcends the limitations of the tribute system, while neither abandoning its terms or the sociological interpretative framework he prefers. Beginning with the observation that scholars of Qing statecraft "discussed foreign relations not in terms of tribute but in terms of defense," Wills refigured the tribute system as one, and not necessarily the most important, form of that defense.

At the same time, however, Wills retained a critical feature of Fairbank's system when, for example, he drew attention to the fact that tribute missions preserved "the appearances of the ceremonial supremacy of the Son of Heaven in the capital" (1984:188). Put another way, what Wills, and virtually all of those who followed Fairbank, faithfully reproduced was an insistence upon seeing the tribute system as dualistic in nature. Such dualism was maintained through the use of binary oppositions such as tribute and trade, ritual and diplomacy, ideology and pragmatism, culture and practical reason, or, as Wills suggests above, appearances and political realities.

Such distinctions provide a way to separate the ritual or cultural functions of the tribute system from the statecraft tradition of historic China, the latter of which at times allowed officials to respond creatively to historical contingencies (Wills 1984:187). Interestingly enough, it is in those instances where culture gets sidetracked, where the bureaucratic institutions in play do not add up to a comprehensive whole, that Chinese bureaucrats look rational and capable of dealing adaptively with changing conditions. (Indeed, it is precisely within this context that Wills argues against the image of a stagnant China.) There are, however, inherent limits to this flexibility, which Wills variously describes as bureaucratic passivity or defensive-mindedness, both of which might be accounted for by the failure of China's bureaucracy to rationalize beyond a certain point. For Wills, that point is quite clearly where ritual performance and foreign relations remained part of that "peculiar jumble of functions under the Board of Rites" (1968:255).

25. For critiques of functionalism see Giddens 1977, Nisbet 1969, and A. D. Smith 1973.

China is, therefore, not only an empire without neighbors (Elisseeff 1963), but, as Wills seems to construct it, an empire without empire builders. Caught up in illusions, unable to rationalize beyond a certain point, China's bureaucrats can only distinguish between appearances and reality when the two mesh — that is, when outsiders were willing to accept the Chinese definition of the situation. When outsiders did not, Qing officials could do little more than respond defensively and cling to the illusions fostered by ceremonialism, while even the most clearheaded drifted unawares toward an inevitable confrontation with the West (1984:189).

Clearly there are questions that could be raised about these conclusions, particularly for the Qing period. The Manchus may not have been particularly interested in maritime matters, but they understood land warfare, and spent most of the first century and a half in which they occupied China aggressively engaged in it. Second, it is very difficult to understand why Qing bureaucrats are rational with some foreigners at certain times and not others; why were they able to deal with the Dutch and Russians (Mancall 1971) pragmatically, yet resorted to ideology with the British? In addition to these misgivings, there are also good reasons for questioning the distinction between culture and reason that infects the dualisms on which Wills and others rely, particularly when one tries to use a tribute-system logic to understand Qing textual production and imperial practices more broadly. Specifically, my concern is with those texts and practices that are associated with one of the most overdetermined of Chinese words, *li,* variously translated as ritual, ceremony, or etiquette.

1.4   The Problem of Ritual

Ritual is a thorny subject to address because within the academic division of labor it has long been the special concern of religious studies and anthropology. In these disciplines, it is often associated with the beliefs of premodern peoples and the non-Western world about the sacred or cosmological and their actions in relation to the transcendent. Ritual is also understood in these disciplines as processes by which society is made, legitimated, or transformed through rites of passage that alter the status of members (Van Gennep 1909, Durkheim 1915, and Turner 1969). In a more vernacular usage, ritual might be understood as part of formal, rule-bound, or compulsive behavior as opposed to informal or more natural behavior. For purposes here, these various views of ritual are significant because they are often appropriated to explain aspects of the tribute system, particularly those involving tribute itself and court audiences before the Chinese emperor.

At the same time, the term *li* has a prominent place in Qing records of the Macartney embassy. In fact it was the *Binli* or Guest Ritual, one of five categories of imperial rites involving the constitution of rulership as outlined in *The Comprehensive Rites of the Great Qing* (*Da Qing tongli*), through which officials organized this and other embassies to the Qing court. The question that I want to deal with, however, is not whether *li* is important to Qing relations with other kingdoms. It is rather whether the *li* of Qing imperial texts is the same as the *li* discussed in the tribute system. Granting that translation is always a slippery business, if attention is limited to foreign relations and imperial audiences, the answer would have to be no. I say this not because I think ritual is an inappropriate translation for *li*, but because writers on this subject have conceptualized ritual far too narrowly.

While many scholars of Chinese history have attempted to reconstruct the meaning of the term *li* from Chinese sources, particularly classical Confucian writings,[26] there has also been a tendency, as suggested above, to conflate *li* with a historical Western understanding of ritual, one that is linked closely to secular/intellectual discussions of religious beliefs and practices.[27] In this configuration, reason and rationality occupy one pole of a continuum, the other of which is ritual and ceremony. From the point of view of a reason-centered secularism that is heavily influenced by the natural sciences, the claims made about rites cannot be possible (consider, for example, transubstantiation in the Roman Catholic mass); therefore, they must be about something outside themselves. In this sense, the fact that people engage in rituals needs to be accounted for. This accounting usually takes two forms.[28]

26. For a recent effort see Wechsler, who provides a comprehensive review of the anthropological, sociological, and political science literature that constructs ritual as functional and symbolic (1985:1–36). He also finds in ancient China comparable notions of ritual and symbol (24, 31).

27. For a discussion of this tendency within Euro-American studies of Catholicism in particular see Asad 1993. Also see Zito 1993.

28. Here I follow Hirst and Woolley, who, in their engagement with Evans-Pritchard's work on witchcraft in Africa, succinctly summarized these issues and approaches:

> The entities posited by witchcraft beliefs cannot exist because of what is claimed about them. The issue is then to explain why people *capable of rationality* persist

The first, or symbolic, approach to ritual treats elements of the rite as either culture-specific or archetypal signs that communicate the meaning of the rite to the minds of participants. If we consider certain aspects of the Catholic Mass from this point of view, then the host and wine are not actually the body and blood of Jesus Christ, but symbols of them, ones which express Christ's sacrifice for humankind. The second, or functional approach, treats ritual as an instrument by which social and political structures are made legitimate. Returning to the Catholic Mass, one might argue that its performance legitimates the authority of the Catholic Church (or Rome, the Papacy) and/or solidifies the community of worshippers. Weddings, funerals, first communion, confirmation, and so on can in turn be read in similar ways or as rites of passage. Each of these approaches to ritual has been projected by sinologists onto Chinese materials, and they have read texts related to foreign embassies through such lenses.[29]

Consider, for a moment, how scholars have dealt with tribute. As noted above, Fairbank decided early that tribute did not have any "economic" value for a Chinese ruling house. Therefore, tribute must have had some other meaning in Chinese culture. It was, like the koutou, a symbol of acceptance on the part of the giver or performer of the suzerainty of the Chinese emperor. Tribute expressed or communicated submission. At the same time, as part of the larger process of the tribute system, tribute could also be understood as an instrument by which the ruling house was legitimated, Chinese society was solidified, or foreigners were incorporated into a social whole enlarged by their presence. The same interpretation could and has been applied to imperial audiences.[30] Now, while these various arguments may seem harmless, or even commonsensical, their overall effects are far from benign. Indeed, they are very much entrenched in the pervasive Euro-

---

in practices deriving from mystical beliefs about nonexistent entities. They do so, on the one hand, because the structure of their thought does not permit them to discover their error and, on the other, because their beliefs are implicated in social relations which they cannot dispense with. (1982:259)

29. Imperial audience rituals, like other rites in which the emperor was involved, have been treated in much the same way described by Asad for ritual in general—rites are understood to represent or symbolize something that lies temporally prior to or outside the activity proper (1993:60). In this interpretation, ritual is a performance of something else.

30. See, for example, Fairbank 1968:273, Wills 1979b, and Jochim 1979. For a critique see J. Farquhar and Hevia 1993:489–492.

American intellectual practices that Said and others have identified as Orientalism; they are also part of more general cultural projects which have served to constitute the "West" as a privileged area of intellectual, political, and economic activity since at least the middle of the last century (see also R. Young 1990 and Herbert 1991).

Among other things, the consequence has been to find ample evidence to confirm truisms about the archaic or traditional character of pre-twentieth century China. So, for example, scholars take rites such as the imperial Grand Sacrifice to Heaven quite seriously because, as real ritual should, these rites address well-articulated cosmologies and may be understood as sharing universal characteristics of religion in archaic or premodern societies.[31] Indeed, it would hardly be controversial to say that it is perhaps here more than anywhere else that the term ritual might be best applied to a Chinese practice.

When, however, such practices appear to defy expectations, to slip out of preordained taxonomies, far less ecumenical judgments of imperial rites are offered. This seems to be especially the case when scholars consider the Qing court's insistence to treat foreign relations as ritual. Insofar as such categorical errors can be excused, they are explained on the grounds that the Chinese emperor (misguidedly) claimed to be a universal ruler. On the other hand, many observers have used the occasion of discussions of foreign relations to highlight major shortcomings of historic China. Mark Mancall, for example, in explaining the "symbolic" value of tribute, argued that in "traditional societies" matters of form held "paramount importance since the distinction between symbol and reality was very vague," and that for Chinese society forms were taken as reality (1971:85).[32] In a similar vein, John Wills has argued that since the Song period, Chinese officials have had a "tendency to focus on ceremonial appearances rather than on the realities of power. ..." "Ceremonies," he continues, "are, after all, formalizations of *appearances*. ..." (1984:21–22).[33] These particular features of ritual or ceremonial thinking, coupled with an insistence, almost (one is given the im-

31. For a useful discussion of features imputed to ritual in archaic societies see Masuzawa 1993, especially 26–30.

32. Also see his 1968 where, among other things, he argues that tribute formed contractual arrangements between Chinese society and other groups. In this interpretation, issues of rulership discussed below are inconsequential.

33. In his 1979b, Wills explained that he preferred the term "ceremony" when speaking of court audiences because "ritual" had cosmological connotations (56).

pression) pathological at times, on maintaining appearances or bending reality to fit appearances, was, in the end, the great Achilles heel of the imperial order. It meant that Chinese officials were prone to dwell in illusion, never confronting the real challenges that faced China in the nineteenth century. In this sense, the Qing government must bear the responsibility not only for its own collapse, but for Western gunboat diplomacy as well.

Similar kinds of logic are discernible in arguments that treat ritual as a legitimating instrument. While it might have provided a sanction for political power, *li* is supposed to have prevented rationalization beyond a certain point in Chinese civilization. As indicated above, this was particularly the case in the domain of law, which in modern societies (and one cannot emphasize this point too strongly) *legitimated the power structure*. China produced no disinterested body of law, and hence no rationalized relations between culture, political power structure, society, and the individual.[34] Ritual might have been useful for maintaining internal political order, preserving Chinese civilization and the illusions of imperial power,[35] and orienting policy toward defense (presumably instead of offense or, perhaps, imperialism?), but it was also the great anchor preventing traditional China from responding creatively to the West.

In summary, scholarly treatment of Qing imperial rites and the tribute system has, over the last half-century, rehearsed well-known symbolic and functional-instrumental interpretations of ritual. Rituals refer to things outside themselves; their actual content is, therefore, of less importance than these referents. Rituals are a typical feature of archaic or premodern societies. As such, they indicate an absence of fully conscious rationality, a confusion of categories, and a limited understanding of cause-and-effect relationships. Ritual action cultivates or inculcates shared beliefs (read culture) in order to produce group solidarity, while providing autocratic rulers an instrument for maintaining social control. All these features of ritual are discernible because of the superior analytical tools that scientifically informed modern social theory provides. Like the orientalist construction to which Said drew attention, it matters little what Qing sources have to say on the subject; all such sources can easily be translated into the regulari-

34. For an elaboration of this argument see Parsons 1966 and, more recently, Myers 1991.

35. Some have argued that imperial audiences and tribute-system ceremonial were primarily designed for internal consumption in China; see, for example, Wills 1984:178 and Wechsler 1985:36.

ties of the observer's discourse, producing knowledge which quite clearly claims to be superior to that of historical Chinese subjects who are under the sway of appearances and illusions.

Very little produced in the new China-centered history has called either the symbolic or the instrumental interpretations of ritual into question; nor have there been efforts to confront the implications of this formation for the study of Qing relations with other kingdoms. Most writers still treat tribute and imperial audiences with foreign emissaries as symbolic, and the rites themselves as highly rigid formal appearances that only occasionally mesh with an external "reality." Few have challenged the assertion that these Qing failures had a direct causal relation to the conflict that developed with the West in the nineteenth century. Presumably, if the Qing imperium had been able to shed ritualized foreign relations, the conflict with the West would either have been avoided, or its outcome would have been quite different.

1.5   Beyond Symbolic and Functional Ritual

The way in which sinologists have tended to treat Qing imperial rites is reminiscent in certain respects of observations Jean Comaroff has made about first-world scholarship of "third-world" others. In her study of bodily regimes in South Africa, Comaroff notes that in the colonial context, practices of the colonized are often categorized by Euro-American social science as "primitive," "sub-political," and "ritualized" (1985:551). The effect is to objectify these practices—that is, to place them at a spatial and temporal distance from oneself, to see them as cross-cut with false consciousness and as signs of the failures or inadequacies of the non-Western world adequately to grasp the nature of reality (Fabian 1983 and de Certeau 1988: 1–17, 209–243). In this sense, ritual often carries a pejorative connotation, particularly when it involves a bodily regime such as koutou that already bears a negative burden in sources written by men from North Atlantic nation-states. Moreover, when it is not linked directly to "practical" results, like making community or providing psychological relief in times of hardship, ritual is habitually relegated to the vague and inchoate realm of the symbolic. Such constructions on the part of analysts are not merely passive reflections of reality; they participate, as do all representations, in the production of the real.[36]

36. See my 1992 and 1995; the latter provides a number of examples of how koutou retains negative connotations both here and in China.

Offering an alternative interpretation of the relation between ritual practices and an event like the first British embassy to China is not a simple task, primarily because, as Comaroff suggests, the notions involved are deeply embedded within social science, and, I would add, Euro-American intellectual practices. A brief return to Fairbank's division between power structure and culture will help to clarify this point. In her recent book on sociological theories of ritual, Catherine Bell finds that since the beginning of this century studies of "sacred kingship" have tied ritual, political power, and legitimation of that power closely together. More often than not the relationship posed is consistent with the instrumental treatment of ritual discussed above: rites are an "artifice" designed to disguise brute power. Building on the work of Geertz, Cannadine, and Bloch,[37] Bell rejects this notion. In its stead, she argues that ritual activities are "themselves the very production and negotiation of power relations." This insight then allows her to substitute for the authoritarian notion of power one that sees ritualization as "a strategic mode of practice" which "produces nuanced relations of power, relationships characterized by acceptance and resistance, negotiated appropriation, and redemptive reinterpretation of the hegemonic order" (1992:193, 196).

The reorientation that Bell has accomplished serves to dissolve the distinction between power structure and culture so that ritual practices themselves produce power relations. But the relations so produced are no longer unidirectional, nor reliant upon a domain external to them for their rationale. Moreover, by drawing attention to strategies, nuances, acceptance, resistance, and negotiation, Bell takes ritual out of the domain of an acted script, and radically historicizes its practices themselves. Among other things, this suggests that older ritual forms might be appropriated to say or do new things — or might themselves be open to revision. One of the virtues of Bell's reworking of ritual is to provide some sense that such activities move within a contested space, that harmony and the affirmation of communal affiliations may be only one element of a general sociology of ritual (cf. Taussig 1987). Recent empirical work in China studies demonstrates the appropriateness of Bell's critical position.

In his study of calligraphy and pulse theory, for example, John Hay demonstrates that terms we might associate with anatomy were widely diffused in other areas such as art theory, kinship relations, topological siting, and literary theory. Hay further suggests that this vocabulary was not neces-

---

37. See Geertz 1980:122–136, Cannadine 1987:1–19, and Bloch 1987:271–297.

sarily used in a metaphoric sense, in which a primary meaning would be extended to other contexts, but rather in a direct sense, as in a macrocosm-microcosm relationship (1983a and b). One way of thinking about such a relationship is to imagine the macrocosm writ small in the microcosm. Another way is to think in terms of part-whole relationships (synecdoche) or of structural similarities (homology) between things that might have different ontological status (see chapter 5).[38]

These insights are, I believe, useful for thinking about Qing imperial ritual in at least two ways. First, we might consider the way *li* is dispersed and diffused across various domains of practices and through various textual traditions. In the reign of the Qianlong emperor, *li* was deeply embedded in the Qing imperium's world-ordering processes, in Confucian, Daoist, and Buddhist philosophy and practices, in household rules and management, and in the worship of ancestors, gods, and spirits, as well as in diplomacy. Moreover, as Angela Zito's work has demonstrated, *li* not only informed imperial practice, but was itself a subject of textual production par excellence. As such, it was enmeshed in rich and variegated discussions, researches, and writings, including those of the *kaozheng* or empirical research scholars (Zito 1989 and forthcoming). The very multiplicity of discourses on *li* challenge, therefore, simple definitions, or efforts to organize ritual unproblematically into a category such as culture as opposed to reason.

A second significance of Hay's work is to draw attention to macrocosm-microcosm relationships. The implications of this notion are especially pertinent for reconceptualizing Qing imperial rites. In order to demonstrate this point, let me begin with a review of the five imperial rites (*Wuli*) as outlined in the *Comprehensive Rites of the Great Qing*: (1) Auspicious rites (*Jili*) deal with sacrifices to Heaven and Earth, rites in which the emperor is the Son of Heaven; (2) Felicitous rites (*Jiali*) are concerned with the south-facing ruler, the ruler addressing his domain, and include the assembly of the entire official domain before the gaze of the emperor, the presentation of memorials to the emperor, and the handing down of imperial edicts (presentation and handing down are designated as hearing [*ting*] and governing [*zheng*]); (3) Martial rites (*Junli*) have to do with the emperor as

38. In addition, Susan Naquin's study of Miao-feng Mountain (1992) poses a site as a contested space of ritual, while Valerie Hansen (1990) discusses the dynamism of gods and religious worship in Song China.

warrior; (4) Guest rites (*Binli*), the primary focus of this study, are about the emperor's relations with other lords, and serve as a model for host/guest relations between all peoples in the imperial domain; and (5) Inauspicious or Funerary rites (*Xiongli*) begin with rituals for the interment of the emperor and end with accounts of funeral rites proper to the common people.

In general, the rites defined the activities of the emperor temporally throughout the year, including both solar and lunar time, and spatially in terms of all beneath, yet embedded in, the Cosmos (*Tianxia*), meaning the whole world. No absolute outside was acknowledged, only relative degrees of proximity to a center. This center was, in turn, frequently constituted anew through ritual practice. Degrees of proximity of participants to the body of the emperor were both made and displayed in rites. The spatial disposition of participants and things (such as imperial regalia) using principles of cardinal directionality, upper-lower, and closer-farther signified and produced specific states of political relations. By manipulating space, by disposing bodies, the imperial court demonstrated that cosmic change was being appropriately acknowledged, worked on, formed, and included in the emperor's rulership. In this sense, each of the five rites involved macrocosm-microcosm relations. Thus, there is no need for analysis to draw distinctions between rites with cosmological and those with practical import [39] — cosmology and practicality were always already involved in any practice classified as *li*.

Such an argument gains added weight when the relations between the rituals in the *Comprehensive Rites* are understood in synecdochic and homologous terms. These kinds of relationships are perhaps best demonstrated in the Grand or Extra-Mural Sacrifices of the Auspicious rites. Grand Sacrifices are the observances discussed first in the ritual text; they address the cycle within the year considered to be the most significant, the solstices and equinoxes that divide the year into four equal parts. As Angela Zito has noted, the *Comprehensive Rites* provides the fullest narrative for the Winter Solstice sacrifice (1984). The Summer Solstice portion of the text, then, simply refers back to the winter rites when the actions to be taken are the same, indicating that the winter sacrifice is logically superior to the summer, forming its basis, as it were. The equinox sacrifices are, in turn, organized as lesser and only partly varied versions of the solstice sacrifices,

39. Or other versions of the distinction, for example that some tribute is symbolic, while other tribute is pragmatic.

with spring superior to fall. In addition to their points of similarity, the text also draws attention to processes of differentiation: what is described in the sections following the Winter Solstice sacrifice are chiefly the points that differ from it. Zito concludes, quite correctly I believe, that the relationship between the pairs, normally construed as being of equal significance and proportions, as if they were a kind of harmonious system of eternal oscillation, is actually asymmetrical, with the superior of the pair encompassing and including the inferior through logical signs of presence, absence, and difference.

It is not, therefore, simply a matter of proposing hierarchy as an organizing principle in "traditional" China. Rather the notion of hierarchy to which the *Comprehensive Rites* appears to refer is materialized via a logic of inclusion or encompassment which simultaneously maintains difference. These adroit uses of macrocosm-microcosm, synecdoche, homology, *and* differentiation as exemplified in the substance of Auspicious rites strike me as fundamental imperial powers, ones that emanate throughout Qing rulership and indicate the source from which the Qing court constructed its sovereignty and claimed legitimacy.[40]

The works I have reviewed in this section offer other ways of approaching Qing imperial ritual — ones, I would argue, which do not demand either totalizing or essentializing the subject of investigation. They also encourage us to reconsider other, taken-for-granted assumptions about Sino-Western relations. Suppose, for example, we hold in suspense for a moment the claim that rather than ritualizing diplomacy, the British, like other Europeans in the late eighteenth century, were busy rationalizing international relations via a body of rules known as the "Law of Nations." The questions that might then be put are these: (1) did ritual play any role at all in British diplomatic practice, and (2) did the British imagining of nation-to-nation relations have cosmological content? While both of these questions will be taken up more comprehensively in chapters 3 and 4, from my understanding of the record of Lord Macartney's embassy to China, the answer to both these questions is yes. In fact, while at times the British ambassador looked askance at the "formal" practices of the Qing court, seeing them perhaps as akin to enlightened reason's critique of the practices of the Roman Catholic church, he also saw ceremony as a crucial means for establishing mutual recognition of sovereignty, thereby enabling diplomatic negotiations to

---

40. These notions of hierarchy and sovereignty might be contrasted to what was in Europe at the same time; see chapter 3, section 6.

proceed. As for the cosmological aspect of the "Law of Nations," one need hardly go further than to point out the many references to God and Nature found in the letter from George III to the Qianlong emperor. To treat such references as so much hyperbole or formality is to dismiss or marginalize them in much the same manner as has been done with Qing imperial notions of ritual.

1.6 Considerations in the Organization of This Study

It is not my purpose to present a new model of Chinese history, or to offer a new grand narrative to replace that of the tradition-modernity confrontation. I will attempt, however, to bring back into consideration (albeit in somewhat modified form) the political order that dominated the Qing and British imperial formations.[41] One way of accomplishing this is to cease interpreting the Macartney embassy as an encounter between civilizations or cultures, but as one between two imperial formations, each with universalistic pretensions and complex metaphysical systems to buttress such claims. Under the sway of area studies exclusionism, twentieth-century Chinese nationalism, and notions of China's uniqueness in the age of European global domination (i.e., China as a semicolony), commonalities between the Qing and British imperial formations have been ignored or denied, while their differences have been distorted. My subject will be, therefore, the contact between two expansive colonial empires, each organized around principles that were presumably incompatible with those of the other. I will not emphasize the collision of cultures.

Throughout this work, I will treat Qing and British principles of organization as discourses of power, each produced by a ruling bloc for the maintenance of its position and the reconfiguring of its social world. While

---

41. In part, my concern here parallels the concerns of Naquin and Rawski 1987:xi and the critique of social history found in Skocpol 1985. In bringing the state back in, however, one must be aware of the danger of reproducing a state-society split that the social history movement had in part reacted against. As a way of avoiding such divisions, I use the term "imperial formations," which, as defined by Inden, "refers to a complex agent consisting of overlapping and contending polities that more or less successfully relate themselves to each other in what they consider, or at least concede as constituting, a single way of life, one that its more active proponents seek to represent as potentially universal in extent." Inden adds that polities should be understood as provisional because their ruling agent is continually engaged in the process of making the polity (1990:29). These particular theoretical insights are, I believe, particularly helpful for discussing and exploring the Qing and British formations of the late eighteenth century.

I will indicate below a number of distinctions between these two modes of power, I want to begin by drawing attention to a few of their similarities. Qing and British imperial discourses were each in their own way absolut-ist; that is, both strove to contain what were recognized as threats to the methods through which they produced power. Neither was, in other words, egalitarian or democratic; rather they operated to consolidate an imperial formation that placed the users of the discourse at the pinnacle of sets of complex hierarchical relationships. In this sense, power was unquestion-ably coercive. People, Chinese and Irish peasants for example, suffered and died through the application of imperial power in China *and* Great Britain. Yet power was also productive. It not only reordered and transformed the social world of the Qing and British empires, it produced particular kinds of agents who operated in those worlds, agents who believed that imperial power, as they understood it, worked for the common good; that "order" was better than other alternatives; and that order should therefore be pro-tected through the judicious application of productive as well as coercive power. I would argue that if any of us are to avoid either seduction or de-spair in the face of such power, it behooves us to understand its nuances. To do so requires both historical engagement and critical self-reflection: en-gagement not only with the Macartney embassy as "event," but with later imaginings of its meaning; and self-reflection which recognizes that the "self" is also a product of that which it seeks to interrogate.

It is also helpful, I believe, to acknowledge that there is more than a minor connection between the subject of this study and European colonial-ism. "China" was, after all, that most superlative object of European expan-sionist fantasies from the fifteenth century to the present, and need not be treated in isolation from such global processes. Moreover, Lord Macartney was an exemplary representative of British imperial ambitions. In addition to once having been ambassador to the court of Catherine the Great, he also served as the governor of Grenada, Madras, and Capetown (Roebuck et al. 1983). Many of those on his embassy assisted him in these duties in other places, and at least one of them wrote a comparative analysis of Afri-cans and Chinese (Barrow 1806). For reasons having more to do with the amorphousness of categories such as "tradition" and "modernity," and the "Orient" and the "Occident," as well as the tendency to separate the history of Great Britain from the history of the British empire,[42] the implications of

42. For a critique and examples of work that bring the empire back into British his-tory, see MacKenzie 1986a and b, and 1992.

these connections between Macartney and empire, and between empire and
modes of knowledge production, often go unremarked in the literature.
Much the same could be said for the Qing court, with the understanding
that its imperial knowledges were informed by a different epistemology[43]
(see chapter 5).

Finally, it is also worth bearing in mind that although understandings of
events in China in the fall of 1793 have been (and in the absence of evidence
to the contrary continue to be) conditioned by a number of modernist assumptions about the *meanings* of ceremonial behavior, international law
and relations, and embassies, there was at the time, and continued to be for
some time after the embassy, far from complete agreement in Europe on
whether there were or ought to be universal codes of diplomatic exchange.
Napoleon Bonaparte argued, for example, that Macartney ought to have
complied with local customs in his dealings with the Chinese because each
sovereignty had the right to dictate how it was to be approached within its
own territories (cited in Peyrefitte 1992:513).

These considerations have led me to a number of conclusions which account both for the way the study is organized and for the particular emphases to be found in it. First, with a number of poststructural critics such
as Donna Haraway, Bruno Latour, and Michael Taussig, I would argue that
knowledge is always situated, interested, and hence political. Second, I have
worked from the assumption that international relations as defined in part
through international law is a naturalized hegemonic discourse that exists
today as an artifact of European global expansion from the sixteenth century forward. It is naturalized in the sense that it has become accepted as
a commonsense way that nations should engage in relations among themselves. It is hegemonic in a Gramscian sense, in that states where such traditions cannot be found have more or less willingly given their consent to
participate in international intercourse under rules defined by alien (in this
case Euro-American) others.

Third, I believe it impossible to coherently translate or evaluate Qing
imperial behavior in managing relations with other kingdoms by relying
on these commonsense principles of international relations. Macartney's
evaluation of his encounter with the imperial court is a prime example of
this impossibility. Moreover, most other studies of the embassy start from
the position that a Euro-American version of international relations is suf-

---

43. Dealing with more recent history, J. Farquhar (1987) has elucidated a different
kind of epistemology with respect to Chinese medicine in contemporary China.

ficient for comprehending most other kinds of historical relations. Here the yardstick used is international law, and other situations are evaluated according to the degree to which they correspond with or deviate from these "norms." Conflict is then often accounted for on the basis of a failure of one party to act normally or reasonably. I will address this issue in more detail in the final chapter when I consider the significance of the Macartney embassy in the history of Sino-Western relations.

Fourth, I will argue that while it may be impossible to translate Qing imperial forms of interdomainal relations into international relations, it is not impossible to reconstruct the particulars of those forms in their own terms. By so doing, I believe one can work toward an understanding of the Qing imperial practices that Macartney found confusing. I take up the nature of Macartney's confusion in chapter 4, and engage Qing practices in chapter 5. In the latter case, I will offer an alternative way of understanding imperial ritual that need not rely on the sorts of interpretations critically reviewed above. In particular, I will consider the challenge Qing sources pose to our commonsense ideas of human agency when, for example, a foundational metaphysics, notions of a universal human nature, and instrumental understandings of thought and action are not involved.

Fifth, since I challenge the view that constructs culture as a realm of primarily beliefs and ideas, I do not think it correct to characterize the encounter between the Qing and British empires as a case of cultural misunderstanding. Rather, I will insist that actors on both sides of the encounter were quite aware that what was at stake were competing and ultimately incompatible views of the meaning of sovereignty and the ways in which relations of power were constructed. Each attempted to impose its views on the other; neither was (at the time) successful.

Finally, a few words on how I have approached the Chinese and English language source materials dealt with here. In general, I have taken both the Chinese and British writings to be far from transparent. In addition to their "factual" content, they are comments on and attempts to organize the world in specific ways. Regardless of the claims they make, they cannot encompass the entire world or account for all phenomena in it any more than any other discourse can. One question I will ask of these texts, therefore, involves their acknowledged and unacknowledged limits, for I believe that it is precisely at the edges of discourses that we may begin to write historical cultural studies.

2 A MULTITUDE OF LORDS

The Qing Empire, Manchu Rulership,

and Interdomainal Relations

Chinese and Euro-American scholars uniformly treat the Qing imperium as a stage of Chinese history, the last in a string of dynasties beginning with the reign of Qinshi Huang (221 B.C.E.).[1] This sinocentric approach to Manchu rule obscures many differences between the Qing and earlier imperial formations in East Asia. For example, with the exception of the Mongol Yuan (itself a conquest dynasty), the Manchus forged the largest and most culturally heterogeneous empire in East Asian history—by the Qianlong reign it had also become the most populous. If the effort to fit the Qing dynasty into "Chinese" history appears awkward at times, it also does not sit comfortably with the rhetoric of the post-1911 Chinese nation-state.[2] Twentieth-century Chinese nationalists and state agents have at times condemned and at other times applauded the Manchus, seeing them sometimes as the cause of China's backwardness and at other times as the transmitters of Chinese traditions.

There are, however, growing reasons to doubt that the Manchu emperors and their advisors were the passive receptors of Chinese political and cultural institutions as they are normally portrayed.[3] While there is still no

1. I do not believe it a great exaggeration to say that the Manchus have only been of interest insofar as they were part of Chinese history. This particular view of the Qing has been shared by American sinologists and by Chinese nationalists on both sides of the Taiwan straits.

2. Twentieth-century Chinese nationalism opposed itself both to European imperialism and to the Qing dynasty. At the same time, however, it never acknowledged Manchu imperialism as such, preferring instead to include territories conquered by the Manchus into the "natural" sovereign nation-state of China.

3. In portions of their work, Chia 1992; Crossley 1992; Elliot 1990, 1992, and 1993;

consensus on this issue, there is sufficient evidence to indicate that at least until the nineteenth century the Qing leadership not only adopted existing Ming institutions to their rulership, but set off in highly innovative directions of their own. It is the purpose of this chapter to provide an introductory overview of the Qing empire and to suggest areas in which Qing rulers constructed an imperial formation that deviated in a number of significant ways from its predecessors.

2.1   The Qing Empire in the Eighteenth Century

A central precept in the Qing imagining of empire was the notion that the world was made up of a multitude of lords over whom Manchu emperors sought to position themselves as overlord.[4] Such concerns are quite evident if, for example, we consider some of the titles associated with and claims made about Hongli, the Qianlong *huangdi*, an epithet which might be more informatively rendered as "supreme lord" or "king of kings" rather than the conventional term "emperor." Hongli was also the Chinese Son of Heaven; the successor to the rulership of Genghis Khan, and to the Jin and Yuan dynasties, and hence Khan of Khans; cakravartin king and "Chinese *Aśoka Dharmarāja*" (Lessing 1942:61–62); overlord of Mongolia, Xinjiang, Qinghai, and Tibet; pacifier of Taiwan, Yunnan, Vietnam, Burma, and the Zungars and Gurkhas; the incarnate bodhisattva Mañjuśrī; and head of the Aisin Gioro, the dominant clan among the Manchus.[5]

These titles were not hollow hyperbole, but signifiers which indicated the nature of the Qing empire and Manchu imperialism. The Qing domain was multinational, multiethnic, and multilinguistic, comprising all of what had been Ming China and much, much more. Military campaigns from the reign of the Kangxi emperor forward extended Manchu dominion of the most powerful imperial formation in eastern Eurasia to the borders of Tsar-

---

and Millward 1993 and 1994 suggest as much. From conversations, it appears that Evelyn Rawski's forthcoming study of the imperial family is in tune with this shift in emphasis.

4. I use the notion of a multitude of lords because it focuses attention on concerns that appear throughout Qing imperial rites, especially Guest Ritual. The notions of rulership I develop here and in other parts of this study have certain affinities with the work of Crossley, especially her 1992 article. Where we differ is in her overt use of organic-functional metaphors to describe Qing rulership.

5. See Hevia 1989; Crossley 1992 provides details on these many claims of Qing emperors. On cakravartin kingship in Buddhism see Tambiah 1976:39–53.

ist Russia on the north and west, and to the Himalayas on the south. The khanates of Inner Asia, Buddhist and Muslim, scattered along the old Silk Road as far west as Yarkand and Kashgar, were added in campaigns during the Qianlong reign. As the *Poems and Prose of the Ten Great Campaigns of the Qianlong Reign (swsqj)* indicate, the final "pacification" of Inner Asia was completed by the 1770s and the Manchu position in Tibet strengthened by the successful repulsion of a Gurkha invasion in 1790–1791. By the time Lord Macartney arrived at the Qing court bearing George III's letter, the Qing empire was the largest, wealthiest, and most populous contiguous political entity anywhere in the world.

In order to maintain their paramount position over this diverse polity, Qing rulers formulated policies designed to guarantee that no combination of forces came together to challenge the supremacy of the Aisin Gioro house and its claim to paramount overlordship in East and Inner Asia. Fully aware of their own minority position, the Qing elite developed a number of geopolitical strategies for maintaining their dominant position. The strategies involved at least three main considerations: (1) subduing potential counterclaimants to supreme lordship in Inner Asia, while building coalitions that acknowledged Qing supremacy;[6] (2) pacifying and maintaining control over China's diverse population; and (3) assuming a defensive position in the Pacific coastal regions of the empire. In the following sections of this chapter, I will review some of the characteristic features of Qing imperial power and empire building, beginning with their construction of multiple capitals and palace complexes.

2.2   Multiple Centers, Multiple Powers

Faced with numerous lords, all of whom were potential rivals to the Manchu claim of overlordship in East and Inner Asia, Qing emperors maneuvered to include the powers of other lords in their own rulership. Inclusion involved participation in guest rites and the court audiences that were part of it, a process which organized a center relative to the peripheral

---

6. One of the central ways of building such coalitions was through marriage ties, first with the clans that came to be designated as Manchu and then with sublords that headed various Mongol and Turkic groups; see Rawski 1991 and Millward 1993:329. According to Lattimore (1934:60) such coalition building was an important factor in the Qing conquest of Inner Asia (cited in Rawski 1991:178).

kingdoms of other lords. The same principles appear to have been at play whether the lord in question was a Mongol prince or the king of England. The relationships constituted in Guest Ritual were hierarchical, with the Qing emperor accorded the position of supreme lord (*huangdi*) and the lords of the periphery that of lesser lord (*fanwang;* see chapter 5 for a detailed discussion). In addition, the audiences themselves were held at sites of historical import, ones which might evoke the genealogy of Manchu overlordship and/or address new conditions in the distribution of lordly powers in the world.

The palace complex at Shenyang (Mukden), for example, recalled the Jin dynasty and Nurhaci's reconstitution of it. It also made reference to the more recent enfeoffment of the Korean king by Nurhaci's successor and founder of the Qing, Hung Taiji.[7] The Yuan and Ming capital at Peking was the site where Qing emperors established themselves as descendants of the Jin and as Sons of Heaven over China proper. Embassies from the lords of Burma, Siam, Vietnam, and other Southeast Asian kingdoms as well as European emissaries were granted audiences there in the Hall of Supreme Harmony (Taihe dian). Rehe (present day Chengde), located north of Peking and west of Shenyang, was established during the Kangxi emperor's reign to encompass Inner Asian lordship and Tibetan Buddhism. There Qing emperors received Mongol and Turkic lords in a tent reminiscent of that of the Mongol Great Khan, and the Qianlong emperor built replicas of the palaces of the Dalai and Panchen Lamas as emblems of his patronage of Buddhism (see Chayet 1985 and Forêt 1992). By segmenting and zoning other lordships in this way, it would appear that the Manchu emperors attempted to position themselves as the only agency capable of addressing the diverse population of the *Da,* or Great, Qing.[8]

These multiple "capitals" or "in-state" residences of the emperor were augmented by audience halls located at the Encompassing Illumination or Yuanming and Eternal Spring (Changchun) Gardens northwest of Peking. In the former, buildings modeled after the palace styles of France and

---

7. H. Chun notes that Korean embassies stopped in Shenyang on their way to Peking, where they presented part of their tribute; see 1968:97.

8. See, for example, Hongli's claim of a great unity (*datong*) that transcends the linguistic differences of the imperium's peoples. Hongli is, of course, the pivot of such unity. The citation is in Millward 1993:269. Also see Zito's discussion, wherein Hongli appears to make reference to having extended cities to nomads (1987:347). Also see Crossley 1987:779.

Italy were erected by the Qianlong emperor's European missionaries and then enclosed within the walls of the larger Chinese-style palace complex (see Malone 1934). Once it is acknowledged as a significant aspect of Qing rulership, palace building might be understood as part of a general process through which the Qing domain addressed contingencies that arose in their efforts to organize hierarchical relations between themselves and other centers of power. Palaces were, in other words, sites where audiences took place, and as such point to the political nature of the relations formed in imperial ritual. These relations were not predetermined, nor were they easily organized and maintained. They required ongoing dialogues which were often charged with competing claims and explicit strategies designed to delimit such claims.[9]

From the time of the establishment of the Qing in China, Manchu rulers had to find innovative ways for managing these complex relations. In China proper, for example, where they were a tiny minority, the Qing court developed a number of strategies for holding their paramount position. First, while they retained the core of the Ming governmental structure, they staffed the highest-level offices with equal numbers of Manchu and Chinese officials.[10] Second, over the course of the seventeenth and eighteenth centuries, Qing rulers inaugurated a number of new institutions and launched campaigns either to circumvent the routine practices of the administration, or reform and discipline it.[11] Third, they sought to maintain control over the intellectual and economic center of China proper, the lower Yangtze or Jiangnan region, with carrot-and-stick approaches. Members of powerful groups found positions open to them at the highest levels of the Qing government, including the Grand Secretariat, the Grand Council (see below), and the various governmental boards. At the same time, emper-

9. This was particularly the case in Inner Asia where the Qing repeatedly exhibited a high degree of flexibility; see Fletcher 1978a, the recent studies by Chia (1992) and Millward (1993), and section 2.3 below.

10. See Hsü 1990:47–59 for an overview of governmental structure. For figures on the distribution of Manchu and Chinese in the positions of governors-general, who oversaw two provinces, and provincial governors, see Kessler 1969. Also see Naquin and Rawski's 1987 survey of eighteenth-century China and their accompanying bibliography on this and other topics covered by my all-too-brief discussion.

11. Such institutions included the Imperial Household Department, which, among other things, oversaw the imperial salt monopoly and maritime customs; see Spence 1966 and Torbert 1977. On problems of corruption, see Zelin 1984, especially 241–252.

ors frequently railed against "factionalism" as a way to curb the power of the Jiangnan literati, particularly as it was centered in private academies.[12] Fourth, the Qing rulers appear to have taken a keen interest in the minute details of rulership, particularly as it related to the conditions of the common people. Part of this interest no doubt involved concern over the possibility of disorder from below that might challenge Manchu hegemony (Kuhn 1990). It also seems to have included concern for the people's livelihoods and, as Rowe has argued, a willingness to use market mechanisms to improve general economic conditions (1993).

While these various concerns and strategies might very well have been conditioned by a sense of the Manchu minority position, it might also have involved a more general acknowledgment of how lightly the imperial order touched the lives of its subjects, how much room there was in fact for all sorts of "heterodox" and heterogeneous practice, especially among a rapidly growing population, many of whose members had about as much connection to the classic books in the Qianlong emperor's text-editing projects as they had to the editors themselves. There is, in other words, evidence of fear of "disorder" from below, but such would probably have remained the case if a Han emperor (however defined) had sat on the throne.

If China proper posed a number of challenges to Qing overlordship in East Asia, so, too, did the regions to the north and west of China. To deal with Mongol lords who submitted to the Qing, in 1638 Hung Taiji established the *Lifan yuan*, or Ministry of Outer Dependencies.[13] Eventually, the duties of the Ministry were extended to include Qing relations with all Inner Asian lords, whether Mongol or Turkic, Buddhist or Islamic. To facilitate matters, the Qing had the Ministry train linguistic and "cultural" experts,

12. For an overview of Jiangnan see Naquin and Rawski 1987:147–158. Bartlett provides figures on Chinese membership on the Grand Council. The majority from the Qianlong reign forward are from this region, see 1991:181–182. On the Jiangnan literati and Qing concerns with factionalism see Elman 1989 and 1990. Kuhn has characterized Manchu attitudes toward Jiangnan as combining "fear and mistrust, admiration and envy" (1990:70–71).

13. The term has been translated variously as Barbarian Control Office and Court of Colonial Affairs. For a comprehensive discussion on the translation of the term, see Chia 1992:84–86; here is also offered the Manchu term, which she translates as "Ministry Ruling the Outer Provinces." I think this a useful corrective except for the reference to province. As I will argue in chapter 5, the Qing court constructed relations with the various leaders of the groups that came under *Lifan yuan* jurisdiction as sublords; therefore, I believe an English rendition that hints at feudalism is appropriate.

and supervise what might be called imperial knowledge projects. These consisted of the creation of dictionaries and grammars, and research on the geography, history, and the genealogies of important personages of Inner Asia.[14] As will be discussed in more detail in section 2.3, during the Qianlong reign, projects were extended to include research into and translation of Tibetan Buddhist sources. In addition, the Qianlong reign saw the compilation of the *August Qing's Illustrated Account of Tribute-bearing Domains* (*HQZGT*), a text in which the costumes of the subjects of sublords are pictured and the special products of their domains listed.[15] In these various textual projects, Qing emperors, especially Qianlong, positioned themselves and the Aisin Gioro as the singular political authority that bound together the disparate parts of the far-flung Qing imperium and linked them to the Cosmos.

Like the more famous *Four Treasuries of the Emperor's Library* (*SKQS*), the powers associated with constituting these imperial knowledges had, by the reign of the Qianlong emperor, come under the purview of the Grand Council, an inner court of advisers and administrators, whose authority was such during the Qianlong reign that they gave Qing rulership a strong hint of collective or collegial decision making.[16] A few words should be said about the Council both because of its important role in Qing internal and external affairs, and because it was primarily members of the 1792–1793 Council who managed the British embassy and with whom Lord Macartney had almost exclusive contact.

The Grand Council has become the acceptable form of translation for the Chinese term *Junji chu;* a more literal translation might render it the Office of Military Strategy.[17] In her study of the Council, Bartlett has noted

14. For some idea of these sources, see Fletcher 1978a and b and the citations in Millward 1993. Also see the entries in Fairbank and Teng 1941:209–219.

15. The same sorts of concerns that generated these Qianlong-era projects also appear present in efforts to compile histories of the Manchu banners and research the origins of the Manchus; see Crossley 1985 and 1987, especially 779. The significance of these projects may lie in establishing unimpeachable sources on the genealogy of Qing rulership. Hongli's efforts to clarify Manchu origins had the effect of placing the Aisin Gioro at the head of the Manchus and himself at the head of the clan, while undercutting the authority of the other Manchu clans.

16. The extent of council oversight of the SKQS project is discussed by Guy 1987:79–104. On the origins of the Council see Wu 1970 and Bartlett 1991.

17. Although I will use Grand Council throughout, a sense of the literal translation seems especially important during the Qianlong reign.

its shifting responsibilities from the Yongzheng to the Qianlong reigns (see Bartlett 1991, part 2). Though never made up of more than five or six members at a time, most of the councillors were Manchus who, by the Qianlong reign, frequently had close personal ties to the Aisin Gioro through marriage. The Council oversaw the many military campaigns of the eighteenth century, with at least one of its members, Agui, frequently serving in the field.[18] It was also responsible for the production of the official history of these campaigns (*swsqj*) through the Office of Military Archives (*Fanglue guan*); the organization of Hongli's southern tours (which themselves seem to have been run much like military campaigns); the management of matters pertaining to Rehe and imperial hunts at Mulan; and the oversight of the Imperial Household Department (*Neiwufu*). Councillors frequently held concurrent positions in other government bureaus, providing emperors with eyes and ears across the discretely compartmentalized agencies.

The seeding of councillors in multiple offices and agencies highlights one of the central roles of the Grand Council, that of providing emperors with extra-administrative sources of information on the workings of the imperial government in the form of private palace memorials. In this capacity, the Council acted as the center of a vast, secret communications network running parallel to the official administration. Eventually, the palace memorial system, and hence the Council's staff, expanded under the Qianlong emperor. By the end of the reign, the Council dealt with an average of sixteen memorials per day. The memorials themselves were recopied by clerks into a common, easy-to-read script; the emperor then made comments in vermilion ink (hence the name "vermilion rescripted palace memorials" or *zhupi zouzhe*). Nearly all of the communications from officials handling the British embassy traveled to the court through this channel.[19]

18. On Agui see *eccp*, 6–8. Many members also held concurrent posts in other government departments; see, for example, the posts of Fuheng, father of Fuchang'an (himself a Grand Councillor), and Fukang'an, in Bartlett 1991:186. I mention the sons of Fuheng here because both figured prominently in the British embassy; for biographies of all three see *eccp*, 249, 252–255.

19. On the palace memorials see Wu 1970, Bartlett 1991:171, and Kuhn 1990:122–124. The palace memorials can be contrasted with the routine form of memorial (*tiben*). With respect to the Macartney embassy, the emperor's responses were in the form of instructions (*shangyu*) dispatched via court letters (*tingji* or *ziji*) under the names of Grand Councillors. See Kuhn 1990:124 on the form of these communications.

2.3   Qing Inner Asia

Qing Inner Asia comprised the territories of present day Outer and Inner Mongolia, the provinces of Xinjiang and Qinghai, Tibet, and Manchuria. Sparsely inhabited, these vast territories were populated by Mongol and Turkic nomadic herders, as well as some sedentary farmers around the oases of Xinjiang and in the Tibetan highlands. The oases were also commercial centers linked to the markets of Khokand, Bukhara, and Samarkand via caravans that traveled along what is familiarly known as the Silk Road. Most of the peoples of these regions were organized around headmen whose basis of authority was both competency and lineage. In the latter case, whether Buddhist or Islamic, leaders often claimed descent from Genghis Khan. In other cases, especially where Tibetan Buddhism was influential, they might also claim to be reincarnations of famous historical personages or use titles associated with Buddhist kingship such as cakravartin king.[20] These various claims and associations were staples of politics in Inner Asia. From the time of the Mongol conquests of the thirteenth and fourteenth centuries, they were also central elements in any assertion of rulership over this region. Qing emperors made similar claims.

By the reign of the Qianlong emperor, Qing hegemony in Inner Asia was virtually complete. It had been achieved through direct conquest, marriage alliances, and peaceful submissions.[21] When Lord Macartney arrived in 1793, the various Inner Asian lords had been organized into a rotational system (not unlike that of the Tokugawa *sankin kōtai*) by which they, Mongol lamas, and Turkic Muslim nobles were to appear at the Qing court periodically.[22] In fact, Macartney participated in one such occasion where members of all three categories were present — the annual celebration of the Qianlong emperor's birthday at the palace complex of Rehe.

Qing emperors also attempted to consolidate the imperium by patron-

20. Ligdan Khan (1603–1634), for example, bore the following epithets: Cakravartin Saint, Conqueror of the Directions, Turner of the Golden Wheel, King of the Law, Tang Taisong, Wise emperor of the Great Yuan, and Marvellous Genghis Daiming Setsen (Bawden 1968:34). On reincarnation and Tibetan Buddhism see Wylie 1978.

21. See Bawden 1968 and Rossabi 1975 for an overview of the Qing conquest of Inner Asia. On Tibet see Petech 1950. On Qing relations with Turkic lords see Millward 1993. Also see D. Farquhar 1968.

22. See, for example, Jagchid 1974:46–50. This process appears to be what Chia refers to as "pilgrimage" (1992 and 1993).

izing Tibetan Buddhism, and did so to a degree and on a scale unmatched by previous dynasties. Manchu interest in Tibetan Buddhism is instructive. In the first place it went beyond simply conceding the importance of Buddhism for the empire's subjects; it included, for example, the construction of monasteries and temples at sites such as Rehe, the launching of military campaigns that during Qianlong's reign helped to extend the dominion of the dGe-lugs-pa sect of Tibet (see, e.g., Martin 1990), and the participation of emperors in Tantric initiation rites. Because of its significant place in Qing rulership, I will briefly discuss the relationship between Qing emperors, especially Qianlong, and Tibetan Buddhism.[23] I have selected this particular example because it touches on many of the issues of imperial politics during the Qianlong era, especially as it relates to Mongol rulers and other Inner Asian lords.

2.3.1   *Manchu Rulership and Tibetan Buddhism*

In his *Pronouncements on Lamas* (*Lama shuo*, 1792), the Qianlong emperor indicated that Qing interest in Tibetan Buddhism was connected to previous relations between the Yuan and Ming dynasties and Tibetan lamas from Inner Asia. In the Yuan period, a lama-patron (Tib. *Mchod yon;* see Ruegg 1991) relationship was forged between Khubilai Khan and the lama 'Phags-pa of the Sa-skya-pa sect of Tibetan Buddhism. During the early Ming period, the Fifth Karmapa Lama visited the court of Ming Chengzu (the Yongle emperor) in 1407. In both cases, emperors bestowed titles on the lamas and lamas bestowed tantric initiations on emperors. In the Ming case, Tibetan sources add that the lama recognized the emperor and empress as the incarnations of the bodhisattvas Mañjuśrī and Tārā.[24]

In addition to these historical affiliations between Tibetan Buddhism and the two dynasties that preceded the establishment of the Qing, the Manchu ruling house was perennially concerned with the possibility of the reemergence of a Mongol kingdom in Inner Asia that might challenge their own preeminence.[25] Such concerns existed before the formal inception of

23. For empirical accounts of Qing Inner Asia, see, for example, Bawden 1968, Fletcher 1978a and b, Millward 1993, and Rossabi 1975.

24. A printed version of the text of the *Lama shuo* can be found in *wztz*, 1:23–26. Also see Lessing 1942:58–62 for a translation. On Yuan relations with Tibetan lamas see Franke 1978 and 1981; and Rossabi 1988. On the Karmapa Lama's visit to Peking see Sperling 1983, especially 80–99, and Wylie 1980. On Tibetan incarnation see Wylie 1978.

25. See Rossabi 1975 and Petech 1950. Here it is useful to follow Crossley's distinction

the dynasty in China and were fueled by more than simply the fact that some Mongol Khans refused to submit to Manchu overlordship. Among other things, only a few decades before Nurhaci began to consolidate the Manchus, Altan Khan and the Third Dalai Lama had met in Mongolia and, invoking the relationship between the lama 'Phags-pa and Khubilai Khan, forged a lama-patron relationship (Bawden 1968:29–30 and Rossabi 1975: 118). Matters were further complicated when in 1639 the Tüsiyetü Khan, Gombodorji, had his son, later titled by the Dalai Lama as the Jebtsundamba Khutukhtu, accepted by the Khalkha Mongols as an incarnate lama. According to Bawden (1968:53–54), the Khan's purpose here may have been to provide a counterforce to the power of the Tibetan dGe-lugs-pa sect, while at the same time hedging against a potential alliance between the Tibetans and the newly declared Qing dynasty of Hung Taiji (Abahai). For their part, the Manchu rulers seemed to have been intent on preventing either the dGe-lugs-pa sect or the Khalkha Khutukhtu from providing a focal point for Mongol restorationists (Grupper 1984:51–52).

With the founding of the Qing dynasty, the triangular relationship between Manchus, Mongols, and Tibetans became more elaborate. The Dalai Lama and occasionally the Jebtsundamba Khutukhtu acted as if they themselves were rival lords. They invested, entitled, and provided seals for Mongol Khans, arbitrated disputes between Khans, and, like emperors and Khans, received and dispatched embassies, commanded populations—in some cases, even armies.[26] In addition, each of these lamas professed to be incarnate bodhisattvas, the Jebtsundamba Khutukhtu, Vajrapāni and the Dalai Lama, Avalokiteśvara, two bodhisattvas who with Mañjuśrī formed a triumvirate.[27] It is perhaps not so surprising, therefore, that a cult of the emperor as the bodhisattva Mañjuśrī would emerge under the early Qing emperors (D. Farquhar 1978).

At the same time that Manchu emperors showed concern over the activities of lamas and khutukhtus, they also demonstrated a keen interest

---

(1990) between the dynastic house and the Manchu clans in general. This is particularly the case in the Qianlong era, when Manchuness was literally constituted by order of the emperor; see Crossley 1987, which admittedly does not draw the same conclusion I have drawn here.

26. See Bawden 1968:31, 34, 48–50, 63–69; Ishihama 1992; Rossabi 1975:112–114, 119; and Ruegg 1991:450. Also see Rahul 1968–1969.

27. These celestial bodhisattvas embodied the universal totality of the three aspects of the Buddha: power (Vajrapāni), compassion (Avalokiteśvara), and wisdom (Mañjuśrī).

in the doctrines and practices of Tibetan Buddhism. They built temples, worshipped specific Tibetan deities such as Mahākāla, and, in the case of Hongli, authorized monumental projects of translating and editing texts of the Buddhist canon.[28] Qing emperors also joined with Tibetan and Mongol Buddhist hierarchs in the promotion of the cult of Mañjuśrī on Mount Wutai.[29] It also seems significant that emperors received consecrations from Tibetan Buddhist lamas (Grupper 1980 and 1984) and were willing to accept names and titles such as cakravartin king and the bodhisattva Mañjuśrī.[30]

The last of these titles is particularly interesting. According to Grupper, various Tibetan works "urged consecrated sovereigns to adopt the twin goals of Bodhisattvahood and universal dominion" (Grupper 1984:49–50). Equally compelling are those aspects of Buddhist notions of divine rulership which seem to make a link between the bodhisattva Mañjuśrī and a cakravartin king. Snellgrove has observed that there had been an association of rulership with Mañjuśrī from very early on in Buddhism. In a text that discusses the construction of a maṇḍala for the deity, Mañjuśrī is placed at the center like a "great cakravartin-chief," he has the color of saffron, and turns a great wheel (Snellgrove 1959:207). While this description may be usefully compared to the various pictorial representations of the Qianlong emperor as a bodhisattva,[31] it extends, more importantly, the range of possible meanings for imperial interest in Tibetan Buddhism.

For example, consider some of the implications of claims that Manchu emperors were involved in Tibetan initiation rituals. This issue is especially important because it seems just as plausible to assume that emperors could have achieved the sort of political manipulations of Buddhist populations

28. I have dealt in greater detail with this subject in my 1993b:249–251.

29. On Wutai see D. Farquhar 1978:12–16. On lamas and emperors at Wutai see Bawden 1961:58, Hopkins 1987:28–29, and Pozdneyev 1977:336. On the basis of these and other examples, Grupper argues that the early Manchu kingdom was "indistinguishable" from those of Mongol Khans (1984:52–54, 67–68).

30. While it seems to be the case, at least in Chinese sources, that Qing emperors did not claim to be the reincarnated bodhisattva Mañjuśrī, they also seem to have done little to discourage others from making the claim on their behalf; see D. Farquhar 1978. Emperors may also have been drawn to Tibetan Buddhism because lamas possessed extraordinary supernatural powers. For some examples see the discussion and sources cited in Hevia 1993b:252–253.

31. Depictions of the Qianlong emperor as the Bodhisattva Mañjuśrī have him dressed in saffron robes and holding a wheel in his left hand; see D. Farquhar 1978:7, Kahn 1971: 185, and Palace Museum 1983:117.

with which they are often charged simply by patronizing Buddhism from a distance. It was not, in other words, necessary for them to participate in these rituals to benefit from being identified with Buddhism. What, then, could have been the motive of Manchu emperors? One explanation may have to do with the promises implicit in the ritual technologies of some tantric teachings. They offered the possibility of achieving buddhahood in a single lifetime, rather than through eons of rebirth (Snellgrove 1987:236). Of great significance in this regard was the knowledge certain lamas commanded for the construction of maṇḍalas and for the initiation of others into rites that allowed them to achieve buddhahood.

By the time of the reign of the Qianlong emperor, certain changes in lama-emperor relations had occurred. The Sa-skya-pa sect, which had had close affiliations with Nurhaci and Hung Taiji, seems to have been downgraded; in its stead was the Yellow or dGe-lugs-pa sect. Of particular interest in this respect was the association between the Qianlong emperor and the Mongolian scholar and dGe-lugs-pa adept, the Lcang-skya Khutukhtu.[32] Lcang-skya (1717–1786) studied Manchu, Chinese, and Mongolian at the court of the Yongzheng emperor, where he became close friends with a classmate, the emperor's fourth son, Hongli, the future Qianlong emperor. In the early 1730s, he journeyed to Tibet, studied with the Dalai Lama, and was ordained by the Panchen Lama in 1735. In addition to placing his magical powers at the service of Hongli, he was also involved in translating Indian commentaries and tantras from Tibetan into Mongol and Manchu; teaching Hongli Tibetan and Sanskrit; establishing colleges (1744) for the teaching of philosophy, tantrism, and medicine at the Yonghe Palace; and, according to the Tibetan biography of the Khutukhtu, bestowed Tantric initiations on the Qianlong emperor.[33] Finally and perhaps most significantly for the subject of this study, Lcang-skya acted as the emperor's personal emissary and mediator between Tibetans, Mongols, and

32. He appears in Qianlong era Chinese sources as Zhangjia Hutuketu and was the second incarnation, the first having been enfeoffed by the Kangxi emperor and given the title "Teacher of the Kingdom" (*guoshi*).

33. On one such initiation occasion, the emperor relinquished the highest seat to Lcang-skya, knelt before him during the consecration, and later bowed the top of his head (*dingli*) to the Khutukhtu's feet; see Wang 1990:57–58. For a full Chinese translation of the Tibetan chronicle of the Khutukhtu's life, see Chen and Ma 1988. I am indebted to Evelyn Rawski for bringing these sources to my attention. The significance of the emperor's action will be taken up below.

Manchus.[34] The many duties and achievements of Lcang-skya, as well as his special role as the bestower of Tantric initiations on the emperor, highlights the degree to which Hongli was involved in Tibetan Buddhism. Through the agency of the Lcang-skya Khutukhtu, the emperor apparently sought to center Tibetan Buddhism within his own rulership and patronize it with the wealth Qing emperors drew from the Chinese part of their empire.[35]

This brief review of Manchu affiliations with Tibetan Buddhist hierarchs suggests a connection between such relations and the constitution and reproduction of Qing emperorship. Far from being discrete aspects or images of rulership, politics and religion appear to have been fused, both embedded within cosmologies. The overall significance of such fusion might be more apparent when considering the form of encounters between emperors and lamas. In particular, I will focus attention on audience rituals, bodily practices within these rites, and differential accounts of such meetings. My purpose is to demonstrate that the events of the Macartney embassy having to do with audience form were in fact not unusual. These were contentious issues across East and Inner Asia, issues which indicate the contingent and provisional nature of Qing overlordship.

2.3.2 *Encounters between Emperors and Lamas*

Meetings between emperors and lamas involved attempts by both parties to encompass and include the other in their own cosmologies. In imperial audiences, for example, Qing emperors frequently tried to establish with lamas relations of the kind that obtained between the supreme lord and a lesser lord, and thereby negate any claims by lamas to political superiority. But even this gesture was not without ambiguity. At the same moment they attempted to include lamas in their emperorship *as if* the latter were worldly lords, emperors also sometimes distinguished them from the category of sublord (see below on the Khalkha submission to the Qing).

For their part, Tibetan lamas and Mongol hierarchs sought at various times to assert a long-standing Buddhist view that placed the lamas as the

---

34. On Lcang-skya's life I draw primarily from Hopkins 1987:15–35, 448–449; *The Collected Works of Thu'u bkwan blo bzang chos gyi nyi ma* (1969); and Grupper 1984. The Lcang-skya Khutukhtu's activities on behalf of the Qing court led the Qianlong emperor to designate him "Teacher of the Kingdom," the only lama ever so titled by the court (WZTZ, 1:23).

35. Chia (1992:224–227) has also argued that the Qing court attempted to make Peking a center of Tibetan Buddhism.

intellectual/spiritual superior of a lord of the "mere" earth. In this relationship, referred to above as that of lama and patron, the lama claimed to command superior spiritual powers. As such he could recognize a lord, including an emperor, as a cakravartin king, instruct him in Buddhism, initiate him into tantric mysteries, and receive offerings from him for sustenance of the sect. The patron, in turn, would be expected to accept a position as inferior, protect the lama, seek his teachings, and promote Buddhism in his (the patron's) domain.[36] In either case — supreme lord–lesser lord or lama-patron — the relationship was hierarchical, with one party assuming the position of a superior, the other of an inferior.

To summarize, emperors and lamas made various claims to preeminence; no one could completely ignore the claims of the others. Nothing highlights these political realities more than the contradictory accounts of meetings between Qing emperors and various Buddhist hierarchs from Inner Asia. What these accounts tend to show is that while the Qing court did at times defer to Tibetan Buddhist hierarchs, increasingly over the course of the eighteenth century, Manchu emperors asserted supreme lord–lesser lord, rather than lama-patron, relations in their intercourse with Tibetan lamas and Mongol khutukhtus. In the face of these Qing hegemonic gestures, lamas and khutukhtus attempted to retain the high ground of spiritual superiority.

After the establishment of the Qing dynasty in China in 1644, and well before the Manchus asserted hegemony over Tibet, the first significant encounter between an emperor and a lama occurred when the Fifth Dalai Lama journeyed to Peking in 1653. The court of the Shunzhi emperor was split over where the lama should be received. Thinking that it might be a useful way for winning over Mongol groups who had yet to submit to Manchu overlordship, the emperor's Manchu advisors thought it wise to meet the lama in Mongolia. His Chinese councillors objected, arguing that cosmic portents indicated that the lama sought to challenge the emperor's supremacy. In keeping with the spatial principles of imperial ritual, therefore, if he left his capital and went to Mongolia, he would be acknowledging the lama's superiority (*szzsl*, 68:1b–3a, 31b).[37]

---

36. Ishihama (1992:507) notes that when granting titles the lama was the clear superior to an earthly lord. Ruegg (1991) argues that it is misleading to see the lama-patron relationship in terms of oppositions between secular/spiritual and profane/religious (450), but as historically variable.

37. Bartlett provides an example of the significance of the movement of an emperor

The emperor decided to give audience in Peking, but with certain modifications that vary from guidelines to be found in ritual manuals. The *Veritable Records* (*Shilu*) of the Shunzhi emperor of January 14, 1653, notes that

> the Dalai Lama arrived and visited (*ye*) the emperor who was in the South Park. The emperor bestowed on him a seat and a feast. The lama brought forward a horse and local products and offered them to the emperor. (*SZZSL*, 70:20a–b)

The differences in question include the holding of the audience in the large park to the south of Peking rather than in one of the outer palaces of the imperial city[38] (ritual manuals suggest the Supreme Harmony Hall) and the fact that the audience was characterized as a visit (*ye*), rather than as a "summons to court" (*zhaojian*), the usual form for recording such events in the *Veritable Records*. In the latter case, while *ye* connotes a visit from an inferior to a superior, I believe it suggests some sense of deference in this context. On the other hand, certain things were done in accordance with imperial audience as outlined in other sources such as the Ming and Qing ritual manuals. The emperor bestowed a seat and a feast on the lama. The lama, like other loyal inferiors, made offerings of local products (*fangwu*).

If this entry on audience appears anomalous when compared to imperial audience protocols, the account of the same audience in the autobiography of the Fifth Dalai Lama is even more unusual. While he does not mention the site at which the audience took place, the lama claims that the em-

---

outside the imperial city. She notes the Qianlong emperor's greeting of Agui on the outskirts of Peking after the latter's defeat of the Jinquan; see 1991:183.

38. The South Park referred to here is probably the Nanhaizi or Nanyuan haizi, located outside the south wall of Peking. Apparently used as a hunting park by the Manchu court, it can still be seen on maps from the early part of this century; see Clunas 1991:46. I am indebted to Susan Naquin for this information. One cannot help wondering if the solution to the problem posed by the lama's visit might help to explain the use of other sites around Peking to address relations with Inner Asian lords. The example of the Pavilion of Purple Brightness (Ziguang ge) to the west of the main audience halls of the imperial city is well known, but audiences and feasts also might take place at the Yuanming gardens. The *DQHDT*, 1818 edition, *juan* 21:6a–7a, diagrams a feast in a round tent at the Yuanming yuan.

Holding audiences outside the main halls of the palace for problematic guests continued through the end of the dynasty. Between 1870 and 1900, no diplomat — European, American, or Japanese ambassador — was received in the Hall of Supreme Harmony. They were hosted at the Pavilion of Purple Brightness or other halls; see Rockhill 1905.

peror descended from his throne, advanced for a distance of ten fathoms and took his hand! The lama also reports that he sat in audience on a seat that was both close to the emperor and almost the same height. When tea was offered, the emperor insisted that the lama drink first, but the lama thought it more proper that they drink together. On this occasion and over the following days the lama recorded that the emperor gave him numerous gifts fit for a "Teacher of the Emperor" (*Dishi*). The emperor is also said to have requested that the Dalai Lama resolve a dispute between two other lamas. On his return trip through Mongolia to Tibet, the lama displayed the presents given by the emperor and appears to have distributed some of them along the route (Ahmad 1970:175–183).

What is especially interesting about these two accounts is not simply that they differ, but that the dimensions along which they diverge involve ritual practice. The imperial records mention the lama's offerings to the emperor, all of which may be construed as his acceptance of a position of inferiority. The lama's account emphasizes offerings made by the emperor to him and includes many examples of the emperor deferring to the lama as a person of superior spiritual insight. The imperial records solved the problem of a meeting with an important and potentially dangerous personage by shifting the location to one outside the imperial audience-hall complex proper. The lama's account emphasizes that the emperor came down from his throne to greet him, an act of considerable deference.

A similar pattern of divergent accounts emerges in connection with meetings between the Shunzhi emperor's successors and the Jebtsundamba Khutukhtu. Here, too, the court seemed willing to accord a degree of deference to the Khutukhtu, while still working to establish a supreme lord-lesser lord bond. So, for example, at the famous submission of the Khalkha Mongols to the Qing at Dolonnor in 1691, the *Veritable Records* indicates that when the Kangxi emperor received the Khutukhtu in an audience on May 29, the Khutukhtu knelt (*gui*) before the emperor. The emperor bestowed tea and other gifts on the Khutukhtu. The next day another audience was held for other members of the Khalkha nobility; they performed three kneelings and nine bows (*sangui jiukou*).[39] At the same time, all of

---

39. The Khutukhtu appeared in this audience with the Tüsiyetü Khan, who was also recorded as kneeling. In the entry for the following day, however, the Khutukhtu is not mentioned, only Khalkha Khans and ranks of nobles, which would include the Tüsiyetü Khan; see *SZRSL*, 151:8a, 10a.

the activities that occurred at Dolonnor were cataloged under the general
rubric for classifying relations between the supreme lord and lesser lords,
that is, "cherishing men from afar" (*huairou yuanren;* see SZRSL, 151:23a). It
appears, therefore, that the Khutukhtu assumed the position of a loyal inferior, but one who was in some way differentiated from the remainder of
the Khalkha nobility by the greater deference with which he was received.

On its side, Mongol versions of encounters between the emperor and
the Jebtsundamba Khutukhtu closely parallel in form the Dalai Lama's version of his meeting with the Shunzhi emperor, a pattern which continued
into the Qianlong era (see Bawden 1961:49–60 and Pozdneyev 1977:332–
336). In 1737, for example, the Second Jebtsundamba Khutukhtu journeyed
to Peking, where he was met and honored by high officials and lamas at the
Anding Gate. When he arrived at his quarters, the Qianlong emperor met
him. Upon seeing the emperor, the Khutukhtu knelt, but the emperor insisted he not do so. Later in an audience that included a tea bestowal, the
emperor asked the Khutukhtu to sit closer and higher than other guests
(Bawden 1961:71 and Pozdneyev 1977:341). In addition, the Qianlong emperor lavished gifts on him and acknowledged his powers.[40]

Much the same sort of conflicting presentation occurred when the Panchen Lama visited Rehe and Peking in 1780. According to the Lama's account, the emperor left the throne and greeted him at the door to the reception hall. Taking his hand, the emperor led him to the throne, where
the two sat facing each other and "conversed as intimate friends." Later the
emperor visited the Lama at the special residence that had been prepared
for him, a reproduction of the Panchen's palace at Tashilhunpo, and sought
his teachings. Banquets and gift giving followed over the next several days.
Various sources claim that during his stay the lama initiated the emperor
into the Mahākāla and Cakrasaṃvara tantras.[41] Here again the lama is cast
as teacher, the emperor as patron and pupil.

The *Veritable Records* provides quite another point of view, one that
differs from both the Tibetan account and the *Veritable Records*' version
of the visit of the Fifth Dalai Lama discussed above. In these records the

40. See Hevia 1993b:264 n. 35 for a discussion concerning the problem of dating
this event.

41. I follow Das's translation from an abridged version of the Panchen Lama's life; see
1882:39–42. On the initiations see Das and also Grupper 1984:59. Also see Cammann
1949–1950 on the lama's visit.

emperor summoned the lama to audience (*zhaojian*) in the Hall of Luxu-
riant Clarity (Yiqingkuang dian) at Rehe. Three days later the Lama was
again summoned to the round tent in the Garden of Ten-thousand Trees
(Wanshu yuan), where Inner Asian lords of various ranks looked on while
the emperor bestowed caps, gowns, gold, silver, and silk on the Lama.[42]
While these audiences constitute the encounter as one between the supreme
lord and lesser lords, the lama was differentiated from the various Inner
Asian lords, looking on much as the Jebtsundamba Khutukhtu had been
at Dolonnor. According to a directive in the *Rehe Gazetteer* (RHZ, 24:10b),
the Lama was allowed to kneel (*gui*) before the emperor instead of bowing
(*bai*), provided he was sincere (*cheng*).[43]

These records indicate that conflicting and contradictory accounts of the
signifying practices of participants in ritual space (i.e., movement in time
along east-west and high-low axes, as well as bowing, kneeling, and enunciating) were possible when emperors received lamas in audience. Such differential presentations of bodily practices tell us much about the efforts of
Manchu emperors and Buddhist hierarchs to incorporate each other as sublords, patrons, or pupils. Even when honoring lamas and altering audience
protocols for them, the Qing court insisted that they were recipients of imperial grace (*en*), making it quite clear, at least by the time of the Qianlong
reign, that the lama was a loyal inferior of the supreme lord. In contrast,
Tibetan and Mongol accounts seem concerned with the superior knowledge or expertise of the lamas relative to that of their imperial hosts as
well as with specific acts of bodily practice that differ from those described
in imperial ritual manuals. They also tend to construct the emperor as an
offerer of gifts, and hence a devotee/pupil, and the lama as receiver of alms.

42. GZCSL, 1111:4a and 10a–b; other occasions of feasting and bestowal followed, including one in the Hall of Preserving Harmony (Baohe dian) at Peking on October 29,
1780; see GZCSL, 1112:17b–18a and 1116:4a.

43. The reason given in this case for allowing the Lama to kneel was that it was
customary in Buddhism to bow (*bai*) only to the Buddha. This particular reference to
respect for the customs of others was not unusual. See the instructions to the imperial
envoy to Tibet, Songyun, in 1795. To accord with the teachings of the Yellow sect, he was
ordered not to bow his head to the ground (*koubai*) before the Dalai Lama; see GZCSL,
1458:34b–35a.

There was another sort of deference that may have occurred at Rehe as well. According to a diagram to be found in the 1818 edition DQHDT, 21:7a, during feasts held at
the round tent in the Garden of Ten-thousand trees, khutukhtus and lamas were seated
closer to the emperor than Mongol nobles.

For both emperors and lamas, therefore, meetings appear to have been a kind of pivot at which asymmetrical hierarchies were fashioned, in which the present and future were significantly addressed, and in which bodily action constructed highly consequential relationships (Hevia 1994b). In these senses, the disposition of bodies and the organization of ritual space were about who was actually submitting to whom, with the mutual recognition that such submission had wide political consequences. Yet, since participants vied to hierarchize each other in audiences, submission was a complicated affair. On their side, Manchu emperors wanted lamas to offer themselves sincerely to the emperor—that is, to accept loyally a position as inferior in a relationship with the supreme lord. For their part, lamas wanted emperors humbly to accept a position as patron and pupil of the lama. I do not think it would make much sense to either party for submission in such relations to be coerced. I suggest, therefore, that at least on the Qing court's side, meetings between lamas and emperors were about constructing scales of sincere loyalty. Participants scrutinized the bodily movements of others as outward signs of inner conditions in an effort to determine whether verbal statements or other kinds of action (such as gift giving), all of which presumably manifested loyalty and submission, were indeed sincere.

The Qianlong emperor's casting of the relationship between the Qing court and the Yellow sect in terms that privilege hierarchies of lords over hierarchies of spiritual powers makes, I would argue, the concerns of the Manchu court easier to understand. Lama hierarchs posed a threat because they challenged the very premises upon which an encompassing imperial sovereignty was grounded. That is, they embodied a competing and equally powerful hierarchical view of the cosmos that placed them above the multitude of earthly lords, even if the latter be patrons. Moreover, if Tibetan lamas had been able reliably and consistently to incorporate Manchu emperors as pupils, then any claims emperors made in Inner Asia to supreme lordship could be challenged on cosmological grounds. Lamas were also dangerous because they had the potential for confusing the loyalties of lesser lords, such as Mongol Khans. Yet the problems lamas posed to imperial sovereignty were not easily resolved (cf. Ruegg, 1991:451). And if Hongli and other emperors were interested in tantric initiations, who is to say that they might not have seen them as one among other ways of fulfilling their cosmological responsibilities in a Manchu (as opposed to a Chinese) empire? The Qianlong emperor's solution seems to have been to construct an alternative center of Tibetan Buddhism under his auspices at Peking's Yonghe Palace and in Rehe. But the problems themselves hardly disappeared; the potential for fashioning claims on cosmo-moral grounds could never be eradicated.

2.4   The Coastal Frontier

Qing policies along the eastern seaboard of their empire were, among other things, designed to organize the rulers of smaller kingdoms such as Korea and the Liuqiu Islands as Qing sublords, to ward off pirates, to prevent potentially seditious links between the mainland Chinese population and overseas Chinese communities, and to manage the "West Ocean" merchants who began to arrive in increasing numbers around the time the Qing was established.[44] From this perspective, what eighteenth- and nineteenth-century Englishmen termed Chinese "jealousy" and "exclusionism" was, in fact, no more than the practical politics of the Qing court. And, like its management of Inner Asian frontiers, the Qing imperium seemed to treat the Pacific coast of China as an area of both opportunity and of potential threat.

Controlled and managed trade allowed the court to tap a source of funding outside the usual bureaucratic channels, funds that could be used not only for the maintenance of the imperial lineage, but in various imperial projects, including warfare.[45] The maritime customs provided the court, in other words, with monies for empire building. At the same time, by limiting and managing contact on the eastern seaboard, the court also tried to prevent links between Chinese merchants and overseas communities, connections which they seemed to suspect might produce well-financed anti-Manchu factions. It also allowed the court a means of preventing collusion between "seditious" natives and foreigners. Finally, limiting contact to a select few coastal ports may also have allowed the Qing court to manage the flow of technologies, particularly military ones, into their empire. In this sense, they may have been close to the thinking of their contemporaries, the Tokugawa leadership in Japan. Military technologies from Europe had

44. See Fairbank 1983:9–20 and Wills 1979a, 1988, and 1993. I also draw on remarks made by Erhard Rosner at the Chengde conference marking the bicentenary of the Macartney embassy, September 18, 1993.

45. On maritime customs and their link to the Imperial Household Department (*Neiwufu*) see Chang 1974; Wakeman 1975:19; and Torbert 1977:99–100.

their uses for gaining and remaining in power, but they were far too dangerous if they became available to rival lords.[46] In the following sections, I will survey Qing relations with kingdoms to the East and South in the order given in the *Comprehensive Rites of the Great Qing* and related texts.

2.4.1   *East and Southeast Asian Kingdoms*

In addressing the differences among the many lords who might wish to form a relationship with the Qing emperor, the court utilized its various capitals to provide discrete zones of ritual activity for encounters with other domains. In the main, kingdoms on the east and south who sought audience with the emperor were received in Peking.

Korea appears to be the one exception to this general rule. The embassies of the Korean king, one of the first lords to submit to the Manchus, sometimes participated in rites at Shenyang, the first capital of the Qing, as well as in Peking. Korea also stands out because it sent embassies annually. These unique features help to account for the fact that Korea emerges in Qing court records as the loyal domain par excellence. For example, in the *Comprehensive Rites,* Korea appears first among other domains, and imperial envoys dispatched to the Korean court are always of a higher rank (*DQTL,* 45:5a). In a section that deals with dispatching an imperial instruction to the court of a lesser lord, Korea is used as the example of a correct reception (*DQTL,* 30:3b–5a). Special reference is also made to Korean emissaries in Audience and Feasting rites (*DQTL,* 19:9a and 40:34b).

Between 1637 and 1881 Korea sent a total of 435 special embassies to the Qing court.[47] These embassies gave thanks for imperial grace (*en*); offered congratulations, especially on the emperor's birthday; offered condolences; delivered memorials; requested the imperial calendar; and requested investiture (H. Chun 1968:92–93). Given this record, Qing-Korea relations appear clear-cut; the Korean king was a sublord to the Qing emperor. At the same time, however, the Korean king constituted his rulership through rituals similar to those of the Qing emperor, organizing, as it were, a cosmo-moral order unmediated by Qing rulership.

Similar observations could be made about Liuqiu and Annam, which ap-

---

46. Waley-Cohen (1993) has recently written about Qing interest in European technology; see especially 1534 ff.

47. These were in addition to the annual appearance of Korean emissaries at the Emperor's Birthday, Winter Solstice, and First Day of the Year rites; see Kim 1981:6.

pear to rank just below Korea among the domains to the South and East. During the Qianlong reign, Liuqiu, like Korea, received Chinese envoys for the investiture of Liuqiu's lord in a rite apparently prescribed by the Qing court.[48] And it, too, was supposed to send embassies to the Qing court annually. Yet, it also appears that Liuqiu was related as a lesser lord to the leader of the Satsuma domain on the island of Kyushu in Japan (Sakai 1968).

Relations with Annam, which was also to send annual embassies, were equally complex[49] and, in the instance considered here, indicative of the responsibilities implicit in the lord-servant relationship between the Supreme Lord and a lesser lord. During the Qianlong reign a rebellion occurred in Annam which eventually toppled the existing dynastic house, itself a loyal dependency to the Qing emperor. As the rebel forces approached Hanoi, the Le emperor sought sanctuary in Guangxi. Upon hearing of his loyal servant's plight, the Qianlong emperor dispatched an army to Annam. By 1788 imperial forces had retaken Hanoi, but were later forced to retreat. Soon afterwards the lord of the insurgent forces petitioned the emperor and was received and enfeoffed at Rehe in 1790 (Lam 1968:167–179).

The recognition by the Qianlong emperor of the passing of one dynastic house and the emergence of another in a domain perceived as loyal to him did not end the relationship with the Le emperor, however. Rather, it was reconstituted in another form. The Le family and its loyal supporters were incorporated into a Chinese banner, and the former lord of Annam was bestowed a military rank (ECCP, 680–681).

Relations with other kingdoms of Southeast Asia varied, but appear to have been organized, like those already discussed, to deal with context-specific situations. Siam, for example, sent several embassies in the latter half of the eighteenth century, which included large contingents of ships desiring trade. Usually the embassies arrived to coincide with the emperor's birthday or to give thanks for imperial grace. Requests to carry on trade were in most cases granted. In addition, Siam was bestowed special rewards for aiding the Qing in a war with Burma (1766–1770; Viraphol 1977:140–159).

48. Ch'en discusses the investiture of Liuqiu kings, see 1968:145–149. His description is virtually identical to that found in the *DQTL*, 45:5a–7a.

49. Woodside has noted that the Annamese king was supposed to "domesticate" Chinese cultural elements, while including in his kingship elements particular to Southeast Asia; see 1971:12 and 23.

Relations with the Burmese kingdom indicate another aspect of interdomainal relations. The Burma wars were not a resounding success for Qing forces, yet afterwards the Burmese lord again sent embassies to the Qing court.[50] Near the end of the Qianlong era, Burmese ambassadors participated in the many rituals that celebrated the length of the reign and long life of the emperor.[51] One might well wonder about the details of handling embassies from domains which appear to have effectively resisted Qing armies.

In addition to Siam and Burma, the Laotian kingdom of Nanchang sent at least ten embassies during the Qianlong reign, most of which corresponded to the emperor's birthday. On one such occasion, the emperor was in Rehe celebrating his mother's birthday. The ambassador, who normally would have been received in Peking, was given permission to proceed to Rehe (RHZ, 24:7a).

This review highlights some of the vicissitudes in relations between the Qing emperor and the domains of East and Southeast Asia, indicating that they were often in flux and that even in cases of loyal sublords, relations were far from unambiguous. Moreover, armed conflict did not preclude the possibility of reconstituting supreme lord–lesser lord relations. On the other hand, there is no reason to believe that the imperial audiences in which such relations were forged were any less problematic than those discussed above concerning Inner Asian kingdoms.

2.4.2   West Ocean Kingdoms

Qing relations with West Ocean kingdoms, the name for Europe in Qing court records, have often been characterized as confused because the imperial court lacked a clear idea of the different nations of Europe (Fairbank and Teng 1941:187). The *August Qing's Illustrated Accounts of Tribute-bearing Domains,* for instance, lists England separately, but also says that it, like Sweden, is another name for Holland (HQZGT, 1:47a, 61b). This "confusion" might be accounted for by the fact that only the Dutch and Portuguese had actually sent embassies to China when the text was published

50. The Qing campaigns were led by such prominent Qianlong era figures as Agui and Fuheng; see ECCP, 7, 252. On the Qing-Burma war see Luce 1925.

51. The clustering of embassies in the last ten years of Qianlong's reign is quite clear from the chart organized by Fairbank and Teng 1941:195. The Burmese ambassador was present in Rehe to celebrate the emperor's birthday when the British embassy arrived in 1793.

in 1761. Put another way, since contact with other domains was organized into lord-servant relations, these "mistakes" are somewhat understandable. The problem the Qing court faced with Europeans lay in distinguishing between an embassy from another lord and the random arrival along the coast of China of an undifferentiated collection of merchants who came to trade.[52] Either activity could be accommodated by the court, but classification distinctions had to be maintained if a properly ordered vertical hierarchy of supreme lord and lesser lords was to be realized. The point to bear in mind about this contact is that trade was entirely possible with or without an embassy actually making an offering to the emperor, because it was assumed that the largess of the land made possible by the emperor's virtuous conduct would naturally attract men from afar. Provided such men maintained a proper sense of decorum, they ought to be allowed to share in the imperial bounty. If they did not behave properly, then benefits would be denied. When, however, a kingdom dispatched an embassy and it was henceforth possible to identify a merchant as the subject of a specific lord, treatment might be altered.

Secondly, while the treatment of Europeans might at times have appeared arbitrary to participants and later observers, Qing officials in Canton had a relatively clear set of considerations to address when a European ship arrived. Are these men the subjects of an identifiable lord? If not, have they come as emissaries of a specific lord to constitute a lord-servant relationship with the emperor and, if so, do they have a communication from their lord addressed to the emperor naming them as his emissaries? Have they brought offerings and have they prepared a list of these offerings? If they are the subjects of an identifiable lord, have they come to renew the relationship with the emperor? Is that relationship verifiable? If they did not seem to fit any of these categories, or if there were questions about their status, advice would be sought from the court and further inquiries made of the visitor.

If it proved that these men had come with no intent to make offerings, but to trade, then matters were easily disposed of. Officials would not have direct contact with the visitors, but would place them in the hands of a specially designated merchant guild (*gonghang* or Cohong), who were responsible for making all necessary arrangements to accommodate their requests

---

52. It is also worth mentioning that from 1644 the Qing court was undoubtedly in a position effectively to deny European traders any sort of access to coastal ports, yet did not.

to trade.[53] In other words, the visitors would be organized through channels outside imperial Guest Ritual, but within the regulation of the imperial domain. This process, which would be similar for any domain, sought to determine the proper classification of the visitors. In this sense, lordship was the paramount issue in organizing interdomainal relations, and as such provided the context in which trade was located.

Embassies from West Ocean domains were sporadic, while merchant vessels arrived on the China coast much more frequently. During the latter part of the seventeenth century and the beginning of the eighteenth century, European trade was allowed at a number of ports. At the same time, however, such contact created a number of problems, among which conflicts between local people and a ship's company were of particular concern to imperial officials. If it was determined that Europeans were at fault, the responsibility lay on the entire group, a proposition that often made Europeans bristle.

Finally, Qing officials presumed hierarchically organized social relations among a ship's company which, from their perspective, implied that superiors had obligations and responsibilities for the conduct of inferiors. This perception of social relationships had implications for exchange. Trade was organized through a complex of relations that linked the trader to linguists, *gonghang* merchants, local officials, and, since trade was perceived as a bestowal of imperial grace, to the emperor. This network of relationships provided the conditions of possibility for exchange. Without them, certain excessive attributes (e.g., selfishness, *si*) would be likely to emerge in the actors concerned and would adversely affect processes by which the Qing emperor's domain was properly ordered.

Trading privileges were bestowed by the emperor on a number of occasions to reward the loyalty of specific West Ocean peoples. For example, the Portuguese establishment at Macao was originally granted because the Portuguese had served the Ming court in driving pirates from the area and intercepting mutinous imperial troops (A. Chun 1983:190–191). Similarly, they were bestowed special trading privileges in the late 1670s because the Qing court desired Dutch naval support in their campaign against Ming

---

53. In general, these arrangements appear to have been the responsibility of the Imperial Household Department; see Torbert 1977:97–103. The merchant guilds also dealt with merchants coming from Southeast Asia and other areas, as well as Europe; see Hsü (1990:143), who also provides an excellent summary of the Canton trade (142–154).

remnants on Taiwan. When, however, a Dutch fleet failed to materialize after the emperor had requested their services, privileges were withdrawn (Wills 1968:136–142). At the same time, however, the Dutch seem to have remained in a unique position among West Ocean domains. In the Guest Ritual section of the *Comprehensive Rites of the Great Qing*, Holland is the only European domain specifically mentioned (45:1b).

The eventual defeat of Ming remnants by Qing forces brought peace to the China coast and the establishment by the Kangxi emperor of customs stations at Macao, Ningbo, Yuntai Shan, and in Fujian. In 1686, however, the imperial court reduced levies and allowed ships to anchor at Whampoa Island in an effort to draw the West Ocean traders to Canton (Fu 1966, 1:61, 87). By the middle of the eighteenth century, trade was the dominant form of contact with West Ocean peoples. The British, whose king had yet to send an embassy to the emperor's court, were prominent both in trading activities and incidents involving conflicts with local people and officials. Such incidents, coupled with the vast increase in merchant vessels requesting permission to trade, led the imperial court to restrict contact with Europeans to Canton. A variety of measures were introduced and continually evaluated that were apparently designed to clarify responsibilities and obligations for the conduct of West Ocean peoples and to provide a means by which they would be best organized to benefit from the largess produced through the emperor's virtuous actions.

This chapter has attempted to provide an overview of the Qing imperium and introduce some themes that are of importance to the remainder of the study. I have tried to show that Qing rulers were fundamentally concerned with claims about the proper way of constituting supreme lordship in a world made up of a multitude of lords and multiple centers of power. Ritual techniques established cosmo-moral dominion, while extending Qing rulership spatially and temporally.

In exploring a few specific instances of the nature of these Qing claims or the means by which they were advanced, I have suggested that Qing notions of rulership informed relations with other domains. Rather than being a pre-given structure in interdomainal relations, Qing lordship was constructed through complex dialogues involving substantive claims by other lords, claims that any Qing emperor had to address if he were to establish himself as supreme lord, while still cherishing these men from afar. Just how such authority was realized through ritual practice remains to be explored (see chapter 5). Before doing so, however, I want to place the British embassy in the context of eighteenth-century European notions of relations between "nations" and British perceptions of the Qing empire. Working from these sources, it will then be possible in chapter 4 to reconsider Lord Macartney's account of his embassy to China as an artifact of the broader cultural issues involved in British expansion.

3 PLANNING AND ORGANIZING

THE BRITISH EMBASSY

3.1 Introduction

The motives behind the first British embassy to China have usually been interpreted as fundamentally and almost exclusively economic. Under pressure from commercial interests, the British government attempted to employ diplomacy as a means for improving the conditions of trade and gaining greater access to China's markets.[1] On the face of it, this explanation seems not only reasonable, but fully supported by the documentary evidence related to the embassy. More importantly from an interpretative perspective, the economic causation argument appears irrefutable whether approached from the direction of classical political economy, classical Marxism, or the Leninist critique of imperialism.

Yet it might also be noted that the British East India Company (EIC), presumably the major beneficiary of any increase in trade that might be realized from an embassy to China, was less than enthusiastic about the undertaking. Company directors argued, for example, that the "first and most important object [was], neither to impair nor injure" the existing relationship with China, because, since the Commutation Act of 1784, trade

---

1. This particular position might also be called the "free trade" interpretation, and has most recently been repeated by A. Peyrefitte (1993). However, as Secretary of State Henry Dundas emphasized during the planning of the aborted Cathcart embassy of 1787, if the embassy succeeded in reaching an agreement with the Chinese government, the English were under no obligation to "communicate the benefit either to other Nations, or even to British Subjects other than the East India Company." Second, while the British government did seek greater access to Chinese markets, they did so on behalf of the EIC, which held an exclusive monopoly on trade with China; see Morse 1926, 2:155.

with China had markedly improved. They were concerned, therefore, that any imperial edict that might result from the embassy would only serve to prejudice the Company in the eyes of Canton officials. They also argued that the Cohong system had definite advantages for trade, especially in that it appeared to be a monopoly in name only. In addition, Company officials were sensitive to any incursions by the British government into areas that might threaten their authority, particularly if the government decided to station a consul in Canton. On the other hand, Company directors felt the embassy could be of practical use by collecting intelligence on the production of tea, silk, and cotton in China, while also gauging Chinese reaction to the varieties of manufactured goods that the embassy might take along.[2]

If the economic causation interpretation is suspect because of the EIC's uncertainty over dispatching an embassy to China, it also might be questioned because of the way in which it relegates a large number of activities related to the embassy to peripheral or minor occurrences. Of particular significance in this regard was the insistence by British Home Secretary Henry Dundas and Lord Macartney that the interests of the British crown came before those of a commercial company.[3] Such a distinction was implicit in the division of the embassy into two parts, a ceremonial and a business phase, the first of which would establish sovereign equality between Great Britain and the Chinese empire, thus making possible success in the second or business part of the embassy. For the ceremonial portion, Macartney envisioned an elaborate rhetorical display, the purpose of which was to capture the attention of the Qianlong emperor in order to make him aware of the English "national character." Macartney intended to accomplish this objective by demonstrating the intellectual and scientific accomplishments of Great Britain and by maintaining a high sense of "éclat." He also hoped to appeal to some basic Chinese characteristics that he had discerned from reading the China lore of the period.[4] For example, he was

2. IOMC, 91:63–68. Also see IOR, "First, Second and Third Report...," 1–10, and Pritchard 1938:210–221.

3. See IOMC, 91:48, 50–52 and Morse 1926, 2:155. Dundas had long been a critic of the Company and champion of Crown interests. In the 1780s, he was in the forefront of efforts to wrest political control in India from the Company and invest it in a government body termed the Board of Control. He also argued for the replacement of Company military forces by the king's troops; see Phillips 1940:23–60, especially 49–55. For his part, Macartney placed the interests of the British national government above all others; see T. Bartlett 1983:87 and Fraser 1983:175, 177–197, and 209–210.

4. See section 3.5 below for a discussion of China lore that circulated in England in

convinced that the Qing court was probably the most sophisticated in Asia,[5] requiring that the rhetorical display remain sensitive to "oriental customs and ideas" (IOMC, 20:108, 132–133; Cranmer-Byng 1963:122). Such concerns were especially significant in the situation at hand because Macartney was also convinced from his reading of a variety of sources that the Chinese judged people on the basis of "external appearances" (IOMC, 91:43).

These assessments of China served to structure the content of a number of key documents organized into the ceremonial portion of the embassy. I refer, for example, to such things as King George's letter to the Qianlong emperor; the gifts selected by Lord Macartney to be given to the emperor and the accompanying gift list; the British plan for approaching the Qing court; and Macartney's scheme for convincing Chinese officials to alter the imperial audience in such a way that it would set Great Britain apart from all other nations with which China had contact.

My purpose in considering the issues just mentioned is not to substitute one cause for another, but to propose that the embassy might better be understood as a peculiar mode of cultural production unique to late eighteenth-century Great Britain. Moreover, rather than drawing distinctions between economic activity and other forms of practices, I intend to treat "diplomacy" and "trade" as notions embedded in discourses, the effects of which were to naturalize the two as expressions of principles whose meanings and efficacy were self-evident to a broad range of the British public. In exploring diplomacy and trade, I want to draw attention to (1) interpretations placed on British self-identity by the planners of

---

the eighteenth century. Sources for these and other representations of China came from European embassy accounts such as Lange 1763 and Bell 1762, and missionary accounts like those of Du Halde 1735, which appeared in an English translation in 1736. Prior to Macartney's departure for China, the EIC had included in a packet for him accounts of earlier embassies to China; see James Cobb, "Sketches respecting China and Embassies sent thither," dated 1792, in IOMC, 91:85–90. On the content of the packet see Pritchard, 1936:409.

A catalog of Macartney's library, dated 1786, in the Wason collection at Cornell includes Du Halde and Liebnitz, as well as works on Anson's and Cook's voyages and the writings of Samuel Johnson, Locke, Voltaire, and Hume; see Cranmer-Byng's comments in MD, 42. Macartney's library suggests that he approached the ideal of the well-informed gentleman; see below.

5. IOMC, 91:46–47. Here Macartney may have been drawing from his own experience of difficult dealings with Indian princes while he was governor-general of Madras; see Fraser (1983:177–197), who notes that Macartney often showed "unconcealed contempt" for Indian rulers (194).

the embassy, (2) British notions of China and "oriental" sensibilities, and (3) the way in which the two came together to provide a rhetorical structure to speak the "public sphere" (see below) to the emperor of China. As a way of introducing the issues at stake, let me begin with a review of the letter sent from George III to the emperor of China, a letter which, unlike the famous reply of the Qianlong emperor, has seldom been treated in any detail by nineteenth- or twentieth-century historians.

3.2   The Letter from George III to the Qianlong Emperor

> His Most Sacred Majesty George the Third, by the Grace of God
> King of Great Britain, France, and Ireland, Sovereign of the Seas, De-
> fender of the Faith and so forth, To the Supreme Emperor of China
> Kien-long worthy to live tens of thousands and tens of thousands
> thousand Years, sendeth Greetings.[6]

So begins the English king's letter. It comes from one who claims the thrones of northwestern Europe and universal dominion over the oceans and is addressed to the emperor of China in a form that attempts to mimic pronouncements made by the "tens of thousands thousand" subjects of the emperor. This structure also serves to establish at the outset a commonality and, it is implied, equality between the king of Great Britain and the emperor of China—they are both sovereigns. As such "His Most Sacred Majesty" and the "Supreme Emperor of China" are involved in a mutual endeavor, ordained by God, to take up the responsibility of overseeing the "peace and security" of humankind and extending the benefits of the "peaceful arts" to the entire "human race."

In fulfilling these responsibilities, the English king had directed his people to venture out into the larger world. Referring perhaps to the Cook voyages,[7] George III explained that he had fitted out ships for the purpose of discovering new regions of the globe, for extending knowledge of the world, for finding the various productions of the earth, and for "communicating the arts and comforts of life to those parts of the world where it

6. All citations are from the version of the letter in Morse 1926, 2:244–247. Much of the phrasing in this letter was suggested by Lord Macartney in a communication to Henry Dundas dated January 4, 1792; see IOMC, 91:37–42.

7. On these and other voyages see Marshall and Williams 1982. Marshall notes that the personnel categories on the Macartney embassy closely paralleled those of the Cook voyages; see Marshall 1993.

appeared they had been wanting." All of these efforts were done unselfishly, with no thought of acquiring new territories, additional wealth, or even for the sake of favoring the commerce of the king's subjects. The result had been peace and prosperity and universal acclaim for the "prudence and justice" of the British king and his nation. The reason given for dispatching the embassy is likewise couched in virtuous motives. Having a desire to know more about the "arts and manners of Countries where civilization has been perfected by the wise ordinances and virtuous examples of their Sovereign," George claims to be eager to become "acquainted with those celebrated institutions" of China "which have carried its prosperity to such a height as to be the admiration of all surrounding nations."

A second purpose of the embassy involved the matter of commerce, but commerce seen from the point of view of a benevolent and disinterested sovereign. Since a presumably mercantilist God had seen fit to create the world with abundances of certain things in one area and absences of them in others, George was certain that "the interchange of commodities between Nations distantly situated tends to their mutual convenience."[8] While this notion of international exchange will be taken up in more detail in section 3.6, it is perhaps worth emphasizing here that George III's letter gives no hint that the "interchange of commodities" might not be the concern of all sovereigns.

At the same time, however, the commonality of purpose among sovereigns exemplified in their efforts to gather knowledge and redistribute the goods of the world confronted one major obstacle. Laws and customs differed from one country to another, meaning that peoples remained in various degrees of ignorance of each other. The difficulties that naturally resulted from such a situation were clearly present in current relations between Great Britain and China. But, like other such problems between nations, they could easily be resolved if resident ministers from one sovereign were placed in the court of the other. In this way, the king concluded, "every misunderstanding could be prevented, every inconvenience removed, a firm and lasting friendship cemented and a return to mutual good offices secured between our respective Empires."[9]

8. See Vattel 1916, 3:121, for an identical argument. Vattel adds that given the imbalances of distribution, nations have an "obligation" to promote mutual commerce.

9. The link between diplomacy and commerce, particularly with respect to the issue of resident ministers, can be found, for example, in A. Smith 1978:552–553, in a lecture dated 1766.

The embassy came, therefore, to establish amicable relations and create institutions designed to prevent future problems by means of a free exchange of ideas and goods. To achieve success in the venture, the king had selected an extraordinary person as his representative. George Lord Viscount Macartney, "well beloved Cousin and Counsellor, former ambassador to Russia, former Governor-general in India, Knight of the Bath, Privy Councillor, member of the royal order of the White Eagle, nobleman of high rank, one possessed of great virtue, wisdom, and ability," had been made the king's "Ambassador Extraordinary and Plenipotentiary."

This, then, is the content of the letter Lord Macartney carried to China and delivered to the Qianlong emperor in a bejeweled box. While it might be easy to dismiss many of the king's pronouncements as hyperbole only marginally related to the actual conditions of Anglo-Chinese relations, I would argue that it is precisely the content of the letter and the way in which the British ambassador insisted on presenting it that provides a point of entry into the cultural world from which the letter came. For in addition to references concerning the British government's understanding of the duties, obligations, and rights of monarchs and their representatives, and the meaning of the interchange of commodities between nations, the text also signals a British understanding of the object to which this overture was directed, the Qianlong emperor, the *absolute ruler* of the world's most "populous and extensive" empire. In order the better to understand the complex of elements involved in George III's letter, I begin with an exploration of the cultural sphere that produced these statements and, in a manner of speaking, George Lord Macartney as well.

3.3   The Public Sphere and the Intellectual World of Lord Macartney

In the second half of the eighteenth century, British government officials as well as political economists and moral philosophers understood diplomacy and commerce as two specific mechanisms for communicating across national boundaries. Among other things each form of communication involved negotiations, through which rational exchange produced "reciprocal advantages" (see, for example, Staunton 1797, 1:18). Such notions of exchange were, in turn, a product of a new kind of social formation that arose out of eighteenth-century bourgeois civil society, the so-called public sphere (Habermas 1962). Made up of novel institutions such as coffee houses, salons, assembly rooms at spas and resorts, gardens of the wealthy, men's clubs, the new weekly and monthly magazines, and various organizations designed to produce and disseminate the arts and sciences, including those under kingly patronage such as the Royal Academy and Royal Society, the public sphere generated a new source of authority in society called "public opinion." Construed as "the universal reason of the generality of thinking individuals continuously engaged in open discussion" (Baker 1992:183), bourgeois public opinion pitted itself on the one hand against inherited privilege and on the other against the "vulgarity" of the "lower" orders (Stallybrass and White 1986:80–100). Ideally, the authority of public opinion was supposed to produce a social order governed by enlightened human rationality, a rationality defined with reference to methods of scientific inquiry.[10]

Much ink has been spilled of late over the issue of whether the public sphere ever actually existed in late eighteenth-century Europe, whether it might not have been an unrealized and perhaps unrealizable ideal, or whether it might not have been an effective propaganda device for the establishment of bourgeois hegemony.[11] Rather than enter this debate, I simply wish to draw attention to the fact that this new sense of the public coincided with European empire building in the Americas, Asia, and Africa, an imperialism that was directly or indirectly advanced by many of the luminaries of the British public sphere, however it may be defined. And yet, whether the public sphere was a reality for eighteenth-century Englishmen is in some ways beside the point. A number of the people dealt with below acted as if what contemporary scholars have termed the "public sphere" was real enough and saw themselves participating in and shaping it. Such beliefs on their part help to explain certain features of the planning and organization of the British embassy.

10. One of the major strengths of the Habermasian model is to draw attention to the specificities of history and the possibility that a given economic form may not produce a universal social form. The description of the public sphere I provide here might better be understood as an idealization. Frequently lost in the euphoria over this notion in recent academic debate is reflection on the processes of exclusion by which this space of the public was constituted. Women, children, workers, the poor, and Africans, native Americans, and Asians (to give but a few examples), seldom entered debates except as objects of contemplation for "enlightened rationality." On the construction of a bourgeois space that provides an alternative to the Habermasian notion see Stallybrass and White 1986.

11. For various views on the issue of the public sphere see Stallybrass and White 1986, the articles in Calhoun 1992, and Eagleton 1990.

One might begin with a discussion of the Literary Club, to which Lord Macartney was elected in 1786. As an expression of public-sphere culture, one would be hard-pressed to find a more exemplary institution. The Club was founded in 1764 by the noted portraitist Sir Joshua Reynolds, court painter to George III and first president of the Royal Academy. Its original membership included Samuel Johnson, who, among his many other talents, was the guiding intellectual force behind one of the more long-lived publications of the era, *The Gentleman's Magazine;* political philosopher Edmund Burke; poet and dramatist Oliver Goldsmith; classical scholar Bennet Langton; and bibliophile Topham Beauclerk. By the time of Macartney's election, the club membership had grown to include orientalist Sir William Jones, naturalist and president of the Royal Society Sir Joseph Banks, actor David Garrick, historian Edward Gibbon, political economist Adam Smith, politician Charles James Fox, James Boswell, and a number of clergymen and titled nobility.

Made up of what historian Lewis Curtis calls the "intellectual aristocracy" of Georgian England, the Club was organized around the principle of diverse membership. Meetings provided occasions where such diversity, "strengthened . . . by the ideal of precise, informed statement," produced the "manly conversation" that Gibbon seems to have found so engaging. Spatially gendered in this way, public-sphere institutions such as the Literary Club organized discourses in which men agreed to disagree, and "thus hoped to find truth" (Curtis and Liebert 1963:36), the masculinized "laws" which governed the natural and social world. The notion of manly exchange is crucial here; spirited, informed conversation (not gossip), when combined with a sound British empiricist faith in experience and a belief that rationality and morality were inseparable, offered the only possibility of finding truth. These principles of truth production also help to explain Macartney's election to the club. What he had to contribute was a kind of experience that few of the other members possessed, that of the seasoned diplomat who had served in the West Indies, India, and Russia.

The rules that governed the organization of the Literary Club also inform a number of notions that seem central to an understanding of Macartney. First and foremost, the attributes associated with the Club were also those of the idealized bourgeois gentleman. The gentleman kept himself informed of the events of the day, took a keen interest in the arts and scientific progress, cultivated an informed sense of taste (see below), and was disinterested, meaning that he was unbiased, impartial, and, rather than being self-seeking, worked for the general good. Moreover, and this was especially the case with members of the Club, his loyalties lay with the crown, while he himself was supposedly above corruption.

The attributes of Club members may seem overstated, particularly when we recall that the gentlemanly ideal emerged at a time of intense factional politics and political corruption in England.[12] Parliamentary seats were bought and sold; official positions were difficult to obtain without influence; and political patronage was the key to advancement, a situation that Macartney himself not only recognized but participated in actively to advance his own career.[13]

The real/ideal dichotomy in the writings of Britain's "intellectual aristocracy" as well as contradictions in Macartney's own behavior suggest the possibility that representations of and attitudes about conditions in Great Britain were transposed onto other national and social realms — in this case, China and the Chinese. Repeatedly Macartney's account, as well as those of other members of the embassy, used the valorized attributes of public sphere culture to structure their writings — judgment, evaluation, pronouncements to the Qing court, and the organization of the accounts themselves are written through these ideals. Equally important, negative attributes of the contemporary political scene in Great Britain such as corruption and influence peddling were, consciously or not, projected onto China. They provided rich metaphors for translating "Chinese action" into familiar behavioral categories. The embassy accounts also draw discursive authority from commonsense beliefs about China to be found in discussions of national character and in changing notions of aesthetics exemplified by debates over taste, which circulated among the intellectual aristocracy of Georgian England.[14]

12. On political corruption in the reign of George III, see Namier 1930:4–7 and 1965: 158–172 and Watson 1960:8–9. Namier argues that "corruption" may also be seen as a way in which the nouveaux riches entered politics, without which the House of Commons would have been represented by only one class, the landed gentry (5). Among the new moneyed interests were the EIC "nabobs" (see Watson 1960:163), who drew a good deal of criticism from intellectual aristocrats such as Edmund Burke; see his attack against the EIC in 1866, 8:11–113.

13. See, for example, Cranmer-Byng's discussion of Macartney's career in MD, 17–23. Macartney characterized himself as above corruption, while serving as a loyal public servant who received few rewards; see Pritchard, 1936:274, 294.

14. See IOR, "First, Second and Third Reports...," which notes that the Chinese government is the "most corrupt in the Universe," that the Chinese are jealous, suspicious, timid, superstitious, and "disinclined to innovation" (1793:4).

3.4   National Character

As indicated earlier, Macartney and Dundas agreed that the Chinese empire had an erroneous impression of the English national character. But what, we might ask, did they mean by national character? With this term, eighteenth-century Englishmen usually referred to the *morals and manners* of a people that lived within a definable territory. According to this taxonomic scheme, nations were definable by characteristic features, many of which were carried by the population of a given nation. Members of one nation shared common features of behavior, attitudes, beliefs, and practices, which distinguished them from the inhabitants of all other nations. In turn, people acquired characteristics through social intercourse, with one generation passing on specific traits and *usages* (customs or habits) to the next. The morals and manners of various groups made it possible to distinguish Englishmen from Spaniards, Frenchmen, Chinese, Pacific islanders, and each of these from the others. In England, knowledge of these differences was, in part, produced by those voyages that George III alluded to in his letter to the Qianlong emperor.

The origin or source of such differentiating characteristics was, however, somewhat in dispute. One school of thought, found for example in the mid-eighteenth-century writings of Montesquieu (1748:221–234), held that climate was the determining factor in shaping the common characteristics of a given population. Writing at the same time as Montesquieu, David Hume granted the importance of climate or of "physical causes," but only insofar as they affected human physiology. Far more significant, Hume claimed, were "moral causes"; these included "the nature of government, the revolutions of public affairs, the plenty or penury in which the people live, the situation of the nation with regard to its neighbors..." (1898:244).

Hume developed his argument against climatic determinism through historical analogy, the content of which he organized under nine observations. For purposes here the most significant of these are the first and the last because, interestingly enough, they deal with China and England, forming two poles of a diametric opposition. Where government has long been established, Hume tells us, "it spreads a national character over the whole empire, and communicates to every part a similarity of manners. Thus the CHINESE have the *greatest uniformity of character imaginable:* though the air and climate in different parts of those vast dominions, admit of very considerable variations" (1898:249, emphasis added). China was, as he argued in another essay, an enormous unity, "speaking one language, governed by one law, and sympathizing in the same manners" (1898:183).

If the principle of China was one, the principle of England was many, a proposition that led Hume to a rather startling conclusion.

> ... the English government is a mixture of monarchy, aristocracy, and democracy. The people in authority are composed of gentry and merchants. All sects of religion are to be found among them. And the great liberty and independency, which every man enjoys, allows him to display the manners peculiar to him. Hence the ENGLISH, of any people in the universe, have the least of a national character; unless this very singularity may pass for such. (1898:252) [15]

i.e, diversity / no uswall

The English were distinguished, therefore, by their diversity of manners, by a well-balanced structure of authority, by the absence of autocratic power, by religious tolerance, and by liberty, all of which figure England as a universal exception. What strikes me as important about Hume's construction is that his opposition between China and England provides a ground upon which English exceptionalism could be founded. The characteristic features which set England apart from all other nations also dovetail rather nicely with the values espoused by intellectual aristocrats in organizations such as the Literary Club.

While it is doubtful that Lord Macartney would have found anything in Hume's definition of Englishness disagreeable, he was less interested in displaying English diversity to the Qing court than in presenting a particular facet of the national character, one quite visible in the English king's letter. English curiosity about the world, the desire to learn about the morals and manners of other peoples, the voyages sponsored by the king to gather knowledge, the institutions George III patronized to disseminate this knowledge, and the interest in developing benevolent ties with a great empire like China — all of these are part of the morals and manners of English gentlemen, of the men who made up the Literary Club, men of taste, discernment, intellectual curiosity, disinterestedness, circumspection, and high moral principle. This was the English character that Macartney wanted to present to China.

---

15. March (1974:39–45) reviews claims similar to those of Hume in other European writers, especially J. S. Mill. The Royal Pavilion of George IV in Brighton is a case in point, see Nash 1991.

But what of the object he thought he was addressing? How did he imagine it? What were China's morals and manners and how did they relate to Macartney's evocation of "oriental customs and ideas"?

3.5   Discussions of Taste and Images of China

In the middle of the eighteenth century, Great Britain was swept by a China vogue. Under the rubric *Chinoiserie,* "Chinese style" found its way into garden design, architecture, and painting. A similar phenomenon occurred in literature and moral philosophy. The Chinoiserie craze peaked twenty years before the Macartney embassy, but its effects were still felt early into the nineteenth century. Macartney himself viewed China in part through these English-made images, while occasionally being disturbed by them.

Beginning in the sixteenth century, accounts about China began to filter into Europe. Some were produced by Jesuit missionaries, some by seaborne voyagers who touched the China coast, and others by members of embassies from various European countries. From these sources a highly idealized China emerged, a utopia in which a benign despotism directed a rational and wise government staffed by an educated elite, China's "mandarins." The result was a nation rich in wealth and agricultural abundance, capable of sustaining the world's largest population. China's positive attributes could be contrasted, as the French physiocrats demonstrated, to the shortcomings of contemporary European society (Allen 1937, 1:182–183 and Appleton 1951:37–52).

By the middle of the eighteenth century, a veritable cult of Confucius had emerged in France, where the Chinese sage came to stand for all of China's ancient wisdom. Moral philosophers such as Quesnay praised the virtues of the Chinese system and urged Europe's monarchs to model themselves after the emperor of China. In Austria, the Holy Roman emperor Joseph II seems to have taken these suggestions quite literally: there are pictures of him plowing the first spring furrow in imitation of a Chinese emperor (*Europa und die Kaiser von China* 1985:304). Even England was not immune to these positive representations of China. In the late seventeenth century, Sir William Temple authored a number of favorable pieces on Confucius, while other English writers saw in China a partial realization of More's utopia. Such sentiments were still in vogue in the middle of the next century. On the occasion of reviewing the essays of the Jesuit missionary Du

Halde for the *Gentleman's Magazine,* Samuel Johnson wrote enthusiastically of Confucius and China (Appleton 1951:42–51 and Fan 1945).

As trade increased between Europe and China, Chinese porcelain, lacquerware, furniture, and textiles circulated freely in England and inspired new design patterns among artisans. By the 1750s, books such as William and John Halfpenny's *New Designs for Chinese Temples, Triumphal Arches, Garden Seats, Palings, etc* (1750–1752), Charles Over's *Ornamental Architecture in the Gothic, Chinese and Modern Taste* (1758), and Paul Decker's *Chinese Architecture Civil and Ornamental* (1759) influenced architectural and garden designs. Further stimulating interest in Chinese design was the account of the emperor's gardens at the Yuanming yuan by the French Jesuit Attiret, which was translated and widely circulated in midcentury English magazines. Probably the most influential of the artistic design works, however, were those by Sir William Chambers. In his *Designs of Chinese Buildings* (1757, with opening paragraphs by Samuel Johnson) and *Dissertation on Oriental Gardening* (1772), Chambers, a former East India Company supercargo at Canton, strongly advocated the use of Chinese styles as part of larger projects.

Yet, at the same time he was championing Chinese design, Chambers also struck a cautionary note by indicating that he did not wish to be numbered among "the exaggerators of Chinese excellence."[16] The refusal by Chambers to join wholeheartedly in praise of China was paralleled by a growing opposition in England to Chinese influence in the arts and in moral philosophy. The attack came from a variety of quarters—outraged classicists defending Greek and Roman "purity," clergymen, and staunch Englishmen extolling English values and "taste." Criticisms of things Chinese, presented either in a satirical manner or as antagonistic attacks, shared a number of common features. First of all, according to critics, it was primarily the nouveaux riches and women who were attracted to Chinoiserie. The former were probably suspect because they were also seen as one important source of political corruption and influence peddling in the British Parliament; the latter because women were considered to be incapable of aesthetic judgment. Secondly, for some, the forms present in Chinoiserie ran directly against considerations of artistic standards by deviating from "Nature and

16. For this discussion of the China vogue in England, I follow Appleton 1951:90–120. He cites Chambers on 102. Also see Allen 1937, Bald 1950, Ch'en 1936, and Steegmann 1936.

Truth." Although the use of these terms varied significantly among critics, notions of simplicity, order, and symmetry appear to have been essential to most definitions. By any calculation, Chinoiserie was none of these things. Third, some critics like William Whitehead argued that Chinoiserie wasn't Chinese at all, but rather a fabrication of European designers (see Appleton 1951:103–119). This last criticism was especially damaging because for the aesthetically concerned it meant that art was being transformed into fashion and, hence, a commodity.

Eventually, the reaction against Chinoiserie became a wholesale criticism of China. In periodicals such as *The Connoisseur* and *Gentlemen's Magazine*, Chinese style was denigrated much along the lines of the following attack on Chinese painting that appeared in *The World* in 1755.

> The paintings, which, like the architecture continually revolt against the truth of things, as little deserve the name of elegant. False light, false shadows, false perspective and proportions, gay colours without that gradation of tint, that mutual variety of lightened and darkened objects ... in short every combination of forms in nature, without expression and without meaning, are the essentials of Chinese painting. (Cited in Appleton 1951:119)

These failures in art, these false productions, all pointed to the same thing — a failure of the Chinese mind to demonstrate the capacity for accurately representing reality either in the natural or social worlds.

This shift in attitudes toward Chinese art was conditioned by another phenomenon as well. Throughout the eighteenth century, and running alongside discussions of national character, there emerged a new kind of history, circulated in part through the new periodicals. Set against a comparative background of Greco-Roman antiquity, a primarily secular historiography took the nation as a primary object of analysis. Under the influence of the perceived pattern of scientific developments, the narrative principles that ordered this history were notions of qualitative progress, which, in turn, were closely tied to claims about the growth of knowledge of the natural and human world. Progress was, on the one hand, material; it could be read in the enormous increase in commodities available in the marketplace, in the emergence of technologies that replaced human labor power, and in the wealth that now flowed into England from other parts of the world. But progress was also a sign of something else: it indicated a rapid movement from the past, a leap away from the domination of the

Church, from ritual and ceremony, superstition and magic, and from custom and habit. It signified a shift from a world supposedly caught up in surface appearances to one that was discernible and representable in language when viewed from a thoroughly masculinized and, hence, *reason*able perspective informed by correct moral, aesthetic, and scientific sensibilities. Moreover, if one were viewing the world in these terms, it would reveal secrets previously obscured by deceptive appearances.[17] In this shift of perception, the image of China suffered immeasurably (and, for many Euro-American intellectuals conditioned by these views of world historical processes and the nature of reality, to a large extent still does).

The perceptual change I allude to here is particularly evident in re-evaluations of China among England's intellectual aristocracy. Hume, for example, saw little or no progress in the Chinese sciences since the time of Confucius and, tellingly, tied this absence to an inability to break with the past. Although China's uniformity of morals and manners made the people polite, it had also produced intellectual stagnation (1898, 1:183). In a famous dialogue recorded by Boswell, Dr. Johnson, whose early enthusiasm for things Chinese seems to have waned with age, dismissed China as having produced little more than pottery (Allen 1937, 1:187). That other prestigious member of the Literary Club, Sir William Jones, could find little good to say about China in 1790, two years before the departure of Lord Macartney from England. According to Jones,

> their *letters,* if we may so call them, are merely the symbols of ideas;
> the popular *religion* was imported from *India* in an age compara-
> tively modern; and their *philosophy* seems yet in so rude a state, as

17. It is generally held that eighteenth-century Europe saw the birth of universal history and the notion of continuous time. While I do not dispute this view, I am also struck by the presence of national and particularist histories in contemporary English periodicals. See, for example, the *Annual Register,* which was begun in 1758 and carried sections on the history of the past year in Great Britain, chronicles, and state papers. One would like to say that perhaps this marks a distinction between a more rigorous, philosophically oriented approach and popular culture, except that Hume also wrote a history of England, while Edmund Burke edited and contributed to the *Register* for a number of years. For an overview of changing perceptions of history in the eighteenth century, see Collingwood 1946:59–85 and Nisbet 1969:104–125. On connections made between eighteenth-century Europe and European antiquity, see Bernal 1987:192–204. On reason and progress, and the gendering of both, see Lloyd 1984:57–73. On perceptual changes and new ways of seeing the world, see Lowe 1982 and Reiss 1982.

hardly to serve the appellation; they have no *ancient monuments,*
from which their origin can be traced even by plausible conjecture;
their *sciences* are wholly exotick; and their *mechanical arts* have
nothing in them characteristick of a particular family; nothing,
which any set of men, in a country so highly favoured by nature,
might not have discovered and improved. They have indeed, both
national musick and national poetry, and both of them beauti-
fully pathetick; but of painting, sculpture, or architecture, as arts
of imagination, they seem (like other *Asiaticks*) to have no idea.
(Teignmouth 1807, 3:147–148)

Like other totalizing repudiations of China in English discourse, this by
Jones had little to do with any new empirical knowledge about China, nor
was it (and this seems rather a curious position for empiricists to have
arrived at) based on any firsthand experience. Rather, as Greg Blue has
pointed out, the rejection is grounded in "a change in Western perspectives" (1988:108), just as, I might add, the earlier idealization of China had
been. Which brings up a rather interesting point. The peculiar representations of China that emerged in England after 1750, exemplified in the comments of Hume, Johnson, Jones, and others, appear unseemly and out of
proportion for an intelligentsia that prided itself on the rational exchange
of ideas and a judicious balance in human affairs. The disparity between
these values of the English intellectual elite and their pronouncements on
China might lead one to conclude that perhaps China annoyed Englishmen precisely because it stubbornly resisted European penetration and the
public-sphere definition of "reason," while continuing to function outside
a Eurocentrically imagined world.

More to the point, perhaps, China's "self-sufficiency" and refusal to meet
Europe on Europe's terms seem to have generated both awe and frustration.
The records of the Macartney embassy abound with both. Vice-ambassador
George Staunton, himself a member of the Royal Society and Doctor of
Law from Oxford, observed that unlike other places where native populations had assimilated European "manners, dress, sentiments, and habits,"
the Chinese, after one hundred years of contact with British traders, had
not changed at all! Making matters worse was the fact that Great Britain
was *dependent* on China; that irreplaceable commodity tea had become "a
necessary of life in most of the ranks of society in England" (1797, 1:16–
According to the wisdom of the time, the cause of this sad state of af-

fairs was not far to seek. It is inscribed in successive generations of reports by East India Company supercargos at Canton and in traveler's accounts of China-coast ports. Those same "mandarins" who had been praised by an earlier generation of sinophiles were now held to be the single obstacle to improving relations between Great Britain and China. They made up a ruling class that seemed incapable of acknowledging the fantasy world it lived in, and which, perhaps most importantly, viewed those engaged in mercantile activities as the "lowest [social] class." China's "supercilious and arbitrary magistrates" (Staunton 1797, 1:14) were prejudiced against and jealous of strangers, while remaining aloof and self-deluded about their own superiority. From the point of view of England's intellectual aristocrats, there was absolutely no ground in the past, as Jones would have it, and certainly not in the present, for any sense of superiority. These sentiments were repeated almost verbatim by successive generations of Englishmen until the fall of the Qing dynasty. In a sense, the British assault on China in the nineteenth century was a repetition of a prior discursive violence; China was destroyed in writing well before a single British gun was leveled at a Chinese person.

But if Chinese resistance suggests one reason why British intellectuals felt it necessary to bring China low rhetorically, it is only part of the story. In their discussion of the British public sphere, Stallybrass and White emphasize that it was forged in large part through negations, ones which produced a "new domain" by "taking into itself as *negative introjections* [emphasis in original] the very domains which surround and threaten it. It *produces and reproduces itself through the process of denial and defiance*" (1986:89, emphasis added).

I would suggest that this is precisely what transpires in the constitution of a negative China. The negation of Chinese style, morals, and manners or Macartney's more general "oriental customs and ideas" produces bourgeois taste, an aesthetics that, as Terry Eagleton recently noted (1990), provides evaluative criteria in numerous domains of bourgeois practice. With respect to representations of China in British discourse, the effect is twofold. On the one hand, it feminizes China; much like female, as opposed to male, sensibilities, China is jealous, misguided, caught up in appearances, irrational, arbitrary, and whimsical. On the other hand, this imaginary China functions to produce bourgeois masculine identity as that which is equivalent to the good, the true, the real, the rational and the upright. Among other things, this suggests that the negation of China, particularly of the Chinese past, produces the "West," with a living China simultaneously a negativity for constructing a superior English national identity and for demonstrating that England had now transcended all past global orders. And denial and defiance lie on all sides. If the "West" is impossible without "China," that discursive regularity is repeatedly elided; and such elision is accomplished in large measure by defying the imaginary China. The first British embassy is a good case in point, for Macartney not only anticipated, but, in the end, claimed that as a result of his acts of defiance—in particular, his refusal to participate in certain forms of Qing court ceremony—his embassy was a success.

3.6   Ceremony, Sovereignty, and Diplomacy

Ceremony was a problem for enlightened reason. Increasingly under the sway of instrumentalism and utilitarianism, public-sphere rationality pitted itself against ancient usages such as those to be found in royal pomp and splendor. To the reasoning eye, ceremony was contentless form designed to mask the mechanisms of power and awe the unenlightened mind. At the same time, in what would become a conservative defence of traditionalism also based on reason, ceremony had its uses. Edmund Burke, for example, may have been referring to the spectacle of royal ceremony when he spoke of pleasing illusions "that made power gentle and obedience liberal" (cited in Eagleton 1990:58). But there was a bit of illusion even in exposing such illusory aspects of power. For in the case of the British embassy to China the question is whether diplomacy as a process of establishing "reciprocal advantages" was imaginable or even possible without ceremony, and if not, what did ceremony do? Why, for example, was court audience and the form it took so crucial to British thinking on the embassy? Why was mere form so important to a seasoned diplomat like Lord Macartney?

In late eighteenth-century Europe, concern over ceremony was linked to the dignity and honor of the sovereign represented by an ambassador. As much political theory indicated, the sovereign stood for the unity and independence of his nation (an important point made in ceremonial court audiences throughout Europe).[18] In his influential work, *The Law of Nations,*

18. Discussions of sovereignty can be found in seventeenth- and eighteenth-century debates on the origins of civil society, which run the gamut from social contract theories to theories of the divine right of kings and are involved fundamentally with identifying

Vattel argued that in the sovereign, as "the depository of the obligations and rights relating to the government," was found "the moral person ... clothed with the public authority and with all that goes to make the moral personality of the Nation." As the corporeal and transcendental center of the nation (Kantorowicz 1957), the sovereign was consequently "sacred and inviolable." When the ambassadors of sovereignties imagined in this fashion entered other nations, their person, too, was sacred and inviolable (Vattel 1916, 3:21–23, 371). To threaten the lofty station of the sovereign or his representatives was thus to threaten the identity of the nation.

In Europe, diplomats attempted to avoid affronts to their sovereign and themselves by focusing attention on matters of precedence and on mastering a variety of ceremonial forms to be found in different courts.[19] No less an authority than John Adams makes clear the importance of ceremony in European courts and how it must be endured before diplomatic negotiation can begin. Yet Adams himself did not think it wise to forego ceremony if it meant that the newly created United States of America would not be treated on an equal footing with European nations.[20] These concerns suggest that, in theory at least, it was through ceremony that mutual recogni-

---

the sources and representations of authority. For a review of sovereignty in a "history of ideas" format, see EB 1911, 25:519–523, which indicates the historical ambiguities of the concept; also see ESS 1934, 14:265–269. More recently, Hinsley notes that the current notion of sovereignty as it relates to international relations is a relatively recent invention, dating roughly from the Congress of Vienna, see 1969 and 1986. Through a reading of Hobbes's *Leviathan*, Ryan (1982:4–8) has argued that sovereignty was constituted in discourse by the systematic exclusion of other views of authority, which serves to establish the absolutism of the sovereign's position. This last position is consistent with that discussed above concerning the formation of the public sphere.

19. Vattel himself dismissed precedence as a "mere matter of custom"; however, he also explains that various rankings of officials were created below that of the ambassador to circumvent the problems posed by it (1916, 3:367–368). The question of precedence in relations between European nations in the eighteenth century has been little studied. In general, the subject has been obscured because historians of European diplomacy assume that the 1648 Treaty of Westphalia established the equality of European nations. Yet substantial evidence indicates that questions of precedence continued to exist and could at times lead to violent confrontations. For some examples of incidents that occurred in London, see Lachs 1965:108–109; Horn 1961:205; and E. Turner 1959:131, 159–160, and 216. Martens provides a section in his work on "avoiding disputes concerning precedence" (1795:136–144). Horn claims that the section was appended by Cobbett; see 1961:205–206.

20. On the importance of ceremony in European courts, see Martens 1795:136–144. John Adams's observations on ceremony are included in his account of an audience with George III in 1785; see C. F. Adams 1853, 8:251–259.

tion of sovereignty was asserted and state-to-state equality achieved (Hevia 1989). Such ceremonial recognition was a prerequisite for the business of embassies, for the negotiation of substantive issues, and for the codification of agreements in the form of treaties.

But given what has already been said about the negative constructions of China during this same period, how could Lord Macartney hope to achieve mutual recognition of sovereignty in a country whose leadership was presumed to be so benighted? The answer to this question lies in a set of mutually reinforcing propositions or beliefs generated out of the history of Anglo-Chinese contact, and out of the British construction of China.

The first of these propositions is linked to the notion that the reason the Qing court did not have an appreciation of English character was because its contact with Englishmen had been limited to "vulgar and uninstructed" British seamen and "other persons of inferior station" (Staunton 1797, 1:15). Indeed, the EIC itself admitted in its instructions to Lord Macartney that British sailors at Canton were "dissolute and riotous," which accounted for trade having been confined to that single port and for the view among China's "superior Mandarins" that the British were "barbarous" (Pritchard 1938:213). Chinese officials had, in other words, never met an Englishman they liked, and certainly none of the stature of Lord Macartney, who was not only a nobleman, diplomat, and member of England's intellectual aristocracy, but, as George III's letter indicated, cousin to the king (!), a fabrication designed to further impress Chinese officials.[21]

The second proposition had to do with British perceptions of the emperor himself. In fantasies that are most likely linked to sinophile constructions of benign despotism, the attributes associated with the emperor, unlike his empire, were given a positive valence. In the absence of any empirical evidence to the contrary, except perhaps for some impressions generated by missionaries at the court in Peking, a few East India Company supercargos in Canton argued that the emperor was of a liberal, open disposition and, in fact, was probably completely unaware of the abusive conditions under which Englishmen suffered at the hands of his officials. Most

---

21. In researching previous embassies to China, Cobb noted that the Dutch had once had difficulty at Canton when they could not answer in the affirmative that the ambassador was related to the Dutch royal house; see IOMC, 91:68. Ewart, the physician on the Cathcart embassy, had made the same point in a letter to Dundas (142). In a rather testy reply to this and other suggestions made by Ewart, Macartney indicated that this was common knowledge (155).

importantly, their accounts were influenced in London during the time the embassy was planned. Having constructed the ruler of China as the exception to the rule of China, Dundas and Macartney believed that all that need be done was to find some way to lay the facts before him. If all went well, following a court audience, Macartney would do so in the business portion of the embassy; so enlightened, the emperor would then presumably alter conditions to the satisfaction of the British.[22]

Proposition two created a certain quandary, however—how could the many obstacles (corrupt officials in Canton, antagonistic French and Portuguese missionaries in Peking) between the British ambassador and the emperor be circumvented, and on what pretext could this be accomplished? In the end, Macartney and Dundas decided (1) to present the embassy to Qing officials as a mission to congratulate the emperor on his eightieth birthday and (2) to avoid the Canton establishment and an overland trek to the capital by landing in as close proximity as possible to Peking—that is, at Tianjin. The landing site was justified to Chinese officials on the grounds that the presents being brought to China were of such a large and delicate nature that an overland journey might damage them.

A third proposition had to do with the British gifts and the role Macartney envisioned for them in impressing the Qing court with Great Britain's arts and superiority. Well aware that China's ruler already possessed large number of European manufactures (derisively dismissed by Staunton as "toys and sing-songs," 1797, 1:48), Macartney decided to provide the emperor with a means of distinguishing between "treasure," "trifles of momentary curiosity," and things "more glittering than useful" and the items brought, "whose merit lay in their utility" (IOMC, 20:109).

The centerpiece of the gifts was an elaborate planetarium, accompanied by a variety of astronomical devices. A descriptive catalog prepared upon arrival in China emphasized either the ability of these technologies to represent the universe accurately or, in the case of telescopes and measuring devices, their usefulness in creating such representations. Samples were also brought of pottery and chinaware produced in modern kilns, tapestries, carpets, saddles, two yellow carriages, muskets, pistols, swords, cannon, cloth and woolens, and lustres. According to the catalog, all were of

22. See Dundas's instructions to Macartney in Morse 1926, 2:233–234. Dundas notes that "the representations of various Travellers afford the strongest reason to believe that the Emperor himself is accessible...."

the highest quality and produced through the most modern methods available. In addition, there were representations "taken from Nature" of the royal family; of cities, towns, churches, gardens, castles, bridges, and the lakes of England; of sea and land battles, volcanoes, antiquities, dockyards, horse races, bullfighting, and "most other objects curious or remarkable in the dominions of his Britannic Majesty, and other parts of Europe"; and "a complete model of a Ship of War," the *Royal Sovereign* (!), with one hundred brass cannons of "immense calibre or size."[23] All of the gifts had a single purpose—to catch the curiosity of the Qianlong emperor. As Staunton put it, "whatever tended to illustrate science, or promote the arts, would give more solid and permanent satisfaction to a prince whose time in life would, *naturally,* lead him to seek, in every object, the utility of which it was susceptible" (1797, 1:49, emphasis added).

This is a rather revealing turn of phrase, for it indicates again the transposition of normative British beliefs onto others as if they were self-evident and universal. One might say, therefore, that Staunton's allusion to the emperor's maturity is to recognition of utility as "manly conversation" is to rationality, or as negotiation is to reciprocal advantages. But why might such analogies be attractive? Recall the negative constructions that were at the same time producing a feminized China. By the internal logic of the relationships produced in that process, it was necessary to construct the emperor of China as masculine if the embassy was to have any success at all in placing relations with China on a new footing. Only an agent so constructed was capable of entering an agreement that might be legitimate; only a masculine subject (particularly one in an otherwise feminized sphere) could sign a treaty and be relied upon to live up to its provisions.

There is, however, reason to question the extent to which Macartney or Staunton actually believed in the attributes they assumed to be those of the Qianlong emperor. To put it another way, Macartney appears to have guarded against the possibility that the emperor might not be capable of understanding the utility of the British gifts by cloaking the display in his notion of "oriental customs and ideas." This assumption, in turn, was grounded in the general belief that Asian courts and "Oriental voluptuaries" (to use Kant's quaint phrase, 1987:134) loved pomp, splendor, and elaborate display; and that it was on the basis of such "external" appear-

23. See IOMC, 20:142–144, and Cranmer-Byng and Levere 1981:520–525. A Chinese translation is in ZGCB, 22b–24b. The name of the ship appears in Waley-Cohen 1993:1534.

ance that the oriental court of China judged people. It was probably these considerations more than any others that account not only for the way the embassy presented itself for the imperial audience in Rehe,[24] but also for the decision to include items among the gifts that were "imperial" or yellow in color (Pritchard 1936:281). Such concerns may also account for the elaborate decoration done to the planetarium. It was ostentatiously embellished with gilt and enamel, and festooned with pineapples and other decorations by the Pall Mall watchmaker Vulliamy (Cranmer-Byng and Levere 1981: 512). From what can be deduced from descriptions and surviving sketches, the net effect was to clothe this "utmost effort of astronomical science and mechanic art . . . ever made in Europe" in something akin to Chinoiserie design!

Closely related to these considerations was a final one involving the court audience in which Lord Macartney planned to present the letter from George III. Even if one granted that the emperor was exceptional, the problem still remained that to "enlightened" Englishmen, the empire he ruled was a despotism, demanding of all those who approached the emperor's throne total submission in the form of humiliating "genuflections and prostrations." Such demands were disgraceful on two counts. First, they hit at the very core of British notions of sovereignty by attacking the dignity of the sovereign. To perform such acts would, therefore, preclude the possibility of mutual recognition of sovereign equality, and end Macartney's mission before the business of his embassy had begun.

Secondly, touching the body to the ground, especially the head or face, seems to have conjured up all sorts of distasteful images in the imagination of the bourgeois gentlemen, not the least being the conflation of ground/low with dirt and the "vulgar" orders. Prostration, in fact, would become in large measure the sign par excellence of Asia's slavish and feminized masses. Examples abound of the revulsion Englishmen felt when they saw Asians perform such acts; invariably they associated them with humiliation, degradation, and, as they became conscious of what they took to be Asian religions, the worship of false gods (Hevia 1995). In this respect, perhaps what also might have bothered "rational" Englishmen was that the closer one came to the ground, the higher the object before one was elevated.

24. See Macartney's description in MD, 122, and the picture on the cover of Peyrefitte 1992 and in Singer 1992.

But how to avoid such humiliations? While in England, Macartney remained rather vague on this issue, arguing that any form of ceremony would be negotiated on site (IOMC, 91:159). Yet, it also seems fairly clear that he was fully prepared to defy court officials on this point, wagering that the embassy's display of "éclat" and decorum, the pronouncements in the king's letter, and the quality of the gifts would provide sufficient leverage to influence Chinese opinion. Dundas was rather less equivocal on the subject. In his instructions, he told Macartney to conform "to all ceremonials of the Court which may not commit the honor of your Sovereign or lessen your own dignity, so as to endanger the success of your negociation [*sic*]" (Morse 1926, 2:236). As will be clear in the next chapter, Macartney eventually hit on a strategy thoroughly consistent with the British notion of reciprocal advantages.

3.7   From Diplomatic Ceremony to the Business of Diplomacy

> Nature rarely produces in one district all the various things men
> have need of; one country abounds in wheat, another in pastures
> and cattle, a third in timber and metals, etc. If all these districts
> trade with one another, *as nature intended,* none of them will be
> without what is necessary and useful to them, and the intentions of
> nature, the common mother of mankind, will be fulfilled. Moreover,
> since one country is better adapted for growing one product than
> another ... each Nation will be assured of satisfying its wants and
> will use its land and direct its industries to the best advantage, *so that
> mankind as a whole will gain thereby* (emphasis added).[25]

The above quotation taken from Vattel's *The Law of Nations* might stand as a fuller elaboration of George III's reference to the benefits nations derive from the "interchange of commodities." Like Vattel, George places ultimate agency in a transcendental subject (a masculine God, the creator) with mercantilist and/or physiocratic desires, who seems to be encouraging human beings to engage in trade, and thus redistribute commodities to "his Creatures scattered over the surface of the earth" (Morse 1926, 2:

---

25. Vattel 1916, 3:121; this section ends with a notion that sounds much like one of the British justifications to use force against China in the nineteenth century: "such is the foundation of the *general obligation* upon Nations to promote mutual commerce with one another" (my emphasis).

245). This construction of exchange, referred to by Macartney as a principle of the soundest philosophy (IOMC, 91:39), can be located within a general discourse on political economy that focused attention on the duties and obligations of the sovereign in fostering the circulation of commodities and the increase of wealth in his kingdom. This idea of economic activity draws metaphorically from views of the proper management of a household.

In one version, the king, like the head of a household, was the lord and steward of the nation. As such he protected the polity and, through his judicious regulation, augmented the circulation of goods and money in the nation. The aggregate of circulating goods and money was termed wealth, and wealth as such provided a measure of the strength of the nation. Strength, in turn, was not conceived in economic terms, but rather as the total product of the proper regulation of the domain. When mobilized by the monarch, the nation's strength/wealth was used in conflicts with other domains.[26]

To insure circulation and augmentation, the king had a moral duty to guarantee the unobstructed flow of goods and money. He could do this internally by promoting public works, providing a system of justice that prevented members of society from encroaching on each other's property rights, and securing the borders of the nation. Externally, he accomplished it by promoting and protecting the exchange of goods and money with other nations.[27] The business of diplomacy was to further such reciprocal advantage.

Facilitating the exchange of commodities was, however, only one part of the business of diplomacy. To put it another way, commodity exchange might be better thought of as one means for balancing and regulating relations between nations, placing them (to use the language of the day) on a "definite and permanent footing" (Vattel 1916, 3:122). Once he had the emperor's attention, Macartney was to explain the many long-term advantages that would result from closer ties with Great Britain and increases in commodity circulation; even the opium trade was negotiable. If possible,

26. See Steuart 1966, 1:16–17. Similar constructs of the monarch appear implicit in Vattel, who refers to the king as a "wise and tender father and faithful administrator"; see 1916, 3:21. My discussion of political economy follows Tribe 1978:80–109.

27. See Vattel 1916, 3:35–36, 47–52, and 75–77, and A. Smith, whose discussion of the duties, obligations, and rights of sovereigns is in the often ignored "Book Five" of *Wealth of Nations;* see 1976:689 ff, as well as his 1978:5–6, and under "sovereign's rights" and "authority."

any understandings that arose from these conversations should be codi-
fied in a treaty of friendship and alliance. Macartney was also instructed
to attempt to acquire an imperial edict extending commercial relations to
additional ports on the China coast.[28] Finally, if the rhetorical presentation
of the public sphere failed to open the business of the embassy in mutually
beneficial directions, Macartney was instructed by EIC directors to gather
information on tea, cotton, and silk production in China with an eye to
transferring them to another area of scarcity, the British colony in India
(Pritchard 1938:217–219).

3.8   From the Court of St. James to the China Coast

On May 2, 1792, George Lord Macartney, former ambassador to Russia and recent governor of Madras, entered the Court of St. James, where,
in an audience with King George III, he was formally invested as the king's
ambassador to China. After his presentation to the king, Macartney knelt
on one knee and kissed his monarch's hand. The following day he was
named "Embassador Extraordinary and Plenipotentiary from the King of
Great Britain to the Emperor of China" and sworn in as a privy councillor.
In June, he was elevated to the rank of Viscount and given permission to
carry with him to China the "plate, canopy, pictures, and equipage of the
Crown" (Pritchard 1936:292–295).

Three days after this ceremony, the East India Company, which was to
pay the entire cost of the embassy, achieved one small victory in its efforts
to protect its interests and retain a degree of autonomy in China: Company
directors convinced Macartney and Dundas that they should be allowed
to announce the embassy. A three-man contingent titled the Secret and
Superintending Committee, made up of Henry Browne, Eyles Irwin, and
William Jackson, sailed from England on May 5 and arrived in Canton on
September 20, 1792. Once there, they sought an immediate audience with
the governor-general of Liangguang.[29]

28. IOMC, 91:39–43 and Morse 1926, 2:237–241. Macartney was also empowered to
seek to open Japan, as well as Southeast Asia, to British trade.

29. For the committee's account of events in Canton, see IOMC, 93:5–141. The account
left by Qing officials can be found in chapter 6. It is clear from both sources that the
EIC's insistence on sending the committee, rather than having the government depute a
royal commissioner to announce the embassy, greatly confused matters. The committee
interpreted the uncertainty it caused in the usual manner; it was just another case of the
obstructionism of local officials in Canton.

On September 26, 1792, Lord Macartney and fifty-six members of the embassy set sail from Portsmouth harbor aboard the H.M.S. *Lion,* a sixty-four gun warship, under the command of Captain Erasmus Gower. The remaining thirty-nine members of the embassy and the gifts for the emperor of China sailed on the *Hindostan,* a vessel of the East India Company's fleet, under Captain William Mackintosh. Nine months later the embassy arrived off the south coast of China, where Macartney learned that the emperor had given permission for the embassy to proceed to Tianjin (MD, 23 and 63).

As the fleet approached Tianjin, Macartney issued a proclamation on July 16 announcing his authority over the officers and crews of the EIC vessels and outlining the conduct he expected of his subordinates. Read on the deck of the *Lion* and *Hindostan,* the proclamation noted that one of the major problems in relations with China was the negative impression the Chinese had of Englishmen. Accordingly, Macartney warned everyone that their conduct at all times must be "regular" and "circumspect" and that if incidents occurred, he would not intercede in matters covered by Chinese law. Those who performed well would be reported favorably at home; those who did not would be suspended or dismissed on the spot. No one was to go ashore or wander about once there without the permission of a superior. No boxes or packages were to be removed from the ships or landing sites without the express permission of the ambassador. Trade of any sort was forbidden, unless Macartney himself determined that the object of his mission could be more readily obtained through such transactions. The reason for the ban was that both the architects of the mission and the Company agreed that trade might prejudice the embassy in the eyes of the imperial court (IOMC, 20:132a–134a). With these matters disposed of and with the supreme confidence of a seasoned diplomat well briefed on his mission, Macartney awaited the moment in which he could begin to speak the ideas and values of the public sphere to the Chinese empire.

4 KING SOLOMON IN ALL HIS GLORY

The British Embassy in China

The events that occurred between the arrival of the British embassy off the south coast of China on June 20, 1793, and its departure from Canton on January 15, 1793, have been well documented in a number of narrative accounts.[1] Rather than duplicate these works in this chapter, I focus attention on the representation of events in Lord Macartney's own account, including his personal journal and reports he prepared for Henry Dundas and the East India Company.[2] My purpose is to explore how the emerging eighteenth-century public-sphere discourse, inherited China lore, and enlightenment notions of exchange structured these accounts of events and provided them with an aura of authority that remains potent to the present day. The central question will not be the accuracy of Macartney's representations, but rather what Macartney said he saw when he looked at *China*, and what sort of understanding and knowledge that gaze produced.

4.1 The Naturalist's Gaze

Public-sphere culture generated a new form of writing in England in the second half of the eighteenth century. In conjunction with the voyages launched under the auspices of the British crown, members of the Royal Society and intellectual aristocrats made various proposals for systematic record keeping that would allow for better organization of the informa-

---

1. See Pritchard 1936:312–345, Cranmer-Byng 1983:216–243, Singer 1992, and Peyre-fitte 1992.
2. In addition to MD, these include IOMC, 20:106–121, a cover letter in a packet of materials sent to Dundas, and Pritchard 1938:378–396, 495–507.

tion flowing into England from the world at large. In general, the scientific method was applied to the natural landscape and the social world of other peoples, producing the taxonomical projects of natural history and human ethnology. Global phenomena were to be collected and placed into a meaningful set of hierarchized units, which could then be comparatively evaluated through exact description. Charting the world in this form had a corollary in writing, a writing which assumed a subject and author who captured the objective world in disinterested prose. Taken together, mapping the world and capturing it in prose pointed toward a utopian dream of total knowledge, of reducing the vast temporal and spatial dimensions of the world to objects at the command of a contemplative subject (Richards 1993).

That preeminent public intellectual and member of the Literary Club, Dr. Johnson, usefully summarized the relationship between this newly imagined subject and its objects. To begin, Johnson argued, the observer was not to be intent

> like merchants, only on the acts of commerce, the value of commodities, and the probabilities of gain, nor engaged, like military officers, in the care of subsisting armies, securing passes, obviating stratagems, and defeating opposition, but vacant to every object of curiosity, and at leisure for the most minute remarks. (Cited in Marshall and Williams, 1982:269)

Cleansed of self-interest and other diversions, Johnson's subject opens his sensorium to collection—in particular, it would seem, to that which is scarce or nonexistent in his own locale, otherwise defined as the curiosity.[3]

---

3. In his discussion of the late eighteenth-century notion of curiosities, Nicholas Thomas argues that, for natural historians,

> the abstraction of artifacts into a scientific enclave was a double operation, that recursively authorized the natural philosopher's travel and collecting, as it made the particular claim that a curiosity was a specimen, something in a scientific enclave rather than an object of fashion or mere commodity, which those lacking scientific authorization might traffic in and profit from. (Forthcoming)

It is worth noting in this regard that although he made his journal available to his second-in-command George Staunton and to his secretary John Barrow, Macartney himself never published his observations, nor in any other way materially profited from the "knowledge" of China he produced.

Equally important, without the concern for those calculations which distract merchants and military officers, he performs these tasks unhurriedly, at leisure, which presumably helps to tune his senses to the most minute of things.

The model of the observing subject outlined by Johnson provides a useful way of approaching Macartney's account of the British embassy. For instance, it helps to explain journal entries that position China vis-à-vis the most meaningful of imperial centers, the 0° longitude point of Greenwich from which all the world was spatially located (mapped) and temporally positioned by Englishmen (MD, 70 and 116).[4] Johnson's suggestions also make Macartney's occasional remark that— "nothing material occurred"— sensible; it marks an absence of useful sense data for processing by the gaze of the naturalist.

Such empty moments were rare, however. Once ashore, Macartney's sensorium was filled with an abundance of recordable data, data which in turn often stimulated recollection (perhaps unconscious) of the representations of China made by previous observers. In an entry of August 12, for example, Macartney admits being "troubled" by mosquitoes, moths the size of humming birds, and "very obstreperous" cicadas lodged in the "sedgy banks" of the river. Distracted, he notes that their chatter "seems to be occasioned by a strong oscillation of the wings where they articulate with the dorsal vertebrae." "Upon further inquiry," however, leisurely contemplation produces the truth that the sound is made by the motion of two flaps which cover the abdomen, a signal of the male to "allure" the female. Yet no sooner is naturalism satisfied, than a cliché about place is generated from the stock of China lore in which Macartney had immersed himself— "It would seem that in this country everything that has life *is multiplied to the highest degree...*" (emphasis added). This is, of course, the Asia of numerical extremes, of superabundance, a perception deeply embedded in European thought at least from the time of Marco Polo forward (March 1974: 23–45). Perhaps more important is the order of the form: the generalized observation follows upon naturalist contemplation so that the former

---

4. Also see entries from July 22–27, especially his description of a thunderstorm on the night of July 26. On the journey overland from Peking to Rehe, Macartney mapped the route, including place names, distances, and longitudinal and latitudinal calculations (noted but not reproduced in MD; see p. 116). Like the calculations at sea, these records were, of course, completely new "knowledge."

is authenticated by the latter, obscuring the possibility that the generalization is hardly as disinterested as Johnson's methodology promised.

Captured in discourse are not only those curiosities which, like the cicada, could be removed for even more leisurely contemplation at "home," but the nontransportable as well—the Great Wall, for instance. When the embassy reached the wall on September 5, Macartney filled what now comprises two pages of the published text of his journal. "The wall is built of bluish coloured brick," he begins,

> not burnt but dried in the sun, and raised upon a stone foundation, and as measured from the ground on the side next to Tartary, it is twenty-six feet high in the perpendicular. The stone foundation is formed of two courses of granite equal to twenty-four inches or two feet. From thence to the parapet including the cordon which is six inches are nineteen feet four inches, the parapet is four feet eight inches. From the stone foundation to the cordon are fifty-eight rows of bricks and above the cordon are fourteen rows; and each row, allowing for the interstices of the mortar and the insertion of the cordon may be calculated at the rate of four inches per brick. Thus then fifty-eight and fourteen bricks equal to seventy-two give two-hundred and eighty-eight inches, or twenty-four feet, which together with the stone foundation make twenty six feet. (MD, 111)[5]

And so on. A similar descriptive operation is performed on the towers of the wall. Only when the measurements are complete, only when the wall has been sited in his discourse, does Macartney then produce generalizations on the wall. As with the observation on the superabundance of life in China that followed the scrutiny of the cicada, the history and purpose of the wall, whatever its sources may be, cannot be addressed until the wall itself is made "real" in naturalist prose.

Moreover, the process of capturing the wall does not end here. In a note, Macartney later adds that he had been informed that the bricks were indeed fired and not sun-dried. Meanwhile, one of the embassy's scientists, Dr. Gillan, carried out experiments to determine the source of color in the bricks, while Lieutenant Parish of the Royal Artillery completed an engi-

---

5. Macartney's diary entry on the Great Wall is rather modest in comparison to that of Staunton, where description and measurements proceed for over seven pages; see Staunton 1797, 2:372–380.

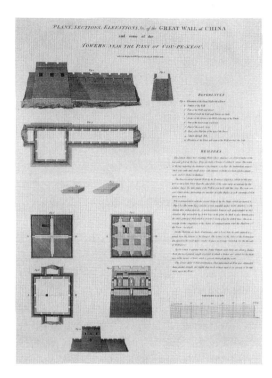

Figure 1. Plans, sections, and elevations of the Great Wall of China.

neer's drawing of the wall, one that Macartney called "highly valuable," superseding "everything that had hitherto been written on the subject" (MD, 111–112; see figure 1). This last observation is extremely interesting, for it suggests that a technical form of visual representation might take precedence in certain instances over discursive description. But perhaps this is only the case when the tools of the engineer are applied, producing a kind of triangulation on the object from the point of view of (a) previous representations, (b) written description, and (c) the draftsman's renditions. In the last case, the results could be quite spectacular, creating a point of view that defied gravity. In what might be called a levitational gaze, Parish produced overhead drawings of the assembly of officials before the tent in which Macartney was received by the Qianlong emperor at Rehe, as well as a similar view of the Rehe Potala as seen from above (see figure 2). The naturalist's gaze fell equally on a variety of other objects. Boats on rivers, crowds on shore, hair, skin color, the physical features of men, women, and

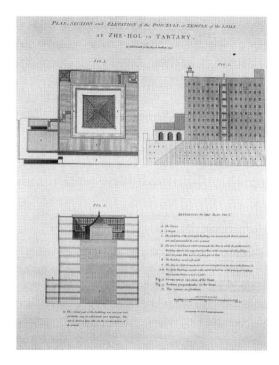

Figure 2. Plans, section, and elevation of the Poo-Ta-La, or Temple of the Lama, at Zhe-hol in Tartary.

children all lend themselves to similar contemplative analysis and generalization (MD, 72–74, 81–82).[6]

This procedure of recording phenomena produced, moreover, a new kind of knowledge about China, a kind lodged now in the detail of description, measurable and quantifiable, and hence generalizable. It carried added weight because it was gathered firsthand, and perhaps even more significantly, because in the process of its production it clearly identified its debased other. In a "little anecdote, however ridiculous," which he claims

6. In the case of the common people he saw, Macartney couldn't "refrain from crying out with Shakespeare's Miranda in the 'Tempest':

> Oh, Wonder!
> How many goodly creatures are there here!
> How beauteous mankind is! Oh, brave new world
> That has such people in it!

An interesting selection of plays and images, to say the least.

to include in his journal on the grounds of fairness, Macartney recorded the following account of the British gifts taken from the "Tianjin gazette." The articles included:

> several dwarfs or little men not twelve inches high ... an elephant not larger than a cat, and a horse the size of a mouse; a singing bird as big as a hen, that feeds upon charcoal, and devours usually fifty pounds per day; and lastly, an enchanted pillow, on which whoever lays his head immediately falls asleep, and if he dreams of Canton, Formosa, or Europe, is instantly transported thither without the fatigue of travel. (MD, 114)

Ridiculous indeed, when compared to the naturalist's jottings, to the superior knowledge created through "colonizing" the Great Wall, but fair only in the sense that all data finds equal access to the observer's sensorium, especially when it can confirm the truth-value of his own procedures and representations.

The routines of the naturalist were, moreover, not limited to the sorts of observations discussed here—perhaps more importantly it took the measure of the men Macartney had come to deal with, sorting them into higher and lower ranks, the more or less "agreeable," and in the process marking out a field of play upon which the ambassador calculated his moves.

4.2   First Encounters

In his dealings with Qing officials, Macartney almost obsessively concerns himself with their rank, a fixation which seeks to locate a counterpart of equal rank to his own, and, failing that, someone of sufficient authority who appears as disinterested as himself. In this search, his gaze invariably falls upon the color of the buttons on their caps, and whether or not they wore peacock feathers in them, signs of rank which he no doubt drew from his readings on China. In most cases, his first encounters with officials begin with determining rank in this way. Once having sited them, he proceeds to speak of his business, thus dividing his encounters into two distinct temporal phases, ceremonial and business portions.

This is the case, for example, when he first meets Wang Wenxiong and Qiao Renjie, the two officials who appear in his journal as Van-ta-gin and Chou-ta-gin, and with whom he was in almost continual contact through most of his embassy.[7] Macartney notes that Wang had a peacock feather and red coral button, while Qiao's cap had a blue button, "a degree inferior to the red." Then "after a number of compliments and civilities in the Chinese manner, we proceeded to business..." (MD, 71). This seemingly effortless move by mandarins from "civilities" to "business" led Macartney to note that they were "intelligent men, frank and easy in their address, and communicative in their discourse." At dinner they soon mastered the use of forks, tasted of European spirits, and shook hands "like Englishmen" when they left. They were impressed with the guard contingent drawn up to see them off, while listening attentively and expressing pleasure with music provided by the accompanying band. Before departing, Wang and Qiao were "very inquisitive" about the presents intended for the emperor and requested a list, which Macartney promised (MD, 71–72).

A week later, on August 6, Macartney had his first meeting with a high-ranking official, Liang Kentang, the governor-general of Zhili. Accompanied by George Staunton, Staunton's son, and his interpreter, Macartney was carried on a palanquin, with a mounted military escort, to the governor-general's audience hall. Liang greeted him at the front gate, led him into the hall, and offered him tea. They then withdrew to an inner hall, where they "entered upon the business." Liang inquired after the ambassador's health, indicated the emperor's great satisfaction over the arrival of the embassy, and informed Macartney that the emperor awaited him in his summer residence at Rehe.

After making reciprocal compliments, Macartney requested spacious quarters in Peking and added that due to the delicacy of some of the gifts, he preferred to leave them in the capital, rather than risk damaging them on a journey to Rehe. He also requested permission to send his ships the *Lion* and *Hindostan* to Chusan. Appearing at ease, polite, dignified, attentive, and unaffected in manner, Liang responded positively to each of the requests. He even offered the ambassador a year's provisions for his fleet, which Macartney, fearing that Liang's generosity might signify his desire for the speedy departure of the embassy, declined. The entire proceeding appears to have made a deep impression upon Macartney, especially the "apparent kindness and condescension with which people of rank speak to, and treat, their inferiors and lowest domestics" (MD, 76; also see IOMC, 20:108b).

These early encounters were, in turn, accompanied by vast outlays of

---

7. For biographies of these two officials see MD, 325–331.

provisions for the entire fleet, on the first occasion of which Macartney made a complete list in his journal (MD, 71). Liang's displays of generosity and kindness led Macartney to confirm a general characteristic of the Orient, that the "hospitality, attention, and respect" the embassy received was "such as strangers meet only in the Eastern parts of the world" (MD, 71; also see IOMC, 20:108b–109a).

At the same time, if some elements of contact could be worked through received ideas, others could not. In the evening on August 11, as the embassy was being transported up the Bei River to Peking, a number of officials from Tianjin came to visit the embassy. With a great deal of curiosity they scrutinized Macartney's dress, the books, and the furniture of the foreigners in a "very inquisitive, lively, and talkative" manner, "totally devoid of that composure, gravity, and seriousness which we had been taught to believe constituted a part of the Chinese character" (MD, 80).

This chain of positive responses, combining confirmation of known Chinese characteristics and new knowledge produced through the encounter, should be placed, however, beside negative features simultaneously emerging in Macartney's analysis. They begin with the arrival on the scene of Zhengrui. A "Tartar Mandarin" styled the "Emperor's Legate," Zhengrui was to escort the ambassador to Rehe and would also help to make him conscious of the emperor's "partiality to the Tartars in preference to his Chinese subjects" (MD, 86). In a meeting at Tianjin on August 11 between Macartney, Liang Kentang, and the Legate, the first serious difficulty between the parties arose. Zhengrui took issue with the plan to leave some of the gifts in Peking. According to Macartney, he was unwilling to accept the British rationale for safeguarding the more delicate items because, as he said, the emperor would desire all the gifts to be presented at once. Certain that he could not dissuade him, Macartney told Zhengrui that if he was adamant on the issue, the Legate, rather than the British ambassador, would have to accept full responsibility for the safety of the gifts. This proposition "startled" him, and he acquiesced when it was clear that Liang also supported the ambassador's proposal. From Macartney's point of view the incident was significant. For the first time he had encountered an official whose behavior contrasted with "the urbanity and graciousness" of a Chinese official like Liang. He recorded that he "easily discovered a perverse and unfriendly disposition in the Legate toward all our concerns" and, consequently, "could not avoid feeling great disquiet and apprehension from the untoward" behavior "so early manifested" by him (MD, 78–80).

A second incident involving the Legate occurred on August 16. Zheng-rui mentioned that reports had been received of British involvement with rebel forces then engaged with imperial troops in Tibet. After vehemently denying the allegation and adding that the British dominion in Bengal was far removed from the Tibetan frontier, Macartney surmised that the subject was raised in an effort to draw out information on British strength in the general vicinity. When Zhengrui asked if the English would assist the emperor against the rebels, clearly feeling uncomfortably manipulated, Macartney replied in the negative; to do otherwise would have shown that the British were capable of aiding either the emperor or his enemies.[8]

Macartney's representation of these encounters with Zhengrui contrast sharply with his treatment of early ones with Wang, Qiao, and Liang. For the first time he begins to differentiate between Chinese and Tartars, as well as between good and bad officials. Tuning his senses more finely to "minute remarks" allows, in turn, increasingly sensitized perceptions and altered generalizations.

> In all the different visits and conferences that have passed between us and our conductors, I observe, with great concern, a settled preju-dice against the Embassy in … the Legate, *though often attempted to be concealed by him under extravagant compliments and professions.* I have taken great pains to conciliate him, but I suspect he is not of a conciliable nature. (MD, 85; emphasis added)

Significant here is an assertion that external behavior is a mere façade, a notion absent, for instance, in his earlier pronouncements about the hos-pitality of the East.[9] And as the gaze now shifts to what lies behind the "refined politeness and sly good breeding," behind the "artifice" of these

---

8. MD, 86–87, and IOMC, 20:109b–110a. Unknown to Macartney at this time, the British government in Bengal was involved to a degree in the war between the Nepalese Gurkhas and Qing forces in Tibet. The King of Nepal had made overtures to the British for aid; see IOR, Bengal Political Consultations, for October 3, November 2, and November 30, 1792. Copies of these records were sent from Bengal to Canton and awaited Macartney upon arrival there. See note 17 and section 8.3.

9. A similar shift occurred in Macartney's perceptual abilities when, on another occasion, he demonstrated field pieces he had brought as gifts for the emperor, weapons which he was certain had no match in China. The audience of Qing officials appeared little impressed, leading the ambassador to conclude that they were concealing their mortification at "this small specimen of our art and superiority" (MD, 90).

"Mandarins," what had before been welcome now becomes suspect, requiring retrospective analysis and revaluation.

> We have indeed been very narrowly watched, and all our customs, habits and proceedings, even of the most trivial nature, observed with an inquisitiveness and jealousy which *surpassed all that we had read of in the history of China.* But we endeavoured to always put the best face upon everything, and to preserve a perfect serenity of countenance upon all occasions. (MD, 87–88; emphasis added)[10]

Indeed, without such "serenity," without remaining "vacant to every object of curiosity," Macartney would not have been able either to function in the negotiations over imperial audience protocol that were commencing at this time, or to penetrate to the "truth" that lay beyond Chinese artifice. I will have more to say on the latter below. For now, let me provide one example of Macartney's contemplation of the information he has gathered, one which draws attention to the relationship between received wisdom and the discovery of new knowledge. In this case, it concerns the reworking of preconceived notions of "despotism" made necessary by the discovery of differences between Tartars and Chinese.

Macartney made references to despotism more than once in the early days of his arrival in China. As the British fleet sailed along the China coast, for instance, pilots came aboard the *Lion* to aid navigation in unknown waters. Seeing a picture of the emperor in the ship's cabin, they "immediately fell flat on their faces before it, and kissed the ground several times with great devotion" (MD, 64–65). Such exaggerated expressions of devotion were, in turn, paralleled by "sudden and summary" administrations of justice, as in the demotion of "superintending Mandarins" and the caning of servants when tainted food was delivered to the embassy (MD, 83). The same despotic state that punished swiftly also had at its instant command the enormous body of labor required to transport the embassy from the Gulf of Beizhili inland.[11]

10. Macartney's newfound awareness wouldn't allow him to enjoy what otherwise might have appeared a gain. On September 1, in Peking, he was visited by Jin Jian, who told him that the requests he had made to Liang Kentang regarding the removal of the *Lion* to Chusan had been approved by the emperor himself. Macartney noted that "every circumstance concerning us and every word that falls from our lips is minutely reported and remembered" (MD, 105).

11. MD, 83, 88–89. At the same time that he made his observations about labor, he was

While these observations confirmed the received wisdom on oriental despotism, additional information led Macartney to modify his earlier representations of China. In his concluding commentary, he argues that although the emperor was "styled despotic, and decorated with all the titles and epithets of oriental hyperbole," his power was, like Zhengrui's "extravagant compliments and professions," an external appearance, one that led the unenlightened to fall down on their faces before pictures of the despot. The truth of the matter was that the government was actually the "tyranny of a handful of Tartars over more than three hundred millions of Chinese" (MD, 236).

For purposes here, it is not the fine distinction between despotism and tyranny that is of interest; rather it is the process that allows Macartney to make the distinction itself. Again he deploys the kinds of techniques that exposed the secrets of the cicada and the Great Wall: observation, measurement, calculation, and comparison, all of which operate from the position of the "disinterested" observer to produce new knowledge.

At the same time, however, the supposedly neutral process of information gathering is disrupted by another movement, one that destabilizes the ideal position of the contemplative subject. When Macartney's expectations are met, when business proceeds easily after ceremony, when officials appear to admire the things he values and are straightforward with him, he does not question their motives, but praises them for their openness, honesty, adaptability, and ease of delivery in communication. When his expectations are not met, however, he becomes suspicious, eventually seeking hidden causes, like the real nature of despotism, behind or below external appearances. At other times, he must shut his eyes (close the sensorium) to flags on the vessels carrying the embassy toward Peking, flags inscribed with Chinese characters saying "The English Ambassador bringing tribute to the Emperor of China" (MD, 88). And he forgets distinctions previously made. The "Chinese" character becomes "inexplicable" at a moment when he is actually speaking of the Tartar Legate (MD, 98); and it is forgotten that the emperor is, to use Macartney's frame of reference, himself a Tartar.

In these cases, the naturalist's effort to constitute a space across which

---

surprised to find that people went about these tasks *readily* and *cheerfully*. Also curious was the fact that although the government was under a single "omnipotent" head, there was "no rational, established state religion." The people were left to pursue any superstition they wished.

the world may be viewed as objects is displaced onto desires for manipulation or control. Thus others, the Chinese and Tartar actors with whom he has dealings, are either instruments to be employed in the service of "universal" values or obstacles to be got around; allies or enemies on an uncomplicated field of play, many of whom would loom large in Macartney's explanation of why the embassy failed to accomplish all its goals.

4.3   Field of Play

In Macartney's initial assessment of the situation in China, there were at least three groups who could aid or obstruct his mission. The first of these was, of course, Chinese "mandarins," who, when Macartney discovered the "significance" of the distinction, were further divided into Chinese and Tartars. The two other groups were foreign missionaries in the emperor's service and foreign merchants at Canton.

When the embassy had arrived off the south coast of China, Macartney sent Staunton to Macao to learn if his ploy for landing at Tianjin had worked. In addition to returning with a positive answer to this question, Staunton also reported that the announcement of the embassy had "excited great jealousy and apprehension in the minds of Europeans at Macao, particularly the Dutch and Portuguese." The former didn't concern Macartney to any great extent. Having stopped in Batavia, the Dutch colonial establishment in Java, and obtained written approval from the governor for his mission, Macartney was certain that the Dutch traders had effectively been neutralized. The Portuguese were, however, entirely another matter. Macartney remained suspicious of their motives and maintained a cautious attitude in his dealings with Portuguese missionaries in Peking.[12]

The missionaries who were then in Peking, all Roman Catholic, were divided into two main groups, French and Portuguese, with the former playing a positive role in Macartney's eyes, and the latter a negative. Among the French missionaries were Joseph-Marie Amiot, Jean-Joseph de Grammont, Louis de Poirot, and Nicolas Raux. Infirm at the time of the embassy, Amiot wrote Macartney at least one letter and met with him briefly after the imperial audience in Rehe. At this meeting, Amiot suggested a number of reasons why the embassy's achievements had been limited (see 4.8 below).

The other French missionaries also played important roles in shaping

---

12. MD, 63, and IOMC, 20:106a. On the Dutch, see Lamb 1958:57–68.

Macartney's views. Grammont, for example, suggested that he consider giving personal gifts to the high-level officials with whom he dealt, while at the same time encouraging Macartney's propensity to divide the world into two camps, those for and against the embassy. On one occasion, he told Macartney that the missionary who had been appointed by the Manchu court to meet the embassy at Rehe, a Portuguese named Joseph-Bernard d'Almeida, was decidedly anti-British, a conclusion that Macartney also arrived at after meeting the priest (MD, 94). On another occasion, Grammont confirmed Macartney's assessment of Zhengrui's attitude toward the embassy. Raux and Poirot served as important intermediaries with court officials, and in Raux's case, acted as an interlocutor on Chinese behavior, confirming what Macartney had read in histories. He also helped to translate Macartney's proposal concerning his forthcoming audience with the Qianlong emperor into Chinese, and together with Poirot, translated the emperor's response to the letter of George III from Chinese into Latin (MD, 99, 102–103, 372). Poirot later wrote Macartney, contradicting Grammont's views on d'Almeida (see Pritchard 1935). The remainder of the missionaries, like the ambassadors from "oriental" kingdoms he would later see in Rehe, drew very little of Macartney's attention. The main exception is d'Almeida, and that contact alone was formative. It seems to have convinced Macartney that "the Portuguese have formed a sort of system to disgust and keep out of China all other nations" (MD, 103).

In general, the French missionaries occupy much the same place in Macartney's account as that of the Chinese officials Wang and Qiao. Like the Chinese, the missionaries are outsiders at a court partial to Tartars. But they are also insiders who wear the buttons and feathers of rank. Macartney relies on the Chinese and French court officials when he discerns sympathy for his mission, considering them useful sources of dependable information. But he also holds them at a certain distance, creating a comparative reference point for his evaluations of the behavior of less-cooperative Qing officials.

4.4   The Audience Negotiations: Speaking the Public Sphere

By establishing a series of referential points, be they other human agents, nature, degrees of longitude or latitude, or the products of human physical labor, Macartney was able to domesticate the landscape upon which he had to operate. In doing so, he created a secure position from which he could safely husband resources for intellectual labor necessary for negotiations. In negotiation, Macartney kept himself open to minute detail, but was no longer merely a passive receptor — he deployed strategies and argued with reason, while maintaining an exterior that was "calm" and dignified. The focal point of these energies was negotiations over the ceremony he would perform at his audience with the Qianlong emperor.

The audience question was first broached on August 15, as the embassy neared a landing site east of Peking at Tongzhou. Zhengrui, Wang, and Qiao had come to Macartney's boat to explain various logistical arrangements and the plans for the embassy's participation in the emperor's birthday celebration at Rehe. They then introduced the subject of court ceremonies "with a degree of art, address, and insinuation" that Macartney could not "avoid admiring." Observing that dress differed from one "nation" to another, the Qing officials said they preferred their own because it was "loose and free from ligatures" and thus did not obstruct the "genuflexions and prostrations" done before the emperor. Since the British wore constraining devices (knee-buckles and garters), they said it would be acceptable to remove them before seeing the emperor.

Macartney parried that regardless of what the Chinese might do before the emperor, he supposed that "the emperor would prefer my paying him the same obeisance which I did to my own Sovereign." This hint at reciprocal exchange led the officials to speculate that perhaps ceremonies in England and China were somewhat alike, but that

> in China the form was to kneel down upon both knees, and make
> nine prostrations or inclinations of the head to the ground, and that
> it had never been, or never could be, dispensed with. I told them
> ours was somewhat different, and though I had the most earnest
> desire to do everything that might be agreeable to the emperor, my
> first duty must be to do what might be agreeable to my own King;
> but if they were really in earnest in objecting to my following the
> etiquette of the English Court, I should deliver to them my reply in
> writing as soon as I arrived in Peking.

At that point Zhengrui intimated that given the length and danger of Macartney's journey, his king would probably be anxious for his return. Macartney replied that his stay was up to the emperor, including the time necessary to transact the business his king had charged him with. Then, as if suddenly conscious of "oriental customs and ideas," he closed by saying that his own goal was "to describe to my sovereign the glory and virtues of the emperor, the power and splendor of his empire, the wisdom of its laws and moral institutions, the fame of all which had already reached to the most distant regions" (MD, 84–85). This is, of course, flattery, but it is something else as well. These are all categories of useful knowledge, the details of which Macartney will deliver to a state interested in gathering such information on a global scale.

Three days later, with the embassy now ashore at Tongzhou, Wang and Qiao again raised the issue of ceremony. "It seemed to be a very serious matter with them," Macartney observed,

> and a point which they have set *their hearts upon*. They pressed me most earnestly to comply with it, said it was a mere trifle; kneeled down on the floor and practiced it of their own accord to show me the manner of it, and begged me to try whether I could perform it (emphasis added).

Note how Macartney places the concern with ceremony on the Qing officials, while eliding any interest he himself might have in it. Moreover, as he operates this displacement, he confirms a well-known Chinese characteristic. They are "not very scrupulous in regard to veracity"; their "ideas of the obligations of truth" are very lax, and when he hints to them of "contradictions" or "deviations from their promises in our affairs," they make "light of them," and seem "to think them of trifling consequence" (MD, 90, and Montesquieu, 1748:304).

Matters rested here until the embassy arrived in Peking. On August 29 Macartney put up the state canopy in the embassy quarters, hung portraits of the King and Queen in a "presence chamber," and made good his promise to deliver a written response. Translated by Raux, recopied by young George Staunton, who was precociously studying Chinese, and placed in a yellow envelope,[13] the proposal asserted a representational equivalency between Macartney and his king and offered reciprocal exchange as a solution to the impasse. Certain that the emperor had no intention of asking him to perform an action that "could be construed, as in anywise unbecoming the great and exalted rank, which his Master whom he represents,

---

13. MD, 99–100, and IOMC, 20:112b. The translated version of the proposal is in neither the India Office archives in London nor the Qing archives in Peking; see chapter 7 for further discussion.

holds among the independent Sovereigns of the World," Macartney suggested that the danger of unintentionally doing so could be averted by an imperial order

> that one of the Ministers of his Court, equal in station to the Embassador shall perform before His Britannic Majesty's Picture at large in his royal robes and in the Embassador's possession now at Peking, the same ceremonies, as shall be performed by the embassador before the throne of his imperial Majesty. (IOMC, 20:153)

The proposal was delivered to Zhengrui, whose response was negative. Wang and Qiao, however, approved and wanted to perform the ceremony themselves on the spot. Macartney declined their offer because they were obviously not of an equal station with him (MD, 99–100). Moreover, in a letter to Dundas, he explained that he would be doing more than he had asked of the Chinese; the Qing minister's prostration would be performed in a "private" room, while Macartney's would occur "on a solemn festival before all the tributary Princes and great subjects of the State, and would be described in the Gazetteer published by authority" (IOMC, 20:112b).

On September 8 the embassy arrived in Rehe. Matters concerning the audience protocol had yet to be resolved and were further complicated when Zhengrui announced that he had yet to show Macartney's proposal to anyone. At this point, an intricate dance commenced. According to Zhengrui, Macartney would personally have to deliver the proposal to the chief minister, Heshen, in order to receive a reply. Later, Wang and Qiao visited Macartney to tell the ambassador that due to an injury Heshen was unable to venture out, but hoped that Macartney would visit him. Macartney demurred, saying he would send Staunton in his stead. The same afternoon Heshen called for Staunton and opened the interview by asking about the contents of the king's letter to the emperor. After Staunton promised to deliver a copy, Heshen attempted "to contrive means of avoiding" the reciprocal act to the portrait of George III. Staunton suspected that Zhengrui had actually shown the proposal to Heshen, but, in keeping with the ambassador's order, he formally delivered a new copy. The next day Zhengrui asked Macartney to waive the reciprocal ceremony, suggesting instead some other form that the ambassador alone would perform (MD, 117–119).

As proposal followed counterproposal, Macartney's confidence was bolstered by a report that probably came from a missionary. It indicated that the "emperor is not acquainted with the difficulties that have arisen on this subject, but that when he is the matter will probably be adjusted as I wish." Apparently safely ahead at this point in the negotiations, Macartney met with Zhengrui, Wang, and Qiao on the morning of September 10. On the assumption that kneeling and bowing his head to the ground was not merely qualitatively, but quantitatively distinct from kneeling on one knee, Macartney insisted that it was "not natural to expect that an ambassador should pay greater homage to a foreign prince than his own liege Sovereign, unless a return were made to him that might warrant him to do more." The Qing officials asked about the ceremony performed before the English king and Macartney explained that he knelt on one knee and kissed the king's hand. When asked if he would be willing to do the same before the emperor, Macartney answered in the affirmative. Zhengrui returned later to say that the ceremony was acceptable, but that kissing the emperor's hand was to be omitted (10MC, 20:113a).

Later the same afternoon, Zhengrui announced that the English ceremony was acceptable, but that since it was not the custom of China to kiss the emperor's hand, Macartney should kneel on two knees. When Macartney refused, Zhengrui accepted one knee, without the hand-kissing. "To this I assented," Macartney records

> saying 'As you please, but remember it is your doing, and according to your proposal, is but half the ceremony, and you see I am willing to perform the whole one.' And thus ended this curious negotiation, which has given me a tolerable insight into the character of the Court, and that political address upon which they so much value themselves. (MD, 119)

But the dance was not quite over. On September 11 Macartney met with Heshen, grand councillor Fuchang'an, and the directors of the Boards of Rites and Revenue. Heshen explained that because of the great distance the embassy had traveled and the "value" of its presents, certain Chinese customs would be relaxed so that the Englishman could perform the ceremony of his own country before the emperor in an audience that was set for September 14, a day of great festivities. In the following conversation, Heshen noted that Cochin China was a "tributary" of the empire and wondered if perhaps Italy and Portugal were tributaries of England. Macartney answered that while England had at times afforded Italy and Portugal protection, they were not tributaries. Macartney learned from this exchange that "such are the avowed and affected notions here of superiority and independence of the Empire, that no transaction is to be admitted with foreign nations on the ground of reciprocal benefits, but as grace and condescension from the former to the latter."[14]

Nevertheless, the "negotiations" over the content of the ceremony to be performed before the emperor convinced Macartney that it was possible to deal with the Chinese court when approached as he had done. Speaking the public sphere, as it were, while carefully gathering and deploying intelligence led him to the eventual conclusion that

> with regard to their immutable laws, what laws are so I know not; but I suppose the phrase has no very precise meaning, and is only made use of as a general shield against reason and argument, for we know that they have broken through some of their laws that were declared unalterable. The recent instance of the ceremony in my own case is one, not to mention others, which the accession of the present dynasty to the throne must have often rendered necessary. (MD, 153–154).

And yet, in truth he had not achieved reciprocal exchange, but rather a concession allowing his audience with the emperor to proceed. Macartney ignored this, preferring instead to believe that his rhetoric and stratagems verified his assumptions about China and Chinese behavior. Such certainty received added support from what he understood as the extremely positive impression the British gifts and manufactured items were having on Qing courtiers and officials, objects which, he became convinced, were superior to anything he received as presents from the emperor.

4.5   The Gifts and British Manufactures

The scientific instruments, examples of British arts, and British manufactured items were, as noted earlier, designed to impress upon the emperor and his court the superior stature of Great Britain. When the embassy first arrived in China, Macartney was determined that nothing should diminish the effect he wished the gifts to make. To further insure success, he decided to add some additional and special gifts that he could personally give to the

14. See MD, 120–121. Macartney told Dundas that he had even been willing to negotiate on terms that acknowledged Chinese superiority, but the officials were not interested; see IOMC, 20:113a.

emperor. From Henry Browne at Macao he bought a telescope and later acquired two watches of "very fine workmanship" from Captain Mackintosh (MD, 69 and 101). He also purchased from Mackintosh "Parker's Great Lens," some twelve or sixteen inches in diameter, an "object of singular curiosity," about which Macartney says he

> was apprehensive that if it fell into the hands of the Chinese merchants and were presented through their channel to the emperor it might tend toward the disparagement of our fine things, and perhaps be imagined to eclipse them. I therefore thought it advisable, for the public service and the honor of the Embassy, to join it to the other presents. ... I flatter myself we have no rivalship to apprehend at Peking from the appearance of any instruments of a similar kind.[15]

With the market in high technology cornered, as it were, Macartney tuned his senses to the reactions of the Chinese to British things. In the beginning of September, he notes that "their admiration" was "much excited" by the gifts and "specimens of different manufactures," as well as by "little articles of use and convenience which Europeans are accustomed to." Of special interest were Birmingham sword blades and fine clothes, all of which he advised the Company to consider adding to its exports (MD, 105). Court officials also showed interest in British musical instruments, of which they had drawings made for the purpose of reproducing them in China (MD, 104). Rather than being disturbed by the implications of this revelation (that is, if they wanted British goods, they could simply copy them), Macartney concluded that "not withstanding their vanity and conceit, they are not above being taught" (MD, 104). This last turn of phrase is rather telling, because it suggests the possibility that "business" involved pedagogy, as well as the working out of reciprocal advantages (see chapter 8).

Having thus established his own credentials as the first in a line of British imperial pedagogues in China, Macartney concerned himself with the disturbing fact that although eagerly curious about the superior British things, the Chinese were awkward in handling them (MD, 105). Moreover,

---

15. MD, 69, and IOMC, 20:108a. Macartney noted to Dundas that British technologies had come into the emperor's possession by way of Canton officials; he termed the imperial collection "Cox's Museum," an actual place in London; see Altick 1978:69–72. The designation by Macartney is double edged; Cox not only designed and displayed such devices in London, but produced them for export to China.

as Macartney began to feel that the embassy was being "narrowly watched," he became concerned over the degree of curiosity exhibited by courtiers, officials, and, more disturbingly, others who fit neither category. At one point, for example, the crowds who came to view the pictures of the King and Queen that now hung in his Peking quarters were so great that Macartney asked Wang "to regulate the number and quality of the visitors and the hour of admittance" (MD, 104).

At times, such annoyances were deflected by certainties that the central pieces among the gifts, the planetarium, orrery, globes, clocks, and lustres, could not but have a spectacular effect. When, for example, he was taken to see the hall at the Yuanming Gardens, where it had been decided to display these items, Macartney saw in it a musical clock made in England of "wretched old taste." After recording where each of the items he had brought would be arranged, he concluded that it would be "an assemblage of such ingenuity, utility and beauty as not to be seen collected together in any other apartment, I believe, of the whole world besides" (MD, 96; see figure 3 for the schematic diagram of the placement of the gifts).

His certainties regarding the efficacy of the gifts received objective confirmation on the day they began to be set up at the Yuanming Gardens. Staunton had accompanied the British artisans, including John Barrow and James Dinwiddie, to the designated hall and reported the following exchange. Fearing that Chinese workmen had little skill with objects of such a delicate nature, Barrow and Dinwiddie insisted that the unpacking of them cease, explaining that until the pieces were assembled they remained under British care. Zhengrui interceded, saying that they were tribute (*cong-so*) to the emperor, and consequently the British had no more to do with them. The interpreter replied that they were not tribute, but presents, at which point Jin Jian, whom Macartney styles the Grand Secretary, but who was actually an official in the Imperial Household Department (*Neiwufu*), "put an end to the conversation by saying that the expression of *song-lo,* or presents, was proper enough" (MD, 97).

One might expect Macartney to make much of this, especially given that earlier he had had to close his eyes to the flags on the boats sailing up the Bei River, but he does not. Perhaps the triumph is too self-evident to necessitate commentary; perhaps, as with Qing officials he finds sympathetic, he need not belabor the obvious, he need not probe deeper because he is content with external appearances. Whatever the case, with the exception of those dissonant notes struck by Zhengrui, his occasional concern with the inexplicable nature of the Chinese character, and his discomfort at being

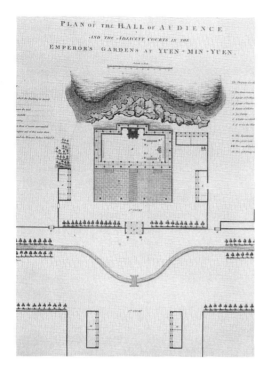

Figure 3. Plan of the Hall of Audience and the Adjacent Courts in the Emperor's Gardens at Yuen-Min-Yuen.

closely watched, Macartney had little reason to doubt that the strategies for attracting the attention of the Qing emperor were working out quite nicely. After his triumph in the audience negotiations, he approached the Qianlong emperor with supreme confidence that scientific naturalism and public-sphere values were producing the encounter in the ways he had anticipated. He walked into the audience fully confident that once he had successfully asserted the sovereignty of his king, the business of his embassy would be able to proceed accordingly.

4.6   Macartney's Audience with the Qianlong Emperor

At four A.M. on the morning of September 14, 1793, the English ambassador, escorted by Wang and Qiao, mounted a palanquin and set out for his audience with the emperor of China.[16] Over a velvet coat, Macart-

16. Anderson's account of the disorderliness of the procession to the tent is in striking contrast to that offered by Macartney; see Anderson 1795:180.

ney wore the Order of the Bath, a diamond badge, and a diamond star. On his head was a richly plumed hat. Staunton, also in velvet, wore over his coat the scarlet silk of an Oxford Doctor of Laws. Macartney wrote that he had dressed in this fashion to indicate the attention he paid to "oriental customs and ideas" (MD, 122). The audience was to be held in a large tent. When he arrived at the site, the ambassador was taken to a smaller side tent, where he waited for approximately an hour. The emperor's approach was announced by drums and music, and the British embassy left the tent to greet the emperor. While others prostrated, Macartney and his retinue knelt on one knee.

As soon as the emperor was seated on the throne, Macartney proceeded to the entrance of the tent and entered. Carrying his king's letter in the bejeweled gold box, he "walked deliberately up and ascending the side-steps of the throne, delivered it into the Emperor's own hands, who, having received it, passed it on to the Minister [Heshen], by whom it was placed on a cushion." In return, the emperor handed him a jade scepter, called by Macartney a ju-eo-jou or giou-giou (*ruyi*). Although the Chinese seemed to prize it as a symbol of peace and prosperity, as noted earlier, Macartney found no "great value" in it (MD, 122); this conclusion is similar to the one he had drawn about gifts given to him by Liang Kentang when he first arrived in China. He then presented the emperor with the two enameled watches he had acquired from Mackintosh.

Again, no mention of success, no indication that he had achieved one of the fundamental goals of the embassy, that he had, from his point of view, established equality in sovereignty at the moment the emperor had stretched out his hands to accept the box containing his king's letter. Rather, this supreme moment of ceremonial exchange is instantly displaced onto objects and their value, to the implicit comparative difference in value between the jewel-encrusted gold box, the watches themselves inlaid with diamonds, and the jade scepter. It is as if, defying Dr. Johnson's dictum, Macartney cannot help thinking like a merchant, cannot help comparing the watches and the scepter in terms of market-exchange, no matter how strongly the gentlemanly ideal and the naturalist ethic cut against the grain of this lowly form of evaluation. Or, perhaps, he must reposition himself once he arises from his one knee, seek protective ground in the face of the oriental despot in all his splendor, regain his balance and his discerning eye. For the sight before him is grand and elegant, and clearly seductive.

The tapestry, the curtains, the carpets, the lanterns, the fringes, the tassels were disposed with such harmony, the colours so artfully varied, and the light and shades so judiciously managed, that the whole assemblage *filled the eye with delight,* and *diffused over the mind a pleasing serenity and repose* undisturbed by glitter and affected embellishments. (MD, 124; emphasis added)

And therein lay the danger. Oriental splendor was delightful, even sensuous; it muddled the reasoning faculties and put them at rest. In such a state, one was no longer wary of external appearances such as those provided by "glitter" and "affected embellishments," but instead was enticed into the Oriental scene. "Every function" of the proceeding, Macartney tells us, was performed with "silence and solemnity as in some measure to resemble the celebration of a religious mystery" and "the commanding feature of the ceremony was that *calm dignity,* that *sober pomp of Asiatic greatness,* which European refinements have *not yet attained*" (MD, 124; emphasis added). One wonders what Dr. Johnson's response to these lines might have been had he lived long enough to read them; what might he have thought of the effect of the Orient on the naturalist's gaze or of the serenity Macartney evokes? And Burke: would he have found this particular "clothing" of power felicitous?

And yet, at the very moment that he seems on the verge of immersing himself in something like pleasure, Macartney's gaze is arrested. He recalls that there are other ambassadors also present, "but their appearance was not very splendid." This realization works to transport him to other times and places, to refix the proceedings in such a way as to undercut his own histrionics.

Thus have I seen 'King Solomon in all his glory.' I use the expression, as the scene recalled perfectly in my memory a puppet show of that name which I recollect to have seen in my childhood, and made so strong an impression of my mind that I thought it a true representation of the highest pitch of human greatness and felicity. (MD, 124)

An odd association, possibly, but rather significant when one considers Macartney's concern with the "ceremony" of diplomacy and the assumptions he held about the organization of the Qing empire. Assaulted by "disturbing" sensory evidence of oriental splendor, an idealized childhood memory emerges to rescue Macartney's objectifying gaze. He is able to place what is before him in the past tense, while suggesting that in spite of the high pitch the performance achieves, the emperor and his court are little more than a theater for children, or perhaps children themselves. He has recovered, in other words, from the waking dream-state into which he has been lulled, and is soon producing useful knowledge again.

In tours of the imperial park at Rehe, he discovered, for example, that Chinese gardens fell "very short of the fanciful descriptions which Father Attiret and Sir William Chambers have intruded upon us as realities" (MD, 133). Macartney also had a number of fruitful conversations with a young Mongol (he calls him a Tartar), by the name of Songyun, who was interested in the fact that he had been British minister to Russia. Civil, intelligent, and polite, Songyun explained that he had once negotiated with the Russians at Kiakhta and seemed to want to compare notes (MD, 127). On other occasions, he met courtiers who told him that the emperor was descended from Kublai Khan and believed that the soul of Fo-hi (a term he uses rather than Buddha or Buddhism) had "transmigrated into his Imperial body" (MD, 130, 136). He also visited the Potala temple, where he learned that the ceremonies of its monks were like those of the "Romish Church" and that the worship of Fo-hi was the religion of the Tartars (MD, 135–136). On September 17, he participated in the emperor's birthday celebration, and further distanced himself from the effects of the Orient by now styling the emperor "Nebuchadnezzar" (MD, 131). On a less felicitous note, he also discovered that the palaces throughout the park were filled with "spheres, orreries, clocks, and musical automatons of such exquisite workmanship, and in such profusion, that our presents must shrink from the comparison and 'hide their diminished heads'" (MD, 125).

4.7   On to Business

During his tours of the imperial gardens, Macartney was accompanied by Heshen and other high officials, providing him with an opportunity to evaluate those with whom he expected to begin negotiations. He describes Heshen, for example, to be a well-bred courtier. However, after commenting to him that he understood the gardens to be the work of the emperor Kangxi, Macartney notes a perceptible cooling in Heshen's attitude toward him. Such hints of jealousy were more overt in the case of Fukang'an, the former governor-general of Liangguang, whom Macartney characterizes as "formal and repulsive," and filled with "great coldness and a mixture of un-reasonable vanity." Soon after, the ambassador's suspicions that Fukang'an was indisposed toward the embassy were confirmed. During a conversation with Heshen over the two ships at Chusan, Macartney asked if Mackintosh, the captain of the *Hindostan,* could rejoin his ship. Fukang'an immediately objected that such an action would be improper and against the laws of China. Macartney's efforts to change his mind failed (MD, 127–128).

During these encounters, Macartney repeatedly tried to introduce the "business" of his embassy. When officials proved evasive, he sought a private audience with Heshen. The minister said that he was unable to grant the request because of his involvement in the emperor's birthday celebration and the impending departure of the court from Rehe. Heshen did, however, agree to receive a note from Macartney. On September 18, Macartney and his retinue were invited to an audience that was part of the imperial birthday celebration. Summoned before the throne by the Qianlong emperor, Macartney attempted to turn the conversation toward the aims of his embassy, but the emperor chose instead to bestow additional gifts on the English king, his ambassador, and his retinue. At the conclusion of these festivities, Wang announced that the ceremonies at Rehe were at an end and that the emperor planned to leave on September 24, three days after the embassy was to depart (MD, 128–129, 134, 137, and IOMC, 20:115a–116a).

With the stay in Rehe rapidly drawing to a close and no "business" as yet transacted, Macartney immediately prepared the letter that Heshen had agreed to receive. In it he asked that Mackintosh be permitted to proceed to Chusan, that the *Hindostan* be allowed to trade there, that two European missionaries aboard the ship be allowed to land and enter imperial service, and that he be allowed to correspond freely with the British factory in Canton (MD, 141, and IOMC, 20:155).

On the evening of September 19, Zhengrui removed a piece of paper from his pocket and informed Macartney that Mackintosh would not be allowed to separate from the embassy, but that the other matters were manageable; for example, the *Hindostan* could trade at Chusan exempt from duties (MD, 142). Apparently desiring to have on paper the trade concession or perhaps some sign that business had in fact been conducted, Macartney requested a copy of the paper Zhengrui was holding. After the Legate refused, Macartney concluded that he remained hostile to the embassy. But Zhengrui was a minor irritant at this point. Through sources he does not identify, Macartney heard of a meeting between Heshen, Fukang'an, and the disgraced Hoppo of Canton, who had to be transported from prison to attend (MD, 142). While he did not know the particulars of the meeting, Macartney felt it boded ill for his mission.

On September 20, the emperor's presents for the British king were packed up and Macartney had "George III. Rex" marked on each box. The gifts themselves did not appear very fine, but as usual those who delivered them "affected to consider them of great value" (MD, 142). Meanwhile, preparations were completed for the departure of the embassy and Zhengrui visited to inform the ambassador that he would accompany the embassy on its return journey to Peking. Thus, Macartney left Rehe having achieved little beyond the ceremonial delivery of his king's letter into the hands of the Qianlong emperor.

4.8   Events in Peking

Arriving back in Peking on September 28 and suffering from a severe case of gout, Macartney turned his attention to the unfinished assembly of the British gifts at the Yuanming Gardens. Apparently still holding hopes that the gifts would favorably impress the emperor and thus facilitate the negotiation process, Macartney was disturbed by reports he received on October 1 that Chinese officials were pressing the British artisans to complete the operation so that the emperor could view them as soon as he returned to the capital. When they were told more time was required, the officials expressed astonishment. Macartney noted that the incident demonstrated again their ignorance and showed that the Chinese believed labor, not skill "was the only thing necessary, and that so complicated a machine as a system of the universe was an operation as easy and simple as the winding up a jack [*sic*]" (MD, 145–146). Further disappointment was to soon follow. When the emperor finally did see the display of the gifts, he was, according to James Dinwiddie, far from awed by British genius. He is said to have commented, "These things are good enough to amuse children" (Proudfoot 1868:53).

As if insult were being added to injury, Macartney also learned on September 28 through unidentified sources that high officials, claiming that under Chinese law embassies were allowed to remain in China no longer than forty days, wanted the British to depart. Immediately sending a note to Heshen, he acknowledged the concession regarding trade at Chusan and again asked permission to send Mackintosh there with the explanation that his presence would guarantee amicable commercial intercourse. He then stated his determination to depart Peking soon after the new year and travel overland to Canton at his own expense. Heshen responded by requesting a meeting at Yuanming Gardens the next day (MD, 146, and IOMC, 20:157).

The meeting of October 2, 1793, would prove to be the only opportunity the British ambassador had to discuss the "business" of his embassy with officials in the capital. Present were Heshen, Fukang'an, and Fuchang'an. The meeting began with the delivery of some letters that had arrived from Canton. Upon request, Macartney disclosed the contents and "freely" put the letters into Heshen's hands. They were from Admiral Gower, who, having reached the island of Chusan off the Zhejiang coast, reprovisioned the *Lion,* rested its crew, and was now prepared to depart. The *Hindostan,* which was also at Chusan, awaited the return of Captain Mackintosh. Heshen expressed hope that the *Lion* had not yet departed, for he was certain that Macartney was anxious to return home. The emperor, Heshen said, was aware that the climate of Peking often adversely affected foreigners and had indicated concern over Macartney's health. Therefore, there was no reason for him to delay his departure, especially since the feasts of the new year were identical to those Macartney had already seen at Rehe.

Brushing aside the climate issue, Macartney reminded Heshen that he had been promised opportunities for negotiations once back in Peking. After offering to pay his own expenses for a longer stay in order to cement a "firm friendship" between his king and the emperor, he explained that his monarch wished to receive a reciprocal embassy from China. Avoiding a direct response, Heshen returned to the emperor's anxiety over the ambassador's health, which led Macartney to conclude that the officials were unfavorably disposed to his business. When he rose to leave, however, Heshen and the others were "gracious" and "flattering" to him. Macartney's interpreter congratulated him, explaining that these negotiations could only lead to the "happiest issue" (MD, 147–148).

When he returned to his quarters, however, Macartney learned that the emperor's answer to his king's letter required only translation into Latin to be complete, a signal, according to his understanding, for the embassy to depart. His apprehension increased when Wang and Qiao, in a dejected state, due, from Macartney's view, to a loss of advantage that might have been gained if the embassy had succeeded and to little hope of promotion from having attended the embassy, informed him that he would be summoned to the palace to receive the emperor's letter the next day. The events which ensued, including another letter of requests from Macartney to Heshen and the ceremonies of departure, will be taken up in chapter 7. It is sufficient to note at this point that the ambassador continued to be frustrated in realizing the objects of his embassy.

In this regard, it is worth considering an interview Macartney had on the evening of October 4 with Father Amiot. The Chinese, said Amiot, considered embassies temporary ceremonies and lacked favorable ideas of treaties. As a result, nothing could be expected of them suddenly; rather, patience, caution, and adroitness was necessary over a period of time. The embassy had made an excellent impression, one that could be built upon through regular correspondence between the two monarchs. Appointing a king's commissioner to Canton, suggested Amiot, would be a way to further communication and provide the English with a viable representative to participate in court-related activities. Macartney should not be disappointed or discouraged at this stage. Momentary satisfaction was best foregone in "favour of the more solid and permanent advantages which must gradually follow from" deliberate proceedings. Amiot then urged Macartney to request permission to depart (MD, 151).[17]

Although he appears to have appreciated the priest's comments and been gratified by confirmation that the embassy had succeeded in its object of impressing the imperial court, Macartney had such high expectations of success that he could not easily reconcile himself to what appeared to be a singular failure. After his meeting with Amiot, he ruminated on the possible causes of failure. The priest had remarked about the court's concern over disorder in Europe occasioned by the French revolution and how it might have temporarily prejudiced the Chinese against all Europeans. Macartney gave a good deal of credence to this suggestion. Equally plausible was the continued jealous nature of the court and its adherence to immutable laws, as well as the possibility that the ambassador himself might have made some "trifling" error. He concluded, however, that the central cause was the court's aversion to innovation, especially at this late date in the emperor's life and in light of the various intrigues that he suspected among its members (MD, 153).

In his letters to Dundas over the next few months, Macartney repeated many of these observations. In particular, he emphasized court intrigue,

---

17. Macartney immediately drafted such a request and had it delivered to Heshen (IOMC, 20:163).

that is, the obstructionism of Chinese officials, as a major element. Later, when he learned in Canton the details of the British efforts to mediate the dispute between Tibet and Nepal, he became convinced that Fukang'an, the military commander in the Tibetan campaign against the Gurkhas, was behind much of the intrigue against him. The motive Macartney imputed for this was that Fukang'an feared he would lose the merit he had garnered in the campaigns if the truth were known. He had worked, therefore, to get the British embassy out of Peking as quickly as possible (IOMC, 20:194).[18]

Grounds for optimism were also present. Macartney found many Chinese officials not indisposed to foreigners. Equally encouraging was what he could discern of the Chinese people. "As for the lower orders, they are all of a trafficking turn, and it seemed at the seaports where we stopped that nothing would be more agreeable to them than to see our ships often in their harbors." Macartney's evaluation here reproduces some of the assumptions of the discourse on wealth and international commerce that he had carried with him to China. Again there is a familiar division between the head of government, recalcitrant officials, and the psychologically accessible lower orders. Also present is the assertion that a dialogue was possible with some "good Chinese" on the basis of frank and reasonable discussion. Unfortunately these Chinese officials were not in a position to immediately aid the embassy. Instead, an aging emperor was surrounded by suspicious and jealous aides.[19]

18. The Qing court had received several reports from Fukang'an, the commander of Qing forces in Tibet, concerning contact he had had with Bengal. In them he noted that the governor of Calcutta, head of a people identified as the Pileng, had dissuaded the Gurkhas from continuing military action in Tibet. The Manchu general read this as an indication of the spread of imperial virtue in the world and added that the Pileng of Calcutta may be related to people who traded at Canton. He does not, however, directly connect the Pileng to the British (*KEKJL*, 51:4b–5a, 7a–8a). Also see Rockhill 1910:58–62, and Fu 1966, 1:324.

What influence this situation had on the Qing court's attitude toward the British embassy is difficult to discern, but after Macartney left Peking, the court consulted a Gurkha by the name of Ganggele Tazhexijiang about whether the British were the Pileng people from Calcutta. He said no, Pileng was actually a pejorative term referring to a kind of people. On the other hand, he noted that the British he had seen in Peking looked like and dressed like people from Calcutta, so that maybe the people from Calcutta and the British were the same (*GZSY*, QL 58.9.14, 68:85–86).

19. On October 6, Macartney recorded in his diary that many at court were pleased with the embassy and wished the British would remain longer. Just who these officials were and where this information came from is not clear; see MD, 155.

On October 7, 1793, the embassy departed Peking. Zhengrui accompanied them as far as Tianjin, where Songyun, the official who had impressed Macartney while at Rehe, took up the duties of escort. The conversations between Macartney and Songyun (see section 8.2) coupled with the lavish reception when the embassy arrived in Tianjin led him to ruminate on the treatment he had been accorded by the Qing court. "They receive us," he wrote in a diary entry of October 13,

> with the highest distinction, show us every external mark of favour and regard, send the first Minister (Heshen) himself to attend us as a *cicerone* for two days together through their palaces and gardens; entertain us with the choicest amusements, and express themselves greatly pleased with so splendid an embassy, commend our conduct and cajole us with compliments. Yet, in less than a couple months, they plainly discover that they wish us gone, refuse our requests without reserve or compliance, precipitate our departure, and dismiss us dissatisfied; yet, no sooner have we taken leave of them than we find ourselves treated with more studied attention, more marked distinction, and less constraint than before. *I must endeavour to unravel this mystery if I can. Perhaps they have given way to impressions which they could not resist, but are ashamed to confess; perhaps they begin to find their mistake, and wish to make amends.* (MD, 164; emphasis added)

As a summation of his experiences in China, this statement nicely combines Macartney's confusion with what he claims to be contradictions in Chinese behavior. Here as elsewhere he projects outward onto others responsibility for problems caused by his own limitations. As such his conclusions stand as a profound comment on the analytical tools he brought to bear to understand China. It is not simply that his naturalist's gaze fails to deliver truth, producing in the end mystification, conspiracy, or psychological shortcomings in others. His confusion is also a product of the certainties and sense of superiority over the Qing empire that informed the planning and organization of the embassy. These attitudes, in turn, were firmly embedded in public-sphere discourse; and they articulated smoothly with the discourse of the imperial state that Macartney quite effectively represented as it came into contact with another imperial formation. It seems appropriate, therefore, to leave Macartney's account of his embassy at this point and consider in more detail the kind and order of treatment the

Qing empire deemed proper for the reception of embassies from the edges of its empire. After reviewing some features of Qing imperial practices particularly relevant to relations with other kingdoms, I will explore principles that inform Guest Ritual, the category under which relations with other lords were organized. In subsequent chapters, I will construct the encounter with the British from existing imperial court records, occasionally juxtaposing British accounts to highlight, rather than reconcile, their differences.

5 GUEST RITUAL AND INTERDOMAINAL RELATIONS

During the sixty-year reign of the Qianlong emperor (1736–1796), as throughout the Qing period, the imperial court engaged foreign lords in a political discourse for which Manchu-Chinese imperial rituals were a ruling idiom. As discussed in the introduction (1.5) and chapter 2, the Qing court organized encounters between emperors and other lords under the rubric "Guest Ritual" (*Binli*), one of five categories of imperial rites. In Guest Ritual, the emperor was accorded the position of supreme lord (*huangdi*)[1] in relation to lesser lords (*fanwang*) as guests. Various textual materials, including the main one relied upon below, *Comprehensive Rites of the Great Qing* (*DQTL*),[2] provide rich details on the organization of these occasions.

1. The emperor is designated as *huangdi* in a variety of court audience situations. Guest Ritual is only one of these and, in part, appears to be organized with reference to other occasions of court assemblage. The Imperial assembly or audience is to be found in textual sources among the Felicitous rites (*Jiali*). As part of the Felicitous rites, the court audience is divided into the Grand audience (*Dachao*), held on the first day of the year, the winter solstice, and the emperor's birthday; the regular audience, *changchao*, held two or three times a month; and the rite for "attending to the affairs of the realm" (*ting-zheng*), held several times a month for the purpose of presenting memorials to the court and for the dissemination of imperial edicts. In both the Grand and regular audience, provision is made for the participation of lesser lords or their emissaries. See chapters 18 and 19 in the *DQTL*.

2. The *Comprehensive Rites* was first edited and compiled under imperial auspices and published in the twentieth year of Qianlong's reign (1756). My references throughout are to the 1883 reprint of the 1824 re-edited edition. There are variations between the reprint and the 1756 edition, which was also published in the *SKQS* (see under *Da Qing tongli* in the Bibliography). The differences mentioned here are consistent with a notion that rites

This chapter will explore in more detail the textual sources of Guest Ritual and the metaphysical assumptions which informed this body of Qing practices. I have tried to write within the logic of Guest Ritual, a logic that is discernible from the authoritative Qing texts considered below. Examples of this logic at work can be found in chapter 2 and in chapters 6 to 8, where I reconstruct the British embassy from Chinese-language court records.

Before proceeding to a discussion of the principles that inform Guest Ritual, however, a few words are in order about my use of the term "guest." In English, guest connotes a narrow range of social situations. Generally, it is used to designate someone who is entertained by invitation in a home or in a public setting. Normally, we conceive of such persons as holding a social ranking similar to our own. If they do not, the word guest is likely to be modified by terms such as "honored" or "special," indicating, however unclearly, a recognition of difference. Nevertheless, implicit in our notion of guest is a foreknowledge of the person (either directly through experience or indirectly through a mutual acquaintance) and an a priori assumption of equality in the context of guest and host. For several reasons, none of these assumptions finds equivalencies in imperial Guest Ritual.[3]

In the first place, the guest is not invited to the Qing court. Rather, the lesser lord requests permission to enter the imperial domain. Second, because the entire process appears to be about forming superior/inferior relations, equality is irrelevant. Third, these features of Guest Ritual appear, in turn, to be infused with an explicit morality, rather than influenced by etiquette or manners that may, but by no means must, be buttressed by moral principles. Finally, the use of the term "guest" implies a certain kind of host. To interpret the position of the emperor (as it is constituted in Guest Ritual) to be that of host is highly misleading because it could reduce him to little more than the head of one household among others, which, if maintained, would obscure the fundamental distinction in the rite between the one (*huangdi*) and the many (*fanwang*). The Guest Ritual section of the *Comprehensive Rites* begins by asserting this very distinction.

---

must change as cosmic-earthly conditions alter. Also see the QLHD, *juan* 56; LBZL, *juan* 180; and HCTZ, *juan* 46 on Guest Ritual.

3. Hocart noted a similar difficulty when considering the Greek notion of guest. In Homeric times, a "guest" was protected by Zeus and might even be thought of as a god. To mistreat a stranger was an act of one who had no regard for the gods; see Hocart 1952: 78–86.

5.1   Locating Guest Ritual in Qing Imperial Discourse

The Guest Ritual section of the *DQTL* is made up of two chapters (45 and 46). The first deals with meetings between the emperor and guests, which will be the focus of this chapter, and the second with various rankings of people below the emperor. Chapter 45 opens with prefatory comments about the rite, beginning with a reference to practices of the Zhou dynasty (1027–481 B.C.E.).

> In the *Rites of Zhou* the Grand Conductors of Affairs (*Daxingren*)[4] handled (*zhang*) the rites and ceremonies of the guest. Kingdoms external to the nine provinces were called foreign kingdoms (*fanguo*). Each of these kingdoms took its most precious things (*guibao*) to be the offering (*zhi*). (*DQTL*, 45:1a)

Having suggested that some of the particulars of Zhou rituals are related to those found within the *Comprehensive Rites*, the Preface continues with an explanation of why lesser lords come to court for audience.

> In our time the enunciated teachings of the imperial family (*guojia shengjiao*) have reached the foreign peoples of the four directions who come as guests. The various kingdoms from beyond mountains and seas have recorded this. For over a hundred years, the Board of Rites, by Imperial Order, has feasted and rewarded them. (*DQTL*, 45:1a)

These references to an exterior are then linked, via processes of text editing, to the imperium proper, organizing the meetings of categories of people below the emperor as lesser and varied versions of imperial Guest Ritual.

> Various ceremonial canonical writings have been examined, combined, and thus compiled to make Guest Ritual. Then the ceremonial usages for visiting the multitude of officials, the gentry, and common people were appended afterwards, each according to its correct place. (*DQTL*, 45:1a)[5]

---

4. The *HCWXTK* adds that the Grand Conductors of Affairs "regulate (*zhi*) spirits and men" and "harmonize (*he*) high and low" (115:1a). Here the designation used for the conductors is *zongbo*. Also see *WLTK*, 220:1a.

5. These ceremonial usages are in chapter 46 and include protocols for visits between

The Preface then concludes by defining the lesser lords and their offerings more precisely.

> In the ceremony of offering up the most precious things at court (*chaogong zhi li*), the foreign peoples of the four directions (*siyi*) are classified as domains (*guo*) and order their offerings according to the proper season. [The princes] of these domains send their servants to present petitions (*biaowen*) and local products (*fangwu*). They come to Our court in the capital. (DQTL, 45:1a)

In considering some of the implications of this construction, note first that the text begins by invoking aspects of Zhou rulership. This is a rather intriguing move because the particulars of imperial Guest Ritual that follow the Preface appear to have more of a structural affinity with Tang and Ming guest rituals than with those of the Zhou period. At the same time, Qing editors made a number of changes in the procedures to be found in the Tang and Ming texts, and, perhaps more importantly, expanded the category itself. Apparently to accord with their understanding of guest ceremonies in the *Rites of Zhou* (compiled in the second or third century B.C.E.), editors not only added guest rites involving grades of people below the emperor, they also included a section on the dispatching of an embassy to enfeoff a foreign prince. These additions signified a general trend in the Qianlong reign to transcend the practices of previous dynasties and to recover the spirit, if not the exact form, of the guest rites of the Zhou dynasty.[6]

Second, in its account of why people come to the court of the Qing emperor, the text implies that some form of emanation and attraction occurs. This suggests something akin to Waley's translation of *de* (usually glossed as virtue) as exemplary power capable of moral ordering (1958:89, 93).[7] The

---

imperial princes of the blood and foreign nobles graded into five ranks; visits among capital officials; and visits between capital officials and provincial officials, among provincial officials, and among commoners. On the significance of the constitution of Qing notions of rulership related to text editing see Zito forthcoming.

6. See the Guest Ritual sections of the DTKYL, 81–90 and the MJL, 30–32. The Tang, Ming, and Qing imperial ritual texts are all different in the sequential ordering of the five rites. In addition to the *Rites of Zhou*, ritual specialists in these dynasties probably also drew on the *Records of Rites* (*Liji*) and *Ceremonies and Rites* (*Yili*), the latter of which contains a large section on host-guest ceremonies. For English translations see Gingell 1852, Legge 1967, and Steele 1917.

7. The Kingly Rites section of the HCWXTK describes the processes of rituals performed by the king as follows:

"enunciated teachings of the imperial family" might be thought of in these terms. Specifically, these enunciations appear to embody the attributes of the king who faces south, the position the emperor assumes, for example, in imperial audience.[8] In all forms of audience, the emperor addresses the imperial domain and the world at large by instructing, admonishing, cherishing, and rewarding his servants (*chen*).[9] The reigning emperor both generates this instruction and continues the attributes of previous emperors through his act of enunciation. His instruction extends outward to encompass the whole world (*siyi,* the four directions). Domains at the farthest extent of the world record the supreme lord's teachings. Their rulers are attracted to his court, where they are feasted and rewarded by order of the emperor. While this process will be dealt with in greater detail below, the passage cited here suggests that imperial instruction embodies aspects of sagely and virtuous kingly rule and, as such, has the power to reorient others, including lesser lords.

Third, the foreign lord and the population he commands are organized under what appears to be a generic heading of *yi,* rendered as "the foreign peoples" above. Usually it is glossed as "barbarians." I believe, however, that in the context of Guest Ritual the latter translation is somewhat misleading, particularly when other sources indicate that the purpose of the rite was to bring close (*qin*) other domains (*yi binli qin bangguo;* e.g., WLTK, 220:1a). As a noun, *qin* is translated as family or relative. Here, however, it is used as a verb meaning "to love," "to be close to," as one would be toward one's own relatives.[10] In either case, the use of this term, along with others that

---

> The practice of rites passes from high to low. Thus, from the King's court it extends (*da*) to the feudal lords, the great men, the king's servants, and the commoners, bringing all together through it. Discussing rites, making measure, and examining texts is to return to the Heavenly production of the "many things emerging from the source." (115:1a).

In addition to providing a sense of the extension of imperial virtue produced by the performance of rites, this passage also suggests that text editing is an element intrinsic to ritual practices, not simply, for example, a resource for them.

8. See the *Book of Rites* for additional glosses on the south-facing king (Legge 1967, 2:61).

9. All of these kingly attributes can be contrasted with the attributes associated with him when, for example, he faces in other directions to sacrifice to the Cosmos as the Son of Heaven or to his ancestors as a filial son (see the Auspicious rites of the DQTL).

10. This is also the word in the much disputed opening phrase of the Great Learning (*Daxue*). Beginning with Cheng Yi (1033–1107), Neo-Confucian thinkers preferred to

refer to showing compassion for lesser lords or cherishing them, seems to be pointing toward a process of inclusion, rather than one designed to affirm a dichotomy such as civilization and barbarism.[11] Moreover, the kingdoms of these lords are classified as domains (*guo*), a designation that also denotes the Qing empire. This suggests a world imagined as one made up of a multitude of lords ruling numerous domains, each of which exists in a part-whole relationship to the imperial domain. Implicit in this imagining is, I believe, a notion that the lordship of the lesser lords is somehow linked to that of the supreme lord.

Fourth, lesser lords are said to come to court and make offerings. That is, they present petitions and local products (*fangwu*), things unique or special to their domain. This latter notion is particularly intriguing; it implies that local products are a means for differentiating one domain from another. Moreover, the same term is used to define "tribute" presented to the court from within the Qing imperium.

To summarize, the general structure of the Preface indicates the following pattern: an emanation outward of imperial instruction followed by a movement of people and their precious things from outer and lower to inner and higher.[12] The prefatory comments of chapter 45 serve, therefore, as a useful introduction to some of the key principles and patterns that make up the Guest Ritual process. This, however, is only part of their significance. Recall the introductory discussion of macrocosm-microcosm in ritual (1.5). There I argued that the cosmic was always immanent in earthly forms, thus infusing all ritual action with cosmological principles. It is to the metaphysics embedded in ritual process that I now turn.

5.2   The Metaphysics of Rites and Imperial Ritual

None of the extensive ritual materials dealing with emperorship can be understood independent of the claim made in imperial discourse that the

---

read it as *xin*, renovate the people, rather than love them; see Chan 1963:85 and Gardner 1986:89–90.

11. The distinction becomes even more difficult to maintain uncritically when, for example, some sources refer to the lords of the other domains as *zhuhou*, the "feudal" lords of Chinese antiquity; see WLTK, 220:1a. These lords came to the court of the Son of Heaven during each of the four seasons and participated in audiences appropriate to those seasons.

12. This is, of course, also the structural logic of the Great Learning, a text quite important throughout the Qing because of its link to *kaozheng* thought; see Peterson 1975.

sage king was the pivot between the Cosmos and the earth. Imperial ritual was the proper action which formed a relationship between the noumenal and phenomenal, the invisible and the affairs of human beings.[13] Ritual texts and Manchu-Chinese records of foreign embassies take their place within this larger context of imperial ritual action.

Certain cosmological principles inform these rites and comprise what I will call a *patterning discourse*.[14] First, the invisible is immanently manifest in the phenomenal world as emerging patterns of relationship between people and things. Second, the name for a thing, the thing itself, and the enunciator are all part of the same ontological order. Third, patterns are perceived and classifications are made on the basis of attributes discernible as phenomena emerge. Fourth, emerging patterns result from a process of generation, regeneration, and transformation. Fifth, patterns are not simply recognizable by human beings; rather the human social world is inseparable from cosmic patterns. Implicit in this last assumption is the view that humans, through their purposive acts, bring to completion cosmically generated patterns by working on manifest phenomena. In other words, human beings, without exception, are active participants in the ongoing process of making the universe; as such, human action affects and shapes these processes. Imperial ritual takes its place within this imagining of the cosmos.

Morally correct imperial rulership is about comprehending cosmically produced manifestations and working on them. As such it is a logical inversion of the perception that the improper performance of imperial ritual could produce natural disasters, indicating the mismanagement of human affairs by an incompetent ruler. Thus, while there is an overall pattern of repetition in the cosmos (i.e., spring follows winter, summer follows spring, etc.), there is also a palpable and continous change in patterns, which if

13. R. Smith (1993:167) makes this proposition quite clear. Moreover, he extends it to divination.

14. I have developed the following notions of patterning from two sources. The first derives from Reiss's discussion of a discursive order preceding that of natural science in Europe (see 1982:21–54). The particulars of these European developments are, of course, quite different from those to be found in China. The second source is the writings of John Hay, especially 1983a and b and 1993:66–76. As noted above, Hay sees the metaphysical principles he elucidates as implicated in painting, calligraphy, and other practices. I believe that they are also important for understanding ritual in general and imperial rites in particular.

misrecognized could open the door to chaos, the dissolution of the specific rulership, and its possible replacement by another.

The recognition of patterns is encoded in imperial texts as classification (*shu*). Classification serves to organize (not fix) people and things (i.e., as unfolding temporal processes) in conjunction with cosmically emerging patterns. The engagement between cosmic pattern and human classification continually channels action away from extremes and toward a contingent spatial center that temporarily constitutes a cosmo-moral order made up of the Cosmos, earth, and humanity. This process is discernible in a variety of textual sources under the rubric "centering," *fengjian shi zhong*, negotiating a mean between overabundance and scarcity. Centering is also implicitly evoked in criticisms of those who go too far or do not do enough, in reminders to officials that they should be neither too humble nor too haughty, and in distinctions that are drawn between the gravity and triviality of situations. In general, one has a sense of directed movement along a path made between extremes of excess and deficiency. Moreover, centering appears to have cut across many domains of imperial practice, linking what some might consider the most mundane activities of administrators to very large cosmic processes.[15]

The significance of centering will become evident through consideration of the particulars of the Macartney embassy in the following chapters. At present, it is sufficient to note that actions of all the participants are continually reviewed for signs of excess and deficiency that would move the action toward extremes. We might say, therefore, that human actions are channeled between extremes, and that this channeling embodies the centering process. As it does so, channeling organizes hierarchical relationships that are considered to be the proper order of the world at the moment of ritual constitution. To put it another way, the centering process allows the differentiation and inclusion of the powers of others into the emperor's rulership as desirable superior/inferior relations.

The principles by which difference was included within imperial sovereignty (principles which appear to be common to all imperial rites) extend far beyond the organization of texts and forms of intertextual reference. Relationships so formed appear to have the following characteristics: the power of the superior lies in his capacity to generate conditions necessary

15. See Rowe 1993:10. n. 6, where the issue is posed in terms of official involvement in economic activities.

for the inclusion of inferiors; the power of the inferior lies in his capacity to bring to completion what the superior sets in motion. The Manchu-Chinese imagining of imperial sovereignty took this form.

The asymmetry and interdependence of the superior/inferior relationship is signified as such in several ways in imperial rites. First, and perhaps most importantly, not everyone is the Son of Heaven or supreme lord, not all knowledge and human capacities are equal. In other words, the meanings that might be ascribed to the emperor's capacity to pivot from his position facing north when he addresses the Cosmos and his ancestors to one facing south when he addresses the earth are different from similar actions of, for instance, the head of a lineage. At the same time, however, the rites performed by others are not absolutely separate from those performed by the emperor; they exist in part-whole (synecdochic) and homologous relations with imperial rites. Such affiliations make the point that neither the imperial order nor the lineage can be maintained without the participation of loyal inferiors. Superiors initiate, set affairs in motion, are a source; but inferiors bring affairs to completion. What I take to be significant here is that at the very pinnacle of imperial ritual, plural human agency and the constitutive properties of such agencies are proposed — people can be both generators and completers depending on the relationship being formed. It was in and through rites that these contingent human attributes were realized and made the world in a specific way; ritual (*li*) was the name given to purposeful human activities, which, for a time, constituted a cosmo-moral order.

If we look closely at the Grand Sacrifice, we may see one way in which this was accomplished. At the solstices and equinoxes the emperor moved out of his palaces in the four cardinal directions, thereby constructing, as it were, a center. In these rites, Heaven (south) and Ancestors (east) initiated, while the emperor, as Son of Heaven and filial imperial son, faced north and completed. Pivoting and facing south, the emperor initiated and Earth (north) and Soil and Grain (west) completed (Zito 1984:76). As if to emphasize a pivotal center and plural human agency, the solstice sacrifices were followed by the Grand Assemblage and Grand Banqueting. In the latter rites, the emperor was located at the north end and on the center line of an audience hall, facing south toward the world of human affairs. In this capacity he was the supreme lord, the lord of lords, the generative principle, and those before him, his servants, were the completing principle. As generator, the emperor commanded the assembly of officials; as completers, officials gathered before him in east and west flanks and knelt three times, each time bowing their heads thrice (*sangui jiukou*).

5.3   Lordship and Guest Ritual

Not all inferiors had the capacity for situationally specific completion; not everyone could enter a relationship with the emperor and prostrate to him. Other lords were among the select few who could. There were several practical reasons why this was so. In the first place, lords commanded domains, that is, they organized relations of power and authority over people and resources in a particular area. The capacity to command others was comparable to that of the emperor, and, like imperial authority, was the foundation upon which a lesser lord's martial strength was built. Moreover, the military strength of lords, be they supreme lord or lesser lords, when focused, could be and indeed often was directed against other lordships.

This martial aspect of lordship, in turn, provides some indication of what the goals of warfare ideally were. One apparently did not utterly reduce a rival; rather a lord had to demonstrate that his command over people and things was superior to that of others, and then include the strength of a defeated rival within his own sphere. Yet such inclusion had to be continually managed and reproduced, because alterations were presumed to be ever present in relations of power.[16] In other words, change continually had to be addressed if any lordship was to remain intact. In this sense, relations between lords were inherently contentious and contradictory, even after an act of inclusion had been accomplished. It was not enough (to use the language of the tribute system) for other lords to be "enrolled" as tributaries (Fairbank 1948:133). Rather, relations were contingent and provisional, requiring continuous renegotiation and refashioning as conditions in the world changed.

In a political situation in which lords vied with each other for supremacy, any claim that the emperor might make to supreme lordship was predicated on his dexterous management of relations with other lords; he must include their strength without diluting it so that he could, if necessary, command them to assist him in the ordering of the world. This was, after all, his Mandate from Heaven (*Tianming*). Without the inclusion of other lordships,

---

16. One good example of such vicissitudes was the Qianlong emperor's relationship with the Inner Asian lord Amursana; see Hummel 1943:11–13.

such order would at best be superficial and sovereignty unstable. And there were very practical consequences to such an eventuality. Any lesser lord, especially one who stood as an inferior vis-à-vis a reigning emperor, could, under the proper conditions, also make a claim to supreme lordship based on the manifest inability of the emperor to fashion links with the invisible and properly order the world. For Manchu kings, this was no small matter, since the dynasty itself was founded when the Qing ruler made just such a claim against the Ming.

Guest Ritual provided the context in which the lesser lord's strength was both acknowledged (that is, differentiated from that of other lords) and shown now to be part of a whole, having been reformed and channeled in such a way that it was encompassed by the supreme lord. Guest Ritual had, therefore, a martial element to it: the strength of the sublord was displayed, but he was also shown the superior military prowess of the emperor.[17] This form of display was accomplished in several ways. First, in imperial audiences the lesser lord was positioned on the west, the side reserved for the emperor's military officers, as opposed to the east, which was reserved for civil officials. Second, present at audiences for lesser lords were large imperial guard contingents. Third, the routes traveled by the lesser lord to and from the capital sometimes had guard contingents displayed along them. And, finally, in audience he might not be the only lesser lord present. In effect, he was shown that others like him also pledged their loyalty to the emperor.

The Guest Ritual process begins with the actions of the supreme lord as generator. In his fashioning of the relationship between the Cosmos, earth, and humanity, he takes and holds a pivotal role in the ordering of the universe. His capacity to do this is the exemplary power (*de*) that suffuses the world; it results from the emperor's performance of the ritual cycle. As many texts tell us, the lesser lord is reoriented sincerely to face toward transformation (*xiang hua zhi cheng*); he manifests sincerity (*cheng*) in the form of reverence (*gong*), obedience (*shun*), earnestness (*geng*), and faithfulness (*zhi*), attributes which stimulate him to come to the emperor's court and make offerings.[18] Having thus been reoriented, the lesser lord requests permission to enter the imperial domain. His request to come to court is

17. This aspect of Guest Ritual appears to have been particularly prominent in the Macartney embassy; see below, especially chapter 8.

18. In the case of the Macartney embassy, see ZGCB, 5a.

understood by the imperium as a desire on his part to continue the process of his own and his domain's transformation in and through actions that will acknowledge the generative capacity of the emperor. In the end, he will give thanks (*xie*) for the imperial grace (*en*) that has been extended (*da*) to encompass him. He will bring to culmination a portion of the process set in motion by the emperor's actions in fashioning a cosmo-moral order. This particular sequence is discernible in the *Comprehensive Rites* and the court documents of the Macartney embassy.

From ritual and related texts, we can then discern the following relationship between superior and inferior, which serves to orient action. The emperor emerges as one who bestows imperial grace (*en*); as bestower, he entitles the lesser lord and gives him such things as clothing, jade scepters, the emperor's calligraphy, the calendar, and food. He also allows him to participate in other rites. The lesser lord, as the completing principle, offers things up to the emperor. These might include his genealogy, the unique products of his domain, and thanks for the extension of the emperor's grace. Moreover by his deportment, including dress, speech, and gesture, such as kneeling and bowing the head to the ground (koutou), the lesser lord is understood to manifest his sincere loyalty. The result is that an inferior center (i.e., that constituted by the lesser lord in his domain) is encompassed: the lesser lord by his movements and gestures actually accepts transformation and is differentiated (maintaining a distance and displacement from the superior center constituted by the emperor on the center line of the audience site).

Throughout the Guest Ritual process, asymmetrical spatial principles are continually evoked as the relationship being fashioned is evaluated and managed by imperial officials. Relations between high and low, near and far inform, for example, responses to contingencies that arise as the rite unfolds and are read in the relationship between this particular encounter and other encounters (precedents) that may have occurred in the present reign or previous reigns.

But there is something more here. Sons become fathers, servants become lords. We see in ritual the generation or enabling of proper conditions and attributes that transform those who bring ritual processes to culmination (sons, servants) into generators (fathers, lords). The completer in imperial audiences in the Grand Harmony Hall (Peking) or the round tent of the Garden of Ten-Thousand Trees (Rehe) becomes the generator in Korea, Vietnam, Kashgar, and Portugal. In other words, ritual action holds the

possibility of temporally extending the cosmo-moral ordering of the world
into the future, as well as outward into the domains of lesser lords.

5.4   Guest Ritual and the Constitution of Rulership

As noted earlier, Guest Ritual does not appear to deal in crude distinctions between civilization and barbarism, but with the way the undifferentiated is incorporated, through centering, into the rulership of the Qing emperor. In this formation, superior and inferior, lord and servant, are, while
equally participants in the process, hierarchically distinct. Central to such a
possibility is the recognition on the part of the lesser lord, however limited
it may initially be, of the nature of the process in which he participates. Such
recognition is enabled, to be sure, by the extension of imperial virtue, but it
continues in practice through specific acts initiated by the lesser lord. Such
acts might be viewed as a manifestation of the knowledge the lesser lord
now possesses as a result of the resonance between his own attributes and
imperial virtue. Certainly, his request to come to court can be viewed in this
manner, but there are other equally significant indications of his response.

One of these is the presence in his petitions of sincere attitudes and emo-
tions appropriate to a servant, and their sincere presentation in his communication (*biao*) to the court. Also significant are the gifts the lesser lord
has brought to offer up to his superior. The lord's offerings are referred to
as *gong* or tribute and are supposed to be local products, or products of
the land (*tuchan*). Further, lesser lords are encouraged to consider these
local products as the most precious things of their domain. These references
suggest that there is more at work here than exchange value or symbolic
value, however they may be defined. The definition of tribute to be found
in ritual texts indicates that objects may not be separable or alienated from
their production in sensuous human activity, that they may in fact embody,
much like a romantic notion of a work of art, human attributes as well as
their own specific characteristics.

Given what has been said about the extension of imperial virtue and the
explicit references to the gifts being native to the domain of the lord presenting them, I would suggest the following possibility, one that I believe is
also consistent with the presentation of gifts from within the Qing empire to
the imperial court. The performance of the imperial ritual cycle is unques-
tionably tied to agricultural seasonality and implies that the actions of the
imperium, coupled with those of the farmer, nurture and bring to fruition

the products of the land. These products, in part, are channeled upward as offerings to the court. At the court, the products of the land become the concrete manifestation of correct temporal practices of organizing and managing a domain. They may, in turn, be offered up by the emperor, as servant and filial son, to the Cosmos and his ancestors in higher-order rites and as bestowals to other lords on different occasions of Guest Ritual.[19] Relations with lesser lords are conceived as an analogous situation.

The extension of imperial virtue throughout the world enables the lesser lord to act in a manner similar to the emperor; within his capacities, he can set in motion the process of nurturing the land in his own domain. He then gathers up the kinds of things that are unique and specific to his domain as if their uniqueness and specificity themselves manifest these processes, and presents them as his offering. But to do so he must have the capacity to recognize these gifts as such and to understand that they are invested with the complex processes that made them possible in the first place.

It is precisely this recognition that the imperium attempts to elicit in its dialogue with the lesser lord and in its viewing of the people and gifts that the lord dispatches to court. This is why not just any gift will do; it must be linked explicitly to the lesser lord's domain. To be gifts made in offering, they must, therefore, be things that are differentiable from other things of other domains, linked in some manner to the constitution of the lesser lord's rulership, and possible to locate in a pattern of the generation and regeneration of the myriad things of the world.

In a similar manner, imperial bestowal is intimately linked to the emperor's rulership, but is distinguishable from the lesser lord's act of offering things up. While it may be taken as a recognition by the emperor of the sincerity of the lesser lord's offering, the importance of bestowal lies in the fact that by flowing down, it completes the hierarchical relationship of superior and inferior. Again, like the offerings made by the lesser lord, the crucial element in this process is embodied in the kinds of things bestowed. Silk cloth or garments emblazoned with imperial dragons, for example, head bestowal lists.[20] In other words, the process of bringing close the lesser lord is realized in practice by bestowals presumably given to only the most important members of the imperium proper.

19. See Hevia 1993a:75 on the last point.

20. See Cammann's discussion of dragon robes and silk cloth used to make these robes (1953).

Imperial bestowal is also caught up in a network of relationships that include the provision of food and lodging, and the hospitable treatment of the embassy of the lesser lord. Furthermore, bestowals are graded according to a determination by court officials of a hierarchy within the embassy of the lesser lord, one that is elicited in the dialogue between imperial officials and the ambassador. The timing of bestowals, as well as the quantities and kinds of things bestowed, are then made contingent upon determinations of the lesser lord's or his servant's intent within the ritual process. Neither market nor symbolic exchange theories seem capable of containing the excess of meaning involved in "tribute" and imperial bestowals, particularly when it seems that items given are not symbolic of anything, but rather the concrete manifestations of moral practice. Any effort to distance them from this specific context transforms the gift and the bestowal into something quite alien to imperial discourse.

Predicated as it is on maintaining difference in the process of inclusion, imperial ritual might be viewed as overdetermined. First, imperial discourse must assume certain universal human attributes and capacities; otherwise imperial virtue would have limited efficacy. Second, it must assume that there is a correct and incorrect order for the world, and that the constitution of a correct order is both desirable and necessary. Third, it must assert that lordly virtue itself can only be generated through the regularities of imperial discourse. Fourth, while it can contemplate and accommodate otherness, it cannot do so in absolute terms. All boundaries are permeable, all difference is transformable, inside and outside are relative to each other. If, therefore, a perceptible failure occurs in any dimension of the rite, the practitioners of the discourse are forced to consider their own actions in determining what went wrong. And since this discourse acknowledges no absolute exteriority, one cannot simply lay the blame at the door of the lesser lord, even if one were to insist on viewing that lord or his servant as barbarous.

5.5   Ritual as Action

The integration and temporal extension of the cosmos achieved through a centering process produces an order of difference that is the embodiment of the true, correct, and proper disposition of people and the things in ritual space at the moment of ritual constitution. This order is hierarchical in that it is a manifestation of situationally specific powers of superiors and inferiors. Hierarchy, as understood here, is embedded in and arises from principles of agency (i.e., human being as agent in integrating and extending the cosmos), which can be observed in the concrete unfolding of temporal processes. It may be seen as contingent positioning wherein individual agents are simultaneously constituted and constitutive of other positions by the up/down–in/out movement of imperial instructions, memorials, people, and things, which, in turn, produces an order of difference.

This order of difference incorporates complex relationships of power deriving from variations in the distribution of the knowledge and experience of agents. Knowledge and experience accumulate in persons as a result of the positions they have occupied in the past, and therefore these qualities both generate effective action and provide the standard by which action can be evaluated. Thus, the possibility of managing the centering process is not premised upon a pre-given pyramidal structure of coercive power relations, but on continuing demonstrations of appropriate action that has been informed by knowledge and experience. Judicious interventions at many levels and at many points in the process generate social relations in a constantly renegotiated production of hierarchical forms. This construction of an order of difference is only realized in the course of specific engagements with others whose power is constrained not only by their position, but also by the degree of knowledge and experience they can bring to bear at any moment.

The generation of this engagement is thus simultaneously free and bounded. Free in the sense that agents can and do make choices throughout the temporal process, but bounded by the kinds of choices open to agents at any moment, options which themselves are informed by the classification of affairs at that particular moment in ritual process. This suggests that ritual action might better be approached as discourses about agency and human capacities, rather than as the rote repetition of a body of fixed rules or as an ideological obstruction masking "real" practices.

Given what has been said about patterning and a centering process, it would seem inappropriate to approach a ritual text and the relationship between such a text and practice in terms of dyads familiar in social science analysis. Models which draw a distinction between form and content, theory and practice, symbolic and real, ideal and actual are formulated in an enlightenment epistemology just as foreign to Christian theology as it is to Qing imperial cosmology. I believe it more fruitful to recognize that while a distinction is made between ritual texts and the practice of rites,[21] this distinction is grounded in a relationship between temporally fixing practices *in* language and realizing processes or bringing them to completion *through* language and other forms of signifying practice (e.g., bodily action). We might then think of the distinction between a given ritual text and the rite itself as a dialogue in which the former proposes a series of acts, an ordered sequence or set of protocols (*jie*), that can be addressed by the latter. The point of such a relationship is that the rite must remain open-ended if centering is to be realized. To constrain it by fixing actions prior to the temporal unfolding of action would be to introduce excesses or deficiencies at the outset of a process specifically imagined as negotiating between such extremes.

Guest Ritual, like all imperial rites, has a sequence, one whose logic can be located in ritual manuals and any court records which deal with an embassy from a lesser lord. The logical sequence is, however, only explicitly referred to when it appears that participants are unaware of protocols or because the rite has markedly deviated from its intended course, that of organizing a relative center.

The temporal sequence of Guest Ritual outlined in the *Comprehensive Rites of the Great Qing* begins with a request to enter by the lesser lord, followed by the imperium's response.[22] It continues with the greeting of the embassy at a periphery of the imperial domain; the presentation of credentials, a list of offerings, and a ranked list of the members of the lesser lord's embassy; the inspection and translation of these communications by officials at the periphery and their forwarding to the court for further consideration; the inspection, management, and caring for the embassy and the offerings by successive peripheral officials, who pass the embassy on to the court; the preparation for audience of the embassy and the offerings as they are channeled upward toward the court; the imperial audience, where the relationship between the lesser lord and the imperium is realized in the space (a relative center) that has been constituted through the dialogue of all the participants; the banqueting of the embassy as a bestowal of imperial grace; the rewarding of the lesser lord, including the presentation of his enfeoffment document and emblems of his lordship; and the seeing off by

21. What Zito refers to as text/performance; see 1989 and forthcoming.
22. Also see the description of an embassy routine in Wills 1984, as well as Fairbank and Teng 1941.

Qing officials as the embassy moves down and out through reconstituted peripheries.

This much can be deduced from the Guest Ritual section of the *Comprehensive Rites of the Great Qing* and Lord Macartney's account. Moreover, we can (and will) follow this sequence through a study of an embassy's record. But, because the performance of the rite cannot be taken as an end in itself, because it is implicated in the constitution of a worldly order appropriate for addressing the invisible, and because this world is assumed to be in a perpetual state of flux, the sequence suggested in the ritual canon cannot dictate what is proper for the specific encounter under way. It can only propose possibilities. Within the space between what ought to occur and what is realizable under the circumstances, ritual becomes radically historical, grounded, as it were, in the materiality of life as the actions of human beings shape the world they inhabit. This sensibility about ritual action is critical if encounters between the Qing imperium and other domains are to be reconsidered in ways that avoid the classic biases of modernist historiography. To see how an encounter is organized, how classification orders a temporal process, and how agents make choices in this process, I turn now to the Qing court record of the British embassy to China in 1793–1794.

6 CHANNELING ALONG

A CENTERING PATH

Greeting and Preparation

6.1 Initial Contact: The Announcement and Request to Enter[1]
(October 22, 1792–December 3, 1792)

Before the entry of an embassy from a foreign lord into the Qing imperium, the lord was required to present a written request for permission to enter and to be received in audience by the emperor. Because permission for audience was not automatically granted,[2] the announcement and request preceding the embassy proper was of importance in determining whether or not entry would be allowed. In examining how Qing officials in Canton and at the imperial court managed the announcement letter, it is clear that the request portion of Guest Ritual provided an opportunity for the imperium to determine the intentions of those seeking an imperial audience.

The normal way for East India Company (EIC) supercargos to communicate with officials in Canton was by passing their petitions (*bin*) through the Cohong merchants. The Secret and Superintending Committee, which arrived in Canton on September 20, 1792, to deliver the announcement of the Macartney embassy, had no desire to see the document transmitted in this way. Instead, through the merchant Cai Shiwen, they requested

---

1. The *DQTL* does not mention the announcement and request portion of the rite. In the court records of the Macartney embassy, however, there is sufficient evidence to indicate the significance of the announcement and its overall importance for the progress of Guest Ritual.

2. Mancall cites two cases in which Russian missions of the seventeenth century were allowed to go to Peking, but were not received in audience because of problems surrounding their petitions and credentials; see 1971:44–56. The Amherst embassy of 1816 also had difficulties after arriving in Peking and was denied an imperial audience, see section 9.1.

an audience with the governor-general of Liangguang, Guo Shixun, saying that they were delivering a message from their king. Unable to discover the exact particulars of this message, Qing officials decided to grant the audience, since to do otherwise would have been contrary to the imperial imperative of "cherishing men from afar."

The audience granted by Qing officials to the EIC messengers caused certain problems, many of which were summarized in a joint memorial from Governor-general Guo and Commissioner of Customs Shengzhu on October 22, 1792. Difficulties began when it became clear that while Browne, Jackson, and Irwin said they bore a message from their king, the letter itself was signed by Francis Baring, who was head of a merchant firm. This led to questions about the relationship of the messengers and Baring to their king. Unable to classify the Englishmen as messengers from their king, Canton officials referred to them by the generic term "barbarians" or foreigners (*yiren*) and, according to the British account, moved them from the audience hall to a side chamber, where they could be dealt with less formally.[3]

Additional difficulties arose when the content of Baring's letter was evaluated through translations made from the Latin and English versions. Noting the reason given for the embassy (to congratulate the emperor on his eightieth birthday), Guo and Shengzhu then recalled the normal way such matters ought to occur. The actual message of the king (*biao*) and a list of gifts (*gongdan*) for presentation at court should have accompanied the request. Not only were these documents not present, but the messengers could give little information about them (ZGCB, 1b). Further inquiries were made about the gifts and when the embassy could be expected. The messengers explained that they had left before the embassy departed and could only vaguely calculate its arrival. As for the gifts, they knew only that some were heavy and might be damaged on an overland journey from Canton.

The memorial continued by observing that the British had long come to Canton to trade and implied that this port would be their proper point of entry to the Qing empire. Yet now they planned to disembark at Tianjin. Aware of their jurisdictional responsibilities and the necessity for correctly

3. The Secret and Superintending Committee's version of events in Canton are in IOMC, 93:25–56. In a letter to London, Browne and the others reported that they had finally received word that the embassy would be received in the manner they had requested. While they assumed jealousy and conspiracies against themselves on the part of local officials, the committee confirmed that the emperor, provided a direct appeal were made to him, was much more open to contact than his officials (93:121).

caring for an embassy, the officials indicated their concern for this situation and the logistical problems it might cause the court. They pointed out that it would probably be difficult to intercept the embassy and direct it to Canton, and suggested that the whole coast be alerted to the possibility of receiving the British at any of a number of ports (*zGCB*, 1b–2a). In evaluating the request, the officials in Canton said that it seemed to stem from loyalty and gratitude on the part of the English king. The memorial and the originals and translations of Baring's letter were forwarded to Peking, where the court addressed them on December 3, 1792 (*zGCB*, 2a).

In a memorial from the Grand Council (*Junji chu*) of that date, the emperor was informed of the request. The councillors explained that it had given the Latin and English versions of the request to West Ocean men in the emperor's service (European missionaries) who, able only to translate the Latin version, provided the following information about the *Yingjili* domain (England). Identifying England as the "Red Haired kingdom" lying to the far northwest, the translators reported that (1) England had a different religion than other West Ocean kingdoms; (2) it had never sent an embassy to China before; and (3) no Englishmen were in the emperor's service. Confirming that the Latin versions translated in Canton and Peking were the same, the councillors then outlined the reasons given by the British for sending the embassy, and their request to land at Tianjin because of the delicate nature of their gifts (*zGCB*, 3b).

On the same day, the emperor responded to Guo Shixun's memorial. Through the Grand Councillors Agui and Heshen,[4] Hongli informed coastal province officials and the Changlu Salt Commissioner of his evaluation of the British announcement and certain decisions he had made concerning the embassy. Reviewing the request, the emperor noted that "the

4. From this point until October 1793, Agui's name does not appear again on imperial instructions. On Heshen see *ECCP*, 288–290. According to Elman, by the late 1780s, Agui and Heshen were the center of two distinct factions in the upper reaches of the imperial bureaucracy (1990:283–284). Arguing for a link between Heshen and Fukang'an, Waley-Cohen has suggested that these rivalries among Manchu elites account in part for the failure of the Macartney embassy (1993:1541–1542). While the latter argument is very intriguing, there is perhaps only one suggestion in the embassy records that would support such an interpretation. See below in chapter 8; after much had gone wrong in the management of the embassy by court officials, the Qianlong emperor ordered that Agui be called in for consultation. From that point forward, his name accompanied that of Heshen on imperial instructions.

feelings expressed in their communications were of the highest reverence (*gong*), obedience (*shun*), earnestness (*geng*), and faithfulness (*zhi*)," all of which indicated their "sincere facing toward transformation" (*xiang hua zhi cheng*). Therefore, since they were coming a great distance, the emperor granted their request. Noting the uncertainties of sea travel, he also warned that the embassy might at any time put in at one of the coastal ports and must be properly cared for by local officials. When it disembarked, the embassy and its gifts were to be put in the hands of someone who could perform his duties with circumspection (*tuo*). This official was to escort the British to the capital without the slightest delay.

The emperor then instructed all provincial coastal officials to inform their subordinates that frequent reports were required from everyone. If the ships should arrive at Tianjin, the Changlu Salt Commissioner was to see to it that small boats were available to ferry the larger gifts to shore. Finally, officials were to be appointed who would escort the ambassador to the capital and avoid his being delayed by the off-loading of the gifts.[5] With the emperor's instruction of December 3, 1792, the announcement/request stage of Guest Ritual ended and the entire coast was alerted to prepare for the reception of the British embassy.

A few observations are in order concerning the way in which the English request was managed by local officials and the Qing court. Provincial officials in Canton were well aware of the proper way of proceeding with an embassy, but were confronted with a series of contingencies that defied regular procedure. As noted above (2.4.2), a series of questions came readily to mind to Canton officials allowing them to differentiate the king making the request from the mass of foreign peoples external to the Qing empire. In the case of the British, the task was made difficult because of the form in which their message came. That is, it appeared to confuse East India Company merchants with royal representatives. The solution of Canton officials was to separate the king of England from the East India Company messengers. At the same time, Guo Shixun and Shengzhu questioned the messengers and compared multiple translations of Baring's letter. Their

---

5. The emperor's instruction is in *ZGCB*, 5a–b. Three extant memorials in response are in the Qing archives. See *ZPZZ*, 24.2–4, for those of Changlu salt commissioner Muteng'e; Zhili governor-general Liang Kentang; and Shandong governor Jiqing. Materials in these and other Chinese sources on the embassy have been translated into French, see Peyrefitte 1991.

object, as the court's would be later, was to sort out what they saw as ir-regularities in the British presentation in order to determine the intent of the English king. In other words, Canton officials were trying to gauge the sincerity of the British king in his claim that he had dispatched an embassy to congratulate the emperor. These officials could not, however, make the final determination or give permission for the embassy to proceed; only the imperial court could do this. Therefore, they gathered as much infor-mation as possible, listed irregularities, made recommendations, gave their opinion of the English king's sincerity, and sent all upward in a memorial to the throne. A similar process occurred in the Grand Council.

The emperor's determination was then sent downward in the form of an instruction (*shangyu*) to the Grand Councillors Agui and Heshen, who directed it to the appropriate lower-level officials. From a study of the in-formation available to him, Hongli decided that the announcement was indeed sincere and that the contingencies posed by the irregularities of the request could easily be dealt with through circumspect management by local officials. He instructed all concerned on the immediate steps to be taken, most necessary of which was the maintenance of continuous com-munication between all levels of the imperium. It was made clear that the emperor was to be kept informed of events and where responsibility for reporting lay. Meanwhile, with the emperor's decision to allow the British embassy to proceed to Tianjin, and the alerting of the coastal provinces to the possibility that the ships bearing the ambassador and gifts might put in at any port, preparations began for reception.

6.2   Preparation for Reception (December 1792–July 1793)

The point at which a foreign embassy entered the Qing empire, its routes, and the jurisdictions responsible for the care of its members was prescribed in the *Comprehensive Rites of the Great Qing*. The military and civil officials at the entry point were to inform the Board of Rites, which would authorize the granting of credentials to the embassy. The embassy was then set on the road to the capital with a protective escort. As it progressed, provincial-level officials were charged with providing food, housing, and entertainment for the delegation. At each provincial bor-der, the embassy was passed to the next jurisdiction, where the process of providing official hospitality repeated itself until they reached the capital (*DQTL*, 45:1a).

Meanwhile, in the capital, the Board of Rites, after memorializing the emperor and receiving his permission to proceed, notified the Board of Works (*Gong bu*) to prepare lodgings; the Board of Revenue (*Hu bu*) to furnish grains; and the Office of Banqueting (*Guanglu si*) to furnish meats, fish, wine, vegetables and fruit. The Board of Rites then ordered the sub-director of the Office of Guest Ceremony (*Honglu si*) to meet and watch over the embassy when it arrived at the capital. Upon arrival, the embassy was directed by the Board of Rites to guest quarters, where it was held for a time and provided with victuals (*DQTL*, 45:1b).

6.2.1   *Mobilization of the Coastal Provinces (December 1792–May 1793)*

While the Macartney embassy was dealt with in most respects as outlined here, the entry rite section of Guest Ritual provides only the barest guide for embassy procedures. One such consideration only briefly touched on by the ritual text had to do with assigning personnel and clear lines of responsibility in caring for the embassy. For example, in June, the Manchu bannerman Zhengrui, recently assigned to replace Muteng'e as Changlu salt commissioner, was put in charge of receiving and escorting the embassy (*ZPZZ*, 24.16). In addition to issues over personnel, officials up and down the coast had to assemble various sorts of land and sea transport vehicles, make preparations for provisions and accommodations, and instruct appropriate subordinates to keep a vigilant watch for the arrival of the embassy fleet.[6]

At the same time, local officials were not passive recipients of orders from the court. In memorials from March to June 1793, some of them made recommendations of their own on how to manage the embassy. Shandong governor Jiqing suggested as early as March that the Portuguese embassy of Qianlong 18 (1753) might provide a useful precedent for the British embassy (*ZPZZ*, 24.5). By June, imperial instructions citing the Portuguese precedent were circulated to officials in all relevant jurisdictions.[7] In another case, provincial officials made recommendations about the necessity to arrange for the British embassy to trade in places other than Canton (*ZPZZ*, 24.11, 12).

6. Memorials reporting preparations began to arrive at the court in March 1793 and continued on a regular basis until the arrival of the embassy off the South China coast in June; see *ZPZZ*, 24.4–17.

7. The first instance I have found of the court citing the Portuguese embassy as a precedent is in *GZSY*, QL 58.5.12, 67:117–124.

One of these latter memorialists was Zhili governor-general Liang Kentang, the provincial official who would be responsible for the embassy if it landed near Tianjin. Among other things, he wondered how the embassy would communicate with local officials and suggested that competent translators ought to be sought (*zpzz*, 24.10).

The concerns expressed by local officials pointed to the general problem of indeterminacies surrounding the arrival of the British. They also raise questions about how officials were to make decisions when contingencies arose. In part, the dialogue between the court and provincial officials, and the wide dissemination of these communications through imperial instruction, explain how some contingencies were addressed. In addition, practice-oriented texts such as the *Comprehensive Rites* provided a field of reference for decision making. The handling of an early problem might be useful in demonstrating these points.

6.2.2   *The Problem of the Investigation Ship (June–July, 1793)*

On July 9, 1793, the emperor sent an instruction to Grand Councillor Heshen for dissemination to coastal governors. In it the emperor cited a memorial received from Governor Changlin of Zhejiang reporting that a ship under the command of the Englishman Captain Proctor had put in at Dinghai near Ningbo. The local military commander Ma Yu and the Ningbo prefect Keshi'na had informed Changlin of the ship's arrival and explained that it was investigating mooring sites for the large gift ship in the British fleet. Prior to receiving authorization from Changlin, the two local officials had allowed Proctor to sail. The Zhejiang governor had requested that Ma Yu and Keshi'na be investigated and punished for this action.[8]

In reviewing Changlin's request, Hongli thought it excessive. He explained that if foreign kingdoms sent ships to spy or make trouble, the ship's personnel ought to be arrested and strict inquiries made. But in this case (as Changlin should have known), the English had announced and requested permission to send an embassy and had received the emperor's permission to do so. This, the emperor said, belonged to the class (*shu*) of meritorious undertakings (*haoshi*). Therefore, the use of an investigating ship was considered appropriate. Officials certainly should make inquiries of such a ship, but in so doing, the emperor cautioned, they should not detain it, since delay might cause the outsiders to become suspicious. He then

---

8. A copy of Changlin's memorial of June 30 is in *zpzz*, 24.20.

honored Changlin's request for an investigation, but tempered it by limiting the punishments that could be meted out to Ma Yu and Keshi'na.[9]

Changlin's failure to understand the proper way of managing this affair did not stop here, however. He had informed other coastal governors of the content of his memorial, an act Hongli classified as an extreme transgression of appropriate practices (*shu shu guodang*). Speaking to all those aware of the situation, the emperor complained that provincial officials were prone to go too far or not do enough. Moreover, officials noted for strict adherence to forms often detained and investigated ships. This was likely to cause outsiders mistakenly to suspect that they were being interrogated and arrested, which could generate fearfulness in their hearts.[10]

A week later, Heshen informed the governor-general of Zhili, Liang Kentang, the governor of Shandong, Jiqing, and the new Changlu salt commissioner Zhengrui of an imperial instruction received that day (July 16, 1793). The instruction referred to a memorial from Changlin to the effect that Ma Yu had reported sighting and communicating with the embassy fleet off Dinghai on July 4. Ma Yu spoke with Macartney, who explained that his ship was too large to enter Dinghai harbor. Since the winds were favorable, Macartney planned to continue north on the sixth. This information was classed with meritorious undertakings, and the emperor was said to be delighted with the news. For promptly reporting and expeditiously handling the matter, Ma Yu was commended by the emperor for his attentiveness (*liuxin*). As a result, neither Ma Yu nor Keshi'na was to be punished and the investigation was dropped. But, in addition, Changlin (who on this occasion quickly reported Ma Yu's meeting with Macartney) and the governor-general of Liangguang, Guo Shixun, were also rewarded for their attentiveness.[11]

9. There are substantial similarities in form between the emperor's criticism of Changlin's judgment in this instance and other occasions reported, for example, by Kuhn (1990) and Elman (1990:280). Such warnings and remonstrances were, I suspect, more than an imperial style; they worked continually to reproduce the authoritative position from which Hongli spoke on all and sundry matters.

10. The emperor's instruction is in ZGCB, 8. On the same day, the Grand Secretariat reviewed the emperor's orders and, after directing responsibility for the investigation of Ma Yu and Keshi'na to appropriate officials, concluded that their actions were not great transgressions (ZGCB, 9a). In response to the emperor's observations, Liang Kentang argued that Ma Yu and Keshi'na had done nothing wrong and, therefore, should not be punished; see ZPZZ, 24.24.

11. The Grand Secretariat repeated the emperor's decision and cited Ma Yu's attentiveness as a case of clear and concise reporting (ZGCB, 10b–11a).

The Qing records of the British embassy provided many similar examples of the handling of unforeseen events like the one just reviewed. For that reason, I want to dwell briefly on problems that arose in this case because they are instructive about how other situations were managed. Once the coast had been alerted about the arrival of the British embassy, the emperor, having decided that the English king appeared sincere in his requests and having given permission for a landing at Tianjin, expected his officialdom to judiciously manage (*tuoban*) the reception of the British and care for them (*zhaoliao*) in the spirit of an event that had already been classified as a meritorious undertaking. In this sense, the arrival of Proctor's ship should not have caused difficulties, since principles of differentiation implicated in the classification of the British undertaking allowed for a distinction to be drawn between this ship and any other ship that might venture along the coast. Once Proctor had identified himself as part of the embassy, he ought to have been treated expeditiously, as Ma Yu had done. The reason for this, Hongli pointed out, was that it was of vital importance to insure that no actions be taken which would generate suspicion among the British. Clearly, Changlin's transgression and the possibility of generating suspicion through inappropriate actions were considered improper for an activity classified as a meritorious undertaking. On the other hand, when Changlin's actions *corresponded* to the classification under which the embassy had been placed, he received an imperial reward. It was probably no coincidence that he was rewarded at the same time as Guo Shixun, the official who had judiciously managed the announcement of the embassy.

The emperor's instructions concerning this incident provide a crucial insight into Guest Ritual, one that draws attention to the formative powers of ritual practice. Hongli indicated that certain kinds of actions by his officials would generate specific feelings in the one toward whom the action was directed. Moreover, he implied that either the acts of his officials and the feelings they elicited in another could be appropriate or inappropriate to the correct unfolding of ritual process, and that such variations were subjects of concern. The Ma Yu case is a good example of that concern; it indicates that properly directing affairs in order to deal with contingencies was more important than compliance with a written rule or adherence to a given form. Just what this proper direction was became clear in an imperial instruction on July 24, 1793, sent through Heshen to Liang Kentang and Zhengrui.

With the embassy now approaching Tianjin, the emperor cautioned his officials about how to receive the British guests.

In dealing with matters concerning outsiders (*waiyi*), you must find
the middle course between extravagance and meagerness (*fengjian
shi zhong*), so that you correctly accord with Our imperial order
(*tizhi*).[12] The provinces have the inappropriate habit of either exceeding or falling short [of the middle course]. In this case, after the
British ambassador arrives, treatment of him cannot be overly grand.
But the ambassador has sailed far to visit Us for the *first time;* this
cannot be compared to Burma, Annam, or others who have come for
many years to present gifts. Liang Kentang and Zhengrui must judiciously care for them and avoid too mean a reception, because that
would make these distant travellers to take us lightly (*qing*). (ZGCB,
12a–b; emphasis added)

Given the number of times Hongli subsequently repeated the form and
content of this instruction, it might be taken as a litany on managing
Guest Ritual: it simultaneously summarizes the direction of channeling (the
maintenance of a centering process between excess and deficiency) and the
appropriate actions that ought to be taken to achieve centering in the specific case of this encounter. The former is achieved through differentiating
the British from others: this is the first time they have come; therefore they
cannot be treated the same as those who come often. The latter is indicated
by drawing attention to the ways in which treatment by imperial officials
generated attitudes in the guest: if we give them a mean reception, they
will take us lightly, a reference that echoes Hongli's earlier concern about
frightening the British with an overzealous application of rules.

After a good deal of uncertainty over whether the harbor near Tianjin
would be suitable for mooring the *Lion*, the British fleet arrived and, to the
relief of local officials and the court, set anchor at the end of July.[13] At that

12. *Tizhi* is most often translated as "system," "structure," "fundamental rules," or
"basic institutions." Hsü has extended this notion, arguing that the term refers to "the
Chinese way of life and proper management of things from the Chinese standpoint,"
supported by the notion of *li*, which he translates as "propriety" (1960:111). This definition strikes me as far too encompassing; see Hevia 1993a:68 for additional comments. I
have rendered *tizhi* here as "imperial order," but I also suspect that it included a notion
of imperial will or, perhaps given the context, the emperor's intentions.
13. Concern over the ability of the fleet to anchor near Tianjin is evident in memori-

point, all energies were directed at setting it on the road to Rehe, where the emperor was then in residence and preparing the ambassador and his entourage for imperial audience. In the latter case, given the unprecedented nature of the British embassy, the ambassador had to be instructed in the proper way of forming superior-inferior relations. Central to these objectives were certain time constraints. In order for the British to fulfill their desire to congratulate the emperor on his birthday and present the gifts of their king, they had to be in Rehe by the beginning of the second week in September, or in about forty days. In addition, the court had to make a number of decisions over the proper rewards to bestow on the British. At one level, such rewards included the daily provisioning of the embassy; at another level, it meant determining the order of precedence among the members of the embassy so that imperial bestowals could be graded on the basis of rank. The Portuguese precedent provided some guidelines, but at this early date specifics were still to be determined (see ZGCB, 11–12). In order to focus attention on issues surrounding the gifts, imperial rewards, and preparation for imperial audience, I deal with gifts and rewards in the next section (6.3), and preparation for audience in the section immediately following (6.4). It should be borne in mind, however, that the court records of the embassy deal with these issues simultaneously, weaving a relationship between the intentions and attributes of gift givers and the qualities ascribed to and discernible in the gifts.

6.3   The British Gifts and Imperial Rewards

6.3.1   *Landing the Embassy and Gifts (July–August 1793)*

In addition to the labor-intensive process of off-loading the British gifts at Tianjin and provisioning the embassy, the issue immediately facing imperial envoy (*qincha*) Zhengrui and Liang Kentang was soliciting from Lord Macartney lists of the gifts and of his retinue, including the ranks of each member down to ordinary seamen in the fleet. As a member of the Imperial Household Department (*Neiwufu*), Zhengrui was given responsibility for obtaining the lists, while Liang was to take care of provisions and lodging.[14] In addition, given the time constraints discussed above, the court

---

als and imperial instructions of late July. The possibility was entertained of landing the embassy at Miao island off the Shandong coast; see ZGCB, 13b, 14b, 16a.

14. In Liang's case, he was ordered to work closely with officials in each jurisdiction

entertained the possibility of dividing the gifts, leaving the larger and more complex items in Peking for assembly, while shipping the less cumbersome ones to Rehe.[15]

The court's concern with provisioning the embassy also provided the emperor an opportunity to remind his officials about the centering process. Hongli's reasoning is worth following closely because of the links it draws between how officials should present themselves to the embassy, imperial rewards, and the way in which the two together ought to elicit feelings of gratitude and humility from the ambassador. In an instruction of August 1, the emperor noted that the embassy had already been rewarded with ample provisions from officials in Zhejiang and Shandong, and that they could expect more once ashore at Tianjin. In addition, the embassy would be feasted and rewarded handsomely once they arrived in Rehe. In light of this, the emperor cautioned that it would be unnecessary to prepare a special feast for them at Tianjin.

In receiving men from afar, he explained, it is important to be neither careless, nor naïve, for this may obstruct their sincere facing toward transformation. While it is permissible to render them a greater measure of compassion, excessive kind treatment might inadvertently elevate them above their proper station in the rite, and lead the embassy members, who, it must be remembered, were ignorant of the court's ceremonial procedures, to take the imperium lightly and become arrogant (*hu*). With this possibility in mind, Zhengrui was to insure that upon greeting the embassy he

---

that the embassy passed through to see that such matters were handled smoothly. It might even be necessary to draw from imperial stores to meet the requirements of the embassy, but if this were done, local officials were to keep strict accounts and report honestly on what was used; see ZGCB, 16b, 17b.

Liang's actions in these matters were classified as judicious management (*tuoban*). Centering between abundance and scarcity so that there were no mistakes or overreporting of supplies was termed "squaring with proper circumspection" (*fang wei tuoshan*). This particular grammatical form recurs often in the court records. It seems to refer to action which accords with an existing classification category. In other words, the *fang wei* construction places recent or unfolding action into preexisting classification schemes, while the classification construction I have previously made reference to, the use of *shu*, constitutes the class at the same time that actions under consideration are placed into it.

15. Zhengrui was ordered to raise this possibility with Macartney and explain to him that such a division would be safer and more convenient; see ZGCB, 15. In addition, for expeditiously handling matters, Zhengrui, who apparently had previously been demoted, was returned to his rank and was given an additional reward (*shang*) (ZGCB, 16a); see the biographical note in MD, 322–325.

was especially attentive (*liuxin*) to his own actions and seek the middle course between humility and haughtiness. In so doing, he would provide the British with an example of proper ceremonial conduct and make clear that the imperium cherished men from afar. This, the emperor said, was of the utmost importance (*ci wei zui yao*) (*ZGCB*, 16b).[16]

In the same instruction, Hongli also addressed the issue of timing. Since a landing at Tianjin had been accomplished, the journey to Rehe was substantially shortened. Moreover, Zhengrui had reported that preparations for the overland journey were almost complete. In light of this, the pace of the embassy's progress could be leisurely. Indeed, all seemed to be proceeding so well that Hongli authorized a slower rate for transmitting memorials (*ZGCB*, 17a-b).[17]

The steady stream of encouraging reports also influenced decisions about the handling of the gifts. In an instruction of August 5, Hongli noted that most of the gifts could now be shipped directly to the summer retreat, especially since the largest of the items, the planetarium, could be easily accommodated in audience halls there (*ZGCB*, 25b).[18]

16. As a practical demonstration of the emperor's compassion and generosity, Zhengrui was also to explain to Macartney that the emperor had fixed an additional reward of a year's supply of grain for the embassy's return journey, which Hongli felt would enhance the embassy's understanding of the empire's benevolence toward strangers and make them grateful (*ZGCB*, 17a).

17. The Qing imperium employed a complex scheme for the overland transmission of memorials and instructions. To this point, the speediest communication channels had been employed, no doubt because of the uncertainty of the location of the British landing. On the transmission of memorials, see Fairbank and Teng 1939.

At this juncture in the *ZGCB* collection, there also appears a memorial dated August 3 and an editorial note stating that it was not issued until September 23 (see *ZGCB*, 18a). It is from the Grand Council suggesting a response to the British king. In his article on these documents, Cranmer-Byng argues that the Qing court had determined its response to the British embassy prior to any of the negotiations undertaken by Macartney (see 1957–1958:138). References in the memorial to events that transpired well after the embassy landed, however, suggest that this could not be the case, but is rather an error on the part of the *ZGCB* compilers.

18. In addition, artisans from the Bureau of Astronomy were notified to proceed to Rehe in order to observe the assembly of the gifts by the British and thus be prepared to repair them in the future. In particular, the court was interested in sending someone who was familiar with mechanical devices made in the West Ocean countries. Selected to lead the group was one of the Christian missionaries in imperial service named Joseph-Bernard d'Almeida (Chinese name Suo Dechao) (*ZGCB*, 26b). This was the missionary whom Macartney suspected of being jealous of the English embassy.

Hongli's relaxation of procedures may also have been a result of memorials indicating that the British ambassador displayed similar characteristics as those discernible in the English king's request to send the embassy.[19] Such reports not only elicited Hongli's vermilion brush of approval (e.g., zpzz, 25.6), they also led the emperor to take a benign view of one of Lord Macartney's first requests. Because of illness among the British crew, as well as a desire to trade, Macartney asked that part of the British fleet be allowed to return to Ningbo. Unaware that Macartney sought to establish an imperially sanctioned precedent for opening new ports to British trade, Hongli granted the request, adding that Zhejiang governor Changlin ought to have little difficulty in making arrangements (zgcb, 26a). As a result, centering became an increasingly complicated affair. Now the actions of the Zhejiang jurisdiction would have to be calculated into assessments of excess or deficiency in the ritual process.

6.3.2   *The Translation of the British Gift List (August 6, 1793)*

As the off-loading of the embassy proceeded, attention turned to the nature and number of the British gifts. This was an especially pressing issue for the court because all items were crated and would not be viewed until they reached the site of assembly. Accordingly, Zhengrui instructed the two officials who had daily contact with the embassy, Qiao Renjie and Wang Wenxiong, to solicit a list of the gifts from Lord Macartney, along with the British king's letter to the emperor and a roster of embassy members.[20] On August 2, 1793, Macartney submitted a document to court officials titled "Catalogue of presents sent by His Britannic Majesty to the emperor of China." The English original, accompanied by Latin and Chinese translations, one of which Liang Kentang reported as having been done by the British themselves (zpzz, 25.9), was received by the court on August 6 (zgcb, 21–24).

Writing in the name of George III, Macartney explained in a preamble that the items sent had been selected because they indicated "the progress of science and of the arts in Europe" and added that between sovereigns,

19. See, for example, memorials of late July and early August, in zpzz, including those of Jiqing (24.34), Zhengrui (24.35, 25.1, 25.6), and Liang Kentang (25.14).

20. I shall take up the issue of the letter below in greater detail. However, it is worth noting that in a memorial of August 3, Zhengrui reported that the ambassador explained that the letter was sealed in a box to be submitted to the emperor only. Hongli's vermilion notation on the memorial indicates that this was acceptable to him; see zpzz, 25.6.

the intent, rather than the gifts themselves, was of greater value. A detailed description of each gift followed, which emphasized their wondrous nature and uniqueness (see 3.6 above). In addition to couching the description of each item in superlatives, Macartney repeated pronouncements in George III's letter concerning the mutual concerns and common interests of sovereigns. An effort was also made to demonstrate English knowledge of the Chinese court. Specifically, mention was made of two carriages whose main color was "yellow or imperial" (IOMC, 20:142–144).

After the court received the list, it was translated into Chinese, probably from the Latin version, by missionaries in the emperor's service (ZGCB, 22a–24b). The most interesting feature of the translation is the way in which it differs from the English-language version. In the first place, all references to the mutual interests of sovereigns are eliminated from the text, along with the reference to the yellow carriages. The description is also toned down a good bit, although a sense of the uniqueness of the items remains. The preamble and various passages in the description of the gifts were altered to refer to offerings made from a foreign king to the supreme lord and some information added about the size of the embassy.

The gift list ought, therefore, to have caused little concern to the court. Its pronouncements appeared consistent with the intentions expressed by the English king in his request for permission to send the embassy. At the same time, however, some of what appeared in the translated version did not address concerns already expressed by the emperor. For example, the list made no mention of the size or weight of items or their ease in handling once they were put together. Given these uncertainties, the emperor called for additional information from the ambassador.

6.3.3 Emerging Concerns about the British Ambassador's Intentions (August 9, 1793)

Lord Macartney and Liang Kentang met for the first time on August 6, the occasion on which Macartney drew clear distinctions between ceremonial practice and the business of his embassy (see above 4.6). It was perhaps at this meeting that Liang questioned Macartney on the gifts, because on the following day, the Zhili governor reported that the ambassador insisted that it would take a month to set up the planetarium (ZPZZ, 25.12). Macartney's response had far-reaching consequences that eventually led to a reassessment of the British ambassador's intentions and the mobilization of court resources in order to determine the truthfulness of the ambassador's claims about the qualities of the gifts. It also revived the plan to split the gifts into two groups, with some going to Rehe and the rest remaining in Peking.

Responding to Liang's memorial of August 9, the emperor observed that the one-month time period was probably an exaggeration, a boast about the ingeniousness of artisans from England. Indeed, Hongli scoffed, if it took a month to assemble the planetarium, it must have taken years to manufacture it. Clearly concerned over what he seems to have interpreted as the sudden emergence of arrogance in the British ambassador, particularly in light of earlier reporting that indicated just the opposite, the emperor considered relieving Liang Kentang of some of his duties involving the embassy. He reasoned that having too many high officials accompanying Macartney to Rehe would be more than enough to "increase his boastfulness and arrogance" (ZGCB, 27b). Hongli's concerns at this moment of the ritual process provide the first clear indications that the intent of the ambassador might be in question. As a result, the emperor opened discussion of future plans and possible contingencies that might arise.

But why should Macartney's claims have generated so much concern? There were at least three mutually related factors at work that may help explain Hongli's reaction. In the first place, reports on the still unseen planetarium and other items made it difficult to distinguish them from other European instruments in the court's possession. Moreover, the gift list and Macartney's response to Liang Kentang failed to clarify matters. Rather, they seem to have called into question Macartney's claims about the uniqueness of the gifts, and may even have led to speculation that perhaps these products were not so local after all.[21] Secondly, it would seem that correlations were being made between qualities ascribed to the gifts and the attributes of the gift giver. Such correlations were one way for the court to judge the sincerity of a foreign king's expressed desire to enter into an inferior-superior relation with the emperor. Presumably, if it were determined that Macartney's claims were insincere, then the court would have to consider other possible motives for the sending of the embassy. Finally, if in fact the ambassador was being truthful and the planetarium and clocks had been so "carefully manufactured" (*yongxin zhizao*) that their reassembly would be difficult and time-consuming, they wouldn't be ready for presentation on the emperor's birthday. More detailed information was obviously

21. Zhengrui reported in a memorial on August 9 that he had said as much to Macartney (ZPZZ, 25.13).

required. At the same time, the emperor also wondered if perhaps Zheng-rui's reporting had been influenced by his fear of difficulties; he therefore ordered his envoy to make additional inquiries of the ambassador and pro-duce an item-by-item description of the gifts (zGCB, 27b–29a).

Not surprisingly, Hongli's concerns over the direction in which matters appeared to be moving also led him to reevaluate recent imperial bestow-als, especially with respect to the portion of the embassy now near Ningbo. After listing the amounts of food supplies that had been allocated to the embassy, the emperor concluded that the rewards could be classified as "liberal and generous" (*you hou*); therefore, no additions need be made by Changlin.[22] Significantly, other local officials were also ordered to avoid being extravagant with the embassy.[23]

6.3.4 *The Decision to Split the Embassy and Gifts (August 14–19)*

On August 14, Zhengrui confirmed that the planetarium would require a month to assemble. In addition, several other items would take some days to set up. Macartney requested that the emperor allow them to be left in the capital. He would then depute four artisans to be responsible for these gifts and they would have them ready for the emperor to view on his return to Peking. Concluding that this was the best course, Hongli issued a num-ber of instructions over the next few days to deal with yet another division of the embassy.

After instructing Zhengrui to personally explain to Macartney that the British would be responsible for setting up the gifts left in Peking and that only items requiring minimum assembly should be brought to Rehe, the emperor designated two officials of the Imperial Household Department, Jin Jian and Yiling'a, to oversee management of the embassy while it was in the capital. Zhengrui was to work closely with these two. Speculation then

22. The order was modified a few days later (August 14) when it was unclear whether the fleet had actually been given a year's supply of grain from Tianjin stores. Moreover, it appeared that the British preferred meat to grain, so that it might be unnecessary to provide so much rice and flour. Changlin was to supply them with more grain from the imperial storehouses only if they requested it (zGCB, 32).

23. The correspondence on bestowals is part of the imperial instructions of August 9 and 11 (zGCB, 27b–28b, 29b). These same sources note a request by Macartney to have an area set aside in Zhejiang so that ailing crewmen could be put ashore for rest and recuperation, and to have an order issued preventing local people from attempting to board the ships. Liang was instructed to inform Changlin that he should judiciously manage all these matters.

turned to suitable sites for display. The emperor made a number of suggestions, the chief being the Hall of Upright Governance, Pervasive Clarity (Zhengda guangming dian) at the Yuanming Gardens, where the embassy was to be billeted (*ZGCB*, 30a–31a).[24]

At the same time, instructions from Hongli and the Grand Council ordered that competent imperial artisans from the Bureau of Astronomy be present when the assembly of the gifts began. Their responsibilities were not only to learn how to dismantle and reassemble the pieces, but to make comparisons with instruments the court already possessed (*ZGCB*, 33b–34a, 42a).

6.3.5   *The Embassy Roster and Recommendations*
        about Imperial Bestowals (August 9–20, 1793)

As decisions were being made over the disposition of the British gifts, officials in the Grand Council were attempting to make preliminary determinations about the kinds and quantities of items to bestow on the embassy. In order to make their recommendations, the councillors relied on the precedent of the 1753 Portuguese embassy,[25] which they attempted to correlate with the ranks of the embassy members to be found on the embassy roster. This, however, was not a simple task. For one thing, the list that Zhengrui had received from Macartney indicated that seven people on the list were designated as family members of either the ambassador or vice-ambassador. Did they have a rank? Were they actually family members or servants? Zhengrui was told to prepare a more complete list specifying ranks and relationships, and quickly forward his report (*ZGCB*, 29a). Approximately a week later, the Grand Council presented the emperor with a list of suggested bestowals to be given the British embassy. In addition

24. The Imperial Household officials were to make all arrangements for the embassy's stay in Peking, including sightseeing. Among other things, this was to include the European-style palaces and its mechanical fountain (*ZGCB*, 33b). They were to be shown, in other words, that the court already had quite sophisticated mechanical devices, a subject I shall return to below. Officials were also told that if the embassy entered the capital city, they were to be housed in the confiscated mansion of Muteng'e, the former Changlu salt commissioner and commissioner of customs at Canton (*ZGCB*, 33b). On the same day, the Grand Council asked if, once assembled, the gifts might be difficult to move. If so, it would be very inconvenient to have them in the great halls that the emperor had designated for their display. Zhengrui was to ask Macartney and clarify the matter (*ZGCB*, 33a).

25. After the Shandong governor Jiqing's reference to the Portuguese embassy, it is taken up again in court records beginning in July; see *GZSY*, QL 58.6.4, 67:15–19 and 58.6.21, 67:119; also see QL 58.6.30, 67:187–190 and 58.7.3, 67:9.

to those specifically for the English king, recommendations were made regarding the ambassador, the vice-ambassador, the military officers in the embassy, and the son of the vice-ambassador. The list also proposed occasions on which awards could be made (*ZGCB*, 34a–40b).[26]

When, however, it became clear that the embassy was to be divided in Peking yet again, the councillors immediately called their own calculations into question. In a memorial of August 20, they began by noting that Macartney's retinue appeared to number ninety-two. The problem was to clarify how many of them would proceed to Rehe and how many would remain in Peking. The councillors also indicated that such considerations were important for the occasions on which imperial bestowals would be made. On the basis of previous practice, they recommended one main reward and four lesser bestowals. Since the bestowals would be graded, the councillors were concerned that if lesser officials in the ambassador's retinue were invited to a banquet to be held at Rehe, this might constitute an increase in their bestowals, thus throwing off calculations for other ranks (*ZGCB*, 42b).

The concerns of the councillors parallel those expressed by the emperor earlier. Like the rewarding of provisions, various forms of imperial bestowals held the potential for influencing the attitudes of embassy members. Finding the middle course between overabundance and scarcity and timing the bestowals for the proper moment in the rite all appear to be crucial considerations in the calculations of the emperor and his officials.

6.3.6   *Initial Resolution of the Placement of the Gifts at the Yuanming Gardens (August 20–26, 1793)*

From August 21 to September 2, the British embassy was in Peking making preparations for its departure to Rehe. During this period of time, questions surrounding the gifts were brought into sharp focus and new determinations made about the current state of the ritual process. The day before the embassy arrived at Peking, the emperor noted in an instruction to Jin Jian, Yiling'a, and Zhengrui that now that the gifts would soon be at the Yuanming Gardens, there would finally be an opportunity to see them. Accordingly, the first thing that had to be done was to view them one by

---

26. Since this list varies from others which were generated later, we may assume that like imperial rewards concerning provisions, the actual bestowals were determined by the court's continuing evaluation of the centering process.

one and make definite decisions on which were to be set up in the capital and which were to go to Rehe. He then recalled that Macartney had given certain indications that once the astronomical instruments were assembled, they could not be moved. If this was indeed the case, then it caused enormous problems for the placement of the gifts, especially since the buildings in question were classified as main halls (*zhengdian*), making it inconvenient for them to remain there. On the other hand, since there were still uncertainties about the nature of the gifts, it was of the utmost importance to have court artisans present as the British uncrated and assembled them, so that an informed assessment could be made.

But evaluation of the objects was only one part of the problem the court now faced. Recalling his earlier assessment of Macartney's claim over the length of time needed to set up the planetarium, Hongli suggested that the ambassador wanted to appear ingenious. Not only did this form of arrogance distinguish him from his king (who appeared sincere and reverent), but his boasts had understandably misled Zhengrui. As a result, it was important for the latter to consult with Jin Jian and Yiling'a in order to make certain that officials from the Board of Astronomy observed fully the English methods of handling the gifts. Having fixed the evaluation of Macartney and the gifts as a matter of collective responsibility, Hongli concluded that such an approach would square with proper circumspection (*fang wei tuoshan*) (zGCB, 42b–43b).[27]

Matters rested here until the emperor issued two instructions, on August 26 and 28, that seemed temporarily to bring problems over the placement and nature of the British gifts to an end. Reviewing an August 25 memorial from Jin Jian (zPzz, 25.19), Hongli expressed satisfaction over the ambassador's reaction to having been taken to the Hall of Upright Governance, Pervasive Clarity. Macartney, Jin reported, had exclaimed that it was more than sufficient for the British gifts. Certain now that Macartney's exaggerations were a product of ignorance (rather than arrogance), Hongli concluded that events were once more moving in the right direction. But there was still an aspect of the gift issue that required attention; this had to do with what the emperor saw as a serious difficulty in the relationship between Zhengrui and Macartney.

27. Two days later, the Grand Council sent a directive to Zhengrui emphasizing the emperor's concerns and adding that a detailed plan should be drawn up showing specifically the placement of the items in the halls in question (zGCB, 44a–44b).

Recalling his envoy's reports on Macartney's statements about the gifts, the emperor concluded that a timid Zhengrui may have been intimidated by the British ambassador. These shortcomings were in some respects understandable. Since his duties to date had not included those of a Commissioner of Customs at Canton, he had little knowledge or practical experience with Europeans or their astronomical instruments. In other words, Zhengrui's shortcomings had been partly responsible for Macartney's boasts! Unfamiliar with devices like those the British had brought, he had been awed by Macartney's claims, and this, in turn, had increased the ambassador's arrogance (ZGCB, 45b–46a). Once Macartney had viewed the audience halls of the imperium, he himself had been awed and, consequently, was now truthful in his assessment.

But the matter did not rest there. Zhengrui had been instructed to present to Macartney the emperor's reasoning about the transport of the gifts from England to the Qing empire and get a response. Since there had been no reply, Hongli ordered Zhengrui to speak to Macartney and report (ZGCB, 44b–45a). We might wonder why the emperor was so insistent on this last point, why he wanted Zhengrui to confront Macartney with the emperor's doubts about the ambassador's claims. Perhaps it had something to do with the fact that even though Macartney had confirmed that the halls were large enough for the English gifts, whether the gifts could be dismantled, moved, and reassembled still required clarification. Hongli made it clear that this consideration was of the utmost importance in an instruction of August 26, when he asked, "if after the gifts are assembled, they cannot be dismantled, how could we accept them?" (ZGCB, 45b).

Moreover, if the emperor's assessment of the situation was correct, the relationship between Zhengrui and the ambassador was off center at a time when his envoy still had to work with the British ambassador on the assembly of the gifts and continue to prepare him for the audience in Rehe. If the relationship between the imperial envoy and the ambassador remained skewed during this period, how could Zhengrui's reporting be relied on? Presumably, by confronting the ambassador with an unassailable argument formulated by the emperor himself, the relationship between Zhengrui and Macartney would be channeled away from extremes of excess and deficiency.[28]

28. The instruction of August 26 also noted that the head of the Bureau of Astronomy, Andrea Rodriguès, and the vice-head, Alexandro Gouvea, along with ten artisans,

6.4   Preparing the Embassy for Imperial Audience

6.4.1   *First Meetings and Issues Surrounding Ceremonies*
in Tianjin (August 3–14, 1793)

At the same time that officials responsible for the embassy were to manage all matters related to the British gifts, they were also supposed to prepare the ambassador and his retinue for audience with the emperor. The records of the British embassy indicate that the process of preparation was caught up in events which transpired during ceremonial occasions at local jurisdictions. It is also clear that encounters between Qing officials and the embassy were an object of intense scrutiny by the court, which evaluated reports from officials for signs of excess or deficiency.

The first such occasion of scrutiny occurred with respect to a feast for the embassy hosted by Liang Kentang and Zhengrui on August 6. Recall that the emperor had advised against any special feasts for the embassy while in Tianjin because they had been sufficiently feted in Zhejiang and Shandong. However, Hongli's instruction did not reach Tianjin in time; Liang and Zhengrui had feasted the embassy after announcing the imperial edict of welcome. Commenting on this, the emperor observed that (in the absence of any order to the contrary), provincial officials had acted according to the proper protocols of the rite (*lijie*) (*ZGCB*, 20a).

Yet it was also clear that the emperor was concerned that officials remain aware of how important these early moments of contact were. After reminding them of the principle of centering (*fengjian shi zhong*), Hongli addressed the issue of greetings between his officials and a foreign ambassador. In a rather extraordinary passage, Hongli observed that if the ambassador performed the rite of kneeling and bowing his head to the ground, then the said high official could not refuse to reciprocate accordingly. If the ambassador did not perform this rite, but rather acted in accord with the customs of his own kingdom, officials should not attempt to force him to do so. They should not, in other words, resort to any excessive treatment, for then the ambassador might become contemptuous (*ZGCB*, 20b).

The emperor's instruction is significant on a number of counts. In addition to once again linking the actions of his officials to the generation of attitudes in the foreign ambassador, it also makes allowances for difference.

---

had proceeded voluntarily to observe the activities at Yuanming Gardens. The emperor lauded their action as proper circumspection (*ZGCB*, 45a).

Interestingly enough, much like claims in George III's letter, it grounds these differences in an assertion that customs and practices vary from place to place. On the other hand, the emperor's warning is not a generality. It comes at a delicate time in the Guest Ritual process, one in which it is clear that the British are not familiar with the imperial court's practices. Thus, any excessive action at this moment might skew the process at the outset. That kneeling and head bowing (koutou) did become an issue in the British embassy at a later date indicates that some other factors were involved, factors which emerged as the rite unfolded.

Questions surrounding the meeting and greeting of the British ambassador took on added significance in the days that followed. In an instruction to Liang and Zhengrui dated August 5, Hongli observed that when ambassadors arrive bearing gifts, the visit (*xiangjian,* mutual viewing) between foreign officials (*beichen,* literally "side" servants) and high court officials should be organized on the principle of appropriate relations, presumably meaning that emperor's men should assume the position of superior and the visitor that of inferior. As an example, Hongli noted that even though he was a king, the ruler of Annam showed the highest reverence and sincerity in his visit with the prefect of Guangzhou. He then focused on the crux of the matter. Noting that officials must find the middle course between haughtiness and humility (*bubei bukang*), the emperor added that since the British had traveled a great distance, it was important not to be careless, "for this would obstruct their sincere facing toward transformation." Demonstrating compassion was permissible, but if excessive, it might stimulate their "covetousness," "arrogance," and make them contemptuous of the court. The emperor also observed that since Zhengrui had been in the court's service for many years, he fully understood the distinction between a light and heavy touch in ritual matters, indicating that he should have little difficulty in managing these matters (*ZGCB,* 20b–21a).

On the same day, however, Zhengrui's judgment and competency were called into question. In a memorial, the imperial envoy reported that the British ambassador and vice-ambassador had an exalted view of their own station and wished a visit with Zhengrui to be on the same level (*ping*). If he went to visit them first, Zhengrui felt it would adversely affect the appropriate relations in the rite. In view of his concern, he had deputed subordinates (Wang and Qiao) to visit the ship and make inquiries about the foreign king's communication and list of gifts.

In the most critical language employed to this point, the Qianlong emperor classified Zhengrui's actions as "straightening what is crooked to the point of exceeding what is correct" (*jiaowang guozheng*),[29] yet another example of provincial officials going either too far or not far enough in carrying out their duties. What was especially bothersome in this case was that the British had traveled such a great distance and, consequently, ought to be shown the compassion of the court. If Zhengrui insisted on adhering to forms, Hongli concluded, he would miss the court's intent in this matter (*ZGCB*, 5.25a–b).

After presumably making further inquiries over the course of the next week, Hongli returned to the issue of meetings between his officials and the British, using the opportunity to instruct his officials in how they should be preparing the British ambassador for imperial audience. Commenting on August 14, the same day it had been confirmed that the planetarium would take a month to assemble, the emperor noted that there were inconsistencies in reports over Macartney's actions at the banquet in Tianjin. According to a joint memorial from Liang Kentang and Zhengrui, Macartney had removed his hat and bowed his head to the ground (*koushou*). Previously, however, in a memorial that Liang had submitted, he had stated that the ambassador had removed his hat and stood awestruck (*songli*).[30] Since he understood that Europeans wore tight bindings around their legs making it difficult for them to kneel and that it was not their custom to bow their heads to the ground, Hongli supposed that it was their custom to remove their hats, bow, and nod their heads. Perhaps the memorial was simply unclear on this point, and the ambassador did bow his head to the ground.

If, however, matters were as earlier reported (the ambassador removed his hat and bowed his head [*dianshou*]),[31] then Zhengrui should bring the

29. The question of appropriate relations in the rite emerged again after the court had received the British list of gifts. The emperor noted that the British ambassador (*shichen*) was styled *qincha*, envoy, a term reserved for the emperor's servants who deal with lesser lords. The emperor speculated that this probably resulted from a mistranslation by the English translator. While he thought it of little importance at present, the emperor stated that if the use of the term continued it would place England on the same level as the imperial court, a situation that had important implications for relations in the rite. He ordered, therefore, that all references to *qincha* be changed to *gongcha*, gift bearer (*ZGCB*, 26b).

30. The emperor appears to be referring to a memorial from both officials dated August 8 (*ZPZZ*, 25.12). Zhengrui, however, had reported on August 3 that in a meeting with Macartney the ambassador had removed his hat and no more (*ZPZZ*, 25.6).

31. If the emperor is referring here to Zhengrui's memorial of August 3 (*ZPZZ*, 25.6), the text indicates that Macartney removed his hat and stood at a respectful distance (*yaoxiang*).

matter up in casual conversation (*xiantan*), explaining that when foreign kingdoms sent embassies, ordinarily the kings or their ambassadors performed the rite of "three kneelings and nine bows" (*sangui jiukou*). Macartney should, therefore, do the same. On the other hand, the court was aware of the European custom of wearing bindings on the legs. Since they would make it difficult to kneel during the imperial audience, the most convenient (*shenbian*) solution would be to remove them for the audience and then afterwards put them on again. Zhengrui was to explain that if Macartney insisted on rigidly adhering to the customs of his own kingdom, he would be proceeding contrary to the intent of his king in sending him here in the first place. Moreover, the ambassador would run the risk of being ridiculed by other ambassadors who would be present at the emperor's birthday celebration. Zhengrui was to add that he doubted court officials would allow the ambassador to deviate. Hongli was sure that if presented in this manner, the ambassador would accord with the ritual protocols, and thus square with proper circumspection (*ZGCB*, 31a–b).

It is worth repeating that Zhengrui was to say all this to the ambassador in casual conversation. His statement to Macartney was apparently not intended as a compulsory directive, but as a general statement of the court's attitude in this matter. Moreover, in light of the confused reporting as to what the ambassador had or had not done, the emperor's suggestions both reminded his officials of what might be expected and worked toward a clarification of the situation. The matter was, therefore, not closed, but opened to dialogue and discussion. Zhengrui, in fact, was to respond quickly about the results of this conversation in a memorial.

The timing of this particular intervention by the emperor might also be noted. With an open possibility that the encounter had been skewed by the actions of imperial officials and/or the British ambassador, the emperor, in raising the question of ceremonial forms, attempted to center the process by insisting on a dialogue between his representative and Macartney. Moreover, Hongli sought to resolve or clarify contradictions between the ambassador's behavior and the attributes ascribed to his king that had arisen over issues related to the British gifts. In this respect, the emperor no longer appears concerned about generating suspicion, but instead with actions that might lead to a convergence of the ambassador's attributes with the sincerity and reverence of his king.

In another instruction on the same day (August 14) Hongli made it very clear that these were not idle concerns. After noting that Zhengrui had reported that the ambassador was extremely reverent and respectful (*gongjing*), the emperor wondered if Macartney might be merely putting on appearances (*fenshi*). Zhengrui must attentively scrutinize (*liuxin chakan*) him to determine whether he was truly reverent and obedient, for it might be that he could not avoid being slightly boastful and arrogant. In his reports, Zhengrui was not to shield (*huihu*) him, but rather prepare an accurate memorial so that the ambassador might be appropriately received at Rehe (*ZGCB*, 32b).

The emperor's observations at this point are very interesting because they raise the issue of discontinuity between the discursive and nondiscursive, between outer forms and genuine intent, suggesting that there are limits to the reading of surface signs in the task of determining inner feelings. It was crucial, therefore, for Zhengrui to be accurate in his reporting and not attempt to protect the ambassador, a possibility that had to be considered due to the ongoing mutual constitution of their positions in the rite as the two who were most immediately engaged in dialogue. Moreover, since it had already been observed that the ambassador might have propensities toward boastfulness and arrogance, especially since he was unfamiliar with the protocols of Guest Ritual, it was crucial for the imperial envoy to make accurate reports on the ambassador's behavior. Recall Hongli's concern over the allotment of provisions; it would appear that erroneous reports might lead the court unwittingly to skew the process, with the result that the relationship produced between the Qing imperium and the foreign king would at best be ill formed.

6.4.2   *Displacement of the Tianjin Ceremony (August 18, 1793)*

On August 18, as the embassy approached Peking, an imperial instruction was issued indicating that questions over ceremony had been resolved. In the first place, Zhengrui had reported in a memorial of August 17 that Macartney had not only removed his hat, but had also bowed his head to the ground (*ZPZZ*, 25.16). In addition, the instruction indicated that another memorial had been received in which Zhengrui explained that the British ambassador and his contingent were ashamed that they were not well versed in Qing court ceremonies; each day the British practiced kneeling and bowing their heads to the ground (!). The imperial envoy was instructing them himself and felt that they would be well prepared by the time they reached Rehe (*ZPZZ*, 25.22).

This startling turn of events hardly seemed to surprise the emperor, however. Hongli read Zhengrui's reports as indicative of the efficacy of the ritual process. The British had in effect been transformed and, with their newfound sincerity, served simultaneously their own king and the supreme lord (zGCB, 41a).[32] Put another way, centering had elicited a recognition of appropriate ritual relations from the British ambassador. The dialogue between the imperial envoy and Macartney led to the emergence of the crucial attribute of sincerity, manifested in the ambassador's willingness to learn proper conduct, thus laying to rest, for the time being, questions about his intentions.

Yet even as doubts about Macartney's ability to participate in an imperial audience were seemingly resolved, others cropped up as soon as the embassy arrived in Peking on August 21. As noted above, the court remained skeptical about Macartney's claims concerning the British gifts. Events surrounding the gifts led Hongli to note signs of boastfulness and arrogance in the British ambassador, but perhaps more importantly, to question the management of Guest Ritual by his own officials.

6.5   Crisis in the Rite 1: Mismanagement by Imperial Officials
        (August 29, 1793)

A week after the embassy arrived in Peking, imperial instructions strongly criticized those most intimately involved in caring for the British embassy. The particular factor which precipitated this crisis had to do with the failure of officials to report on the progress of events at Peking, and eventually led to a thorough review of the process, culminating with questions regarding whether the English ought to be received in audience and their gifts accepted at all.

On August 29 Hongli complained that over the course of the last week he had not received a single memorial about what was transpiring in Peking. Upon making inquiries of the Grand Council, he had been told by Heshen that Jin Jian and Yiling'a expected Zhengrui to memorialize. In a vermilion endorsement, the emperor observed that the situation had become quite ridiculous (zGCB, 46a–46b). While it was true that Zhengrui had been responsible for the majority of the reporting to this point, Hongli explained that this was only because he was in daily contact with the embassy. With

32. Also see the memorandum from the Grand Council to Zhengrui regarding how the imperial envoy should be instructing Macartney (zGCB, 41b).

the embassy in Peking, the emperor expected joint reporting from Jin Jian, Yiling'a, and Zhengrui. Rather than managing affairs together, these officials had simply adhered to forms and avoided responsibility. Singling out Zhengrui in particular, Hongli classified the whole matter as a transgression (*feishi*). The three officials were then instructed to report in detail immediately, with all their names appearing on the same memorial (*ZGCB*, 46b–47a).

On August 30 and 31, an imperial instruction and court letter were issued that thoroughly reviewed the transgressions to date. These two documents are of special interest because they address excesses and deficiencies on the part of imperial servants, while organizing the specificities of each incident into general classifications. The subjects discussed included the way in which Zhengrui handled a letter from Macartney to the commander of the *Lion*, the relationship between Zhengrui and officials in Peking, and the assembly and situating of the English king's gifts.

Among his many duties Zhengrui had been instructed to facilitate communication between the ambassador and the *Lion* at Zhejiang. Aware of the health problems of the British sailors and of Gower's suggestion that the fleet depart before Macartney reached Ningbo, the court agreed that under the circumstances the fleet ought to depart if the British so desired. For reasons found inexplicable by the emperor, Zhengrui had decided that the ship must remain near Ningbo awaiting the ambassador's return and, apparently, had not forwarded Macartney's letter to Gower. The emperor characterized Zhengrui's unfortunate actions as muddled (*hutu*) and confused (*hungui*) (*ZGCB*, 47b).

In reviewing the matter, Hongli classified the imperial envoy's actions as a failure to complete an undertaking (*bucheng shiti*). However, since Zhengrui may not have told the ambassador what he had done (if this were the case, it was Zhengrui's good fortune!), he had an opportunity to correct his transgressions. In any case, the entire matter must be swiftly concluded and Gower informed that he could sail without the ambassador. The emperor added that this was but another example of officials failing to do the correct thing and classified it as excessive adherence to forms (*juni*), muddled (*hutu*), petty (*kebi*), and laughable (*kexiao*) (*ZGCB*, 47b–48a).

Most importantly, Hongli observed, while Jin Jian and Yiling'a were of a higher rank than Zhengrui, they were all responsible for managing the affair together. How then could they differentiate in such a way that Zhengrui alone memorialized? Perhaps Zhengrui, styling himself an imperial envoy (*qincha*), considered himself above them, or Jin Jian and Yiling'a thought Zhengrui beneath them. At any rate, the actions of Jin Jian and Yiling'a were classified as the small-mindedness of Imperial Household Department officials and not the least amusing. Previous instructions regarding the British gifts were repeated, the three officials were sternly rebuked, and a firm order issued for a joint memorial on the progress of the assembly of the gifts (*ZGCB*, 47a–48b).

The next day, another instruction repeated much of the above with a few additional observations. Because Zhengrui had so badly confused communication between the ambassador and the *Lion*, the emperor instructed him, along with Jin Jian and Yiling'a, to explain to Macartney what had happened, pointing out that Zhengrui's actions were not consistent with what the emperor himself had directed. The ambassador should then be told that he could send another letter. Hongli added that this was what was meant by "very meritorious" (*shenhao*). The letter was to be transmitted to Changlin, who would deliver it to the ship, and then memorialize. In addition, those who had been expected to remain in Peking while the ambassador proceeded to Rehe were not to return to the fleet at Zhejiang.

Further on in this instruction, the question of the relationship between the three officials was again raised. The emperor pointed out that Zhengrui had been appointed as escort because he happened to be nearby when the ambassador arrived in the Qing empire, which may have led him to conclude that there was no service greater than the one he was doing. Having deflated the imperial envoy, Hongli added a sarcastic twist: Zhengrui probably also compared himself favorably with the merit that Fukang'an had accrued in pacifying the Gurkhas. The emperor concluded that Zhengrui was unworthy of receiving imperial grace (*en*). As for Jin Jian and Yiling'a, the emperor surmised that they must have been envious of Zhengrui and sat by passively. Again, all were rebuked, instructed to manage matters jointly, and memorialize together (*ZGCB*, 48b–50b).

While the reasons for the actions (or inactions) of the three officials are far from clear, the fundamental issue addressed by the emperor centered on the proper management of an affair that had been classified as a meritorious undertaking. Either in the absence of clear reporting or in the exercise of poor judgment, Hongli's officials were moving the process away from a center path. His intervention, especially through the classification of his servant's actions as excesses, was an attempt to redirect the flow of events, to channel them along the proper path and thereby reorder the relationships among the various participants. The question that lingered, however, was the degree to which the process had already been skewed.

6.6   Crisis in the Rite II: Reappraisal of the British Ambassador's Intentions (September 9, 1793)

In spite of various problems associated with the embassy, it seems that the court anticipated few additional difficulties, particularly now that the British ambassador was preparing himself for audience and the qualities of the British gifts were more clearly defined.[33] Optimism was evident, for example, in a memorandum prepared on the same day the embassy arrived in Rehe (September 8). It outlined a protocol for the audience in which Macartney was to participate, one that was thoroughly in keeping with the structural elements to be found in the *Comprehensive Rites of the Great Qing* for audiences held in the capital, including three kneelings and nine bows (GZSY, QL 58.8.4, 67:31–35).[34]

On September 9, however, matters took a sudden and dramatic turn. In instructions to officials in Peking and local officials responsible for the embassy,[35] Hongli announced that a serious crisis had emerged in the ritual process, one clearly precipitated by Macartney's letter concerning his suggestions for audience (see 4.4 above). Complaining that he was profoundly troubled, the emperor said that the British ambassador had arrived in Rehe completely without comprehension of ceremony, a situation that had been created by excesses on the part of local officials. The result was that the ambassador had become recklessly arrogant (*jiaojing*), requiring immediate reconsideration of the future treatment of the embassy.

33. For example, on August 31 the Grand Council acknowledged receipt of a memorial in which Jin Jian indicated that some of the court's celestial and terrestrial spheres (*tianqiu, diqiu*) were of a more subtle nature than those brought by the English. Jin Jian was ordered to send some of them to Rehe, along with an official observing the assembly of the gifts at the Yuanming Gardens (ZGCB, 50b–51a, 52b).

34. This seems an especially important point to make, since it has sometimes been held that had Macartney been in Peking where the "metropolitan bureaucracy was present, he probably would have been forced to koutou, or presumably forego imperial audience"; see Wills, 1984:185.

35. Since Gower had been given permission to sail from Zhejiang, it was now clear that the embassy's return journey would be overland from Peking to Guangzhou. Therefore, in addition to jurisdictions the embassy already had passed through, all others on the route from Peking to Canton were notified.

Since the British had proven to be "ignorant foreigners" (*wuzhi waiyi*) and thus unworthy of special consideration, the emperor ordered that along the return route, the British were to be treated and provisioned in an ordinary way. Moreover, garrisons were to be turned out to impress upon them the imperium's awesome strength (*ZGCB*, 52b–53a). Officials in Peking were told that the Portuguese precedent concerning entertainments and sightseeing was scrapped. When he returned to Peking, Macartney was to be summoned to an audience with princes and high officials in which they were to remain seated and he was to be given a seat off to the side (!). Further, the British king's gifts would be accepted and rewards made to him, but the embassy was not to remain in the capital awaiting the emperor's return.

What seemed especially to gall Hongli at this point was that when summoned to a meeting with the grand councilors, the ambassador, claiming he was ill, had sent the vice-ambassador Staunton. The latter had presented a communication which indicated that the British did not understand ritual protocols. Heshen had upbraided the ambassador and ordered him to practice the ceremonies (*yijie*), but Macartney continued to claim illness. The emperor concluded that the British remained proud and arrogant. It was crucial, therefore, to limit displays of the emperor's compassion and grace (*en*), because only in that way would foreign kingdoms be properly guided (*jiayu*). Accordingly, Hongli announced that he had called upon that most trusted of senior advisors, Agui, to consult on this matter.[36]

Given the serious impasse that had been arrived at over the form that the imperial audience would take, it is perhaps worth reviewing briefly the sequence of events that produced Hongli's harsh new assessment of the British embassy. Recall that when the embassy arrived in Tianjin, Hongli indicated that in meetings with his officials the British should be allowed to perform ceremonies in keeping with their native customs. The conflicting reports later submitted by Liang Kentang and Zhengrui concerning the ceremony that had occurred at Tianjin led the emperor to seek clarification. In other words, he wanted to know if the English had foregone their own customs. Zhengrui's reporting indicated that this indeed was the case, and there was no reason to think otherwise until Macartney presented his proposal for the imperial audience just before leaving Peking.

36. I have considered together two instructions of September 9 and 10; they are in *ZGCB*, 52b–54a. In his account, Macartney makes no mention of his own illness, saying instead that Staunton was sent because Heshen asked to see him (*MD*, 118).

The British ambassador's suggestions were objectionable on a number of counts. In the first place, the very question of designating someone of an equal station to koutou to the picture of George III was probably incomprehensible because the ambassador of a foreign king (like the king himself) was categorically distinct and inferior to a servant of the emperor.[37] No doubt the ambassador's suggestion that he kiss the emperor's hand was equally peculiar. Macartney's plan for the audience, combined with his refusal to meet with high court officials when he arrived in Rehe, led directly to the decisions outlined in the instructions of September 9 and 10. In addition, as a result of his bald lies, Zhengrui was demoted in rank.[38]

The problem the emperor and his councillors faced now was thus one of extreme complexity given that his servants, as well as the British ambassador, were responsible for having moved the ritual process away from a centering path. Preparation had, in other words, not produced a sincerely loyal inferior, but rather had exposed arrogance on the one hand, and incompetence on the other. While his orders, at this point, might serve to alter matters, questions surrounding the ambassador's intent and Zhengrui's mismanagement were far from completely resolved. If the imperial envoy had lied about Macartney practicing for his imperial audience, had he lied about other things as well? And was Macartney's perceived arrogance a product of Zhengrui's mismanagement, or inherent in the British ambassador? As a temporary solution, Hongli chose to maintain the distinction between the English king and his ambassador, while punishing Zhengrui.[39] Perhaps more importantly, however, with the preparation phase

37. Recall Hongli's own designations of the British as *beichen,* or side officials with respect to his envoy and his example of the king of Annam.

38. While there is no indication of Zhengrui's demotion in the court records, Macartney provides evidence of it. According to what he was told, the envoy was also demoted because of his failure personally to view a portrait of the emperor aboard the *Lion* (MD, 118). On questions surrounding the portrait, see ZGCB, 26.

39. There is one more observation about the ritual process which seems appropriate to make at this point. We have seen how complex preparation and evaluation are, especially in view of the multiple temporal sequences simultaneously brought into play by the division of the embassy and gifts. Because of this and because of the problems such contingencies raised for channeling affairs along a centering path, the preparation phase of the ritual process tended to be organized to exclude as much extraneous contact as possible so that evaluations could be made. This helps to explain the many restrictions placed on the embassy, particularly with respect to its freedom of movement, and for the continuous scrutiny of contacts and communications. It also helps to explain why

of the embassy now thoroughly muddled, Hongli and his chief advisors sought a way either to salvage their original classification of the embassy as a meritorious undertaking (*haoshi*), or completely reevaluate the situation and refuse to receive Macartney in audience.

————————

Macartney was repeatedly told that he and the embassy would, following their audience with the emperor, be allowed a greater degree of free movement.

7 CONVERGENCE

Audience, Instruction, and Bestowal

The intensity of the Qing imperium's concern for the early progress of the embassy suggests the importance of the preparation phase of Guest Ritual. During this period, the emperor, members of the Grand Council, members of the Imperial Household Department, and local officials took great care in evaluating the intent of the embassy. The evaluation procedure was designed to channel actions along a centering path. It was accomplished in large part through viewing the British embassy and carrying on intense dialogue with its members, a process which was additionally complicated by the fact that the embassy had been divided into three parts. During the preparation phase, the court also scrutinized the actions of its own officials. The centering process worked to direct what were now multiple temporal sequences operating within the rite[1] toward a convergence — an imperial audience in which the emperor received sincerely loyal lesser lords or their ambassadors.

On September 14, 1793, the Qianlong emperor received the British ambassador Lord Macartney in a round tent in the Garden of Ten-thousand Trees on the eastern side of the "Mountain Resort for Avoiding Summer Heat" at Rehe. According to Sir George Staunton, one of the few British "eyewitnesses" of the events that transpired on that day, the form the audience took was unusual. Staunton wrote:

---

1. These multiple sequences involved the division of the embassy into three parts. Excesses or deficiencies at Rehe, the Yuanming Gardens, or Chusan would have affected the rite as a whole and, therefore, had to be monitored and coordinated.

[the] mode of reception of the representative of the King of Great Britain, was considered by the Chinese court, as particularly honourable and distinguished: Embassadors being seldom received by the Emperor on his throne, or their credentials delivered into his own hands, but into that of one of his courtiers. These distinctions, *so little material in themselves,* were however understood by this refined people as significant of a change of opinions of their government in respect to the English; and made favourable impression upon their minds. (Staunton 1797, 3:38–39; emphasis added)

In addition to the distinctions that Staunton mentions, there were others that he probably would have thought carried little material value as well. Lord Macartney recalled in his diary that upon entering the tent, he proceeded up a side stairway (probably on the east) and went directly before Hongli. Kneeling down on one knee, he passed the jewel-encrusted box containing George III's letter into the emperor's hands, stood up, and retreated to the left of the emperor (the east side of the tent) where he and his retinue were seated for a banquet.[2]

The British accounts of the audience at Rehe are particularly provocative for reasons that go well beyond the fact that Macartney did not koutou.

---

2. See MD, 122–123. The only other account is that of young George Staunton, the vice-ambassador's son, and it rather provocatively claims that as the emperor passed the British embassy on his way into the tent "we went down on one knee and Bowed our heads Down to the ground." The entry, as Cameron has noted, has the words "to the ground" crossed out (1976:303). Among other written accounts of the embassy, only Anderson was present at Rehe. Although he does provide rather amusing details of the chaos that attended the British procession to the audience tent, he does not give any particulars about the ceremony (1795:219–221). Barrow was at the Yuanming Gardens while Macartney was in Rehe; he notes that a great uproar occurred there, especially among Western missionaries, when word arrived that Macartney had not performed koutou (1804:117–118).

There are no extant sources in the Qing court records that indicated what Macartney did. However, Pritchard reports that Chinese sources in the Palace archives indicate that the particulars of a British ceremony were presented to the emperor prior to the audience (1943:190), presumably referring to Macartney's letter on the audience protocol. The QSG, Annals of Rites (*Li zhi*), 10:4a–b, adds that a special edict was issued allowing the Western ceremony. Neither of these originals have been examined by contemporary scholars, and my own research in the archives was similarly fruitless. The LBZL, 180:10a, notes that the British ambassador knelt (*gui*) in delivering his king's message, but does not mention him either passing it into the emperor's hands or that he was in front of the emperor.

Moreover, the differences were quite marked between the Macartney audience and protocols for audience outlined in Qianlong era sources such as the *Comprehensive Rites of the Great Qing* (DQTL), the *Collected Statutes of the Qianlong Reign* (QLHD), and the *Precedents of the Board of Rites* (LBZL). These texts indicate, for example, that at no time does a foreign ambassador approach the throne, let alone hand something directly to the emperor while kneeling on one knee. They also indicate that messages such as the one Macartney brought were normally delivered to officials of the Board of Rites in a ceremony prior to imperial audience. Finally, and perhaps most significantly, ambassadors and their retinues ordinarily moved through the west or right sides of courtyards and halls, and were expected to kneel three times, bowing their heads to the ground thrice each time on that side of courtyards or halls.[3]

How, then, are we to explain these apparent major deviations from practices prescribed in authoritative Qing texts on audiences? Indeed, from the court's evaluation of Macartney's attitude, we might expect Hongli and his councillors to have insisted on strict compliance with forms found in the texts referred to above, especially when we consider that Macartney had arrived in Rehe in September—an important ritual period of the year. In September the emperor received in audience princes and ambassadors from Inner Asia. Further, Macartney was present during the celebration of the emperor's birthday, which, ritual manuals tell us, was a time when a variety of high-order rites occurred, including Grand Assemblage (*Dachao*) and Grand Banqueting (*Yanyan*, see Appendix for a calendar of events). To have Macartney perform an atypical ceremony on this great occasion before eyes of the many important personages then present in Rehe appears to contradict much that has been written about "traditional Chinese foreign relations."[4] While granting that the available evidence is sketchy, I believe that there are a number of clues in the court record to support not only Macartney's account of the audience, but also the Qing court's insistence that ritual practice was the proper way to form superior-inferior relations between the emperor and the multitude of lesser lords in the world.

3. In his accounts of embassies from Portugal and Holland that preceded the Macartney embassy and the embassies involved in the precedents discussed below, Wills cites European sources that appear to support the DQTL (see 1984:2).

4. In addition, those aware that the audience form was indeed altered have not explained why the imperial court was willing to make such changes; see Pritchard 1943: 190–194, Cranmer-Byng 1957–1958:117–186, and Wills 1984:184–185.

7.1   Alterations to Imperial Audience for the British Embassy

7.1.1   *Adjusting the Ritual Process*

The first sort of evidence indicating that the court was willing to compromise on the issue of ceremony can be found in an instruction to princes and officials in Peking of September 11. In it, the emperor rescinded his earlier decision over treatment of the embassy when it returned to the capital. Now the embassy would be allowed time to rest, while awaiting the emperor's return. Hongli also indicated that the British could be shown the imperial gardens. The reason given for these changes was that Macartney had met with grand councillors that day and had received the imperium's warning. Hearing this, the British ambassador had indicated remorse, while expressing the highest reverence and obedience. As a result of the sincerity discernible in his demeanor, the court considered him again worthy of receiving the emperor's grace (*ZGCB*, 54a–54b).

Hongli's instruction seems to be indicating that centering was back on track, especially since his most competent advisors had had an opportunity to scrutinize carefully Macartney's verbal and physical expressions to discern his inner qualities. What they, in turn, claim to have seen is also significant: although Macartney lacked comprehension of the proper relations in the rite, he had shown that his intentions were proper; that, like his king, he was himself sincere. Such a conclusion not only verified the efficacy of the centering process, but facilitated the process by which the English king's powers, like those of other foreign lords, could now be incorporated into Qing imperial sovereignty. At the same time, all that had transpired was not ignored, for it served to differentiate this kingdom, its king, and this embassy from other kingdoms, other lords, and other embassies.

The pattern of inclusion and differentiation central to the formation of Qing sovereignty was, moreover, indicated in the altered form of audience. In particular, principles of cardinal directionality and bodily action became significant signs of the similarity and difference between the British embassy and the embassies of other lords. The precedent of the Portuguese embassy of 1753 explains some of the changes to audience forms, while other changes appear to have set new precedents. Let me take these issues up in turn.

7.1.2   *Precedent and Innovation*

An investigation of the *Statutes and Precedents of the Assembled Canon of the Qing Dynasty* (*DQHDSL*) indicates that the ceremony performed on the occasion of the Portuguese embassy (Qianlong 18) was the same as that for an embassy in the fifth year of the Yongzheng emperor's reign (the Portuguese embassy of Alexandre Metello de Sousa e Menezes in 1727). Records of the latter embassy refer back, in turn, to one that occurred in Kangxi 59 (a West Ocean embassy in 1720).[5] This earliest entry explains that an ambassador from the West Ocean arrived to present a petition and participate in an imperial audience. A table was placed in front of and at the center of the stairs leading to the Hall of the Nine Classics and Three Obligations (Jiujing sanshi dian) in the Eternal Spring Garden (Changchun yuan), rather than at the Hall of Supreme Harmony.[6] After the emperor had taken the throne, a functionary of the Office of Ceremony (*Honglu si*) led the ambassador to the central table, where the communication (*biao*) was placed. After stepping back from the table the ambassador performed three kneelings, bowing his head to the ground thrice each time.[7] Then, using stairways and gates to the left (or east side) of the emperor, the ambassador delivered the communication into the emperor's hands, who passed it to a high official at his side. Retreating the way he had entered, the ambassador returned to the foot of the stairs leading to the hall and again performed three kneelings and nine bows. Reentering, the ambassador received an imperial bestowal

---

5. *DQHDSL*, 505:8b–9a and 505:5b. The 1720 embassy has caused a degree of controversy because of the difficulty in identifying it in European sources. The *QSG*, 10:2b, claims it as a Portuguese embassy led by ambassador Fei-la-li, but stands uncorroborated by other sources. The only embassy present at the end of December 1720 was a Papal delegation led by Mezzabarba. Fu (1966, 2:501) argues rather convincingly that Mezzabarba and Fei-la-li are one and the same. References to Portugal and Italy were also made in one of the emperor's letters to George III (*GZCSL*, 1435:13b).

The significance of the precedent lies, however, in that it allows an ambassador to deliver a communication from his superior directly into the hands of the emperor, rather than at the Board of Rites as indicated in the *DQTL*. Almost an identical situation occurred during the Russian embassy headed by Izmaylov. According to various sources, after performing koutou, the ambassador was allowed to convey the Czar's message into the emperor's hands; see J. Bell 1762:133–134.

6. The Guest Ritual section of the *DQTL* only deals with audiences in the Hall of Supreme Harmony. However, the Grand Audience section (*DQTL*, 18) of this manual indicates that embassies may be appended to the end of the west flank of officials on other occasions. However, the chapter only mentions audiences at the Yuanming, not the Eternal Spring, Garden.

7. It is unusual for persons to enter the central space of the audience site and koutou. As indicated above, what might be called a "greeting koutou" to the emperor was normally performed below the west stairs leading up to the west door of the audience hall (*DQTL*, 45:2a).

of a seat and tea. He then gave thanks for the emperor's grace and departed (*DQHDSL*, 505:4b–5a).

The treatment of the West Ocean embassy cited here makes it quite clear that an alteration in the Guest Ritual audience similar to that designed for the British had occurred as early as the Kangxi period. In what appears to have been an unusual change in normal routines, the foreign ambassador was allowed to enter the center space of the hall in order to place his king's letter on the table and to kneel and bow to the south of the table, rather than at the west entrance to the hall. He was then shifted to the left or east side of the audience hall, the side normally reserved for the emperor's civil officials, in order to deliver his king's communication directly into the hands of the emperor. In effect, aspects of the "presentation of credentials and local products" ceremony at the Board of Rites, at which the emperor was never present, appear to have been incorporated into the imperial audience itself (*DQTL*, 45:2b–3a). More importantly, perhaps, the ambassador seems to have been allowed to act as if he had been transformed into one of the emperor's civil officials offering up a communication that had originated with a lesser lord. The precedent provided, therefore, a solution to part of the problem Macartney's requests posed and may in fact have helped to reinforce the positive assessment of Macartney's intentions that emerged from the determination of grand councillors that he was indeed sincere.

At the same time, however, not all aspects of the precedent were adhered to; the table for his king's letter and the koutou were both eliminated. And, as if to emphasize this last alteration, rather than being escorted by an official from the Office of Ceremony, as the West Ocean ambassador had been in 1720, higher-level officials—a grand councillor and an officer of the Board of Rites—led Macartney to his audience with the Qianlong emperor.

7.2   Imperial Audience

In chapter 4, portions of Lord Macartney's account of the events of September 14 were presented. As noted at the time, his diary provides abundant information on the scale and splendor of the audience, but it does not point out the unique features of the court assembly which occurred on this occasion. There are several reasons for this. In the first place, Macartney would have been unaware of the routine characteristics of imperial audience and would not have known, unless it was pointed out to him, that in addition to the waiving of koutou, other alterations had been made. Second, his assessment of the difference between this audience and a European royal audience did not go beyond a qualitative evaluation; that is, the audience with the emperor showed a much greater degree of pomp and concern with ceremonial detail. Third, when Macartney's account is placed beside the terse entry found in the *Veritable Records of the Qianlong Reign* (GZCSL), it is easy to conclude from the latter that nothing of substance occurred, or that the court thought so little of these ceremonies, beyond the act of prostrating before the emperor, that no description was required.

This last observation points to a fundamental difference in points of view on audience. Macartney's diary entries are rich in detail, a kind of detail associated with scientific observations of the natural world. It is, in other words, a privileged view from a position constituted by the distinction drawn between a knowing/perceiving subject and passive objects. The observer accumulates detail and, in so doing, presumes that in the act of enunciating, reality is both mirrored and recorded. Since even the most privileged position in the Guest Ritual process could not disengage and distance itself from that process in the way Macartney had, accounts like his are not part of the Qing court record. Indeed, very little is said about that particular day. On the other hand, it is possible to make a few observations on audience in general, placing it in the context of the entire Guest Ritual process, as well as to review aspects of audience to be found in the *Comprehensive Rites of the Great Qing*.

7.2.1 The Guest Ritual Process and Imperial Audience

The various temporal sequences of Guest Ritual were directed toward a convergence which organized a relative center, the spatiotemporal site at which audience would occur. Audience, the moment of convergence of these previously distinct sequences, operating at different tempos, appears to have pivoted the entire ritual process by physically locating people and things in terms of the relevant relationships that had emerged in preparation for audience. In other words, time was apparently spatialized, and it is in this sense that a notion of "fixing" (*ding*) becomes important. For what appears to have happened in audience was the transformation of temporal sequences into a momentary structure, a shift of syntagmatic elements into a specific paradigmatic form.

It is at this moment in the rite (and, I believe, only at this moment), that the ritual process becomes manifestly symbolic; the structure here constituted and momentarily fixed (a simultaneous crystallization of relevant relationships) was meant to be understood by all present as a spatial display of the current conditions of the world and their linkage to broader cosmic processes. The power of ritual at this moment in the rite ought not to be underestimated, for what I am suggesting is that it was precisely the capacity to order and spatialize time that constituted the Qing cosmological claim to be the *guojia*, the chief domainal family, and Hongli to be *huangdi*, the supreme lord and head of that family.

Ritual manuals such as the *Comprehensive Rites* make clear the richness of significations available for use in audience, while indicating how the center should be ritually invested with contingent meanings. Not only the spatial placement of foreign ambassadors and their retinue with respect to the position of the emperor, but also the relative placement of the high officials, imperial regalia (banners, implements, carriages, etc.), lesser officials and the imperial orchestra, and guard contingents are legible. The presence of this or that element in a given audience was probably arrived at through a dialogue among officials responsible for audience and the precedents and principles recorded in ritual manuals.

The *Comprehensive Rites* drew a distinction between Grand and Regular audiences, which were differentiated by the presence of a certain order and quantity of people and things. The actual determination of what would and would not be present was presumably arrived at through an evaluation of the ritual processes under way. This included the determination of the site (the hall, or in Rehe, the tent) of the audience. Once the date and place of audience was arrived at, the positions of participants and regalia in the audience hall were established (*DQTL*, 18:2a–5b). These positions were organized at all levels of audience (and feasting) with respect to the location of the emperor at the extreme north end of the hall, where he was seated facing south on the center line. Other participants were ranked and located on his left and right hands from north to south. The left side of the hall was where civil officials were placed, while the right side was reserved for military officials and members of the eight banners.[8]

Below the throne, the foreign king or his ambassador was appended to the end of the right file of military officials. Directly south of the emperor

8. Left and right were always determined in imperial ritual on the basis of the direction the emperor faced; that is, his left and right hand. This is important to bear in mind, especially when reading Euro-American accounts of audiences or other ceremonies, because observers might indicate directions from their own left or right.

and below this space an orchestra might be placed. It played a variety of music as participants moved from position to position, and stopped when each new position was reached. Regalia and insignia, which varied with the level of audience, might be placed around the hall or in the forecourts leading to the hall; those items outside the hall were organized in east and west flanks (like the people inside). Anyone approaching the throne presumably did so on either side of the center line, meaning that s/he passed between the ranks of people and things to arrive at the left or right of the throne.

During audience, there were numerous occasions on which participants prostrated and at which hymns were intoned. The latter varied with the time of the year audience occurred. Participants were outfitted in their court clothing, which also varied according to the season and level of audience, and which displayed the rank of the participant. Foreign kings or their ambassadors were required to wear the court clothing of their domain. At the proper moment, embassies, in ranked order, were led to the west door of the hall, where they performed koutou. Through his officials and interpreters, the emperor asked "soothing" questions, to which the guest responded. Once this dialogue was completed, the guest performed another koutou, and was led back to the original position at the end of the west flank of military officials. He might return later if he was to participate in a tea ceremony or feast.

7.2.2   The British Audience

Although held in a large circular tent,[9] the audience of September 14 appears to have been on the order of Regular Audience. On the day of the audience and banquet, Macartney, his retinue, and the Burmese ambassador, as well as other participants, were awakened before dawn, escorted to a preparation tent, and then assembled in two flanks outside the entrance to the audience tent. The British ambassador stood at the end of the file on the left side of the road (the emperor's left hand when on the throne, the east side of the hall or tent) leading to the entrance (see figure 4).[10]

---

9. There were, of course, a number of physical differences between a tent and audience halls in imperial palaces—one doorway, rather than several, and no stairs being among them.

10. A British painting of the position of the British embassy as I have described it here has been reproduced many times; see Peyrefitte 1992 or Singer 1992. Figure 4 is William Parish's schematic diagram from the British Library, Add. MSS 19822, folio 8, no. 7716018.

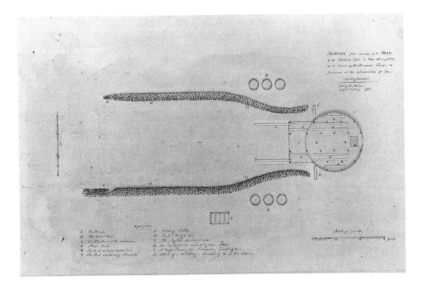

Figure 4. Sketch of the plan of the Audience Tent in the Garden of Ten Thousand Trees. The British embassy is at the left end of the lower file.

Following the delivery of his king's letter and the emperor's "soothing questions,"[11] the British ambassador and his retinue were seated to the left of the emperor in the banquet which followed. In what appears to have been a significant honor, he and Staunton were called forward during the banqueting to participate in a wine ceremony with the emperor. Macartney records that Hongli passed the wine cup directly to him, rather than via one of his officials.[12] These various concessions and honors indicate that at least at the time of the imperial audience, the Qianlong emperor had decided that although untutored in ritual procedures, Lord Macartney was indeed sincere.

11. As Macartney's diary indicates, such questioning occurred on more than one occasion: the following day when he greeted the emperor, who was on his way to a Buddhist temple; at the emperor's birthday feast; and when the emperor returned to Peking.

12. See the wine ceremony in the DQTL, 40:6a. Also see the entry on audiences at Rehe in the DQHD, 65:11, where Mongol princes participate in wine ceremonies with the emperor.

7.3   Imperial Intervention I: The Emperor's Poem

As indicated earlier, the incorporation of foreign kings into imperial sovereignty was not without certain ambiguities. In the case of the British embassy, the elements of imperial audience that were altered provide a useful example of the complexities of political encompassment. The ambiguity of the relationship constituted through the rite was also demonstrated in an unusual act of imperial intervention. According to the *Veritable Records,* the emperor composed a poem about the British embassy at the time of audience. The content of the poem is worth close scrutiny, for it displays this ambiguity quite forcefully and elegantly.

Hongli began the poem with a reference to the Portuguese embassy. Now, he continued, the English have come in all sincerity. Their journey is akin to the wide-ranging travels of Shu Hai and Heng Zhang. Clearly, therefore, the merit of Nurhaci and the virtue of Hung Taiji had extended across the vast ocean. While these men from afar appear ordinary, their hearts are good and true. (In other words, they were sincere in their turning toward transformation and this was visibly displayed by them.) The poem then shifts from the appearance of the embassy to a consideration of the gifts they have brought in offering. The things, Hongli explained, were not precious (*bugui*), but curiosities (*yi*), and their subtlety had been much exaggerated (!). On the other hand, no matter how meager their offerings, they themselves have been treated generously (GZCSL, 1434:11b).[13]

In its conciseness, Hongli's poem emphasizes the original evaluation of the British embassy and summarizes the pattern of the encounter, while also commenting on the feelings elicited in the ritual process. In addition, it locates the British gifts in the contradiction that had emerged between Macartney's claims and the court's own evaluation. Perhaps more importantly, in highlighting British exaggerations versus imperial generosity, Hongli seems to have placed the British as hierarchically inferior to the Mongol nobility, Islamic ambassadors from Inner Asia, and the Burmese,

13. It is impossible to determine if the poem was presented orally by the emperor or one of his officials at the audience. The poem also appears on a Chinese tapestry, presumably showing the British gifts being brought to the Yuanming Gardens. The tapestry is now at the National Maritime Museum, Greenwich, England. For a picture, see Cameron 1976:301. Needham has argued convincingly that it does not depict the British embassy at all, but an earlier one, perhaps from Holland; see 1965, 4.2:471. Also see Cranmer-Byng and Levere 1981:520.

all of whom participated in the same audience and banquet. As if not only to mark this distinction, but also to emphasize the court's magnaminity, Hongli made a number of bestowals to the British during and immediately after the audience.

7.4   Imperial Intervention 11: Bestowals

Bestowals included the jade scepters presented to the ambassador and vice-ambassador and items given to young George Staunton, each of which Hongli personally presented. Other items were sent to the embassy's quarters (DQHDSL, 507:25a–27a and ZGCB, 55a–b). The main point made by the bestowals, however, is their categorization as special ones (*teci*). They appear to have been the result of the emperor's own evaluation of the speech and demeanor of the British ambassador and his retinue.

Bestowals were also made in subsequent audiences in which the British participated. Two such occasions are noted for Rehe and a third, with the emperor absent, upon the departure of the embassy (DQHDSL, 507:27a–31a). What is striking about the list of bestowals is not only their magnitude, but the fact that the entire embassy, including ordinary seamen aboard the fleet, received something.[14] They make the point that the embassy was a unit, and, therefore, each member was worthy of the emperor's generosity. Moreover, since the allotments were graded by rank, they mirrored the list of participants that had been elicited from the British. As such, imperial bestowal acknowledged hierarchical social relations in the domain of the foreign king. Finally, the bestowal lists are different from the lists of items proposed at the beginning of the embassy by the emperor's servants. While earlier precedents may have guided choices, the final disposition of the emperor's generosity was determined through evaluation of the ritual process. The bestowals were intended to display the relations produced in ritual process, rather than to reference an ideal state external to it.

There was another kind of a reward that the embassy received while at Rehe, one that is not recorded in the court record for this period, but that deserves consideration. The day following his audience with the emperor, Macartney and his retinue were conducted on a tour of the Rehe Gar-

---

14. A recommendation for additional rewards for those aboard the ships at Zhejiang was presented in a memorial by the Grand Council on September 21, some of which were eventually made; see ZGCB, 62a–b.

dens by the grand councillor Heshen, Fukang'an (former governor-general of Liangguang, which included Guangzhou or Canton, and pacifier of the Gurkhas), and Fuchang'an (a grand councillor and Fukang'an's brother), all prominent administrative and military officials of the inner circle around Hongli. With so many important people present, the tours of the gardens were no doubt meant as a mark of special favor by the emperor. But they also signified more than this, and were treated as such by both parties.

On the court's side, questions concerning Macartney's pronouncements about the British gifts still lingered. As if to address this issue directly, the embassy was taken to buildings filled with intricate European clocks and mechanical devices. Some of these may have been the ones sent from the capital and, as Macartney was told, more were kept at the Yuanming Gardens. The point being made was that the things Macartney had brought were in no way unique to his king's domain. Many and varied versions of the same devices came from other West Ocean countries and had, moreover, been presented to the emperor in vast quantities. The British had brought nothing special to boast about.

Macartney's response to the display is worth citing because, although it is highly unlikely that he understood the Qing definition of local products, it indicates his recognition of part of what was being communicated.

> (The pavilions) ... are all furnished in the richest manner, with pictures of the emperor's huntings and progresses; with stupendous vases of jasper and agate; with the finest porcelain and japan, and with every kind of European toys and sing-songs; with spheres, orreries, clocks, and musical automatons of such exquisite workmanship, and in such profusion, that our presents must shrink from the comparison and 'hide their diminished heads.' (MD, 125 and 355)

This moment, in which Lord Macartney realized that the grandiose display he had concocted to awe the one person in China who might be positively swayed toward the business of his embassy was perhaps ill conceived, is the closest Macartney actually came to questioning the premises upon which the embassy was founded. Indeed, it is almost as if the centering process had elicited that rarest of all attributes, humility.

7.5   The Period of Grand Assembly and Feasting at Rehe

Between September 17 and 19 the British embassy participated in a number of audiences and feasts, beginning with the celebration of the emperor's birthday.[15] As the festivities were under way, the court considered a number of important matters related to the embassy. In addition to the tour of the Rehe Gardens, these included the translation of George III's letter (taken up below), a memorial from the Grand Council to the throne concerning an interview with the ambassador, and Macartney's testimony about his efforts to bring up the "business" of his mission.

The memorial in question was offered up to the emperor on September 18. The councillors indicated that in compliance with the emperor's instructions, they had passed on to the ambassador a report from Changlin about the state of affairs at Zhejiang. They also took this opportunity to emphasize to Macartney that the emperor daily reviewed memorials from all the provinces in order to insure the proper management of affairs throughout the empire. The British ambassador was reported as being extremely impressed by this and observed that the treatment of the fleet at Chusan was another example of the emperor's extraordinary grace in dealing with men from afar. Although Macartney's diary entries make no mention of it, he was also reported to have showered great praise upon the emperor. Expressing awe and loyalty, as well as wishes for the emperor's long life, Macartney, at least from the perspective of court officials, appeared truly to have been transformed in his encounter with the Qianlong emperor (ZGCB, 58a–b).

At virtually the same moment at which these observations were being made by the Grand Council, Macartney chose to introduce the "business" of his embassy. On the day of the emperor's birthday, he attempted to discuss his mission with Heshen. Finding the grand councillor evasive, Macartney next took the opportunity presented during the assembly of September 18, when he and Staunton were summoned before the throne to raise the issue with the emperor himself. Hongli's only response was to bestow with his own hands a decorated box containing precious stones (MD, 134 and 137). Over the course of the next few days, Macartney appears to

15. As the entry in the *Veritable Records* indicates, on this occasion all imperial officials, foreign nobility, and ambassadors participated in the feast. This assembly and ones that occurred on September 18 and 19 included audience and Grand Feasting, and may have paralleled those described in the *Comprehensive Rites of the Great Qing.* These were rites held only after the Winter Solstice Sacrifice, the first day of the year, and the emperor's birthday. For an outline of "Grand Assemblage" see the DQTL, 18:1a–14b; variations at Rehe are outlined on 12a–b. Foreign ambassadors were also mentioned. As in other cases, they were added to the end of the file of officials on the west flank, see 18:6a and 7a, for example.

have taken whatever opportunities were offered to press requests upon the court. His actions led to a further reappraisal of the embassy, one that ultimately called into question the evaluations that had been made at the time of imperial audience and in the Grand Council memorial just discussed. Needless to say, the ambassador's intent was again the central issue.

7.6 Crisis in the Rite III: Reevaluating the British Embassy

7.6.1 *The Continued Inability of the Ambassador to Understand Relations in the Rite*

Precipitating the new crisis were a series of requests submitted by Macartney to Heshen on September 19, which from the British ambassador's perspective formally opened the business of his embassy. The requests included permission for Captain Mackintosh to return to his ship now anchored off the Zhejiang coast and conduct additional trade there; for two missionaries, Hanna and Lamoit, to come to Peking and enter imperial service; and for letters to be forwarded to Canton as well as for any messages awaiting Macartney to be directed to him. These requests were, in turn, followed by six others made on October 4 at Peking in which Macartney outlined the British government's views for improving diplomatic and trade relations. Taken together, Macartney's communications not only led the court to criticize him, but produced a thorough reevaluation of the classification that had been applied to the embassy. It also precipitated an extraordinary internal critique of the ritual process, including Hongli's evaluation of how he himself might have skewed centering.

The day after Macartney submitted his first set of requests, the Grand Council suggested he be told that it was unnecessary for Mackintosh to go to Zhejiang, since the ship had many competent officers aboard. Moreover, it would entail escorting Mackintosh to Zhejiang and then back to the capital. Trade was permissible, but Macartney should prepare a list of the items desired, give it to a high official, and it would be sent to the governor of Zhejiang, Changlin, under whose jurisdiction the trade would occur. Changlin could then present it to the ship's officers and make arrangements for trade in order to insure that the British were fairly treated. In addition, no taxes would be levied on the trade.

With respect to the missionary issue, the Grand Council argued that Macartney should have made his wishes known when he arrived at Tianjin and arrangements could have been made. Instead, saying nothing, he had allowed the two men to return to Zhejiang with the fleet. This, according to the councillors, was nonsense (*wuwei*). The best thing to do at present would be for the ambassador to prepare a letter for transmission to Zhejiang, and Changlin could make arrangements for the escort of the missionaries to the capital. If, on the other hand, they wished to return with the fleet south, then arrangements could be made for them to be escorted from Canton. It was left for the missionaries to judge what they thought most convenient. Finally, any correspondence the ambassador desired could be handled through imperial post and was classed as permissible (ZGCB, 58b–60a).

Presumably an edict containing these suggestions was issued, because on the following day, September 21 (the day the embassy departed Rehe), the Council reported that Zhengrui had spoken to Macartney. While the ambassador expressed gratitude for the imperial grace extended to him, he still sought an order from the emperor to the governor of Zhejiang allowing direct trade. Moreover, he did not see why he should prepare a list as instructed. Regarding the request to send Mackintosh to Zhejiang, Macartney said that there were no competent officers aboard his ship who could adequately supervise its departure from Ningbo or Chusan. As for the missionaries, the ambassador felt that the court need only issue an order; no letter from him was required (ZGCB, 59b–60a). Having thoroughly investigated Macartney's pronouncements, the councillors could only conclude that he was still ignorant (*wuzhi*) of ritual protocols.[16] Moreover, they suspected that the ambassador also had other requests and that he would become insatiable in his entreaties (*kenqiu wuyan*). They therefore recommended that the matter be deferred until the ambassador arrived in the capital, whereupon he could be criticized and his requests refused (ZGCB, 60a).

The same day an instruction was transmitted to the governor-general of Liangguang and Changlin reviewing the ambassador's requests. Hongli asked the pointed question that if Mackintosh's services were so crucial to the ship, how had it been able to sail from Tianjin to Zhejiang without him? Clearly, Macartney had been untruthful. Moreover, sending Mackintosh

---

16. The record actually says that the emperor's servants have concluded that the ambassador *did* understand the relations (*shang zhi tizhi*) (ZGCB, 8:60a). Based on what preceded this observation and what follows, including an imperial instruction of the same date, I believe this to be a misprint in the collection being considered here. After all, when it was explained to him how properly to proceed, the ambassador refused to comply.

under escort now would be worrisome, expensive, and open the door to even more requests. Given the situation, it was important now for Changlin to expedite matters at Zhejiang and fix a date for the departure of the fleet so that the ambassador could be informed. Hongli urged speed because the British might make excuses to delay their departure. In fact, the Mackintosh request was probably a delaying tactic. Observing that every undertaking has a source and culmination, the emperor suggested the possibility that after being feasted in the capital, the embassy should be ordered to proceed directly to Zhejiang and join the fleet for their return to England. This would allow matters to proceed expeditiously (*ZGCB*, 60a–62b).[17]

These observations by the emperor and his councillors indicate their emerging perception that something was seriously wrong in the rite, that a profound discontinuity existed between Macartney's external pronouncements in giving thanks for the emperor's grace and his inner feelings, as well as a discontinuity between Macartney's apparent hypocrisy and the sincerity that was determined to be present in George III's decision to send an embassy to China. In light of this, the emperor suggested that perhaps the embassy had only come to spy and, once the English requests were denied, perhaps they would attempt to cause other kinds of trouble, especially in Canton (*ZGCB*, 64b–65a and 70b–72a).

Since the court's reaction to Macartney's requests may appear extreme, they deserve some comment. In the first place, the ambassador's refusal to present a petition regarding trade in Zhejiang and the disposition of the missionaries, coupled with his request regarding Mackintosh, was not merely excessive, but, if indulged, would have circumvented the processes by which a relative center was organized through ritual practice. Macartney's intentions seem to have been that he wanted an official statement from the emperor, a kind of contract, that he could use to "legalize" English trade at Zhejiang and which could serve as a precedent for later claims. Even if the court did not understand the import of his request in these terms, it did perceive that granting such a request ran counter to the manner in which interdomainal relations were organized. The intricate process

---

17. The same day, the Grand Council asked Zhengrui if he had mentioned a feast to be held at the Yuanming Gardens to Macartney. If he hadn't, it was unnecessary to do so, since it was now out of the question (*ZGCB*, 62a and 64a). On September 22 Zhengrui was instructed to prepare the embassy quickly for its departure from the capital. A day was to be set for the departure rite in which final rewards would be made and the emperor's instruction to the English king presented to the ambassador (*ZGCB*, 63b–64a).

of channeling communications, people, and things in the centering process organized relations of power and authority and made it possible both to evaluate the processes under way and to assign and take responsibility for actions carried out in such processes. Macartney's refusal to participate can be seen, therefore, as an action which would subvert the very principles that were at work in ritual practice. On the other hand, the problem the court now faced was similar to the one it had to deal with when it became clear that Zhengrui had lied about Macartney practicing koutou. The British ambassador may indeed have been ignorant of the proper relations in the rite, but the excess now present involved more than one agent and his actions.

7.7   Imperial Instructions of September 23, 1793

On September 23 two crucial instructions were issued by the emperor. The first of these was dispatched through the Grand Council to the governor-general of Liangguang and the governors of Zhejiang and Guangdong. It outlined the English king's request that a minister be allowed to reside in Peking and the reasons for the emperor's refusal of the request, speculated on what the British response might be, reviewed the ritual process to date, and instructed provincial officials on how to proceed. The second instruction was one version of the famous letter from the Qianlong emperor to George III.[18]

7.7.1   *The Emperor's Instruction to Officials on the Periphery*

The instruction to provincial officials is a fascinating document if for no other reason than that it reviews virtually all of George III's suggestions for improving relations between England and China, and then explains in terms virtually identical to those directed at the British king why many of his requests either were already in place or were impossible to grant. Hongli began with the issue of a resident minister in Peking. Granting that the purpose might be to care for their trade, and to study and be transformed through instruction, he still wondered how an ambassador could deal with matters occurring hundreds of miles away in Canton. Moreover, Qing imperial ceremony and the customs of England were not the same. Alluding perhaps to the court's experience with Macartney, Hongli wondered

18. A third instruction regarding Macartney's requests concerning British trade in China also carries this date, but it could not have been written before October 4, the day that Macartney submitted his six requests.

whether even someone willing to practice for imperial audience would be able to emulate the court's procedures (*zGCB*, 64b).

Explaining that West Ocean people (missionaries) who asked to enter imperial service wore court dress, lived in official residences, and were not allowed to return to their native land, Hongli reasoned that a British ambassador presumably would not be willing to do the same. His speech and clothing would be different and he would be aimlessly wandering about Peking. Moreover, since they lacked an understanding of appropriate ritual relationships, their requests could be classed as nonsense (*wuyan*). Perhaps, therefore, they had only come to the Qing empire to spy, which obviously could not be allowed.

In addition, it had become clear that the pronouncements in the English king's communication were different from requests made by his ambassador. While the latter had had his errors pointed out in clear instructions, there was still a discontinuity between the feelings expressed by the English king and the troublesome and annoying entreaties made by his ambassador. Accordingly, these foreigners had been classified as ignorant (*wuzhi*). At present it was uncertain what the English reaction would be to the emperor's refusal to grant their requests, but they might try to stir up trouble in Canton. Officials there must be on the alert. Changlin, who was now being reassigned as governor-general of Liangguang, and Guo Shixun must be particularly attentive and circumspect for any signs of discord caused by the British in either Canton or Macao, and act accordingly.

Following these observations (many of which would be repeated in subsequent instructions), Hongli then turned his attention to a review of the ritual process. It is worth citing a substantial amount of the passage because while Hongli criticizes his subordinates, he also acknowledges his own responsibility for the direction the undertaking had moved.

> In caring for the embassy as it passed through their jurisdictions, periphery officials often were unable to negotiate along a centering path. Perhaps this was because We ordered a slight increase in imperial grace. The various governors, emulating Us, went further, and were exceedingly liberal and generous in their treatment to the point of overflow, without regard for ritual protocols, thus increasing the embassy's arrogance and recklessness.
>
> Perhaps when we ordered a slight increase in restraint, officials were excessive in reducing treatment. The way of cherishing men from afar is also lost when not enough is done. On several occa-

sions We sent down instructions regarding this. When foreigners turn toward transformation, We simply consider their intentions in coming. If they are reverent, obedient, humble and respectful, then we increase Our grace. If they do not understand aspects of the rite, then We guide them by means of ritual practices. *The governors must calculate the lightness and heaviness of affairs and care for them accordingly.* This is squaring with proper circumspection. (*ZGCB*, 65a–b; emphasis added)

The problem, therefore, was centering, and centering had gone awry not specifically because of Macartney's actions, but because in their efforts to emulate the emperor, his subordinates failed to make properly refined calculations concerning their actions. This particular criticism is worth bearing in mind, because it points directly to the assumption that the preexisting knowledge and experience of subordinates, when combined with effective dissemination of imperial instructions, ought to have been sufficient for officials to make intelligent calculations that accorded with centering. The problem was, in other words, not a question of cross-cultural misunderstanding, but the failure on the part of the imperial officials to properly organize a process that everyone in positions of authority should have been able to manage.

Given the difficulties as well as the many agents responsible for the present impasse, Hongli advised that the best course now was to bring this undertaking to a speedy conclusion. If possible, the embassy should be put aboard the fleet in Zhejiang; Changlin was notified accordingly and instructed on how to proceed. Indicating that centering did not end with imperial audience, Hongli told Changlin that he must not be extravagant toward them—they were to be supplied with daily necessities, but no more. In his dealings with them, Changlin must accord with the proper ceremonial relations. If they made foolish requests, he must be stern and forthright in pointing out their errors, for if he were lax, the ambassador would only begin again his incessant importunities (*maodu wuyan*) (*ZGCB*, 64b–65b).[19]

---

19. Instructions of September 29 and October 1 covered much the same ground and added that the governors of the jurisdictions the embassy might pass through need not personally see off the embassy. The Jiangsu, Anhui, and Jiangxi governors were also included because the embassy would have to pass through these jurisdictions if it took the overland route to Canton (*ZGCB*, 68b–70a).

7.7.2   *The Emperor's Instruction to the English Lord*

Hongli's other instruction of September 23 is one version of his letter to George III.[20] In it the emperor's concern over the direction the centering process had taken remains quite clear, and is perhaps most evident when he moves from a soothing, instructive tone to one that is more stern. After reviewing George III's reasons for sending Macartney to China and judging them sincere, Hongli explained in detail his treatment of the king's embassy. He then turned to the requests. Repeating much of what he had said to his own officials about why it was impossible for the British to station an ambassador in Peking, he added that he did not wish to force others to comply with the manner in which Catholic missionaries were incorporated into imperial service. Moreover, he was sure that the situation would be similar if he were to send an official to the English court. He did not say that he found the request to be nonsense or that the king was ignorant. At the same time, however, he did indicate that appropriate relations in rites were fixed (*ding*).

The emperor was not unaware, however, that West Ocean domains might organize their relations with other domains differently. Indeed, there is a hint in his response that the British request was not unprecedented. Noting that there were many West Ocean kingdoms, Hongli wondered what would happen if they all made the same request? At any rate, the real issue was why George III felt it necessary to have a permanent ambassador in the capital. He had said that one purpose was to care for the English trade. The English had long traded at Macao and the emperor had extended his grace to them there. Moreover, others such as Portugal and Italy had made identical requests concerning trade and the court had treated them with compassion. When irregularities had occurred, those responsible had been punished. Why, then, was it necessary to have someone in Peking, particularly when it was such a great distance from where the trade took place? Implicit in this question was another: what interests did the British have in China other than trade? The English king also said that he wished to send someone who could study the court's ceremonies—but to what end, Hongli wondered? Such efforts could be classified as useless (*wuyong*).

Hongli then turned attention to the English king's gifts. Elaborating on

---

20. This is the famous letter from the Qianlong emperor to George III; see 10.4 for a discussion of its place in the historiography of Sino-Western relations.

his brief comments made in the poem composed at the time of Macartney's audience, the emperor explained:

> we have never placed great value on unusual and rare things. You have sent gifts from a long distance and offered them with profound sincerity; therefore, I specially ordered my officials to accept them. In fact, because Our fame is known throughout the world, many other kingdoms, who also made difficult journeys, have sent valuable gifts to us. We already have a sufficient number of similar things. Your ambassador saw them personally. But since we do not overvalue such things, we are not eager to have you send any more that are made in your own country. (GZCSL, 1435:14a–b).

Since this passage has long been cited as indicative of Chinese isolationism, sense of self-sufficiency, and misguided sense of superiority, a few comments are in order (see 10.4 below). Note, for example, that Hongli is not speaking of British trade; that is a topic taken up in other parts of the instruction. He is speaking, rather, to the evaluation of the British gifts by his officials, and to the fact that the court accepted the gifts even though it had such instruments in abundance. Macartney had not only been taken to see some of the existing imperial collection, but, as noted earlier, thought that the instruments he had brought were less grand than those the court already possessed. What, then, is the issue Hongli addresses? It would seem that it has to do with the perceptions the court had of Macartney's attitude toward the British gifts. Unlike his king, the British ambassador appeared arrogant about the superiority of the gifts, particularly the astronomical instruments. What was being rejected, I believe, was not trade with Great Britain, not British manufactures, and not the gifts at hand, but Macartney's claims about the gifts, claims which had been elicited in the ritual process and identified as excessive.

In the concluding portion of the instruction, the emperor reiterated the inherent discontinuity between the British king's request to station an ambassador in the capital and proper ceremonial relations. England would not benefit from such an arrangement even if allowed. Detailed instruction had been prepared by the emperor and presented to the ambassador, who was now returning to England. The king only had to understand the ideas presented here and increase his resolve to be reverent and obedient in order to preserve his domain and realize the good fortune of peace. There followed a brief list of imperial bestowals as well as mention of the fact that all of the emperor's bestowals had been incorporated into a list that had been given to the ambassador (GZCSL, 1435:11b–15a).

In reading this instruction one is struck by the lengths to which the emperor went to explain to King George the problems in his requests and in the ritual process as a whole. At the same time, it is also clear that the emperor chose not to raise the more difficult issues surrounding the behavior of the English ambassador. And while blunt at times about the difference he perceived between the Qing empire and Great Britain, he left open the possibility of future encounters.

It is perhaps also worth commenting on the issue of a resident minister, especially since it would become a major focal point of conflict between the Qing and British empires in the nineteenth century. The details of the Qing management of embassies reviewed here indicate that one of its major elements was the constant presence of imperial officials. Indeed, it was in relation to caring for the embassy that classifications such as "properly circumspect," "attentiveness," and "judicious management," as well as designations involving excess and deficiency have their meaning—they allow evaluation of the process and the effective assignment of responsibility. Such classifications of action were further informed by the notion that affairs (in this case a "meritorious undertaking") have their sources and culminations. From the emperor's perspective, therefore, what the English king was asking would require an unending and continuous presence of imperial servants to care for an ambassador. Moreover, such a presence would be impossible to organize in any way relevant to the imperium's conception of relations between the Supreme Lord and lesser kings. Hongli's references to the problems an ambassador would have in Peking because of his different speech and clothing can be understood in these terms, as can his invoking of precedent and "fixed" relations in the rite.

7.8   Preparations for Departure and Further Assessments of British Attributes

On September 24, as the British embassy traveled from Rehe to Peking, the Grand Council memorialized that according to Zhengrui the embassy had additional gifts to present upon its return to the capital. The same day an instruction was sent to Zhengrui informing him that the departure rite for the embassy would be held at the gate of the Hall of Supreme Harmony on October 3 and that he was to insure that all matters concerning the

British gifts were completed before that date. In addition, each of the items dealt with in the emperor's reply to the English king's communication were reviewed and Zhengrui was instructed to respond to any questions Macartney might have in a way identical to that the emperor had outlined (zGCB, 66a–67b). Two days later, Hongli repeated his sense of urgency. Fearing that Macartney might feign illness or refuse to accept the emperor's communication to his king, Hongli ordered Zhengrui to make the schedule for the remaining period of the embassy's stay in the capital clear to the ambassador and make sure matters progressed smoothly until the embassy departed Peking (zGCB, 67b–68b).

After the emperor's return to Peking (September 30),[21] Macartney was summoned to an audience at the Yuanming Gardens with Heshen, Fukang'an, and Fuchang'an on October 2. Heshen delivered letters from Chusan and inquired about their content. Macartney explained that the *Lion* and *Hindostan* were prepared to depart, which prompted Heshen to express hope there was still time to catch them because the court was concerned about the health of the embassy. Taking this as a sign that he was being urged to leave, Macartney protested that he had barely opened the "business" of his mission. He added that his king would pay the expenses for a longer stay. Heshen would not discuss this proposal, but turned his attention to the ambassador's health and the emperor's concern for him (MD, 147–148).

This meeting may well have prompted the imperial instruction of the same date addressed to Changlin and Guo Shixun. In it the emperor presented a remarkable assessment of England in the most critical language used in the court record of the embassy. Noting that the British might react adversely to the court's refusal to allow them to station an ambassador in the capital, Hongli ordered Changlin to be attentive and on guard, for it was now clear that among the West Ocean peoples the English were the strongest (i.e., in a pejorative sense, "brute strength"); they not only plundered other West Ocean ships on the high seas, but were feared because of their lack of restraint. While now aware of the imperium's position, they might still attempt to stir up trouble in Macao. Perhaps the British would try to coerce or intimidate other West Ocean peoples or, having been granted an

---

21. Along with Qing officials, Macartney and part of his retinue turned out along the road leading to Peking to greet the emperor. According to Macartney, the emperor expressed concern about the ambassador's health (MD, 145).

audience and having received an imperial instruction, they might misrepresent themselves to the other West Ocean people or try to collect duties. It was important, therefore, for imperial officials to make the situation clear to merchants from other countries. Hongli also repeated his order to have troops arrayed all along the route the English would take so that they could see the imperium's awesome strength (ZGCB, 70b–72a).

The emperor's assessment of British strength, a strength that was ultimately perceived to be devoid of a moral basis, is worth consideration. The Macartney embassy seems to have convinced Hongli and his close advisors that Englishmen were extremely dangerous because they were capable, to a degree, of masking their true nature. Through the centering process, it had become clear that Macartney could for a time hide his true intent behind false sincerity, a situation that made the British dangerous and perhaps, given their military technologies, capable of reckless and unrestrained applications of force. Macartney's intention of providing a basis on which the court could differentiate England from other European countries was, therefore, a success, although certainly not in the sense that either he or Dundas had planned.

As these harsh evaluations were made, the emperor's servants worked to bring the portion of Guest Ritual involving imperial audience and bestowal to a close. They gathered together the items that would be bestowed on the embassy and its king in a departure ceremony, prepared a list of these things, and worked out the details for the transport of the embassy from Peking to Zhejiang.

8 BRINGING AFFAIRS

TO A CULMINATION

The British embassy's return to Peking signalled the beginning of the final phase of Guest Ritual: the departure rite and the escorting of the embassy out of the Qing empire. In this chapter, I bring into conjunction the Qing and British accounts of what transpired between the beginning of October and Macartney's departure from Canton in early January 1794. Of particular interest in this regard is the fact that the court's work of assessing British intentions did not cease, while Macartney himself came to see this period as the most fruitful portion of the embassy.

On October 3, 1793, the British ambassador was led to what appears to have been the Hall of Supreme Harmony, the first of the great audience halls in the imperial city (MD, 149). In a variation on the departure ceremony described in the *Comprehensive Rites* (outside the Meridian gate [Wumen] instead of within a hall [*DQTL*, 45:3b–4a]), Macartney saw arrayed in the hall before him the emperor's letter to George III, a complete list of imperial bestowals, and additional bestowals from the emperor to his king and the embassy. Heshen made the formal presentation and then explained that all would be sent to his quarters. The councillor also seems to have made it clear that neither he nor other high officials whom Macartney had hoped to influence with "magnificent presents" would accept anything from the British ambassador (MD, 149).[1]

Aware now that his departure could not be forestalled (a proposition that father Amiot confirmed later the same day, see section 4.8), Macartney made one last attempt to open the business of his embassy before

---

1. This refusal does not appear to have been directed specifically at the British. Bartlett notes it as a general ethic of grand councillors; see 1991:185.

leaving Peking. As the departure ceremony came to a close, he mentioned to Heshen that he wished to address some specific issues regarding the British establishment in China, and Heshen said he would be willing to receive a statement in writing. Soon afterwards, Macartney prepared a list of six requests that asked for permission to trade at Chusan, Ningbo, and Tianjin; to establish warehouses in Peking (as the Russians had in the past), Canton, and Chusan, and residences for merchants in the latter two places; and an alteration in transit duties between Macao and Canton (IOMC, 20: 161). When the embassy departed the capital on October 7, the emperor's reply was delivered to Macartney.

8.1   The Emperor's Reply to Macartney's Six Requests

From the assessment of the British reviewed at the end of the last chapter, we might expect that the emperor's reaction to additional "importunities" would be a peremptory dismissal. Instead, he again addressed himself to George III in much the same manner and detail as he had in the first instruction. Noting that West Ocean people, including the British, had long come to China to trade, the emperor, through his grace and compassion, established *hangs* (i.e., the Cohong merchants) at Macao, where things that Europeans desired existed in abundance. Now the English king's ambassador asked to deviate from these "fixed" procedures, a difficult request since the court could only look upon peoples from distant lands with equal human-heartedness (*yi shi tong ren*). Moreover, given that Macartney did not completely understand appropriate ceremonial relations, the emperor feared that the ambassador might not be able to make it clear why the requests had been denied. Hence he had prepared this point-by-point instruction (GZCSL, 1435:15a–16a). The general premise of his observations was that since only Macao had *hangs* and interpreters, trade anywhere else was impossible for foreigners. A simple proposition perhaps, but one that also provides a good deal of insight into how the court conceptualized trade and linked it to the notion of cherishing men from afar.

As noted in chapter 2, the emperor's concerns for lesser lords and their kingdoms were most fully articulated through Guest Ritual. It was also recognized, however, that the extension of the emperor's generosity should allow embassies to acquire other desirable things that were not included among imperial bestowals. Such a possibility was addressed, for example, in Qianlong-era regulations, which established a market at the residence of visiting embassies in Peking (QLHD 56:7b). Trade could also be held at markets on the borders of the jurisdictions that embassies passed through, which, of course, was the case when the *Lion* and *Hindostan* retired to Zhejiang. As in other cases, the primary concern of the court was for officials to make arrangements to insure that embassies were treated fairly and that no antagonisms developed between local people and foreign traders.

This was only part of the issue, however; equally important were the terms in which Macartney's request to trade in Zhejiang were organized and the ways in which the emperor's decision was disseminated. In the opening sections of the instruction being considered here, the emperor noted that the English king's ambassador presented a *bin* or petition to the Grand Council, which, in turn, put his requests into a memorial and offered them up to the emperor (GZCSL, 1435:15a). The emperor's response was then returned through the same channels to the ambassador. This rather mundane pattern finds resonance with the description of communication between the emperor and a foreign ambassador to be found in the *Comprehensive Rites*. The relevant passage is from the audience section of Guest Ritual and reads:

> The emperor asks soothing questions. The Director of the Board of Rites then transmits (*chuan*) the emperor's inquiries to the translator. The translator *turns around* and instructs (*yu*) the ambassador. The ambassador responds (*duici*). The translator translates his words. The Director of the Board of Rites molds the words into a verbal memorial and memorializes (*daizou*) the emperor. (DQTL 45:2b; emphasis added)

Discernible throughout the embassy record, this form of address draws attention not simply to mediated communication, but to the physical positioning of participants in that communication as well. Moreover, something very similar occurred when foreign merchants sent their petitions to *hangs*, who translated them and presented them to local officials. If we also recall earlier observations about the organization and spatialization of hierarchical relations and the role of centering in fashioning these relations, the *hang* appear to be an agency outside of Guest Ritual through which hierarchical relations, in this case commercial ones, were organized. Why, however, would such machinations be necessary?

Addressed to George III and not Macartney, Hongli's response suggests that rather than being antagonistic toward trade — or perhaps better, unable to conceptualize trade as simply involved with exchange value and use value

(of policy)

—the Qing court concerned itself with the social and political implications of commerce. The imperium recognized, as it were, the potential that such activity held for producing antagonisms and conflict among people, as well as greed and avarice in individuals, all of which were the concerns of a virtuous ruler. In turn, these potentially negative human characteristics were only likely to materialize when social relations were not organized through principles of the sort that informed ritual practice. It was the responsibility of the *hang* to do this, to organize trade as a social relationship in which there were superiors and inferiors, and hence clear lines of responsibility.

In so doing, the *hang* centered the engagement with foreign merchants, thus creating the conditions of possibility for varieties of exchange. Along with their interpreters, the merchants organized a hierarchy for the upward and downward movement of communications (requests moving upward as petitions from "foreign" merchants, and instruction from local officials moving downward through the *hang* to foreign merchants) and things (gifts, trade items brought by "foreign" merchants, duties from foreign merchants' trade moving inward and upward, and the downward rewards of the bounty of the imperial domain). The imperium assumed that relations organized in this way would be nonantagonistic.

As a solution to the vexing problem that resulted from the arrival of large numbers of Europeans not easily incorporated into the Qing empire, the *hang* were a reasonable success. The merchants not only guaranteed that the West Ocean people would be treated fairly, but as East India Company sources indicate, the trade in Canton was extremely lucrative for England. Here the major items the "foreign" merchants desired (primarily tea) were readily available, and, moreover, since the West Ocean people approached the Qing empire by ocean from the south, the port of Canton, as Hongli might have put it, was convenient for all concerned.

Returning now to the emperor's instruction to the English king regarding his ambassador's requests, it is understandable why in some sense the requests were treated as self-evidently inappropriate. The *hang* and their interpreters already existed in Macao, the most convenient and appropriate place for West Ocean people to trade. Moreover, the kind of trade that the British desired already existed. And, although the Russians had been allowed to trade in the capital, it was because there was no other place for them to trade at the time. Now a place had been established at Kiakhta and all trade with the Russians was conducted there.[2] Hongli used the

2. The site had been established in 1729; see Fu 1966, 1:160.

same reasoning to reject requests for dwellings and warehouses at places other than Macao. With respect to duties, the emperor emphasized that all peoples from the West Ocean were treated the same and the English should accord with what was the same for all (*xiangtong*) (GZCSL, 1435:16a–20b).

Finally, there is one other element about the *hang* that, although not mentioned in the emperor's letter, is worth some comment. It stems from references in imperial instructions generated around the time of the embassy's departure from Peking and involves relations between the British and Chinese merchants. For example, the emperor wondered how the British could include so much precise information in their requests; perhaps, he surmised, they had gotten information from treacherous Chinese merchants who colluded with foreigners (GZSY, QL 58.8.30, 68:4). He was concerned, therefore, that precautions be taken to insure that all contact with Chinese merchants in Ningbo, Canton, or anywhere else be mediated through Qing officials and that the British be prevented from making private contact with the powerful Chinese merchant groups along the southeast coast (GZSY, QL 58.9.7, 68:49–58). These concerns seem to be similar to Qing fears of links between these same merchants and Chinese communities in southeast Asia. The court worried about possible internal subversion, and about blocs forming that might threaten the Manchu position in China, but couched these fears as concern that the British not be cheated by unscrupulous Chinese merchants. At any rate, the significance of mention made in court records about potential collusion between varieties of groups against the Qing, while perhaps exaggerated in this case, was no different from similar concerns that animated Qing policy along the coast and in Inner Asia. And, since the Qing court was a minority, it was perpetually engaged not only in forming coalitions within which the emperor could be positioned as the paramount head, but in preventing the formation of combinations against itself.

The concerns over the British embassy expressed in Hongli's letters to the English king and in circulars to pertinent officials ought also to be understood in terms of his concern with properly ending the ritual process. In this respect, the embassy still had to be escorted from the capital to the periphery of the Qing empire. Moreover, this final temporal sequence was organized, like the period leading up to audience, as a centering process.

Recall that Hongli had already signaled the state of centering in numerous instructions disseminated to the jurisdictions through which the embassy would pass, alerting officials about possible trouble the British might cause and instructing them on how they should treat the embassy. A few days prior to the embassy's departure, additional arrangements were made. Hongli and his advisors decided that Zhengrui would not accompany the embassy beyond the Zhili jurisdiction to which he was attached. In his place, Songyun, one of the officials who had met Macartney in the Rehe Gardens, was designated as the new imperial envoy responsible for escorting the embassy overland as far as Zhejiang, where Macartney could board the *Lion*. On October 4 the court told Songyun that if the embassy caused trouble along the route, he could draw on local garrisons and use force to restrain them if necessary (*zgcb*, 9:75a).

Moreover, Hongli's concern over possible difficulties with the British did not simply involve his assessment that they were deceitful, greedy, and hotheaded. In a circular of October 5, he also made it clear that since coastal garrisons had slack discipline and poor training, he wondered if they could meet threats the British might pose. He warned officials, therefore, that they should correct this situation immediately and be prepared to provide Songyun assistance if necessary (*gzsy*, QL 58.9.1, 68:1–5).

8.2   From Peking to Hangzhou: Songyun and Macartney
      (October 10–November 9)

When the British embassy left Peking on October 7, 1793, they passed a "pavilion" where Heshen, Fukang'an, Fuchang'an, and other grand councillors waited to see them off. After receiving a complete list of imperial bestowals and the emperor's final instruction to his king (*md*, 155–156), Macartney soon renewed his acquaintance with Songyun, the newly deputed imperial envoy. For his part, Songyun was under orders from the court to keep the embassy on a tight rein and under close supervision. As Macartney departed Peking, officials who had been alerted to mobilize their garrisons along the embassy's route of travel began to send confirmation memorials to Peking (*zpzz*, 26.9, 26.10, 26.11, 26.22, and 26.23).[3]

On October 10, Songyun joined the British embassy along the road to Tianjin. In dealing with Macartney, the new imperial envoy's strategy seems

---

3. It would appear that only some of the memorials related to this portion of the embassy are extant in the Qing archives at Peking. None exist from Changlin, for instance (see below). Macartney also notes in his journal that Songyun received or sent dispatches almost daily.

to have been to soothe the ambassador's anxieties and disappointment in order to discern if the British had any hostile actions in mind. According to Macartney's account, after enlightening each other about the different attitudes of their two countries toward the exchange of resident ambassadors, Songyun addressed differences in customs, practices, and "etiquette" between China and Great Britain. Apparently forgetting his discussions with missionaries and his successful negotiations over imperial audience ceremonial, as well as what he had read about China beforehand and his earlier concern that he might have made some "trifling" error (see section 4.8 above), Macartney objected that he had been kept in "ignorance" and prevented from learning more about Qing practices (MD, 160). Therefore, if he had done something that offended the court, it was not his fault. Songyun assured him that the comportment of the embassy was above reproach and the same day memorialized that there were no difficulties with the behavior of the embassy (ZPZZ, 26.14).

For his part, Macartney remained unplaced. After a conversation with Wang and Qiao which included reference to official corruption in the Qing empire, Macartney seemed reassured of British superiority. "We find," he wrote, "that the boasted moral institutes of China are not much better observed than those of some other countries, and that the disciples of Confucius are composed of the same fragile materials as the children of Mammon in the western world" (MD, 161). Moreover, even though he was soon lauding Songyun's "attention" and "civility" in his journal in much the same tone that he had used toward Liang Kentang earlier, he also made veiled threats that Great Britain might completely quit the China trade if its merchants did not soon realize some relief.

Refusing to be baited, Songyun explained that local customs duties were quite often increased because of contingencies that arose within the jurisdiction in question. In the case of the Canton area, customs duties had been raised to provide funds for military operations in Tibet and along the Vietnam border. But peace now prevailed, so duties could be reduced. While this explanation pleased Macartney, he also lamented that Songyun had not originally been appointed to escort the embassy, rather than Zhengrui; in that way, all misunderstandings about his business might have been avoided (MD, 162–163).[4] But, rather than soothing the ambassador, Songyun's observations soon had him in a state of confusion.

---

4. Macartney may have had a point here, but it is also worth recalling that Zhengrui had the difficult task of not only preparing the British embassy for imperial audience,

On October 13, the day the embassy arrived in Tianjin, Macartney wrote of his inability to understand the erratic treatment he had so far received from the Qing court, treatment which included the contradictory behavior of Zhengrui and Songyun, as well as many small kindnesses like the daily provision of milk for his tea and bountiful supplies (MD, 163; see 4.8 above).[5] Before he could resolve the mystery, however, his attention was drawn to the emperor's answer to his six requests and reference to a seventh he did not make. Curious and resentful, Macartney confronted Songyun.

In the first place he objected to the fact that the emperor's response clearly separated him from his king, implying that the requests were not the sort George III might have made had he been present. Recalling in his journal Louis XIV's aphorism that "there was no point of honour with such people as the Turks," Macartney reported that he asked Songyun why, when he had made no mention of it, the emperor had refused to allow the British to propagate Christianity in China! Granting that Macartney had not mentioned religion, Songyun speculated that it was probably included on the assumption that the British were like other Europeans.[6] Macartney responded that "the English had been anciently of the same religion as the Portuguese and the other missionaries, and had adopted another, but that one of the principal differences between us and them was our not having the same zeal for making proselytes which they had." This denial was followed by another. For some reason, Macartney observed, the court had concluded that the British were engaged in an "unfair design to obtain exclusive privi-

---

but also managing the British gifts. That was quite a different situation than Songyun now faced. At any rate, the different tone to be found in Songyun's reporting, along with Changlin's behavior toward the British, has led scholars such as Dai Yi (1992:431) and Pierre-Henri Durand (1993a–b) to argue that these two officials were less prejudiced toward foreigners than Heshen, Zhengrui, and other members of the Grand Council. While there are certainly clear differences in the extant reports about the British before and after their departure from Peking, I would argue that the different moments in the ritual process better account for the contrast. Songyun and Changlin were, after all, under orders to bring the ritual process to a swift and satisfactory conclusion.

5. Such considerate treatment was, of course, occurring at the same time that the emperor had ordered a reduction in allowances for the embassy, a fact that Macartney's discerning gaze never seemed to detect.

6. The source of this seventh item may have been the Catholic missionaries in the emperor's service. It also may have had something to do with the rites controversy during the Kangxi reign and problems with missionaries during the Yongzheng reign; see Pritchard 1929:105; Fairbank, Reischauer, and Craig 1978:249–251; and Fu 1966, 1:138–168.

leges" in China. Of course, he had made the request for extending trade on behalf of his government and the East India Company, but had never desired that it should not be extended to others. His concern, he reiterated, was to preserve the trade, and if he failed (again the veiled threat), it would have serious consequences for China. Therefore, he requested that the emperor be asked to draft a third letter that would clarify matters. In pressing for "assurances," Macartney was again seeking the elusive "treaty" or "contract" that would place trade with China on a sound footing. Songyun's response, however, was that since the embassy had left the capital, no additional letter was likely. On the other hand, he told Macartney that every day the emperor was more and more pleased with the embassy (MD, 166–169).

The dialogue between Macartney and Songyun continued along these lines for some time, with the ambassador pressing for an additional letter from the emperor to clarify matters, and the imperial envoy reassuring and "soothing" him by presenting positive assessments of the embassy that he said came from the emperor himself.[7] At the same time, Songyun continued to report that he was having little difficulty with the British (ZPZZ, 26.26 and 26.31), reports which were, in turn, incorporated into imperial instructions and disseminated to relevant jurisdictions (GZSY, QL 58.9.17, 68:117 and QL 58.9.23, 68:139). Hongli's envoy also told Macartney that because of the emperor's concern for the treatment of English merchants at Canton, he had appointed a new governor-general by the name of Changlin to look into matters there (MD, 168). Moreover, as it was now clear that the embassy had missed a rendezvous with the *Lion* in Zhejiang, the blame for which Macartney placed squarely on the court (MD, 171–172), Songyun told the ambassador that Changlin would escort him to Canton. These promises of things to come were coupled with new imperial bestowals to the embassy and rewards for officials who had worked with the embassy, included among which were some of the British local products (GZSY, QL 58.9.23, 68:139–143, 189–190).

These favorable developments led Macartney to enter many laudatory comments about Songyun in his journal, comments which clearly were related to a sense that he was finally beginning to address the business of his

---

7. See, for example, the emperor's instructions of October 21 and 27. In the first of these, Hongli notes that the emissary had probably quieted down by now, but that officials must remember that he was cunning (GZCSL, 1437:4a–b). In the second, the emperor spoke of additional rewards to be given the embassy upon its departure from the Qing empire (GZCSL, 1437:9a–11a).

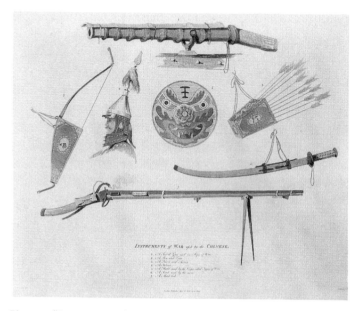

Figure 5. "Instruments of war used by the Chinese." Military intelligence gathered by the British embassy.

embassy with a high-level court official. But success also produced some interesting speculation. As early as October 25, Macartney began to fantasize about the possibility of war between Great Britain and China, and wondered if the court in Peking could be

> ignorant that a couple of British frigates would be an overmatch for the whole naval force of the empire, that in half a summer they could totally destroy all the navigation of their coasts and reduce the inhabitants of the maritime provinces, who subsist chiefly on fish, to absolute famine? (MD, 170)

He also paid closer attention to the garrisons turned out all along his travel route, noting in early November that "these troops have a slovenly, unmilitary air, and their quilted boots and long petticoats make them look *heavy, inactive and effeminate*" (MD, 174; emphasis added). Influenced in part, perhaps, by the differences in military technology (figure 5), by December, he indicated doubts over whether the Qing forces could make anything but a "feeble resistance," leading him to draft a full-blown plan of invasion that would include mobilizing some of the Qing "tributaries" against the dynasty (MD, 203 and 211). And while he attributes to British humanity the fundamental explanation for why force should not be used as long as hope remains for succeeding by gentle means, it also seems clear that the only power Macartney could see benefiting from war, economic collapse, and chaos in China was imperial Russia, that other empire that loomed just over the Qing horizon (MD, 211–213). Such concerns would, of course, become cornerstones in British policy in the next century.[8]

8.3   From Hangzhou to Canton: Changlin and Macartney
(November 9–January 1794)

On November 9, in Hangzhou, Songyun introduced Macartney to the new governor-general of Liangguang, Changlin. At their first meeting, Changlin delivered the additional imperial bestowals announced on October 27. Among them were what Macartney described as the "paper of happiness" written in the emperor's own hand. He prized it as the highest sign of "friendship and affection" that the emperor could give to another prince (MD, 176). While this appears to be something of an overstatement, the transmission of the bestowal by Changlin was significant because it served to organize a relationship between a servant of the emperor now responsible for the jurisdiction to which the English were attached and the ambassador of a lesser king.

Such considerations were important because, like both Zhengrui and Songyun, Changlin was charged with continuing the assessment of Macartney and his retinue. Although his memorials of November and December no longer seem to exist, a court letter from Agui and Heshen indicates that not only did Changlin continue to evaluate the British embassy, but his reports corroborated those of Songyun (GZSY, QL 58.10.28, 68:161–163). The result was that the emperor and his councillors somewhat tempered their earlier harsh judgements.[9] On November 19, for example, Hongli issued an instruction to cancel duties at Macao for one English ship (GZCSL, 1439:3a–

---

8. The competition with Russia over Inner and East Asia was often called the Great Game; see Hevia 1994d.

9. Well into November the emperor continued to use the vermilion brush to warn officials that if one request were granted to the British, others would follow; see GZSY, QL 58.10.10, 68:58.

4a). The following day, the court received via Songyun a petition (*bin*) from Macartney thanking the emperor for his compassion, kindness, and generosity in language consistent with the humility and loyalty demonstrated by his king (*GZSY*, QL 58.10.17, 68:115–118).

In the meantime, Macartney and Changlin were in almost daily contact. In a meeting on November 17, Changlin solicited the ambassador's views on the major problems at Canton, asked for information about improper behavior by imperial officials there, and, like Songyun, attempted to determine British intentions. As on other occasions, Macartney read these direct addresses to "business" as frankness, and responded in kind.

> I told him ... that, from the reception my requests had met with, I naturally concluded that the Court in Pekin [*sic*] to be indifferent, if not unfriendly to Great Britain; and that I should have represented it so in my dispatches home if Songyun had not taken such pains to impress me, as he declared he had the highest authority to do, with the Emperor's favourable sentiments towards us and our concerns, and if he, the Viceroy had not confirmed them at the first conference I had with him in the presence of Songyun. (MD, 181; also see 184)

It would seem, therefore, that the adept actions of Songyun and Changlin had had a salutary effect, indicating that for the time being the Qing court had little to worry about with respect to hostile actions on the part of the British. In fact, Macartney was so buoyed by his exchanges with Songyun and Changlin, so certain that the business of his embassy had begun, that three days later he presented Changlin with his assessment of the conditions of trade at Canton. His evaluation came in the form of requests for changes in the current system.

The first three dealt with the levying of duties. Macartney asked that they be regularized and fixed, with the emperor made aware of them, and that no extra duties be imposed on ships that moved back and forth between Macao and Canton. The fourth and sixth items asked for freedom of movement outside the English factory at Canton, free access to the city, and permission for British merchants to remain at Canton after the trading ships departed. The fifth item asked for the setting aside of a plot of land where sick English seamen could recuperate. Items seven and eight requested permission to trade with merchants other than those in the "hong," while nine asked that the English be allowed to study the Chinese language. Item ten proposed that in the event of a crime committed by an Englishman, only that person be punished. The last read "that the English be not confounded with other Persons who trade to Canton and speak the same language, but are a different Nation and inhabit a very different part of the World, called America" (IOMC, 20:196).[10]

Having already received an answer from the emperor on some of these requests, one wonders why Macartney insisted upon repeating them to Changlin. Perhaps he did not perceive the emperor's earlier answers as relevant to these issues. Or perhaps he felt that now that the real business of his embassy had finally begun, he could reintroduce his basic negotiating position. Whatever the case, the requests, along with a desire that more ports be opened to British trade, succinctly summarize British objectives in China, objectives which would eventually be gained by force a half-century later, after the first Opium War. In this regard, there is one other item that might be mentioned here, one that links these requests to British imperial interests, Macartney's epistemological project, and the concerns of the next generation of Englishmen in China. Macartney "heartily" prayed "that the Chinese Government may adopt a more liberal policy, and open the country to the *free inspection and curiosity* of English travellers" (MD, 199; emphasis added).

Indeed, such "free inspection and curiosity" produced one of the singular successes of his embassy. Recall the instructions of the East India Company to gather information about commodity production in China. In spite of Chinese "jealousy" and "superstition," Macartney not only collected a good deal of information about tea and silk production, but was also able to acquire live specimens of tea plants. He was able to do so by simply asking Changlin, who, having observed the British "curiosity about everything relative to natural history," allowed the removal of several live tea plants from the earth. Macartney intended to ship them to Bengal for cultivation (MD, 186).[11]

This incident indicates a rather interesting contrast in views. Previously, in its evaluation of the embassy following imperial audience, the Qing court

10. After arriving in Canton and discussing the situation there with English supercargos, Macartney amended his list and expanded it to a total of sixteen items; see IOMC, 92:451–460.

11. Also see MD, 291–303 for information gathered by Dr. Gillan on minerals and resources. The tea plants were carried by Dr. Dinwiddie to Calcutta; see Pritchard 1938:501 and Cranmer-Byng's note 57 in MD, 374–375. It is unclear whether anything further came of the experiment.

surmised that the British had come to "spy." From available court records, this appeared to mean the gathering of information about the military strength of the Qing empire. Hence, the court's response was not to hide its power, but to turn out garrisons along Macartney's route and allow him to see what that strength was. The British ambassador, on the other hand, was little concerned or impressed with these displays, except insofar as he thought they were meant to honor the embassy (MD, 202). Meanwhile, Macartney gathered information he perceived to be of commercial value and found that by asking, it was freely given to him. For an official like Changlin, the sort of "knowledge" that Macartney valued appears to have been just another case of showing kindness to men from afar, kindness which produced other "triumphs" as well.

On December 9, for example, Changlin announced receipt of an imperial instruction (GZCSL, 1439:13a–15a). In it the emperor briefly reviewed the encounter to date and indicated that another embassy from the English king would be welcome. Requesting a copy for translation (see IOMC, 92: 431–436), Macartney noted in his journal that the emperor also indicated that any future contact should be via Canton, implying a "sort of disapprobation" of the embassy having sailed north to the Gulf of Beizhili. "Nevertheless," he notes, "I would not for any consideration that we had not, as by these means we are now masters of the geography of the north-east coasts of China, and have acquired a knowledge of the Yellow Sea, which was never before navigated by European ships" (MD, 193). While perhaps overstating his case, the significance of this passage lies in how productive Macartney assumed his defiance to have been. The kind of knowledge he refers to here, much of which now existed as a result of his "free inspection and curiosity" and his acquisition of specimens of China's natural history and commodity production, was immeasurably more valuable than any accompanying censure from the emperor. There is, in other words, discernible at this level of practical material production an imperial project, one that specifically couples disavowal (we have given them no reason to treat us irrationally) with defiance as a means for producing knowledge that demonstrated British superiority. (It also looks like the priorities of spies.)[12]

12. The embassy's new knowledge of China was widely disseminated in Europe and North America through the publication of George Staunton's account in 1797. The work included a separate volume of drawings and diagrams, including figures 1 through 3, and 5, reproduced in this volume. There were also a number of etchings from drawings done by William Alexander, as well as navigation charts of the China coast and profile

Given the failure of the British gifts to transform Tartar and Chinese perceptions of the British, these sorts of "victories" were important to Macartney. Perhaps no better example of this display of "superiority" is evident than in one of his conversations with Changlin. Macartney's account of this meeting stands out in part because it embodies a narrative structure that in the next century will be repeatedly recycled in official sources and British imperial literature. The incident became, in other words, a cliche, and therein lies its power.

On the evening of December 4, Macartney and Changlin were comfortably chatting. With few attendants about, Macartney, having noticed that Changlin's pipe had gone out, took from his pocket a "phosphoric bottle" and kindled a match instantly. "The singularity of a man's carrying fire in his fob without damage," Macartney writes,

> startled him a good deal. I therefore explained to him the phenomenon and made him a present of it. This little incident led to a conversation upon other curious subjects, from which it appeared to us how far the Chinese (although they excel in some branches of mechanics) are yet behind other nations in medical or surgical skill and philosophic knowledge. (MD, 190) [13]

Thus, Macartney became a teacher expounding on the wonders of the Western world. And the reaction? Changlin and his companions "seemed as if awakened out of a dream, and could not conceal their regret for the Court's coldness and indifference to our discoveries," all of which served to elevate Macartney's opinion of them and, perhaps more importantly, to clarify for him the problem of China. Demonstrating a marked change in attitude since the era of the more liberal minded Kangxi, he wrote, the current government, suspicious of innovation, was bent upon "arresting the progress of human knowledge." Yet Macartney was also optimistic; he was certain that any attempt to halt progress would ultimately be in vain because of the soaring nature of the human mind, of the certainty of "com-

---

sketches of Chusan Island and the Shandong peninsula. In the latter case, the drawing indicates that portions of the physical landscape were named after Macartney, Staunton, and Admiral Gower. A collection of Alexander's drawings and paintings of the embassy is in three volumes at the India Office Library, London, while the British Museum holds a two-volume collection. Also see Conner and Sloman 1981.

13. One exception was "hydraulics," about which Macartney had a good deal to say; see MD, 272–274.

mon sense," which, rather significantly, his "enlightened" universalism did not exclude from the Chinese character. Put another way, his gesture toward a universal human nature allows him (1) to doubt if the "Tartar government" would be able "to stifle the energies of their Chinese subjects" for much longer and (2) to assert a commonality between the British and Chinese: both can be proud and vain (MD, 191 and 215).

It is here, then, in this simple exercise of Macartney's show-and-tell, and Changlin's recognition and acknowledgment of British technical superiority, that the imperial project becomes grounded in an inevitability, in an unmistakable certainty that, as Macartney put it, "a better knowledge of the better parts of our character will calm their disquiets, weaken their prejudices and wear away their ill-impressions." Like a force of nature, knowledge generated from public-sphere attributes and values would provide the transcendence necessary for the Chinese to overcome their "jealousy" and for the British to subdue their "contempt of others," allowing both peoples to realize that they were "men formed of the same material and governed by the same passions" (MD, 215). These assertions of commonality, which at the same time maintained British superiority, were, in the end, why Macartney could not but see his embassy as a success.

On December 19, 1793, the embassy arrived in Canton and was feasted by Changlin, Guo Shixun, and Suleng'e, commissioner of customs at Canton. Sometime in this period, Changlin wrote a point-by-point response to Macartney's eleven requests and to five others that were submitted in Canton. First, he temporarily reduced the duties between Canton and Macao, while repeating the court's reasons about why duties could not be fixed. He also promised justice and a greater degree of communication with the supercargos, looked favorably on the idea of a hospital for sailors, and agreed to allow Chinese to teach British students the Chinese language. He added that officials would now note the difference between the English and Americans (Fu 1966, 1:327–331, and Pritchard 1936:366).[14]

These various "successes" led Macartney to emphasize in his reports to London that the objective of providing the Chinese with a more accurate view of British national character and of producing useful knowledge about

---

14. In addition, on January 1, 1794, Changlin announced two proclamations. Although neither appears in the court record, the English language version promised severe punishment for anyone harming or practicing extortion against Europeans; see IOMC 92: 467–486.

China for consumption by the British government, the East India Company, and the British public had been accomplished. In a letter written to Henry Dundas on December 23 at Canton, for example, Macartney made it clear that in spite of the conspiracies he suspected afoot in Peking, particularly regarding misrepresentations of the British establishment in Bengal by Fukang'an, he was fairly sure that going directly to the emperor had produced a number of good results, in particular the invitation for a second embassy. He suggested that the British government seize this opportunity to send another ambassador to Peking, both to build on his own successes and to correct the slanderous statements about the British in Bengal (IOMC, 20:191–194).

The same day, he wrote a lengthy report to the Company detailing his accomplishments. In addition to announcing his success at acquiring tea plants, mulberry trees, and silkworm cocoons, Macartney also noted a number of encouraging signs that might be significant for the extension of British trade in China. In particular, he was excited about the prospects for finer British woolens such as "fleecy hosiery" to penetrate the vast China market. Also encouraging was the fact that the Chinese seemed to understand the advantages derived from the division of labor, suggesting that equivalencies might exist in labor costs between the two nations that would allow the Company to realize a reasonable profit on Chinese manufactures.[15] Moreover, the Chinese, unlike Europeans, held no prejudice about exchanging bullion for acceptable goods. While these elements might work in favor of the extension of trade, Macartney also pointed out that the greatest advantage would be secured by penetrating commodity-producing areas in China. Provided Company authorities could control the behavior of British seamen, he thought this entirely possible. Such control was important because China's despotic government was suspicious of any activities that might threaten the tranquillity and submission of the population it ruled. At the same time, some officials were receptive to the British; Macartney had taught those in Canton the difference between British sub-

15. In a letter to Sir John Shore, governor-general of Bengal, written in February 1794 from Macao, Macartney was somewhat less enthusiastic concerning the prospects for British trade. In this letter, he reviewed a number of circumstances that presently "impeded" the further introduction of British manufactures into China. Among these were the age of the emperor and his disinclination to change, and the cautious nature of the government, which of late had been exacerbated by reports from Europe of the French revolution; see Pritchard 1938:498–499.

jects and Americans, whom the Chinese had now learned to distinguish under the name "Yankies" (IOMC, 20:203–211).

Meanwhile, having learned that England and France were now at war, Macartney turned his attention to making sure a sufficient naval force was on hand near Canton to insure the safe passage of the embassy to England. As he prepared for departure, Macartney determined to build upon the friendship he felt now existed between himself and Changlin. On January 8, he invited the governor-general and local officials to the British factory for breakfast with himself and the East India Company supercargos. The Qing officials promised the British merchants access and special attention. Later that day, Wang and Qiao, in tears and showing marks of "sensibility and concern" that could only come from "sincere and uncorrupted hearts," took leave of the embassy (MD, 216). On January 15, the Canton garrison turned out as Macartney left Canton for Macao. As had so often been the case, he closed his journal with a contradictory gesture. The knowledge generated by the encounter convinced him that "nothing could be more fallacious than to judge China by any European standard." At the same time, he did not "flatter" himself that his recorded observations could "be of much advantage or entertainment to others" (MD, 221–222). How serious are we to take such modesty from a member of the Literary Club?

Word of Macartney's departure appears to have reached Peking a week or so later. On January 25, 1794, the Grand Council formally announced the culmination of imperial Guest Ritual: the British had departed the Qing empire to return to their kingdom. Aware now of war between Great Britain and France, the councillors entered one final note of speculation about why the embassy had bothered to come. Perhaps, they observed, the British sought an ally in their war against France (GZSY, QL 58.12.24, 68:207–212). An impossibility, of course, since Qianlong *huangdi,* the supreme lord, was enjoined to cherish all men from afar and treat them with equal benevolence and compassion.

9 GUEST RITUAL AND DIPLOMACY

Qing imperial Guest Ritual and British diplomatic protocols each incorporated practices for organizing political relations between domains and within powerful imperial formations. Although the ways they accomplished such tasks differed, the two sets of practices and the assumptions that informed them made equally universalistic claims. Moreover, both the Qing court and members of the British embassy could take a certain amount of satisfaction from the fact that their mode of producing relations of power had uncovered or detected strengths and weaknesses in the other. Neither party, however, was able to move very far outside its own particular version of world-constituting practices, nor is there any particular reason to expect them to have done so, particularly when the Qing leadership and Lord Macartney seemed to have concluded that as a result of their meeting they understood the other better than previously. However, the evaluations that emerged were not ones in which the parties shared a definition of the situation. Rather, there was an implicit sense that if either side had accepted the other's version of sovereignty, their own claims would have been significantly undermined.

Lord Macartney's demarcation between ceremony and business, with its specific construction of diplomatic and commercial exchange, could not easily be reconciled with Qing views on the ritual formation of imperial sovereignty. Nor was his deployment of an epistemology based on individualistic enlightened reason in any way compatible with the Qing court's centering process, where knowledge was produced in multiple-agent evaluations of actions involving many actors and numerous temporal sequences. The incommensurability between these modes of action and evaluation produced irreconcilable political differences, differences which were probably only resolvable if one of the parties chose to impose its views on the other. The objects Lord Macartney had brought as gifts for the Qianlong emperor provided a focal point of these differences.

As part of his claim to *represent* universal structures of commercial and international relations, the British ambassador attempted to differentiate the British crown from the East India Company and the gifts he had brought for the Qianlong emperor from the goods the Company wished to trade in China. In making these distinctions, Macartney invested the former with meanings apart from and in excess of the "market value" of the items. The Qing court interpreted this strategy as a claim of superiority and read it as "arrogance" and "ingeniousness." In his poem at the time of imperial audience and in his instructions to George III, the Qianlong emperor distinguished between attributes associated with the most precious things of the domain and the unseemly attributes presumed present in Lord Macartney's claims about the British gifts.

There were at least two discernible effects of the distinction drawn by Hongli in these documents. First, it separated the gifts brought by the embassy from items traded by the British at Canton on the basis of different modes of practice, rather than on the basis of the kinds of things involved. In other words, the court did not treat the gifts as either *representations of* scientific virtue or commodities. This allowed Hongli to maintain that imperial bestowals and local products (*fangwu*) embodied human attributes and were only distinguishable on the basis of the particular context in which they appeared. One suspects that the same logic was at work when Changlin granted Macartney permission to take tea plants, mulberry trees, and silkworm cocoons from China. As the official now most responsible for cherishing these men from afar, Changlin did not treat the items Macartney requested as commodities, but rather as precious things appropriate for bestowing on the servants of the British king. Secondly, in considering the British gifts from the point of view of what might be done with them, the court perceived that certain technologies, the cannon aboard a ship like the *Lion* for instance, posed a threat. This was not because cannon per se were dangerous, but because they could be in the hands of the British. This may explain why British accounts indicate that Hongli showed interest in British gifts such as the model of the *Royal Sovereign* and, at the same time, dismissed the gifts as toys fit for children.[1]

---

1. See Waley-Cohen 1993:1534, citing Staunton, and Proudfoot 1868:53.

The encounter was further complicated by the British division between "ceremonial" presentation and reason-centered "negotiation." Since the Qing court viewed Guest Ritual as a continuous and seamless process with a discernible source and culmination, and was as a result uninterested in drawing such a distinction, it organized Macartney's repeated requests for an opening of the business of his embassy as yet another example of arrogant importunity on the part of these particular West Ocean people.

The irreconcilable differences that emerged in the encounter were also informed by opposing views of the constitution of superiority and inferiority. In the case of the Qing imperium, superior and inferior were realized through complex dialogues continually working toward the inclusion of the powers of others in the emperor's rulership. In the naturalized and naturalizing discourse of the British, superiority and inferiority were intrinsic to agents, aspects of their nature. Under the guise of the mutual recognition of sovereigns, superiority as a self-evident proposition was displayed and benefits flowed from it in the natural direction, from upper to lower. I want to take up these different notions of power in turn, beginning with a discussion of Qing Guest Ritual and rulership.

9.1   Guest Ritual and the Fashioning of the Qing Imperium

In forming hierarchical relations that drew for their coherence on powerful cosmic ordering principles embedded in higher-order rites (a relationship that British imperial representatives remained ignorant of throughout the remainder of the Qing dynasty), Qing Guest Ritual retained the attributes of difference among lesser kings in such a way that their own proper management of their kingdoms could not only be acknowledged, but organized in relation to the extension of the supreme lord's virtue and grace throughout the world. The Qing insistence on including and positioning difference with respect to these criteria of rulership might be seen as a unique response to real sociopolitical conditions in the world, a response that recognized ambiguity in interdomainal relations, particularly with the lords of Inner Asia. Rather than suppress this ambiguity, Guest Ritual appeared to comment on it. In the British embassy, this element of supreme lord-lesser lord relations came out most clearly in Lord Macartney's audience with the emperor at Rehe.

In the audience, the emperor and his councillors summarized the nature of the encounter between the Qing imperium and the *Yingjili* kingdom as it had emerged in the centering process. This summation provided a sense of an initial temporal culmination, achieved by pivoting significant elements of the relationship that had emerged through time onto a spatial plane where current conditions in the world and the history of Qing rulership were brought into conjunction. In other words, characteristics of the encounter that had previously been evident in a diachronic dimension (greeting and preparation) were organized in the synchronic plane (audience).

This suggests that the fashioning of the Qing imperium was more than a dialogue involving the present transformations of the world; it was also a dialogue between the emperor and his ancestors (maintained by means of announcements in the ancestral temple) that worked continually to reposition the present supreme lord vis-à-vis prior lordly experiences. Through text editing (the investigation and compilation of the deeds of rulers and the current emperor, and the rewriting of rites), the actions of imperial ancestors were continually incorporated into the reigning emperor's rulership in a process (analogous to the incorporation of lesser lords) that evaluated former procedures on the basis of the degree to which they could converge with the current state of the world.[2]

At the same time as the past was incorporated into the present, the future was also addressed. A second important outcome of the British embassy was that it provided a precedent, one that included and superseded the Portuguese embassy of 1753 (Qianlong 18). Moreover, the British precedent was invoked within a year of Macartney's departure from Canton when the Dutch in Batavia sent an embassy to Peking under the leadership of A. E. van Braam. Arriving in time for New Year's festivities, rather than the em-

---

2. The Preface to Kingly Ritual (*Wangli*) found in the HCWXTK contains an essay that clarifies the relation between editing ritual texts and the production of the kingly domain; see 125:2a. The following example is one among many references on this relationship.

> Shizu (Shunzhi) united China with the exterior, determined the correct rites, and created the proper music for the court. He dipped into that which was appropriate in the past and present. By means of investigating transformations and numerous texts from prior ages, he published a new set of orders for the sagely court.

Succeeding emperors were then said to extend, expand, and introduce new elements into the ongoing production of ritual texts. Following the Preface, the Kingly Rites section of the HCWXTK continues with lengthy entries on alterations to rituals under successive reigns prior to that of the Qianlong emperor.

peror's birthday celebration, the Dutch experience was somewhat different from that of the British. The Qianlong emperor invited them to his residence in the "Forbidden City," the Palace of Peaceful Old Age (Ningshou gong) where they watched theatricals, granted them audience in the Hall of Protecting Harmony (Baohe dian), and received them in a second audience at the Pavilion of Purple Brightness (Ziguang ge) in the Middle Lake Garden (Zhonghai). While the treatment of the Dutch might be understood as marks of special favor, ones that could have been related to the fact that they had sent embassies during the reigns of other Qing emperors,[3] elements of their reception were partly drawn from the most recent West Ocean embassy (*GZSY*, QL 59.12.1, 71:1). Records of the British embassy were to determine, among other things, imperial bestowals.

The Macartney embassy was also important to the Qing management of a second British embassy, that of Lord Amherst to the court of the Jiaqing emperor in 1816 (Jiaqing 21). Even a cursory review of the court records indicates that the Macartney embassy served as a guide for planning the reception and activities for Lord Amherst.[4] For reasons that may have involved more than the classifications of the first British embassy, namely ongoing conflicts in Canton between English merchants and local officials, the court determined that it would not follow the audience procedure outlined above for the Macartney embassy. In particular, the preparation of the embassy was much stricter, with the court going so far as to issue Amherst a written description of the audience in which he was expected to participate.[5]

3. See Duyvendak 1939:61–66 and Fu 1966, 1:332–334. The extent to which the particulars of this embassy were forgotten is marked in part by the fact that when Euro-American forces invaded Peking in 1900 and marched through the palace complex, many foreigners assumed that this was the first time "white men" had entered these "sacred" precincts; see Hevia 1990b.

4. See the various references to the Macartney embassy in *WXCB*, 10:1–12 and 11:13–40. Fu provides translations of some of the relevant sources as found in the *Veritable Records of the Jiaqing Emperor;* see 1966, 1:402–407.

5. The text may have been taken from the Guest Ritual section of the *Comprehensive Rites of the Great Qing* or from the audience protocol prepared for the Macartney embassy (see chapter 7). An English translation probably done by George Staunton is in IOAC, 197:321–327, and Ellis 1817:497. References to be found in Fu, who cites *QJQCWJSL* 5, indicate that much of the record of the Macartney embassy must have been reviewed; see 1966, 2:618 n. 200.

As a young boy, Staunton had accompanied his father on the Macartney embassy and later lived for a number of years in Macao, becoming proficient in the Chinese language;

In addition, the Jiaqing court appears to have focused attention on the specifics of the earlier ceremony, in which, as we know, Macartney knelt on one knee in presenting his king's communication to the emperor. This time the ceremony of three kneelings and nine bows was not to be altered, and officials conducting the embassy to the court were to instruct the ambassador in this rite. According to Amherst's account, the embassy was rushed to the capital, where, upon arriving, they were to have an immediate audience with the emperor. In the hasty transport, the embassy became dispersed and Amherst found himself without his credentials. Suspecting some sinister motive on the part of the Chinese court, Amherst asked that the audience be delayed because he was fatigued. He also refused to attend an audience with high officials, whereupon a court physician arrived to ask questions regarding the ambassador's health. The next day as he prepared for the audience, Amherst was told that the embassy had been ordered to leave the capital.[6]

Records of the Amherst embassy indicate, therefore, that the court concerned itself with classifications arrived at during the Macartney embassy, for example that the English did not understand proper ceremonial relations. This classification emerged from, among other things, Macartney's refusal on grounds of sickness to attend an audience with high officials when he arrived at Rehe, the confusion that was generated over the forms of the court ceremony, and Macartney's refusal to comply with various responses to his requests. From this pattern, it is not difficult to understand why Amherst's audience was canceled, for once again a serious question had arisen about the sincerity of the ambassador. Like his father, the Jiaqing emperor accepted the gifts of the English king, while clearly differentiating the ambassador from his king in the instruction that was sent to George III (Fu 1966, 1:404–405).

Following the dismissal of the Amherst embassy, the emperor became aware of certain irregularities in the treatment of the English by the conducting officials.[7] For example, the emperor wondered why the ambassador

---

see Cameron 1976:316. The Qing imperium was aware of this and suspected Staunton of being a source of trouble in Macao; see WXCB 10:9b, and Fu 1966, 1:394.

6. See IOAC, 197:285–291. Fu has argued that the main cause of the failure of the embassy should be placed on George Staunton; see 1966, 2:619–620 n. 205.

7. One of these officials was Suleng'e, the same person who was commissioner of customs at Canton when Macartney returned there from Peking. Earlier comments concerning knowledge, experience, and the position an agent occupies are worth recalling. At the same time, it is clear that knowledge and experience are not enough to guarantee the dexterous management of affairs.

had been brought to the capital, if he was unwilling to comply with the required ceremony. He also admonished officials for not informing him that one of the reasons that the ambassador had refused to appear in audience was because his ceremonial dress was in the baggage that had not yet arrived in Peking. The officials responsible were punished and the emperor drafted an instruction to the English clarifying the mismanagement of the embassy by his own officials (Fu 1966, 1:405–407, and IOAC, 197:335–338).

The outcome of the second encounter between the Qing court and Great Britain encourages some general observations about agency and action within centering processes. Centering is one means by which vast and complex hierarchical relations are constituted through the activities of multiple agents, agents who are neither unitary individuals nor individuals who engage in strictly voluntaristic action. Agency in such a process is contingent upon both historical events and the specific actors involved in the temporal process under way. In other words, while each position in the hierarchy is unique (a condition to be distinguished from the uniqueness of persons), it only becomes so in practice, where positions are mutually constituted. What appears significant in the construction of these subject positions is that they are produced by resolving inappropriate actions within a meritorious undertaking and by channeling, through rewards and punishments, appropriate actions in the proper direction for such an undertaking.

In this scheme of action, responsibility for knowing and doing are bound up in the position a participant occupies. For example, in the guest rite the emperor is positioned as the south-facing king who instructs, admonishes, cherishes, bestows rewards, accepts pious offerings, and receives information, advice, and requests from those below. These are the tasks attached to his position, the various aspects of which can be taken for granted; what is salient in practice, though, is the virtuosity with which he performs his imperial duties. The emperor's intervention becomes critical for orienting the temporal process he has helped set in motion, especially when clear category mistakes have been made by otherwise adept officials.

One may surmise, therefore, that the position he occupies, unlike that of other participants, is the only one which offers the possibility of grasping the totality of actions involved in the temporal process under way. From this vantage point, the deeds of participants and the unintended consequences of their actions can be viewed and, if necessary, corrected. This suggests that the points where he chooses to intervene are fundamentally constitutive of the specific process. Or, put another way, since there is no general case of Guest Ritual, since all actions are caught up in concrete practical performances, it is precisely the timing and direction of individual interventions that produce the specific encounter between the imperium and lesser lords.

Slightly different observations can be made about those below the emperor. Their tasks are also contingent on the positions they occupy and their deeds affect the centering process, but their view of the whole is limited by such positioning. Recall, for example, the issue of the investigating ship (6.2.2). Changlin might, in other circumstances, have been praised for bringing Ma Yu's actions to the emperor's attention. But his singular failure to act appropriately in the case at hand led the emperor to remind his officials clearly of what was expected of them in their positions. (Much the same could be said concerning the Jiaqing emperor's admonitions to his officials.) When, however, Changlin's actions corresponded to imperial intentions as embodied in the category "meritorious undertaking," he was rewarded, praised, and eventually promoted.

The second encounter between the Qing and British empires also helps to clarify earlier observations about a "patterning" discourse, particularly in view of the correspondences and categorical affiliations that probably served as the basis for dismissing the second embassy prior to audience. Moreover, the treatment of the Amherst embassy highlights the significance of Guest Ritual in the formation of interdomainal relations. Ritual practice appears radically historical when understood as the processes by which embassies from lesser kings were evaluated, differentiated, and incorporated into an encompassing imperial sovereignty that included the Cosmos and imperial ancestors. A broader understanding of these processes prevents the tendency to reify and abstract ritual, and makes it less plausible to assert that the fundamental cause of nineteenth-century conflicts between the Qing empire and the "modern West" lies in the incompatibility between "Chinese culture" and "Western business."

In its self-consciously reflexive dialogue between present and past imperial formations, the rulership of the Qianlong emperor embodied a coherent Manchu moral leadership over "all under Heaven." Organizing the Manchu domain by means of ritual practice, the Qianlong emperor made a claim to supreme lordship. This claim was, however, subject to contestation in similar (i.e., ritual) terms on the part of lesser lords. In the context of this inherently political ritual discourse, the historical positioning of Qing compilations of ritual manuals (as well as a wide variety of other texts) under Qianlong's auspices takes on additional significance.[8] The conjoining of ritual practice with textual production might be viewed as a specific response to political conditions in East Asia, through which a claim was made to organize both spatial (i.e., the Manchu kingly domain and its outer dependencies) and temporal (i.e., relations to past reigns, and conditions for future peace and prosperity) dimensions of the world.

9.2   Lord Macartney and Diplomacy

Lord Macartney concluded that British diplomatic procedures and public sphere discourse had combined to produce a diplomatic triumph, one which while far from complete, had inaugurated a process that would eventually produce ever more spectacular results.[9] Upon the embassy's return to England in the fall of 1794, Macartney and British secretary of state Henry Dundas moved swiftly to assure the advantages gained in the encounter with the Qing court. At first they thought of sending Sir George Staunton as the king's minister to the imperial court, but had to abandon the plan when he became ill. Instead, they dispatched a number of letters and gifts in the spring of 1795 which arrived in China near the end of the year. This correspondence is of particular interest because it includes the

8. The following can be added to the projects noted in chapter 2: the QLHD (1761), HCTD (1785), and the HCTZ (1785). Zito has written extensively on text production and ritual action; see 1989, 1993, and forthcoming.

9. In England, however, not everyone shared his views. See Pindar 1794–1795, 3:265– 307, 469–473; M. Thomas 1794; and Winterbottom, who argued that the embassy was "better calculated to succeed with a nation of Indians or with a petty African Prince, than the government of China; for if the Court of Peking was to be swayed by splendour, much more ought to have been done" (1795, cited in Pritchard 1936:374). Such conclusions were given added weight from the account by Lord Macartney's servant, Aeneas Anderson, who wrote that the embassy entered Peking like "paupers," remained there like "prisoners," and left like "vagrants" (1795:181).

For a more supportive analysis of the embassy, see *Gentleman's Magazine* for August 1794. In accounting for the limited accomplishments of the embassy, it laid the blame on "Native Princes of India" who had warned the Chinese that once the British had gotten a "footing among them," they had built "an immense empire for themselves" (64: 708–710). Three years later, on the occasion of the publication of Sir George Staunton's account of the embassy, the *Annual Register* published an equally sympathetic review (1797:473–479).

new "useful knowledge" thought to have been accumulated by the embassy in its dealings with Chinese officials.

Five letters in all were sent, each of which was addressed from one British official to his presumed counterpart among those Chinese officials with whom Macartney had apparently dealt successfully. Each of the letters was written in a personal and familiar tone, which was meant to exemplify the more friendly relationship Macartney had cultivated. They began with a letter from the king to the emperor in which gratitude was expressed over the treatment of the embassy. After this "ceremonial" opening, the letter moved on to important "business" by clarifying the situation between the British dominions in Bengal and the Chinese territories in Tibet and concluded by promising that a representative of the king would soon arrive in Canton and proceed to the imperial court when the emperor desired. Following the king's message were letters from Dundas and Macartney to Changlin, and from the chairman of the East India Company to Changlin and the Customs Commissioner or "Hoppo." Each of these letters confirmed in writing the results of the negotiations between Macartney and Canton officials (IOMC, 93:327–330 and 345–374).

An anonymous instruction in the India Office collection of records took up the handling of the letters, each of which was translated into Latin and Chinese. After observing that the translations should bear the king's seal in order to provide "more Authenticity," the instruction continued:

> The original English and the Latin and Chinese Translation should be put in a small Silken bag of Yellow Colour for the Emperor, just large enough to contain the Letters, and the bag kept from being soiled, by being wrapped up in yellow Paper or linen but the Silk bag only containing the Letter in the three Languages to be delivered in form to the Viceroy, after taking it out of the outside wrapper in his presence by the Chief Servant of the Company at Canton.

> The letter for the Viceroy may be put in a bag of green Silk. Among the Chinese, the smaller the Character the more elegant. (IOMC, 93:361)

English concern with ceremonial form is here encoded through a literal mirroring of Chinese signs viewed as significant by the ambassador. Thus, the packaging of the letters in a manner reminiscent of the emperor's communication to the English king, the multiple translations, and assumptions

made concerning what would impress the Qing court all work within a process of establishing equivalent affiliations between British and Chinese categories, thus affirming the achievement of sovereign equality. This process
was extended by the organization of the gifts that accompanied the letters.
They were divided into two groups, one to the emperor and the other to the
Viceroy and Hoppo of Canton, and graded on the basis of quality and rank.

   Taken as a whole, this communication to the emperor and imperial officials at Canton was designed to continue the dialogue that the embassy
believed it had established with the Qing court and to confirm the optimism that had been generated over the possibility of dealing reasonably
with the Chinese. Like the embassy itself, it was organized around assumptions about "oriental" courts that had been confirmed by the embassy, and
included new knowledge that had been accumulated as a result of the care-
ful observations and record keeping of Lord Macartney.

   However, while further communications were sent to China in 1804 and
1811, a king's commissioner was not sent out. The successes that Macartney
thought his embassy had gained were not pursued. The British government,
distracted as it was for some years by the revolutionary developments on
the European continent, did not send another embassy until that of Lord
Amherst in 1816. By then, whatever advantages Lord Macartney seemed to
have gained no longer existed. Instead, as noted above, the Jiaqing court
reviewed the historical record of the embassy, took tensions in Canton into
account, and organized the greeting and preparation phase of Guest Ritual
accordingly.

9.3   An Engagement

   In many ways, the first British embassy to China was a landmark event.
For virtually the first time in its relations with peoples from the West Ocean,
the Qing empire found substantial cause for concern about these particular
men from afar. The British, it would seem, were different from the Portuguese or Dutch; and that point was brought home even more forcefully the
next year when the Dutch arrived and complied with the usual forms of
court protocol. Yet, even granting the court's interest in British technology
and commerce, it is doubtful that the Qing imperium anticipated fully the
threat the British now posed. But then, it is unlikely that Lord Macartney
did either. Indeed, Peter Marshall's insight that Macartney was not Lord
Palmerston also points to certain historical discontinuities between 1793
and 1839 (1993:29).

The British imperialism that emerged in the nineteenth century would break many of the old rules, particularly in the case of China, where it would develop a form of colonialism increasingly dependent upon and driven by technological innovations. The steamship, railroad, telegraph, and rapid-fire weapons, none of which existed in the worlds of either the Qianlong emperor or Lord Macartney, allowed nineteenth-century Englishmen not only to realize the objectives of the Macartney embassy by other means, but to avoid the expense of constructing the sort of political-administrative structure that the British had found necessary for the exploitation of India. At the same time, this unprecedented access to China was paralleled by a new form of colonial penetration: the systematic gathering of comprehensive knowledge about China, much of which took as its object of investigation imperial textual sources, that could be deployed to manipulate the Qing political scene (see Hevia 1994d). The combination of technological versatility and comprehensive knowledge allowed for a colonial presence that could operate without direct political control.

There are, however, other aspects of the late eighteenth-century encounter that provide something like a sense of continuity between the Qianlong reign and the mid-nineteenth century. Some of these are apparent, for example, in the audience question. The waiving of koutou and its replacement with the British ambassador kneeling on one knee invites a consideration of what meanings may have been ascribed to such physical actions in audience ceremonies by Europeans and Qing actors. For Macartney, ritual gestures were less significant in themselves than in terms of some external symbolic order of reference. While he dismissed many ordinary rituals of politeness as "tricks of behavior" (MD, 222), he saw "genuflexions and prostrations" as a possible means of representing political reciprocity, hence his suggestion that an imperial official perform obeisance to his portrait of George III. His separation of ceremony and "business," exemplified here in an attempt to achieve ceremonial reciprocity, betrays an assumption that national sovereignty could be the fixed referent or meaning of an equal exchange of (essentially arbitrary) ceremonial symbols. Such bodily symbols, once exchanged, could only refer to exterior universal realities, namely the internal homogeneity and bounded exclusiveness of sovereign nations. In theory, at least, either a reciprocal koutou or the unilateral performance of an "English" ceremony, could become for Macartney a *representation* of something universal, a mutual acknowledgment of the natural order of relations between states. This perception of bodily action in diplomatic practice, I would suggest, remained fairly constant for Englishmen and other Europeans over the next one hundred or more years. More importantly perhaps, dealings with the Qing court politicized these assumptions and made them objects of contestation.

In this formulation, the bodily movements of Macartney or any other European diplomat before the emperor could not be read as a signifying practice that in itself was constitutive of contingent and continuing relationships. It could only represent or express, at the moment of exchange, the transcendent truth of the internal unity of British and Chinese sovereignty, the *symbolic* recognition of which was the task of "ceremony." Only after this task was completed could the "business" of the embassy proceed. Therefore, a unilateral koutou was dangerous precisely because, by implying allegiance to a nonreciprocating sovereign, it would have destabilized the unity and exclusivity of the type of sovereignty Macartney represented. He would have aborted his mission precisely at the moment it was to have begun in earnest.

In this respect, two further aspects of Macartney's audience with the emperor Qianlong are worth noting. First, recall that following the presentation of his king's letter, Macartney treated the remainder of the day's activities as grandiose displays that, from the position of objective observer, he narrated. Not realizing that the intended "audience" was not simply the human beings present, but a more cosmic order of forms, he believed that the transition from ceremony to "business" in diplomacy had occurred. Therefore, his account attributed to the participants certain presuppositions Macartney had brought with him to China: Asians love pomp; the Chinese judge people on the basis of "external appearance"; the emperor's rule is absolutist and despotic in nature. Second, his "success" regarding the altered form of his audience with the emperor convinced him, in turn, that much of the ritual he saw was mere spectacle for the consumption of the unenlightened, and that China's so-called "immutable laws" would dissolve when met with firmness.

The particular view Macartney offered of ritual became a staple in British thinking in the next century, and equally important, can still be found in contemporary interpretations. With certain modifications, historians continue to separate ceremony from Qing statecraft. Echoing Macartney, they then argue that when the former was in play, the court was essentially caught up in the world of appearances in its relations with Western powers (see 1.4 above). Such reliance on illusion provides, in turn, reasonable explanation for the inability of the Qing court to respond creatively to the Western challenge from the first Opium War forward.

I have attempted to argue against this construction of Qing politics throughout this study, particularly those aspects of it that fail to make a distinction between Chinese civilization and the Qing empire, as well as between "the West" and British imperialism. Instead, I have attempted to refigure the encounter between the Qianlong court and the British as one between two expansive empires, each with its own definition of its concerns and its own security requirements.

In considering the Qing account, my emphasis has been on the way in which the Qianlong emperor and his grand councillors organized the complex agent that was the Qing imperium. Their evaluation of the problem posed by the British or for that matter, Tibetan lamas, was not informed by a neat split between mind and body, between rationality and irrationality, between religion and worldly affairs, or between statecraft and ritual practice, but rather on the ways and means for organizing political power in a world of flux and ultimate indeterminacy. Their solution was the centering process, a mode of action and evaluation that operated within and across emerging patterns, working to channel action away from extremes and toward sites and moments of clarity, however contingent and epiphenomenal they might be. Centering enabled the court to make a number of practical decisions throughout embassies concerning the state of the ritual process, the actions of court officials, and, in this case, the attitudes of the British ambassador and his retinue. It also allowed Qing imperial agents to make a variety of assessments about the British gifts, especially the triviality of some and the potential danger of others.

These particular aspects of the way in which the Qing court organized the encounter with the British had other implications as well. The overwhelming emphasis in ritual texts on the position and disposition of bodies in ceremonial space meant that ritual actions constituted a cosmo-political order in highly consequential ways. To have an imperial official koutou to a picture of the English king, especially outside an ongoing ritual process, might, therefore, have been viewed as logically preposterous. Yet, the court was also bound to include and differentiate the British king and his kingdom or terminate the rite. Since Heshen and other grand councillors had determined that Macartney was sincerely loyal after he arrived in Rehe, Hongli hesitated to end the encounter prior to audience. Instead, he and his advisors were willing to accept within the imperial audience an act of bodily signification appropriate to the English king's kingdom. Macartney's act of kneeling on one knee and bowing his head, the allowance of which one can assume to have been another sign of differentiation, was understood to be no more and no less than a spatial inscription which still realized a supreme lord–lesser lord relationship. In the formation of this relationship, kneeling, like koutou, completed inclusion and differentiation: it provisionally incorporated the strength of the English king in the emperor's rulership.

The audience participated in by Macartney demonstrates quite clearly the degree to which the Qing court was willing to alter a rite in order to realize its own perception of how relations between superior and inferior lords ought to be formed. That koutou could be waived and other actions introduced that would accomplish the same purpose raises interesting questions concerning the nature of conflict between the Qing and British empires in the nineteenth century. Not the least of these is whether to reconsider many areas of contestation in terms of the difference between two modes of ceremony: signifying practices, understood as constitutive of relations of power in a cosmo-political imperial formation, and "symbolic" representations, which are taken to express or reflect transcendent realities of power in a world of discrete sovereign nations.

10 FROM EVENTS TO HISTORY

The Macartney Embassy in the

Historiography of Sino-Western Relations

In his "Observations on China," Lord Macartney concluded that as a result of his embassy "the Chinese had, what they never had before, an opportunity of knowing us, and this must lead them to a proper way of thinking of us and of acting towards us in the future" (MD, 213). To an extent, as I have argued above, Macartney was right, although not quite in the way he presents matters here. Yet, if his assessment of the embassy appears quixotic, particularly when placed beside the evaluations of the Qing court, subsequent reactions in Europe, North America, and China have been no less caught up with problems of interpreting and assessing the significance of the embassy. In this closing chapter, I want to consider some of the themes in the historiography of the Macartney embassy.

In doing so, one of my main purposes is to destabilize the taken-for-granted relationship between sources (facts) and interpretation. What I would like to foreground is a kind of forgetting or erasure that seems particularly pertinent to this study. One example of the kind of problem I wish to address has to do with what transpired when British troops entered the Yuanming Gardens in 1860. While looting the premises, soldiers identified the carriage and cannons Macartney had presented to the Qianlong emperor. Of the carriages we hear no more, but the cannons were shipped back to their place of manufacture, the Woolwich Arsenal. The repatriation of gifts once given by George III to the Qianlong emperor signals a particular assessment of the embassy—perhaps that it was an embarrassing failure that could only be set right by British arms or that it was a sign of weakness ever to have thought that China's rulers would respond in a positive way to such gestures (see Hevia 1994a). Missing, therefore, in most accounts of Sino-Western relations is how the interests of the present, or perhaps more properly, many presents, shape historical recollection of an event like the Macartney embassy. In this sense, reconstructing the past is not simply about bringing new evidence to light, applying new methodologies, or exposing previous biases. It is also about engaging in the politics of the production and distribution of knowledge with which all scholarship is involved. At issue, then, is not how to make accounts *less* interested or *less* ideological, but how to locate our own historiography in relation to multiple interpretative positions and the structures of power that we deal with daily. One way of beginning is by critically evaluating discussions of reality, or, in the context of this study, deconstructing historical reconstructions.

10.1   The British Embassy as Qing Precedent

As noted in the previous chapter, the courts of the Qianlong and Jiaqing emperors treated the first British embassy to China as part of their world-ordering processes. As an aspect of Manchu imperialism in East and Inner Asia, the embassy had a palpable place in the production of a cosmomoral universe that grounded the Qing claim to supreme lordship. It was in this sense that the embassy became a precedent for the treatment of West Ocean ambassadors when they arrived at the Qing court. This was the case with the Dutch in 1794 and with Lord Amherst in 1816. At the same time, however, certain occurrences during the Macartney embassy became objects of political contestation and struggle, particularly with respect to issues surrounding imperial audiences between Qing emperors and European ministers after 1840. At the center of the controversy was whether Lord Macartney had performed koutou before the Qianlong emperor. In this section, I will briefly discuss the koutou issue as it appears in some Qing and British records; below I will take it up again as an object of investigation in the historiography of Sino-Western relations.

The first instance in which the events of the Qianlong-Macartney audience became an object of debate was during the Amherst embassy in 1816. From Qing sources, it is fairly clear that, for whatever reason, the court was not prepared to forego koutou a second time. It is also clear that the Jiaqing emperor had some knowledge of what had occurred in 1793, either as a result of having been present at Macartney's audience or from a perusal of the Qianlong records. At one point, for example, when the two primary officials in charge of preparing Amherst for audience, Director of the Board of Works Suleng'e and Changlu Salt Commissioner Guang Hui,[1] were being urged by the Grand Council to force the issue, the emperor reminded everyone about centering and the fact that it was better to receive them than send them off. In the process he noted that some sort of compromise (*jiangjiu*) had been made during the Macartney embassy (*WXCB*, 30a). Later however, when he explained in a letter to George III why Amherst had not been granted an audience, he indicated that Macartney had knelt and touched his head to the ground (*guikou*) in his audience with the Qianlong emperor (*WXCB*, 37b). These contradictory comments by the Jiaqing emperor remain unresolved in the published Chinese language sources on the Amherst embassy.

After the first Opium War, it was possible to find a number of variations in Chinese sources over what had transpired in 1793. Some, like Wang Zhichun, only indicated that Macartney had been seen by the emperor in a tent in the Garden of Ten-thousand Trees (1879:140). The Guangdong Gazetteer simply recorded that the British had entered to present a tribute of local products, while other official sources mentioned audience and tribute or simply imperial audience, with no mention of particulars related to the ritual. The most interesting of these accounts, however, was a rendition by Chen Kangqi, who, after noting that Macartney was only willing to bend one knee, claims that once in the presence of the Qianlong emperor, the British ambassador fell on both knees and prostrated (*shuanggui fufu*) (see Pritchard 1943:175–179).

The question of what happened in the tent at Rehe arose again during the audience negotiations of 1873. Court records, as well as the reports of the British minister Thomas Wade, indicate that one strategy used by officials from the newly created Zongli Yamen[2] was to suggest that it might

1. On August 15, 1816, the Grand Council instructed these officials to remind George T. Staunton that on the occasion of the earlier embassy, the Qianlong emperor had not allowed the British to perform their own ceremony; it was only when Macartney had relented on this point that an audience had been granted (*WXCB*, 20b). Staunton and other members of the embassy denied that Macartney had performed the koutou; see Pritchard 1943:170 n. 20. Staunton's recollection of events in 1793 is also worth drawing attention to since his "eyewitness" account of the Macartney audience is the only one in English that suggests that the British ambassador might have done more than kneel on one knee and slightly bow his head.

2. The Qing court created this institution to deal with the European legations established in Peking after 1860; see Banno 1964. The title is a contraction of *Zongli geguo*

be appropriate for Europeans to kneel before the emperor at present since others had done so in the past. Wade and his colleagues not only rejected this logic, but made it clear that they were unwilling to go down on one knee as Macartney had.[3]

During these negotiations, the issue of the Macartney embassy was also raised by the Zhili governor-general Li Hongzhang in a conversation with the British consul at Tianjin, Thomas Meadows. According to a report he sent to Wade, Meadows explained that Li claimed to have checked court records on the two British embassies as well as the Dutch embassy of 1795. The records indicated that Macartney and the Dutch ambassador had both performed koutou, but that when Amherst refused, he was not granted an audience. In reply, Meadows told Li that the Dutch had made themselves a laughingstock. Macartney and Amherst had not done so because, in addition to the fact that "we English kneel to Heaven on praying to it, but we never kneel to men," had they complied, they would have had their heads cut off when they returned to England (PRO, FO 748:376–377).

From the 1873 audience negotiations until the Boxer settlement of 1901, Qing authorities and the ambassadors of the European powers continued to struggle over audience forms much as Macartney and the court had in 1793. In what was increasingly constructed as a clear polar opposition, both sides claimed small victories, until in 1901 the allied powers were able to impose Euro-American-style diplomatic forms on the court as part of the Boxer settlement (see Rockhill 1905 and Hevia 1990b). After the fall of the Qing dynasty in 1911, the government of the Republic of China seems to have unquestioningly accepted the forms dictated by the North Atlantic imperial powers. At the same time, the Macartney embassy and the koutou question expired as a living political issue between powerful Asian empires and became history.

---

shiwu yamen or Office of International Affairs Administration. Hsü notes that it was directly under the Grand Council (1990:269).

3. See Wade's account of discussions with Chinese officials on these matters in PRO, FO 748:342–354, 433, and FO 749:11–17, and Wade's own clarification of occurrences during the Amherst embassy in FO 749:22–24. At the same time, however, some high officials were urging the court to forego any forms of kneeling and instead work out favorable terms for other portions of the audience ceremony; see T. Wang 1971:621–623.

10.2 The Macartney Embassy as British Precedent

In addition to its use in diplomatic negotiations, the Macartney embassy was often treated as a point of origin for new kinds of knowledge about China. S. Wells Williams, for example, stressed that as a result of the embassy, more was known about the true nature of China than ever before (1895, 2:455). The embassy also had an important place in treaty port histories produced in the second half of the century (Bickers 1993a,b,c) and figured prominently in numerous popular histories of China produced from the first Opium War forward. In some of these histories, the following epigram became a kind of shorthand assessment of the British undertaking.

> It has justly been observed, that the ambassador was received with the utmost politeness, treated with the utmost hospitality, watched with the utmost vigilance and, dismissed with the utmost civility.[4]

In pre- and post-Opium War English-language histories of the British in China the epigram seems to have derived its appeal as a means for justifying a much more aggressive stance by the British government toward the Qing empire. Recall, for instance, that the codification of rules for diplomatic practice did not occur until the "Concert of Europe" in the 1820s (Hinsley 1969:284–285). Coupled with this development was the breaking of the East India Company's monopoly on trade with China in 1834 and the massive increase in opium imports to China, both of which led to strident calls by British merchants for the opening of China to "free trade" (e.g., Matheson 1836). These developments served to narrow British perceptions and solidify what came to be perceived as the great divide between "East" and "West." Gone was the optimism expressed by Macartney over the possibility of overcoming differences through rational exchange. In its place emerged a discourse that appropriated many of the categories used to characterize the Chinese during the 1790s in order to argue for a direct confrontation with Chinese "jealousy" and "exclusiveness."

In some cases, the absolute difference between Chinese and Europeans was expressed in lurid tones.[5] But this globally dismissive approach was less

---

4. The statement appears in Auber 1834:200; Robbins 1908:461; Willson 1903, 2:323; Pritchard 1936:379; Cranmer-Byng 1957–1958:183; and Hsü 1990:160–161.

5. See, for example, Holman 1835, 4:205–241, where a chapter details the immoral character of the Chinese, including their corrupt nature, hypocrisy, venality, and lack of

popular than one that focused attention on those who were really respon-sible for restraining contact between England and China, namely corrupt and self-interested officials in Canton and, eventually, the monopolistic hong merchants (Auber 1834:397; Matheson 1836:77; and Davis 1836, 1:57–58). The elimination of these officials would, from most perspectives, open China to British penetration because the Chinese people were anxious for contact with Europeans (Gutzlaff 1834:305 and Lindsay 1833:178, 182).

From these premises a typology emerged that took as its point of depar-ture the Macartney embassy. While conflicting views appeared regarding the success of Macartney's embassy, with at least one observer claiming that after it conditions improved for foreign merchants at Canton (Davis 1836, 1:72), there was general agreement that one of the major lessons learned was that Chinese officials would abandon their unreasonable prac-tices and demands when faced with firmness and reasonableness, and if those failed, with force.[6] Any submission to the Chinese was more than an insult to European honor; it accomplished nothing except to perpetuate Chinese isolation, exclusionism, and sense of superiority (Matheson 1836: 17–19), while blocking access to the basically pragmatic Chinese people. In this regard, Lord Napier's mission to Canton in 1834 is particularly instruc-tive. When his efforts to deal directly with Canton officials failed because of their "ignorance and obstinacy" and led to a stoppage of trade, Napier cir-culated handbills among the Chinese population denouncing Qing officials and extolling the benefits of free trade. When this, too, failed to produce the desired results, Napier threatened to move British frigates before the city walls.[7] From the first Opium War forward, firmness and reasonableness were augmented by the use of force, which many viewed as fundamen-tal to the maintenance of treaty rights won as a result of the war. In this atmosphere, some British and American observers questioned the actions of Macartney, implying that he went too far in efforts to please the Chinese and might even have "kowtowed" before the Qianlong emperor (Eames 1909:121 and Rockhill 1905:31).

---

gratitude — features that would be reworked as *Chinese Characteristics* by Arthur Smith half a century later (1894).

6. Davis 1836, 1:29, who also argued that the restrictions on trade were a relatively recent phenomenon, dating from the beginning of Manchu rule in China (20–21). Also see, Holman 1835, 4:245; Matheson 1836:21; and Gutzlaff 1834:305.

7. See Hsü 1990:173–176; Fairbank, Reischauer, and Craig 1978:453; and A. Chun 1983: 213–215.

The significance of the epigram cited above is important in the context of this history because it defines in easily reproducible and memorable form the essential "problem" of China prior to the complete reordering of relations from 1840 forward—the Qing court's refusal to allow British penetration of China in British terms. But though part of the epigram's charm lies in its repeatability, there is something else interesting about it. In a book published in the wake of the first Opium War, an additional clause appears, absent from other sources, that reads "answered with the utmost firmness" (Abbott 1843:232). I would suggest that the reason for the absence of the clause in other sources is that it imputes to Qing officials the very same behavioral characteristic that was to become so critical for the British interpretation of their intercourse with China. In a discourse that was rigidly constructed along lines of absolute binary oppositions, such leakage between poles had, in the end, to be carefully policed.

By the end of the nineteenth century, such dichotomies dominated British perceptions of intercourse with China. For example, Chinese "superiority" stood in opposition to British notions of sovereign equality, Chinese isolation and antiforeignism to British cosmopolitanism, Chinese exclusiveness to British free trade, and the jealousy of Chinese officials to the open-mindedness of British diplomats. From these oppositions, additional ones emerged to define the inner constitution of the Chinese polity. The monarch as despot stood in opposition to the official bureaucracy, the state to society, local government to the village, and officially dominated relations with outsiders to the natural desire among the Chinese people for "free" intercourse (e.g., Morse 1910, 1:1–2). In the last polarity, these same Chinese people could be constructed as xenophobic if, for example, they attacked European or American missionaries or traders.

One suspects, however, that while the sorts of representations discussed above continued to find a place in newer interpretative frameworks (e.g., modernization theory), what sustained them over time were powerful metonymic images that provided stable representational references. I wish to take up in turn two of the most important of these images, not only because of their intrinsic importance to the historiography of Sino-Western relations, but because they are "Chinese" objects brought to England by the Macartney embassy. I refer to the word *kowtow*[8] and the letter from the

---

8. The *Oxford English Dictionary* indicates that the first use of the term was in Barrow's account of the embassy, where it appeared as "koo-too" (1806:213). The first use of kowtow is attributed to Rennie (1864:232). For further discussion see Hevia 1995.

Qianlong emperor to George III, whose careers I will sketch in the next two sections.

It is important to note at the outset, however, that the history of the koutou and the Qianlong letter in Euro-American discourse hardly run parallel to each other. The letter, for instance, is virtually absent from nineteenth-century Western accounts of relations with China, only appearing in print, it would seem, with E. H. Parker's 1896 publication of a version found in the *Donghua lu*. The koutou, on the other hand, was, as might be surmised from a reading of the previous section, extremely prominent in nineteenth-century English language sources on China. Indeed, by the 1840s it had become so thoroughly fetishized[9] that former American president John Quincy Adams claimed that it, rather than opium, was the real cause of the first Anglo-Chinese war. The purpose of the next section is to attempt to explain why this was so.

10.3   The Koutou Question in Euro-American Discourse

> The whole life of the Emperor is ruled by the same petty ceremonial, which sometimes reveals a touch of Oriental imagination, sometimes is merely barbarous. ... Nothing is more curious and comical than a state dinner. ... When the gong sounds, the Emperor enters with his guard and proceeds to a low, golden throne. The favorite courtiers who are present throw themselves on the ground to worship the "Son of Heaven." The chief of the imperial eunuchs thrice cracks his whip, music begins, and the officials who are to serve the Emperor enter, throwing themselves down nine times, and bending their knees five times. (*Literary Digest* 20 [11] [17 March 1900]:344)

In its rendition of the comical and ludicrous behavior of the Chinese, this entry from the *Literary Digest* stands at one side of representations of China. The other was made up of depictions of Chinese as brutal, benighted, or barbarous (MacKenzie 1986a:212). In either case, Qing court ceremony and the koutou loom large in a Euro-American imaginary as objects at which one might hurl ridicule or antipathy. One may well question why so much enmity was expended, especially by North Atlantic diplomats,

---

9. I think it proper to refer to the kowtow as a Euro-American fetish object, one that was constructed on the colonial divide. In using the term to refer to a demonization of a Chinese practice, I follow Pietz 1985.

at an act that could also be seen as humorous. Since such men are usually portrayed as highly rational in their actions, particularly as they sought to maximize gains and minimize losses in their pursuit of their nation's interests in China, it would follow that British diplomats, for instance, ought to have performed the koutou before the emperor of China if they had any hope at all of achieving the objectives of their embassies. Yet, no British diplomat ever did. The question that remains open is why this was the case.

One possible explanation can be found in the remarks of former American president John Quincy Adams in an address he made before the Massachusetts Historical Society in 1840. According to Adams, in shutting out European trade and enclosing themselves behind high walls of exclusion, the Chinese had violated the law of nations that imposed a "moral obligation" on countries to facilitate commercial intercourse. Such obligations were, in turn, rooted for Adams in "*Laws* of Nature" and "Nature's *God.*" Put in these metaphysical terms, Adams was then able to locate the real scandal of the koutou: it was only natural law and God "to which we bow the knee..." (1909–1910:305). Citizens of Christian nations did not, in other words, worship human beings. China's "arrogant and insupportable" pretension that it could hold intercourse with others on the basis of an "insulting and degrading" act was, Adams argued, the sole cause of the conflict with Great Britain.

By presenting his justifications for British actions in China in these terms, Adams enunciated a North Atlantic diplomatic consensus with universalist pretensions, a consensus that became increasingly impatient with what it saw as the backward practices of the rest of the world. The difference between the diplomatic practices to be found in China and those that had emerged in northern Europe from the middle of the eighteenth century forward, particularly with respect to differences in bodily actions, was crucial and animated many accounts of China into this century. For the point was that members of North Atlantic nation-states entered the √ realms of others on their feet; only vassals and slaves entered on their knees. Adams's reference to the "arrogant and insupportable pretension" of China's leaders serves as a kind of refrain justifying the increasingly aggressive Euro-American penetration of China over the second half of the nineteenth century.

Yet why should such "pretensions" be so closely tied to a practice like koutou; why should koutou take precedence in Adams's thinking over all other known aspects of China? Is it simply a question of distaste for acts that are believed to be more proper for addressing a transcendent as opposed to a wordly realm—a Christian god as opposed, for example, to a Catholic Pope? While I believe that there may well be a strong aversion to things that appear to mimic Catholicism running through comments like those of Adams, there is probably more at work here than this.

Kneeling had long been associated in Great Britain with subjugation, but such associations took on added urgency in the nineteenth century as a result of the transformations of physical space in the emerging bourgeois world. The opposition between kneeling and standing upright resonates with others such as high/clean and low/dirty, distinctions which figured not only social class and the geography of the nineteenth-century city, but, as Stallybrass and White (1986) have argued, the feminization of servitude in the figure of the kneeling chambermaid. The Victorian gentleman and maker of empire was just the opposite—stalwartly upright, only touching the ground with more than one knee when wounded or dead at the hands of savage barbarians.

Running parallel to these developments were new notions of court ceremonial that displaced the nineteenth-century practices of the British monarchy from the realm of political ritual onto a new domain that might be called political theater or, perhaps more precisely, the pageantry of British imperialism. David Cannadine has argued that by 1820, attacks on courtly ceremony pivoted on the fact that the enlightenment of humanity exposed such practices as ridiculously hollow shams, as mere artifice.[10] And yet, contrary to what utilitarian thought and instrumental reason might lead us to expect, neither monarchy nor ritual disappeared in Great Britain. Instead, foreshadowed by Edmund Burke's unsettling notion that reason unwisely laid bare the mechanism of state power (see 3.6 above), court ceremonial and other state rituals went public, and in so doing reclothed power. In spectacular displays of grandeur, in international expositions, celebrations of conquest, royal weddings and funerals, and dedications of monuments, all reported in the illustrated press and celebrated in commercial advertising (Richards 1990), representations of state power became objects of mass consumption. As spectacular commodities adorned with old and new sym-

10. Cannadine 1983:101–102. Among the sources that include disparaging remarks concerning court ceremonial see Vattel 1916, 3:367; John Adams, who argued that the business of diplomacy was submerged in ceremonial practice throughout Europe (C. F. Adams, 1853, 8:251–259); Lord Macauley, cited in Crosby 1991; and Thackary 1991:13.

bols of the nation, statist representations helped to build mass consent for imperial adventures abroad.

Curiously, however, the same sort of sensibility that might ground class hegemony in the ability to stage power as spectacular performance had scant patience with the ways in which power was fashioned outside of Europe. A century after Lord Macartney's almost reverential ruminations on the superiority of Asian over European courts with respect to ceremonial splendor and royal pomp (MD, 123–124, 131), his successors not only refused to participate in the "pageantry" of Asia, but set about systematically destroying the structures of "Asian" power and building new ones upon the same ground.

The reasons for this assault are not far to seek; they reside in a second trajectory of reconstituted court ceremonial, one that looked outward, rather than inward. By the end of the eighteenth century, diplomatic ceremonies had been refigured through the "Law of Nations." Ceremonial encounters between the head of one state and the ambassador of another became the primary site for the mutual recognition of sovereign equality (see Hevia 1989 and 1994b). In essence, such recognition necessarily constituted the rational subjects required for the completion of contractual arrangements in the form of treaties. Treaties, in turn, increasingly regulated what had become the partner of European diplomacy on the global stage, commercial exchange. Ambassadors and consuls sought to facilitate the movement of merchants and their goods across the same borders they themselves traversed. And like diplomacy, trade revolved around notions of sovereign equality, exchange, and contract.

It was precisely at the site of inter-state ceremonial that the new notions of diplomacy and commerce converged with emerging pronouncements about acceptable bodily posture for the bourgeois gentleman. By the time of the Congress of Vienna, not only had the definitions of sovereignty, diplomacy, and commercial exchange been worked out in detail and regularized, but diplomatic audiences in European courts had been standardized. Ambassadors entered the presence of the host sovereign, bowed three times in their approach, placed directly into the sovereign's hands credentials or letters, exchanged pleasantries, and retreated as they had entered. They did not kneel on either one or two knees, and when they bowed their heads, they did so from a standing position, bending at the waist. By the beginning of the twentieth century, this form of sovereign recognition and state-to-state equality was "universal" (Hinsley 1969 and Jones 1984:20–21).

The Qing empire was finally forced to comply with these globally imposed standards in the Boxer Protocol of 1901, a little over a year after the publication of the *Literary Digest* piece with which this section opened.

The formal imposition of Euro-American-style audience procedures on the Qing court transformed these events into the kind of spectacle they had become in Europe.[11] It also marked the demise of koutou as a living political issue between the Qing empire and European powers. In turn, representations of koutou also changed. Certainly people still saw it as a humiliation for Westerners, but some began to argue that it had other meanings for the Chinese. The Empress Dowager's portrait painter Catherine Carl argued in 1905 that kneeling and bowing did not "imply any slave-like inferiority" on the performer, but was rather a "time honored" way of expressing thanks to the sovereign (148). Reginald Johnston, the tutor of Puyi, seemed to agree with Carl when he discussed the "*kotow*" two decades later. Refiguring the act as a matter of style and perhaps good manners, Johnston admitted that given the right clothing and training, he himself would have performed it on occasions such as the ex-emperor's birthday (1934:205). In her reminiscence, titled simply *Kowtow*, the popular conveyor of Qing court culture, Princess Der Ling, claimed that her father required it of his secretary as an apology for a slanderous act committed against her (1929:199).

By the 1930s and '40s, the act had undergone several other transformations. In his early discussion of it, John K. Fairbank spoke of koutou as good manners and also in economic terms; it was a kind of repayment for imperial room and board (1942 and 1948; the latter interpretation he would drop from editions subsequent to 1948). At about the same time, E. H. Pritchard published his seminal essay on the koutou and the Macartney embassy. While accepting Fairbank's general characterization, Pritchard also argued that there was nothing intentionally "humiliating or degrading" in

11. From the New Year of 1902, when the protocol was first applied until the fall of the dynasty, thirty-three audiences for the entire diplomatic corps were held at either the Qianqing palace or the new summer palace. Even more extraordinary, during the same period I have counted 158 individual audiences held for ambassadors and visiting dignitaries. There may even have been more. These figures come from printed audience notices in the Number One Historical Archive, Peking. As the number of audiences increased, Sir Robert Hart, director of the Imperial Maritime Customs, was led to exclaim that, in allowing so many audiences, the court was "over-doing it in civility: not only will the Empress Dowager receive Minister's wives, but also Legation *children!*" (cited in Fairbank 1987:139).

the act. Coming very close to treating the Western understanding of koutou as a fetish, Pritchard claimed that it was not a central and ultimate act of submission as generally believed. In contrast, he suggested that the very dispatching of embassies and participation in the embassy routine was submission. "To refuse to kotow," he concluded, "after having conformed to all other parts of the suzerain-vassal relationship was in reality pointless, and grew out of a profound misunderstanding of the meaning of the act itself..." (1943:197–199).

What allowed both Fairbank and Pritchard to cast matters in these terms was not simply the transformation of koutou from an object of political contention to an object of historical investigation. Equally significant was the fact that their revisionism relied on new conceptual apparatuses and categories emerging from fields such as sociology and cultural anthropology. For what these two scholars did was to refigure koutou as a *cultural* issue located within patterns of universal historical development—that is, koutou became part of the cultural scheme of a premodern or traditional society. By the 1950s, such interpretations had been mobilized into Cold War area-studies discourse, where they provided ways to explain China's failure to modernize along European lines as well as the success of communism in China.[12]

It should also be recalled, however, that while the scholars I have just mentioned might have put a more benign face on koutou, the more negative representations did not completely disappear. There were those, in other words, who, while accepting a twentieth-century social-systems approach, continued to treat koutou as a distasteful and scandalous act typical of China's premodern sense of universal superiority. Fairbank himself led the way here by taking a more critical approach from the time of his *Trade and Diplomacy on the China Coast* (1953) forward, eventually characterizing the koutou as one of those "rituals of abject servitude" common in traditional China (Fairbank 1988:14). This line of representation dovetailed in part with the English word "kowtow," which remains a term of derision and ridicule, and gives it a history outside its incidence as a Chinese act (see Hevia 1995).

12. On the theoretical content of area studies in general, see Pletsch 1981. On China studies see Barlow 1993.

10.4   The Qianlong Letter and the Tribute System Synthesis

> The Celestial Empire, ruling all within the four seas, simply concen-
> trates on carrying out the affairs of Government properly, and does
> not value rare and precious things. ... [W]e have never valued in-
> genious articles, nor do we have the slightest need of your Country's
> manufactures.

These few sentences from the letter of the Qianlong emperor to George
III ought to be recognizable to most historians of modern China; they are
perhaps the most frequently quoted lines in histories of Sino-Western relations.[13] Yet, one of the great ironies of such citation is that as far as can be
ascertained, neither the letter as a whole nor this brief passage from it ever
appeared prominently in the considerations of nineteenth-century British
diplomats dealing with China. In fact, the letter seems to have been given
scant attention after Lord Macartney returned it to England, only having
been translated fully into English in 1896 by E. H. Parker and more widely
circulated in the version done by Backhouse and Bland in 1914. When it
did appear in print, it seems that, like the head quote of the last section
concerning "state dinners," the letter was greeted with much amusement.
This was perhaps why, after reading the translation, Bertrand Russell argued that "no one understands China until this document has ceased to
seem absurd" (1922:47).

Russell's interpretation of the letter is consistent with the shift in representations of koutou that were occurring around the same time, and as

13. Among many other places, the Qianlong letter and/or this passage appears or is
referred to in Parker 1896; Backhouse and Bland 1914; MacNair 1923; Teng and Fairbank 1954:19; Mancall 1963:18; Cranmer-Byng 1963:340; Hsü 1990:161–162; Fairbank,
Reischauer, and Craig 1978:257; Rozman 1981:22–23; and Spence 1990:122–123. Lessing,
drawing on the ZGCB, translated portions of both letters to George III, see Hedin 1933:
203–210. Uncited mention also occurs; see the *New York Times* about the visit of the U.S.
secretary of state Warren Christopher to China (27 March 1994, p. 5). It also circulates
prominently in world history textbooks; see Duiker and Spielvogel (1994), who reference Spence citing Cranmer-Byng. Stearns, Adas, and Schwartz (1992) reproduce a large
portion of the letter and ask students, "What do these excerpts tell you about the Chinese view of themselves, the English, and the wider world at the time? How well do these
attitudes correspond to the actual situation? Why were they likely to cause serious problems for the Chinese?" I suppose the correct answer is that the Chinese were awash in
illusions, all of which would lead to trouble; hence the next section in the textbook on
the Opium War.

such heralds the rather swift movement of the Qianlong emperor's letter from the realm of the comical to the land of cultural relativism. For what the letter came to stand for was China's traditional culturalism, isolationism, and sense of self-sufficiency nicely and conveniently compacted into one text. As such, the letter as well as the Macartney embassy were soon incorporated into the tribute system synthesis that defined traditional China's foreign relations and the Chinese world order.

On this line of reasoning, a number of writers during the 1960s argued that broad areas of continuity existed in foreign relations between traditional China and the People's Republic. A spate of articles appeared carrying the message that American policy makers should approach Chinese Communist rhetoric cautiously and be aware of China's long-standing cultural influence within East and Southeast Asia.[14] While it may well be the case, as John Fairbank has suggested (1982:408), that these arguments about tradition within Chinese modernity played a positive role in lessening tensions between the United States and the People's Republic, my concern here is with the effect of representing the Qianlong letter as a cultural essence, as sign par excellence of China's isolation and (false) sense of superiority.

Not only does such citation distort the nature of the encounter between the Qing and British imperial formations, but if current world civilization textbooks are any indication, it also helps to perpetuate the stereotype of a passive East and a dynamic West. Qing "foreign relations" remain, as a result, ahistorically frozen within the boundaries of the "China's response" model, while the inside of China percolates with change.

10.5   From Routines of Empire to the Narrative
       Histories of the Nation-State

By the 1930s, the Macartney embassy had also become a significant historical event in Chinese writings on the history of Sino-Western relations and the process of modernization in China. In the *Qinghua University Journal,* for example, Tsiang T'ing-fu published an article titled "China and the Great Transformation of the Modern World," in which he treated the Macartney embassy as a failure. What is particularly interesting, however, is not only this conclusion, but how Tsiang arrived at it. Citing the work of Zhang Dechang, Tsiang noted that from the Ming period forward China

14. See Mancall 1963; Cranmer-Byng 1965–1966 and 1968–1969; and Fairbank 1966.

had linked trade and tribute together (1934:526). In an address given at the London School of Economics in 1936, he referred to a tributary system that linked trade and diplomacy in a dogma asserting that "national security could only be found in isolation" and in suzerain-vassal relations (1936:3–4). The result of this system was that China had no notion of international relations and no conception of equality between states. Secure in its peaceful traditionalism, Ming and Qing China assumed that it was superior to all other countries in the world until the first Opium War. The Macartney embassy did not alter Chinese perceptions. Rather it demonstrated that China would not give up its traditional notions peacefully (1934:548).

For Tsiang, then, the failure of the Macartney embassy and the struggle that ensued in the nineteenth century were both products of the differences between Chinese and Western civilizations, differences which worked themselves out as a kind of inevitable clash between tradition and modernity. There are a number of points in Tsiang's argument worth emphasizing, especially because they continue to circulate in contemporary representations both in and outside China. First, the entities at play are civilizations or cultures, not specific imperial formations with their own political agendas. They are, in other words, China and the West, not the Qing and British empires. Second, the distinctions between China and the West are grounded on a series of absences within the traditional world: China had no notion of international society or international law. Third, the traditional world is a closed system sealed off from outside communication on all levels critical to modernity. China refused to accept "equal" intercourse in diplomacy and commerce, while, in what was probably the greatest shortcoming for a modernist post-Qing intellectual, turning a blind eye to Western science and technology. In this formation, Tsiang not only anticipated the "China's response to the West" thesis, but positions contemporary Chinese scholars as participants in the construction of a twentieth-century history of international relations. Moreover, those who have followed Tsiang have taken the next logical step in the argument: "Sino-Western" conflict was a case of cultural misunderstanding, rather than an example of aggressive British imperial expansion (see, for example, Wang 1993).

In the post-1949 People's Republic of China, by contrast, there has remained until quite recently a strong emphasis on the role of British imperialism in the history of modern China.[15] In this formation, a distinction

15. To a certain extent the shift in emphasis I explore in Chinese writings on the Macartney embassy are similar to what is explored by Paul Cohen in his discussion of

has often been drawn between feudal China and capitalist Britain, with the former usually presented as passive or defensive in foreign relations and the latter aggressive. Conflict was accepted as inevitable, but its cause was not cultural misunderstanding. Rather, it was seen as an unavoidable product of expansive capitalism and Western imperialism. In recent renditions of this position, Hu Sheng (1981) and Zhu Jieqing (1984) emphasized that Macartney came to China as an agent of the East India Company. The Company's goal was to expand its influence in the China market, preferably by gaining trade concessions and a special site to conduct its commerce. In this regard, Zhu has argued that the long-range British policy toward China was aggression and that once the British had the opportunity, they imposed by force the very demands that Macartney had made in 1793. Accordingly, the Qianlong emperor and the Qing court were wise to reject the British demands, because not only would acceptance have infringed on Chinese sovereignty, but it would have led to much faster expansion of the opium trade (1984: 555–562).

These particular views of the Macartney embassy constituted a consensus within China until quite recently. In the current political climate a number of new interpretations have emerged which, while not directly challenging the anti-imperialism interpretation, have developed in alternative directions, most of which begin with the basic premise that the Macartney embassy was a failure for both sides. In the late 1980s, Zhu Yong completed a study that utilized records from the Qing archives in Peking, as well as the works of E. H. Pritchard and other Euro-American historians of the embassy. Rejecting explanations that focused on Qing xenophobia and a completely closed China, Zhu contended that the Macartney embassy failed because of the Qing policy of "limited contact for self-defense" (*xianguan zishou*), itself informed by a notion of "severity tempered with gentleness" (*kuanyan xiangji*). As a practical consideration, this meant that the Qianlong emperor had to maintain a moderate policy toward the British and avoid going to extremes. This notion of restricted or managed contact was the reason why the embassy was unable to open China more fully to British penetration (1989:280–281).

At around the same time, Zhang Shunhong was completing work in England at the India Office archives and combining them with published

---

the historiography of the Boxer movement in China; see 1992. Unlike Cohen, however, my focus is not on mythologizing the past, but with the politics in which we all engage in representing the past.

and unpublished archival sources in China. He also argued that the embassy
was a failure, but saw the cause as the unwillingness of the Qing court to
communicate with the outside world. Because of this "closed-door policy,"
the Qianlong emperor and his advisers failed to realize the great changes in
the international balance of power then under way. As a result, they lost an
ideal opportunity for catching up with the West (1993).

A third kind of revision can be found in the work of Dai Yi (1992). In his
study of the Qianlong era, Dai moves close to the position expounded by
Tsiang T'ing-fu. Arguing that the Qing empire was isolated and ignorant
of modern international relations (430), he has focused on the debate over
court ritual and koutou as indicative of the great gap between the Western
world of capitalism and science and China's feudal political order, its cultural system (*wenhua zhidu*), and its ideology. The magnitude of difference
meant that it would require a substantial amount of time and change before China could enter the world and adapt to the new situation (426).

While Zhu, Zhang, and Dai emphasize different causal factors, they also
share certain characteristics. In the first place, they generally accept the embassy as a failure, rather than a Qing success. Second, in emphasizing Qing
failures, they locate multiple causes rather than a single one. Third, they
seem less concerned with the question of Western imperialism in China
and more involved with issues of modernization. The Macartney embassy
helps to explain why China remained "backward" and now has to "catch
up" with the West.

An international conference commemorating the bicentennial of the
Macartney embassy was held at Rehe in September 1993, where these
three scholars joined others from China, the United States, Great Britain,
France, and Germany. At this meeting, a number of Chinese scholars, along
with Alain Peyrefitte, the author of *The Immobile Empire*, emphasized the
"closed-door" policy of the Qing dynasty, the conservative nature of the
Qianlong emperor, and China's backwardness (Du Jiang 1993, Guo Chengkang 1993, Liu Yuwen 1993). Although not always overtly stated, this
position suggested that the embassy was a lost opportunity for China.
Presumably, a more farsighted Qing court would have opened its door
allowing European technology and capitalism to flow into China. As a result, the gap between China and the West would have narrowed greatly during the nineteenth century. These arguments appear consistent with those
of the present Chinese government, which has advocated similar policies
since 1980. Thus, the Macartney embassy becomes part of a cautionary tale;
China must never again repeat the folly of the Qianlong court.

The more difficult problem at the conference, however, was accounting for the Qing policy. No particular cause was singled out. Rather scholars emphasized a variety of factors that might account for the court's reaction to the British proposals, including distractions caused by domestic economic and political problems, the Qianlong emperor's disinterest in European technology, and the emphasis placed on ritual in the Chinese cultural tradition (Zhang Jiqian 1993 and Liu Fengyun 1993). Also within this line of reasoning was the view that the closed-door policy was not part of the Chinese cultural tradition, but rather something unique to the Qing period (Ye Fengmei 1993). Most of these arguments also emphasized cultural misunderstanding as a major cause of the embassy's failure.

Thus, with the nation as the horizon or irreducible unit of analysis in these critical engagements, some Chinese scholars appear (wittingly or not) to reproduce Euro-American interpretations of Sino-Western conflict. These interpretations, it will be recalled, tended to discount imperialism as the major source of conflict between China and the West. Instead, they foregrounded cultural difference and the inevitable clash between tradition and modernity. Chinese scholars who point to Qing backwardness and a false sense of superiority seem to be mirroring the American sinological construct of the 1950s and '60s.

These various positions are also of interest because of the distance they have moved away from the anti-imperialist approach of earlier decades and toward arguments to be found in Nationalist Chinese scholarship and American sinology. Indeed, if the conference in Chengde is any indication, imperialism seems to have receded into the background as some Chinese scholars attempt to explain China's "backwardness" on the basis of endogenous, rather than exogenous factors. At the same time, however, the anti-imperialist critique has not completely disappeared. In a 1991 publication, for example, Guo Yunjing argued that there were a number of problems with shifting the emphasis for the failure of the Macartney embassy to the Qing court's "closed-door policy." Guo observed that such an interpretation relieved the British of responsibility for aggression against China and placed the blame on the Qing court (186). Reminding everyone that the Qing had ended multi-port trade because of the behavior of foreigners, she noted that the single-port system at Canton allowed for better surveillance of the foreign merchants and sailors, and fewer incidents of conflict. With respect to the Macartney embassy, Guo argued that the British proposals not only alerted the Qing court to the larger ambitions the British harbored in China, but allowed the court to carry out a series of reasonable actions to combat those ambitions (188). At the same time, however, because of the failure of the embassy, the British became more aggressive on the China coast, leading to harsher policies during the reigns of the Jiaqing and Daoguang emperors. But even if these policies placed certain restrictions on contact, the moves were defensive, reasonable, and in keeping with the right of any country to protect itself (189).

In providing a timely reminder to others, Guo's position appears consistent with pre-1980s interpretations. Imperialism had, after all, served as a crucial component in explaining "modern" Chinese history: it simultaneously accounted for a century of humiliation and served dialectically to explain the coming into being of the consciousness of the Chinese people as a nation. I believe this is not the only significance of her observations. Rather, it strikes me as one among other indications that "reform" in China has produced competing and conflicting views of the nation, and of nation building (see Anagnost 1993).

10.6   Horizons of History

At the risk of stating the obvious, it should be clear that more is at work in these alterations than simply the bringing to light of new evidence, or access to previously unavailable archival sources. How do we account for the twists and turns in the historiography of the Macartney embassy? How do we explain such changes over time? What kind of events are interpretative changes? Is it either possible or desirable to separate the embassy from its historiography? These are not easy questions to answer, particularly when we consider the usual form in which historical knowledge is produced. According to de Certeau, historians seem to be primarily engaged in separating "fact" from "fiction" in various kinds of Popperian falsification projects (1986:199–202). The operation itself is, therefore, a negative one designed (as it were) to purify both event and the writing of history, to cleanse them of fictions so that the narratives of the past can be relied upon. But suppose purification is not the issue? How would we go about conceptualizing a different sort of history—one less concerned with falsification, and more concerned with events through their multiple recountings. Perhaps we might start with a few generalizations suggested by the historiography of the Macartney embassy.

The particulars of the Macartney embassy were displaced in a significant way by the monumental events of the second half of the nineteenth century. Assaulted by rebellion from within and invasion from without, the Qing imperium collapsed, dissolving its empire and its particular notions of rulership. In its stead emerged, however feeble and incomplete, a nation-state comprised of ethnic groups and individual citizens — new identities, new allegiances, and perhaps most importantly new ways of looking at the past. The historiography after 1911 reflects these revolutionary changes. The writings considered above are cross-cut with narratives about the coming into being of the nation; with stories of ancient and contemporary civilizations, with the differences between old China and the new West, with assumptions about the inevitability of conflict between tradition and modernity, and with the particular demands nation-states seem to make of their intelligentsia.

There were at least two dominant moments in this historiography. The first was when Chinese thinkers reworked China's imperial past in Euro-American terms, accepting notions of time and categories of organization quite different from anything that had previously existed in China. This shift was, in turn, part of the more general process of the "Westernization" of Chinese education (Y. C. Wang 1966). The metaphysics of rites and the discourse of pattern that dominated imperial rulership were overwhelmed by this change. Such sensibilities had been broadly defused throughout the Qing imperium, providing common ground for fashioning and resisting the Qing imperial formation. For over half a century, the new discourses from the "West" have provided ways for intellectuals to explain China's "backwardness," and to justify social and economic change.

The second dominant moment was the Cold War. Beginning in the early 1950s, the historiography of China, particularly in the realm of foreign relations, underwent important changes. In the first place, the field was predominantly made up of Americans, most of whom were located at a few key institutions. Second, the Cold War saw both the pervasive application of social scientific terminology to the study of "non-Western civilizations" and the birth of area studies as strategic disciplines.[16] Third, Chinese scholars in the People's Republic of China continued efforts begun in the 1920s to reorganize Chinese history in terms of Marxist categories (Dirlik 1978).

16. I can only draw attention to the latter observation at this point. The history of area studies and the nation-state has only begun to be written; see, for example, Marks 1985 and Barlow 1993. For an excellent introduction to the broader issues involved, see Buxton 1985 on Parsons.

In each of these cases, scholars in both "China" and the "West" were involved in purification and falsification projects. They arranged their narratives in terms of clearly bounded spatial and temporal entities; naturalized the civilization and the nation as stable units of historical analysis; organized events in linear cause-effect relationships; clearly demarcated the social into its religious, political, economic, and cultural components; and drew a clear distinction between stages of historical development. Whether in the service of the state, of the nation, or some abstract notion of truth, scholars have tended to treat all these categories as essential to useful scholarly inquiry. These words, phrases, and categories provided the foundation of research agendas. They also authorized an interpretation of the Macartney embassy that was thoroughly modernist, and hostile or dismissive toward the concerns and beliefs of Qing leaders. The question that remains open is whether there are other possible ways of engaging the past.

I believe that there are, and that we need not venture very far to find them. One reason why this is the case is that the historical projects of building hegemony within modern nation-states have never been complete—there has always been an excess of the social that slips outside the disciplinary apparatus of the state or the authoritative discourses found in the academy or in the public sphere (see, for example, Laclau 1990:89–92). Secondly, modernist historiography, with its emphases on demarcating and creating pure categories for analysis, has never been totally successful. It is not simply that the total knowledge project of the enlightenment remains incomplete (Habermas 1983). It is also, as Bruno Latour has argued, that we have never been modern (1993). Modernism had sought to carve up the world into discrete essences and completely knowable parts. But hybrids not only did not disappear, they have proliferated, while leakage across borders occurs simultaneously with their creation. The imperial audience in which Lord Macartney participated is a case in point. Reducible neither to the naturalizing discourse of European sovereign equality nor to the Qing process of hierarchical inclusion, the audience was a hybrid, which also may account for continued interest in and concern over it.

Or consider the examples, cited above, of the post-Qing Chinese intelligentsia. Appropriating the intellectual framework of the colonizer, Chinese thinkers made their arguments and constructed their narratives in thoroughly hybridized languages. The historiography of their Euro-American counterparts was no less tainted. Fairbank's tribute system, for example, showed signs of functional anthropology, Weberian-Parsonian sociology, fragments of British imperial historiography, and the efforts of Chinese intellectuals to place China in the global history of civilizations. Pollution, in other words, was everywhere.

Processes of hybridization are also worth noting in terms of the subjects of this study. The Qing imperial formation can be dealt with rather quickly on this score. It is difficult to imagine anything more thoroughly hybrid than the Qing notion of rulership. The imperium can easily be pictured as an ever shifting contingent network made up, for example, of ritual sites, lower Yangtze academies and clans, Sons of Heaven, European "sing-songs," Korean and Gurkha embassies, cakravartin kings, the Mountain Retreat for Escaping Summer Heat, and celestial bodhisattvas. Moreover, Qing leaders seem not only to have acknowledged as much, but had a means for operating within such a universe—that's what patterning discourse and centering were all about.

The British imperial formation creates other sorts of problems, but it was no less hybridized. On the one hand, the embassy to China was shot through with easily identifiable modernist elements, not the least being the notion of sovereignty that Macartney presented to the Qianlong emperor. Yet, the sovereign state that Macartney ventured from was also itself part of an empire, one upon which not long afterwards the sun would never set. It is especially dubious to speak of pure forms existing in England at the end of the eighteenth century, since British global empire building provided pathways for all kinds of diversity to leak into Britain. By the end of the nineteenth century, Great Britain was a thoroughly hybridized social realm over which sat a wholly new sovereign, the Queen-Empress. It goes without saying that this was no less the case in the United States. Is it any wonder, therefore, that a major symptom of bourgeois hysteria involved pollution?

I wonder, therefore, how seriously we should take statesmen or historians who talk to us about national uniqueness, national essences, or the special qualities of a people. Or how much credence we should give those triumphalist histories that glorify the present at the expense of the past. Or tell us about the oversights and failures of other peoples in other times and places? How much longer should we limit our inquiries to what increasingly seem to be artificially bounded units such as the individual, the nation, or the culture?

Given these concerns, perhaps conceptualizing a different sort of history is not very difficult. Such a history would focus its attention on networks of relationships among heterogeneous agents, rather than discrete units organized around uncomplicated notions of cause and effect. Moreover, if we are indeed all hybrids of one sort or another, then the presumed gap between past and present, between "us" and "them" may be no more than a particular kind of modernist fiction. It is not a temporal or spatial gap that is at issue here, but an imaginary distance that we must cross. Being born in a particular nation and speaking its language does not give one privileged access to the past of that place. One still has to translate and interpret; they both require empathy and imagination.

In a sense, then, engaging the past becomes part of the ongoing process of hybridization. Our reward for transgressing boundaries is that we might be able to grasp, however fleetingly, that there were other ways of doing things, other ways of being in the world. We also can see that there were other kinds of constraints, other limitations, other forms of power that shaped subjectivities quite different from our own. Without reducing the past to identity with the present or, conversely, without affirming our own superiority over those who preceded us, such engagements with difference allow the possibility of other forms of critique, ones that may be more broadly humanistic than those so far imagined by enlightened reason. Perhaps such considerations will allow us to begin to address the questions with which this section opened. Perhaps they will also allow us once again to sense pattern, where now we can see only the presence or absence of progress.

APPENDIX

Calendar of Events While the British Embassy was in Rehe

September 8, 1793
The emperor bestows a feast for his retinue, imperial princes and dukes, high officials, the Mongol princes, and the prince of Qinghai.
An official is ordered to sacrifice at the ancestral temple.
Three imperial instructions are issued (GZCSL, 1434:3b–7a).

September 9, 1793
The emperor bestows a feast identical to that of the day before with the addition of the ambassador of the Burmese king.
An imperial instruction is issued regarding the shortcomings of the English embassy.
Various rewards are conferred (GZCSL, 1434:7a–8b).

September 10, 1793
An imperial order is dispatched to Liang Kentang on matters unrelated to the British embassy (GZCSL, 1434:8a).

September 11, 1793
An imperial prince is ordered to perform a sacrifice to Confucius.
An imperial instruction is issued amending the revisions to plans for the British embassy (GZCSL, 1434:8a–9a).

September 12, 1793
Imperial princes are ordered to perform two sacrifices.
An imperial instruction is issued and various rewards are conferred (GZCSL, 1434:9a–b).

September 13, 1793
An official is ordered to perform sacrifice to emperor Hung Taiji.
Two imperial instructions are issued (GZCSL, 1434:9b–11a).

September 14, 1793
The emperor takes his throne in the great tent in the Garden of Ten
Thousand Trees and receives the English ambassador Lord Macartney and
vice-ambassador Staunton.
The emperor bestows a feast for the English ambassador, the imperial
retinue, imperial princes and dukes, high officials, the Mongol princes,
and the Burmese ambassador.
The emperor composes a poem about the English embassy (GZCSL,
1434:11a–b).

September 15, 1793
An official is ordered to perform a sacrifice to emperor Nurhaci.
Three imperial instructions are issued (GZCSL, 1434:11b–14a).

September 16, 1793
The emperor receives two Central Asia noblemen in audience, and
bestows a feast for them, the imperial retinue, imperial princes and dukes,
high officials, and the Mongol princes.
Two imperial instructions are issued (GZCSL, 1434:14b–17a).

September 17, 1793
The emperor's birthday is celebrated. Officials are dispatched to the
imperial ancestral temple and twelve other locations to perform sacrifices.
The emperor takes his throne and the imperial retinue, imperial
princes and dukes, high officials and those below them, the Mongol
princes, the Burmese and English ambassadors and others perform the
rite of offering congratulations to the emperor.
The emperor bestows a feast for those offering congratulations
(GZCSL, 1434:17a–18a).

September 18, 1793
Three imperial instructions are issued (GZCSL, 1434:18a–20b).

September 19, 1793
The emperor bestows a feast identical to the one that occurred on his
birthday.
An imperial instruction is issued regarding a request from the
Burmese ambassador (GZCSL, 1434:18a, 20b–21b).

September 20, 1793

Four imperial instructions are issued, including one dealing with requests from the English ambassador (*GZCSL*, 1435:1a–6b).

September 21, 1793

An imperial prince is ordered to perform a sacrifice.

Two imperial instructions are issued (*GZCSL*, 1435:6b–8b).

GLOSSARY OF CHINESE CHARACTERS

bai 拜

Baohe dian 保和殿

beichen 陪臣

Bishu Shan zhuang 避暑山庄

biao 表

biaowen 表文

bin 稟

Binli 賓禮

bubei bukang 不卑不亢

bucheng shiti 不成事體

bugui 不貴

changchao 常朝

Changchun yuan 長春園

chaogong zhi li 朝貢之禮

chen 臣

cheng (sincerity) 誠

chuan 傳

ci wei zui yao 此為最要

da 達

Dachao 大朝

datong 大同

Daxingren 大行人

daizou 代奏

de 德

dianshou 點首

ding 定

dingli 頂禮

diqiu 地球

Dishi 帝師

duici 對辭

en 恩

fang wei tuoshan 方為妥善

fangwu 方物

fanwang 蕃王

Fanglue guan 方略館

feishi 非是

fenshi 粉飾

fengjian shi zhong 豐儉適中

geng 懇

gong (gifts) 貢

gong (reverence) 恭

Gong bu 工部

gongcha 貢差

gongdan 貢單

gonghang 公行

gongjing 恭敬

Gongzhong shangyu 宮中上諭

Guanglu si 光祿寺

gui 跪

guibao 貴寶

guikou 跪叩

guo 國

guojia 國家

guojia shengjiao 國家聲教

guoshi 國師

hang 行

haoshi 好事

he 和

Honglu si 鴻臚寺

hu 忽

Hu bu 戶部

huangdi 黃帝

huairou yuanren 懷柔遠人

huihu 回護

hungui 悃憒

hutu 糊塗

Jiali 嘉禮

jiangjiu 將就

jiaojing 驕矜

jiaowang guozheng 矯枉過正

jiayu 駕馭

jie 節

Jili 吉禮

Jiujing sanshi dian 九經三事殿

juni 拘泥

Junji chu 軍機處

Junli 軍禮

kaozheng 考證

kebi 可鄙

kenqiu wuyan 狠求無壓

ke xiao 可笑

koubai 叩拜

koushou 叩首

koutou 叩頭

kuanyan xiangji 寬嚴相濟

Lama shuo 喇嘛說

li 禮

Lifan yuan 理蕃院

lijie 禮節

liuxin 留心

liuxin chakan 留心察看

maodu wuyan 冒賣無厭

Neiwufu 內務府

Ningshou gong 寧壽宮

Pileng 披楞

ping 平

qin 親

qincha 欽差

qing 輕

ruyi 如意

sangui jiukou 三跪九叩

shang 賞

shangyu 上諭

shang zhi tizhi 尚佑體制

shenbian 甚便

shenhao 甚好

shichen 使臣

shu 屬

shuanggui fufu 雙跪府伏

shun 順

shu shu guodang 殊屬過當

si 私

siyi 四夷

songli 竦立

Taihe dian 太和殿

teci 特賜

Tianming 天命

Tianqiu 天球

Tianxia 天下

tiben 題本

ting 聽

tingji 廷寄

ting zheng 聽政

tizhi 體制

tuchan 土產

tuo 妥

tuoban 妥辦

waiyi 外夷

Wanshu yuan 萬樹園

Wangli 王禮

wenhua zhidu 文化制度

Wuli 五禮

Wumen 午門

wuwei 無謂

wuyan　無壓

wuyong　無用

wuzhi　無知

wuzhi waiyi　無矢外夷

xiang hua zhi cheng　向化之誠

xiangjian　相見

xiangtong　相同

xianguan zishou　限關自守

xiantan　閒談

xie　謝

xin　新

Xiongli　凶禮

yanyan　筵燕

yaoxiang　遙向

ye　謁

yi (foreigners)　夷

yi (curiosities)　異

yi binli qin bangguo　以賓禮親邦國

yijie　儀節

Yiqingkuang dian　依清曠殿

yiren　夷人

yi shi tong ren　一視同人

yongxin zhizao　用心製造

youhou　優厚

yu　諭

Yuanming yuan　圓明園

zhang　掌

zhaojian　詔見

zhaoliao　照料

zheng　政

Zhengda Guangming dian　正大光明殿

zhengdian　正殿

zhi (faithfulness)　摯

zhi (regulate)　治

zhi (offering)　摯

zhonghai　中海

zhuhou　諸候

zhupi zouzhe　硃批奏摺

Ziguang ge　紫光閣

ziji　字寄

zongbo　宗伯

ABBREVIATIONS

DQDH	*Da Qing huidian*
DQHDSL	*Da Qing huidian shili*
DQHDT	*Da Qing huidian tu*
DQTL	*Da Qing tongli* [1824] 1883
DTKYL	*Da Tang Kaiyuan li*
EB	*Encyclopaedia Britannica*
ECCP	Hummel, *Eminent Chinese of the Ch'ing Period*
ESS	*Encyclopedia of the Social Sciences*
FO	Foreign Office Records, PRO (see Bibliography, Archival Sources)
GZCSL	*Gaozong Chun huangdi shilu*
GZSY	*Gongzhong shangyu* (see Bibliography, Archival Sources)
HCTD	*Huangchao tongdian*
HCTZ	*Huangchao tongzhi*
HCWXTK	*Huangchao wenxian tongkao*
HQZGT	*Huang Qing zhigong tu*
KEKJL	*Kuoerke jilue*
IOAC	India Office Amherst Correspondence (see Bibliography, Archival Sources)
IOMC	India Office Macartney Correspondence (see Bibliography, Archival Sources)
IOR	India Office Records (see Bibliography, Archival Sources)

LBZL	*Libu zeli*
MD	Macartney Diary, in J. L. Cranmer-Byng, ed., *Lord Macartney's Embassy* (1963)
MJL	*Ming jili*
PRO	Public Record Office (see Bibliography, Archival Sources)
QJQCWJSL	*Qing Jiaqingchao waijiao shiliao*
QLHD	*Qinding Da Qing huidian*
QSG	*Qing shigao*
RHZ	*Rehe zhi*
SKQS	*Siku quanshu*
SMFBM	Symposium Marking the Bicentenary of the First British Mission to China, Chengde, PRC, September 13–18, 1993
SWSCJ	*Shiwen shiquan ji*
SZRSL	*Shengzu Ren huangdi shilu*
SZZSL	*Shizu Zhang huangdi shilu*
WLTK	*Wuli tongkao*
WXCB	*Wenxian congbian*
WZTZ	*Weizang tongzhi*
ZGCB	*Zhang gu congbian*
ZPZZ	*Zhupi zouzhe* (see Bibliography, Archival Sources)

BIBLIOGRAPHY

Archival Sources

British Library, London, England.
First Historical Archive of China, Peking:
> *Gongzhong shangyu.* Imperial edicts in the palace collection. [Citations in text are to reign date, microfilm reel number, and page number.]
> *Zhupi zouzhe.* Imperially rescripted palace memorials.
India Office Records, London, England:
> Bengal Political Consultations, Range 114, vol. 63, Proceedings of October 3, November 2, and November 30, 1792.
> Cobb, James. 1792. "Sketches respecting China and Embassies sent thither." India Office Macartney Correspondence, vol. 91.
> Col. Cathcart's Embassy to China, 1787–1789, vol. 90.
> "First, Second and Third Reports of the Select Committee of the Court of Directors on the Export Trade with the East Indies." *Early Parliamentary Papers Related to India,* 1793.
> India Office Amherst Correspondence. Lord Amherst's Embassy, 1815–1817, vols. 196–198.
> India Office Macartney Correspondence. Lord Macartney's Embassy, 1787–1810, vols. 91–93.
> ———. Miscellaneous Documents, 1782–1815, vol. 20.
Public Record Office, London:
> Foreign Office Records.

Sources in English and French

Abdel-Malek, Anouar. 1963. "Orientalism in Crisis." *Diogenes* 42:103–140.

Abbott, Jacob. 1843. *China and the English, or the Character and Manner of the Chinese as Illustrated in the History of Their Intercourse with Foreigners.* New York: William Holdredge.

Adams, Charles Francis, ed. 1853. *The Works of John Adams.* Boston: Little, Brown and Co.

Adams, John Q. 1909–1910. "J. Q. Adams on the Opium War." *Massachusetts Historical Society Proceedings* 43:295–325.

Ahmed, Zahiruddin. 1970. *Sino-Tibetan Relations in the Seventeenth Century.* Rome: Instituto Italiano Per il ed Estremo Oriente.

Allen, B. S. 1937. *Tides in English Taste.* 2 vols. Cambridge, Mass.: Harvard University Press.

Altick, R. 1978. *The Shows of London.* Cambridge, Mass.: Belknap Press.

Anagnost, Ann. 1993. "The Nationscape: Movement in a Field of Vision." *positions* 1 (3):585–606.

Anderson, Aeneas. 1795. *A Narrative of the British Embassy to China.* Basil: J. J. Tourneisen.

The Annual Register or a View of the History, Politics, and Literature of the Year. [1794] 1797. London: Robert Dodsley.

Appleton, W. W. 1951. *A Cycle of Cathay.* New York: Columbia University Press.

Asad, Talal. 1993. *Genealogies of Religion.* Baltimore: Johns Hopkins University Press.

Auber, Peter. 1834. *China: An Outline of Its Government, Laws, and Policy.* London: Partbury, Allen Co.

Backhouse, E., and J.O.P. Bland. 1914. *Annals and Memoirs of the Court of Peking.* Boston: Houghton Mifflin.

Baker, K. 1992. "Defining the Public Sphere in Eighteenth-Century France: Variations on a Theme by Habermas." In Calhoun 1992:181–211.

Bald, R. C. 1950. "Sir William Chambers and the Chinese Garden." *Journal of the History of Ideas* 11(3):287–320.

Banno, Masataka. 1964. *China and the West: 1858–1861.* Cambridge, Mass.: Harvard University Press.

Barker, Francis, ed. 1985. *Europe and Its Others.* 2 vols. Colchester: University of Essex.

Barlow, Tani. 1993. "Career in Postwar China Studies." *positions* 1 (1):224–267.

Barrow, John. [1804] 1972. *Travels in China*. Reprint, Taipei: Ch'eng Wen Publishing Co.

Bartlett, Beatrice S. 1991. *Monarchs and Ministers: The Grand Council in Mid-Ch'ing China, 1723–1820*. Berkeley: University of California Press.

Bartlett, Thomas. 1983. "Ireland 1769–72." In Roebuck 1983, 66–87.

Bawden, Charles R. 1968. *The Modern History of Mongolia*. London: Weidenfeld and Nicolson.

———, ed. and trans. 1961. *The Jebtsundamba Khutukhtus of Urga*. Wiesbaden: Otto Harrassowitz.

Bell, Catherine. 1992. *Ritual Theory, Ritual Practice*. New York: Oxford University Press.

Bell, John (of Antermony) [1762] 1965. *A Journey from St. Petersburg to Pekin, 1719–22*. Ed. J. L. Stevenson. Reprint, Edinburgh: Edinburgh University Press.

Belsey, Catherine. 1980. *Critical Practice*. London: Methuen.

Bernal, Martin. 1987. *Black Athena*. New Brunswick: Rutgers University Press.

Bickers, Robert, ed. 1993a. *Ritual and Diplomacy: The Macartney Mission to China 1792–1794*. London: The British Association of Chinese Studies and Wellsweep Press.

———. 1993b. "History, Legend and Treaty Port Ideology." In Bickers 1993a:81–92.

———. 1993c. "Treaty Port History and the Macartney Mission." Paper presented at the SMFBM.

Bloch, Maurice. 1987. "The Ritual of the Royal Bath in Madagascar." In D. Cannadine and S. Price, eds., *Rituals of Royalty: Power and Ceremonial in Traditional Societies*, 271–297. Cambridge: Cambridge University Press.

Blue, Gregory. 1988. "Traditional China in Western Social Thought." Ph.D. diss., Cambridge University.

Brantlinger, Patrick. 1990. *Crusoe's Footprints: Cultural Studies in Britain and America*. New York: Routledge.

Breckenridge, C. 1989. "The Aesthetics and Politics of Colonial Collecting: India at the World Fairs." *Comparative Studies in Society and History* 31 (2):195–216.

Burke, Edmund. 1866. *The Works of Edmund Burke*. 12 vols. Boston: Little, Brown, and Co.

Burke, Peter. 1992. *History & Social Theory*. Ithaca: Cornell University Press.

Buxton, Timothy. 1985. *Talcott Parsons and the Capitalist Nation-State.* Toronto: University of Toronto Press.

Calhoun, Craig, ed. 1992. *Habermas and the Public Sphere.* Cambridge, Mass.: MIT Press.

Cameron, Nigel. 1970. *Barbarians and Mandarins.* Chicago: University of Chicago Press.

Cammann, Schuyler. 1949–1950. "The Panchen Lama's Visit to China in 1780: An Episode in Anglo-Tibetan Relations." *Far East Quarterly* 9: 3–19.

———. 1953. "Presentation of Dragon Robes by the Ming and Ch'ing Courts." *Sinologica* 3:193–202.

Cannadine, David. 1983. "The Context, Performance and Meaning of Ritual: The British Monarchy and the 'Invention of Tradition,' c. 1820–1977." In E. Hobsbawm and T. Ranger, eds., *The Invention of Tradition,* 101–164. Cambridge: Cambridge University Press.

———. 1987. "Introduction." In D. Cannadine and S. Price, eds., *Rituals of Royalty: Power and Ceremonial in Traditional Societies,* 1–19. Cambridge: Cambridge University Press.

Carl, Katherine. 1905. *With the Empress Dowager of China.* New York: Century Co.

Certeau, Michel de. 1986. *Heterologies: Discourse on the Other.* Trans. B. Massumi. Minneapolis: University of Minnesota Press.

———. 1988. *The Writing of History.* New York: Columbia University Press.

Chan, Wing-tsit. 1963. *A Source Book in Chinese Philosophy.* Princeton: Princeton University Press.

Chang Te-ch'ang. 1974. "The Economic Role of the Imperial Household (*Nei-wu-fu*) in the Ch'ing Dynasty." *Journal of Asian Studies* 31 (2):243–274.

Chatterjee, Partha. 1986. *Nationalist Thought and the Colonial World—A Derivative Discourse.* London: Zed Books.

Chayet, Anne. 1985. *Les temples de Jehol et leurs modeles tibetains.* Paris: Editions Recherche sur les Civilisations.

Ch'en Shou-yi. 1936. "The Chinese Garden in Eighteenth Century England." *T'ien Hsia* 2(4):321–339.

Ch'en, Ta-tuan. 1968. "Investiture of Liu'ch'iu Kings in the Ch'ing Period." In Fairbank, ed. 1968:135–164.

Chia Ning. 1992. "The Li-fan Yuan in the Early Ch'ing Dynasty." Ph.D. diss., Johns Hopkins University.

————. 1993. "The Lifanyuan and the Inner Asian Rituals in the Early Qing (1644–1795)." *Late Imperial China* 14 (1):60–92.

Chun, Allen J. 1983. "The Meaning of Crisis and the Crisis of Meaning in History: An Interpretation of the Anglo-Chinese Opium War." *Bulletin of the Institute of Ethnology Academia Sinica* 55:169–228.

Chun, Hae-jong. 1968. "Sino-Korean Relations in the Ch'ing Period." In Fairbank 1968:90–111.

Clunas, Craig. 1991. "Whose Throne Is It Anyway? The Qianlong Throne in the T. T. Tsui Gallery." *Orientations* 22 (7):44–50.

Cohn, Bernard. 1987. *An Anthropologist among the Historians and Other Essays.* Delhi: Oxford University Press.

Cohen, Paul A. 1984. *Discovering History in China: American Historical Writings on the Recent Chinese Past.* New York: Columbia University Press.

————. 1992. "The Contested Past: The Boxers as History and Myth." *Journal of Asian Studies* 51 (1):82–113.

The Collected Works of Thu'u bkwan blo bzang chos gyi nyi ma. 1969. Introd. E. Gene Smith. Vol. 1. New Delhi: Ngawang Gelek Demo.

Collingwood, R. G. [1946] 1977. *The Idea of History.* Reprint, New York: Oxford University Press.

Comaroff, Jean. 1985. "Bodily Reform as Historical Practice: The Semantics of Resistance in Modern South Africa." *International Journal of Psychology* 20:541–567.

Connor, Patrick and S. L. Sloman, 1981. *William Alexander: An English Artist in Imperial China.* Brighton: Brighton Borough Council.

Cranmer-Byng, J. L. 1957–1958. "Lord Macartney's Embassy to Peking in 1793." *Journal of Oriental Studies* 4 (1–2):117–186.

————. 1965–1966. "The Chinese Attitude Towards External Relations." *International Journal* 21 (1):57–77.

————. 1968–1969. "The Chinese Perception of a World Order." *International Journal* 24 (1):166–171.

————. 1983. "China, 1792–94." In Roebuck 1983:216–243.

————, ed. 1963. *An Embassy to China: being the Journal Kept by Lord Macartney during his Embassy to the Emperor Ch'ien-lung, 1793–94.* London: Longmans, Green and Co.

Cranmer-Byng, J. L., and T. H. Levere. 1981. "A Case Study of Cultural Collision: Scientific Apparatus in the Macartney Embassy to China, 1793." *Annals of Science* 38:503–525.

Crosby, Christina. 1991. *The Ends of History.* New York: Routledge.

Crossley, Pamela. 1985. "An Introduction to the Qing Foundation Myth." *Late Imperial China* 6 (2):13–24.

———. 1987. "Manzhou yuanliu kao and the Formalization of the Manchu Heritage." *Journal of Asian Studies* 46 (4):761–790.

———. 1990. *Orphan Warriors: Three Manchu Generations and the End of the Qing World.* Princeton: Princeton University Press.

———. 1992. "The Rulerships of China." *American Historical Review* 97 (5):1468–1483.

Curtis, L. P., and H. W. Liebert. 1963. *Esto Perpetua: The Club of Dr. Johnson and His Friends, 1764–1784.* Hamden, Conn.: Archon Books.

Das, Sarat Chandra. 1882. "Contributions on Tibet." *Journal of the Asiatic Society of Bengal* 51:29–43.

Davis, John Francis. 1836. *The Chinese: A General Description of the Empire of China and Its Inhabitants.* 2 vols. London: Charles Knight.

Der Ling. 1929. *Kowtow.* New York: Dodd, Mead & Co.

Dirks, Nicholas, ed. 1992. *Colonialism and Culture.* Ann Arbor: University of Michigan Press.

Dirlik, Arif. 1978. *Revolution and History: Origins of Marxist Historiography in China, 1919–1937.* Berkeley: University of California Press.

Du Halde, Jean Baptiste. 1735. *Description geographique, historique, chronologique, politique, et physique de l'empire de la Chine et de la Tartarie chinoise.* Paris: Lemercier.

Duiker, William J., and Jackson Spielvogel. 1994. *World History.* Minneapolis/St. Paul: West Publishing Co.

Durand, Pierre-Henri. 1993a. "Langage bureaucratique et histoire: Variations autour du Grand Conseil et de l'ambassade Macartney." *Études chinoises* 12 (1):41–145.

———. 1993b. "Seen and Unseen Sides of the Macartney Embassy." Paper presented at the SMFBM.

Durkheim, Emile. 1915. *Elementary Forms of the Religious Life.* London: Allen and Unwin.

Duyvendak, J. J. L. 1939. "The Last Dutch Embassy to the Chinese Court (1794–1795)." *T'oung Pao* 34 (1–2):1–116.

Eagleton, Terry. 1990. *The Ideology of the Aesthetic.* Oxford: Blackwell.

Eames, James B. 1909. *The English in China.* London and Dublin: Curzon Press.

Elisséeff, Vadime. 1963. "The Middle Empire, a Distant Empire, an Empire without Neighbors." *Diogenes* 42:60–64.

Elliott, Mark. 1990. "Bannerman and Townsman: Ethnic Tension in Nineteenth-Century Jiangnan." *Late Imperial China* 11 (1):36–74.

————. 1992. "Turning a Phrase: Translation in the Early Qing through a Temple Inscription of 1645." In M. Gimm, G. Stary, and M. Weiers, eds. *Aetas Manjurica,* 3:12–41. Wiesbaden: Otto Harrassowitz.

————. 1993. "Resident Aliens: The Manchu Experience in China, 1644–1760." Ph.D. diss., University of California, Berkeley.

Ellis, Henry. 1817. *Journal of the Proceedings of the Late Embassy to China.* London: John Murray.

Elman, Benjamin. 1989. "Imperial Politics and Confucian Societies in Late Imperial China: The Hanlin and Donglin Academies." *Modern China* 15 (4):379–418.

————. 1990. *Classicism, Politics, and Kinship.* Berkeley: University of California Press.

Encyclopaedia Britannica. 1911. 11th ed. S.v. "Sovereignty."

Encyclopaedia Britannica: Micropaedia. 1974. 15th ed. S.v. "Tributary System."

Encyclopedia of the Social Sciences. 1934. S.v. "Tribute" and "Sovereignty."

Esherick, Joseph. 1972. "Harvard on China: The Apologetics of Imperialism." *Bulletin of Concerned Asian Scholars* 4 (4):9–16.

Europa und die Kaiser von China. 1985. Berliner Festspiele Insel Verlag. Berlin: H. Heeneman GmbH & Co.

Fabian, Johannes. 1983. *Time and the Other.* New York: Columbia University Press.

Fairbank, John K. 1942. "Tributary Trade and China's Relations with the West." *Far Eastern Quarterly* 1 (2):129–149.

————. [1948, 1958, 1971] 1979. *The United States and China.* Cambridge, Mass.: Harvard University Press.

————. 1953. *Trade and Diplomacy on the China Coast.* Stanford: Stanford University Press.

————. 1966. "China's World Order: The Tradition of Chinese Foreign Relations." *Encounter,* December, 14–20.

————. 1968. "The Early Treaty System in the Chinese World Order." In Fairbank, ed. 1968:257–275.

————. 1982. *China Bound.* New York: Harper and Row.

————. 1983. "Maritime and Continental in China's History." In J. K. Fairbank, ed., *The Cambridge History of China.* London: Cambridge University Press.

————. 1987. *The Great Chinese Revolution.* New York: Harper & Row.

————. 1988. "Born Too Late." *New York Review of Books* 35 (2) (18 February).

————, ed. 1968. *The Chinese World Order: Traditional China's Foreign Relations.* Cambridge, Mass.: Harvard University Press.

Fairbank, John K., Edwin O. Reischauer, and Albert Craig. 1989. *East Asia: Tradition and Transformation.* Boston: Houghton Mifflin Co.

Fairbank, John K., and S. Y. Teng. 1939. "On the Transmission of Ch'ing Documents." *Harvard Journal of Asiatic Studies* 4:12–46.

————. 1941. "On the Ch'ing Tributary System." *Harvard Journal of Asiatic Studies* 6:135–246.

Fan, Tsen-Chung. 1945. *Dr. Johnson and Chinese Culture.* London: The China Society.

Farquhar, David M. 1968. "The Origins of the Manchus' Mongolian Policy." In Fairbank, ed. 1968:198–205.

————. 1978. "Emperor as Bodhisattva in the Governance of the Ch'ing Empire." *Harvard Journal of Asiatic Studies* 38:5–34.

Farquhar, Judith. 1987. "Problems of Knowledge in Contemporary Chinese Medical Discourse." *Social Science and Medicine* 24 (12):1013–1021.

Farquhar, Judith, and J. Hevia. 1993. "Culture and Post-War American Historiography of China." *positions* 1 (2):486–525.

Fletcher, Joseph. 1968. "China and Central Asia, 1368–1844." In Fairbank, ed. 1968:206–224.

————. 1978a. "Ch'ing Inner Asia c. 1800." In D. Twitchett and J. K. Fairbank, eds., *The Cambridge History of China,* vol. 10, pt. 1:35–106. London: Cambridge University Press.

————. 1978b. "The Heyday of the Ch'ing Order in Mongolia, Sinkiang and Tibet." In D. Twitchett and J. K. Fairbank, eds., *The Cambridge History of China,* vol. 10, pt. 1:351–406.

Fôret, Phillipe. 1992. *Making an Imperial Landscape in Chengde, Jehol: The Manchu Landscape Enterprise.* Ph.D. diss., University of Chicago.

Foucault, Michel. 1972. *The Archaeology of Knowledge.* New York: Harper Torchbooks.

————. 1977. *Language, Counter-Memory, Practice.* Ithaca: Cornell University Press.

Francis, Dave. 1987. "The Great Transition." In R. J. Anderson, J. A. Hughes, and W. W. Sharrock, eds., *Classic Disputes in Sociology* 1–35. London: Allen & Unwin.

Franke, Herbert. 1978. *From Tribal Chieftain to Universal Emperor and God.* Munich: Verlag Der Bayerischen Akademie Der Wissenschaften.

————. 1981. "Tibetans in Yüan China." In John D. Langlois, Jr., ed., *China Under Mongol Rule*, 296–328. Princeton: Princeton University Press.

Fraser, T. G. 1983. "India 1780–86." In Roebuck 1983:154–215.

Fu, Lo-shu. 1966. *A Documentary Chronicle of Sino-Western Relations (1644–1820)*. 2 vols. Tucson: University of Arizona Press.

Gardner, Daniel. 1986. *Chu Hsi and the Ta-hsueh*. Cambridge, Mass.: Harvard University Press.

Geertz, Clifford. 1980. *Negara: The Theatre State in Nineteenth-Century Bali*. Princeton: Princeton University Press.

Gentleman's Magazine. 1794. (London) Vol. 64.

Giddens, Anthony. 1977. "Functionalism: aprés la lutte." In *Studies in Social and Political Theory*, 96–134. New York: Basic Books Inc.

Gingell, William. 1852. *The Ceremonial Usages of the Chinese, B.C. 1121*. London: Smith, Elder, & Co.

Grupper, Samuel M. 1980. *The Manchu Imperial Cult of the Early Ch'ing Dynasty*. Ph.D. diss., Indiana University.

————. 1984. "Manchu Patronage and Tibetan Buddhism During the First Half of the Ch'ing Dynasty." *Journal of the Tibetan Society* 4:47–75.

Guha, Ranajit, and G. Spivak. 1988. *Selected Subaltern Studies*. New York: Oxford University Press.

Gutzlaff, Charles. [1834] 1968. *Journal of Three Voyages along the Coast of China in 1831, 1832 & 1833, 1834*. Reprint, Taipei: Ch'eng-wen Publishing Co.

Guy, R. Kent. 1987. *The Emperor's Four Treasuries: Scholars and the State in the late Ch'ien-lung Era*. Cambridge, Mass.: Harvard Council on East Asian Studies.

Habermas, Jürgen. [1962] 1989. *The Structural Transformation of the Public Sphere*. Trans. T. Burger and F. Lawrence. Cambridge, Mass.: MIT Press.

————. 1983. "Modernity—An Incomplete Project." In H. Foster, ed., *The Anti-Aesthetic*, 3–15. Port Townsend, Wash.: Bat Press.

Hansen, Valerie. 1990. *Changing Gods in Medieval China, 1127–1276*. Princeton: Princeton University Press.

Haraway, Donna. 1989. *Primate Visions*. New York: Routledge.

Hay, John. 1983a. "Arterial Art." *Stone Lion* 11:70–84.

————. 1983b. "The Human Body as a Microcosmic Source of Macrocosmic Values in Calligraphy." In S. Bush and C. Murck, eds., *Theories of Art in China*, 74–102. Princeton: Princeton University Press.

————. 1994. "The Body Invisible in Chinese Art?" In A. Zito and T. Barlow, eds., *Body, Subject & Power in China*. 42–77. Chicago: University of Chicago Press.

Hebdige, Dick. 1988. *Hiding in the Light*. London: Routledge.

Hedin, Sven. 1933. *Jehol City of Emperors*. New York: E. P. Dutton.

Herbert, Christopher. 1991. *Culture and Anomie*. Chicago: University of Chicago Press.

Hevia, James. 1989. "A Multitude of Lords: Qing Court Ritual and the Macartney Embassy of 1793." *Late Imperial China* 10 (2):72–105.

———. 1990a. "Zhou Xirui guanyu Yihetuan yundong jieshuozhongde jige wenti" (Some problems in Esherick's interpretation of the Boxer Movement). *Yihetuan yanjiuhui tongxun* (Boxer Studies Society newsletter) 13 (October):5–8.

———. 1990b. "Making China 'Perfectly Equal.'" *Journal of Historical Sociology* 3 (4):380–401.

———. 1992. "Leaving a Brand on China: Missionary Discourse in the Wake of the Boxer Movement." *Modern China* 18 (3) (July):304–332.

———. 1993a. "The Macartney Embassy in the History of Sino-Western Relations." In Bickers 1993a:57–79.

———. 1993b. "Lamas, Emperors, and Rituals: Political Implications of Qing Imperial Ceremonies." *Journal of the International Association of Buddhist Studies* 16 (2):243–278.

———. 1994a. "Loot's Fate: The Economy of Plunder and the Moral Life of Objects 'From the Summer Palace of the Emperor of China.'" *History and Anthropology* 6 (4):319–345.

———. 1994b. "Sovereignty and Subject: Constructing Relations of Power in Qing Imperial Ritual." In A. Zito and T. Barlow, eds., *Body, Subjectivity, and Power in China*. 181–200. Chicago: University of Chicago Press.

———. 1994c. "Oriental Customs and Ideas: The Planning and Execution of the First British Embassy to China." Paper presented at the SMFBM. *Chinese Social Science Review* 7 (spring):135–157. Also presented at SMFBM 1993.

———. 1994d. "An Imperial Nomad and the Great Game: Thomas Francis Wade in China." Paper presented at the American Historical Association Annual Meeting, San Francisco, California, 9 January 1994.

———. 1995. "The Scandal of Inequality." *positions* (forthcoming).

Hinsley, F. H. 1969. "The Concept of Sovereignty and the Relations Between States." In W. J. Stankiewicz, ed., *In Defense of Sovereignty*, 275–288. New York: Oxford University Press.

————. 1986. *Sovereignty.* Cambridge: Cambridge University Press.

Hirst, Paul, and P. Woolley. 1982. *Social Relations and Human Attributes.* London and New York: Tavistock Publications Ltd.

Hobsbawm, Eric, and T. Ranger, eds. 1983. *The Invention of Tradition.* Cambridge: Cambridge University Press.

Hocart, A. M. 1952. "The Divinity of the Guest." In *The Life Giving Myth and Other Essays,* 76–85. London: Methuen.

Holman, James. 1835. *A Voyage Round the World.* 4 vols. London: Smith, Elder, and Co.

Hopkins, Jeffrey. 1987. *Emptiness Yoga.* Ithaca: Snow Lion Publications.

Horn, David B. 1961. *British Diplomatic Service, 1689–1789.* Oxford: Oxford University Press.

Hsü, Immanuel. 1960. *China's Entrance into the Family of Nations.* Cambridge, Mass.: Harvard University Press.

————. 1990. *The Rise of Modern China.* New York and London: Oxford University Press.

Hume, D. 1898. *Essays Moral, Political, and Literary.* Ed. T. Green and T. Grose. London: Longmans, Green, and Co.

Hummel, Arthur. 1943. *Eminent Chinese of the Ch'ing Period.* Washington: United States Government Printing Office.

Hunt, Michael. 1984. "Chinese Foreign Relations in Historical Perspective." In H. Harding, ed., *China's Foreign Relations in the 1980s,* 1–42. New Haven and London: Yale University Press.

Inden, Ronald. 1990. *Imagining India.* London: Blackwell.

Ishihama, Yumiko. 1992. "A Study of the Seals and Titles Conferred by the Dalai Lamas." In *Tibetan Studies: Proceedings of the 5th Seminar of the International Association for Tibetan Studies, Narita 1989,* 2:501–514. Narita: Naritasan Shinshoji.

Iyer, Raghavan. 1983. *Utilitarianism and All That.* London: Concord Grove Press.

Jagchid, Sechin. 1974. "Mongolian Lamaist Quasi-Feudalism During the Period of Manchu Domination." *Mongolian Studies* 1:27–54.

Jochim, Christian. 1979. "The Imperial Audience Ceremonies of the Ch'ing Dynasty." *Bulletin of the Society for the Study of Chinese Religions* 7: 88–103.

Johnston, Reginald. [1934] 1985. *Twilight in the Forbidden City.* Reprint, Oxford: Oxford University Press.

Jones, D. V. 1984. *Splendid Encounters.* Chicago: University of Chicago Libraries.

Jones, W. 1807. *The Works of Sir William Jones.* 13 vols. Ed. Lord Teignmouth. London: Stockdale and Walker.

Judovitz, Dalia. 1988. *Subjectivity and Representation in Descartes.* Cambridge: Cambridge University Press.

Kahn, Harold. 1971. *Monarchy in the Emperor's Eyes: Image and Reality in the Ch'ien-lung Reign.* Cambridge, Mass.: Harvard University Press.

Kant, I. 1987. *Critique of Judgement.* Indianapolis: Hackett.

Kantorowicz, Ernst. 1957. *The King's Two Bodies.* Princeton, N.J.: Princeton University Press.

Kessler, Lawrence. 1969. "Ethnic Composition of Provincial Leadership during the Ch'ing Dynasty." *Journal of Asian Studies* 28 (3):489–511.

Kim, Key-Hiuk. 1981. *The Last Phase of the East Asian World Order: Korea, Japan, and the Chinese Empire, 1860–1882.* Berkeley: University of California Press.

Kuhn, Philip. 1990. *Soulstealers: The Chinese Sourcery Scare of 1768.* Cambridge, Mass.: Harvard University Press.

Lachs, Phyllis S. 1965. *The Diplomatic Corps of Charles II and James II.* New Brunswick, N. J.: Rutgers University Press.

Laclau, E. 1990. "The Impossibility of Society." In *New Reflections on the Revolutions of Our Time,* 89–92. London: Verso.

Lam, Truong Buu. 1968. "Intervention versus Tribute in Sino-Vietnamese Relations, 1788–1790." In Fairbank, ed. 1968: 165–179.

Lamb, Alistair. 1958. "Lord Macartney in Batavia, March 1793." *Journal of South Seas Society* 14:57–68.

Lange, Laurence de. 1763. "Journal of the Residence of Mr. De Lange, Agent of His Imperial Majesty of All the Russias, Peter the First, at the Court of Peking, during 1721 and 1722." In John Bell of Antermony, *Travels from St. Petersburg to Diverse Parts of Asia, 1716, 1719, 1722,* vol. 2. Glasgow: Robert and A. Foulis.

Latour, Bruno. 1993. *We Have Never Been Modern.* Cambridge, Mass.: Harvard University Press.

Lattimore, Owen. 1934. *The Mongols of Manchuria.* New York: John Day.

Legge, James, trans. 1967. *Li Chi: Book of Rites.* Ed. Ch'u Chai and Winberg Chai. New Hyde Park, N.Y.: University Books.

Lessing, Ferdinand. 1942. *Yong-ho-kung: An Iconography of the Lamaist Cathedral in Peking with Notes on Lamaist Mythology and Cult.* Sino-Swedish Expedition Publications 18, vol. 1. Stockholm.

Levenson, Joseph. 1968. *Confucian China and Its Modern Fate.* Berkeley: University of California Press.

Levy, Anita. 1991. *Other Women.* Princeton: Princeton University Press.

Lindsay, H. H. 1833. *Report of the Proceedings on a Voyage to the Northern Ports of China in the Ship Lord Amherst.* London: B. Fellowes.

The Literary Digest. 1900.

Lloyd, Genevieve. 1984. *The Man of Reason.* London: Methuen.

Lowe, Donald. 1982. *History of Bourgeois Perception.* Chicago: University of Chicago Press.

Luce, G. H. 1925. "Chinese Invasion of Burma in the 18th Century." *Journal of the Burma Research Society* 15 (2):115–128.

Lutz, Catherine, and Jane Collins. 1991. "The Photograph as an Intersection of Gazes: The Example of *National Geographic.*" *Visual Anthropology Review* 7 (1):134–148.

Lynch, Michael, and S. Woolgar, eds. 1990. *Representation in Scientific Practice.* Cambridge, Mass.: MIT Press.

Mackenzie, John. 1986a. *Propaganda and Empire: The Manipulation of British Public Opinion, 1880–1960.* Manchester: Manchester University Press.

———, ed. 1986b. *Imperialism and Popular Culture.* Manchester: Manchester University Press.

———, ed. 1992. *Popular Imperialism and the Military.* Manchester: Manchester University Press.

Macnair, Harley F. [1923] 1967. *Modern Chinese History: Selected Readings.* Reprint, New York: Paragon.

Malone, Carroll B. 1934. *History of the Peking Summer Palaces under the Ch'ing Dynasty.* Urbana: University of Illinois Press.

Mancall, Mark. 1963. "The Persistence of Tradition in Chinese Foreign Policy." *Annals of the American Academy of Political and Social Science* 349:14–26.

———. 1968. "The Ch'ing Tribute System: An Interpretive Essay." In Fairbank, ed. 1968: 63–89.

———. 1971. *Russia and China: Their Diplomatic Relations to 1728.* Cambridge, Mass.: Harvard University Press.

Mani, Lata. 1985. "The Production of an Official Discourse on *Sati* in Early Nineteenth-Century Bengal." In Barker 1985, 1:107–127.

———. 1992. "Cultural Theory, Colonial Texts: Reading Eyewitness Accounts of Widow Burning." In Lawrence Grossberg et al., eds., *Cultural Studies,* 392–405. New York: Routledge.

March, Andrew. 1974. *The Idea of China.* New York: Praeger Publishers.

Marks, Robert. 1985. "The State of the China Field, or the China Field and the State." *Modern China* 11 (4):461–509.

Marshall, Peter. 1993. "Britain and China in the Late Eighteenth Century." In Bickers 1993a: 11–30. Also a paper presented at the smfbm.

Marshall, Peter, and G. Williams. 1982. *The Great Map of Mankind.* London: J. M. Dent.

Martens, Georg Friedrich von. 1795. *Summary of the Laws of Nations Founded on the Treaties and Customs of the Modern Nations of Europe.* Trans. William Cobbett. Philadelphia: Thomas Bradford Sons Ltd.

Martin, Dan. 1990. "Bonpo Canons and Jesuit Cannons: On Sectarian Factors Involved in the Ch'ien-lung Emperor's Second Goldstream Expedition of 1771–1776 Based Primarily on Some Tibetan Sources." *The Tibetan Journal* 15 (2):3–28.

Masuzawa, Tomoko. 1993. *In Search of Dreamtime.* Chicago: University of Chicago Press.

Matheson, James. 1836. *The Present Position and Prospects of the British Trade with China.* London: Smith, Elder, and Co.

Millward, James. 1993. *Beyond the Pass: Commerce, Ethnicity and the Qing Empire in Xinjiang, 1759–1864.* Ph.D. diss., Stanford University.

———. 1994. "A Uyghur Muslim in Qianlong's Court: The Meanings of the Fragrant Concubine." *Journal of Asian Studies* 53 (2):427–458.

Mitchell, Timothy. 1991. *Colonizing Egypt.* Berkeley: University of California Press.

Mohanty, Chandra T., A. Russo, and L. Torres. 1991. *Third World Women and the Politics of Feminism.* Bloomington: Indiana University Press.

Montesquieu, C. [1748] 1949. *The Spirit of the Laws.* Trans. T. Nugent. New York: Hafner Press.

Morse, H. B. [1926] 1966. *The Chronicles of the East India Company Trading to China.* Vol. 2 of 5. Reprint, Taipei: Ch'eng-wen Publishing Co.

———. 1910–1918. *The International Relations of the Chinese Empire.* 3 vols. London: Longhams, Green, and Co.

Moses, Larry. 1976. "Tang Tribute Relations with the Inner Asian Barbarians." In J. C. Perry and B. L. Smith, eds., *Essays on T'ang Society,* 60–89. Leiden: E. J. Brill.

Myers, Ramon. 1991. "How Did the Modern Chinese Economy Develop?—A Review Article." *Journal of Asian Studies* 50 (3):604–628.

Namier, Lewis. 1930. *England in the Age of the American Revolution.* London: Macmillan and Co.

————. 1965. *The Structure of Politics at the Accession of George III*. London: Macmillan and Co.

Naquin, Susan. 1992. "The Peking Pilgrimage to Miao-feng Shan: Religious Organizations and Sacred Site." In S. Naquin and Chün-fang Yü, eds., *Pilgrims and Sacred Sites in China*, 333–377. Berkeley: University of California Press.

Naquin, Susan, and Evelyn Rawski. 1987. *Chinese Society in the Eighteenth Century*. New Haven: Yale University Press.

Nash, John. 1991. *Views of the Royal Pavilion*. New York: Cross Rivers Press.

Needham, Joseph. 1965. *Science and Civilisation in China*, 4.2. Cambridge: Cambridge University Press.

Nisbet, Robert A. 1969. *Social Change and History: Aspects of the Western Theory of Development*. Oxford: Oxford University Press.

Palace Museum, eds. 1983. *Life of the Emperors and Empresses in the Forbidden City*. Peking: China Travel and Tourism Press.

Parker, E. H. 1896. "From the Emperor of China to King George the Third." *Nineteenth Century*, July, 45–54.

Parsons, Talcott. 1966. *Societies*. 2 vols. Englewood Cliffs, N. J.: Prentice Hall.

Peck, James. 1969. "The Roots of Rhetoric: The Professional Ideology of America's China Watchers." *Bulletin of Concerned Asian Scholars* 2 (1):59–69.

Petech, Luciano. 1950. *China and Tibet in the Early 18th Century: History of the Establishment of the Chinese Protectorate in Tibet*. Leiden: E. J. Brill.

Peterson, Willard. 1975. "Fang I-chih: Western Learning and the 'Investigation of Things.'" In William T. De Bary, ed., *The Unfolding of Neo-Confucianism*, 169–411. New York: Columbia University Press.

Peyrefitte, Alain. 1991. *Un Choc de Cultures: La Vision des Chinois*. Paris: Fayard.

————. 1992. *The Immobile Empire*. Trans. J. Rothschild. New York: Knopf.

————. 1994. "Chinese Protectionism versus Anglo-Saxon Free-Trade." *Chinese Social Science Quarterly* 7 (spring): 123–134. Paper also presented at the SMFBM.

Phillips, C. H. 1940. *The East India Company 1784–1834*. Manchester: Manchester University Press.

Pietz, William. 1985. "The Problem of the Fetish, I." *Res* 9:5–17.

Pindar, Peter. 1794–1795. *The Works of Peter Pindar, Esq*. 4 vols. London: John Walker.

Pletsch, Carl E. 1981. "The Three Worlds, or the Division of Social Scientific

Labor, circa 1950–1975." *Comparative Studies of Society and History* 23 (4):565–590.

Polachek, James. 1992. *The Inner Opium War.* Cambridge, Mass.: Council on East Asian Studies, Harvard University.

Pozdneyev, Aleksei. 1977. *Mongolia and the Mongols.* Bloomington: Indiana University Press.

Pritchard, E. H. 1929. *Anglo-Chinese Relations during the Seventeenth and Eighteenth Centuries.* Urbana: University of Illinois Press.

———. 1935. "Letters from Missionaries at Peking Relating to the Macartney Embassy (1793–1803)." *T'oung Pao* 31:1–57.

———. 1936. "The Crucial Years of Early Anglo-Chinese Relations, 1750–1800." *Research Studies of the State College of Washington* (Pullman, Washington) 4:3–4.

———. 1938. "The Instructions of the East India Company to Lord Macartney on His Embassy to China and His Reports to the Company, 1792–1794." *Journal of the Royal Asiatic Society,* pt. 1:201–230; pt. 2:375–396; and pt. 3:493–509.

———. 1943. "The Kotow in the Macartney Embassy to China in 1793." *Far East Quarterly* 2 (2):163–201.

Proudfoot, William. 1868. *Biographical Memoir of James Dinwiddie.* Liverpool: Edward Howell.

Rahul, R. 1968–1969. "The Role of Lamas in Central Asian Politics." *Central Asiatic Journal* 12:207–227.

Raphael, Vincete. 1993a. *Contracting Colonialism.* Durham: Duke University Press.

———. 1993b. "White Love: Surveillance and Nationalist Resistance in the U.S. Colonization of the Philippines." In A. Kaplan and D. E. Pease, eds., *Cultures of United States Imperialism,* 185–218. Durham: Duke University Press.

Rawski, Evelyn. 1991. "Ch'ing Imperial Marriage and the Problems of Rulership." In R. Watson and P. Ebrey, eds., *Marriage and Inequality in Chinese Society,* 170–203. Berkeley: University of California Press.

Reiss, Timothy J. 1982. *The Discourse of Modernism.* Ithaca and London: Cornell University Press.

Rennie, D. F. 1864. *The British Arms in North China and Japan: Peking 1860; Kagoshima 1862.* London: John Murray.

Richards, Thomas. 1990. *The Commodity Culture of Victorian England.* Stanford: Stanford University Press.

————. 1993. *The Imperial Archive.* London: Routledge.

Robbins, H. M. 1908. *Our First Ambassador to China: An Account of the Life of George, Earl of Macartney.* London: John Murray.

Rockhill, W. W. [1905] 1971. *Diplomatic Audiences at the Court of China.* Reprint, Taipei: Cheng Wen Publishing Co.

————. 1910. "The Dalai Lamas of Lhasa and Their Relations with the Manchu Emperors of China, 1644–1908." *T'oung Pao* 11:1–104.

Roebuck, Peter, ed. 1983. *Macartney of Lisanoure, 1737–1806: Essays in Biography.* Belfast: Ulster Historical Foundation.

Rorty, Richard. 1979. *Philosophy and the Mirror of Nature.* Princeton: Princeton University Press.

Rosenau, Pauline M. 1992. *Post-Modernism and the Social Sciences: Insights, Inroads, and Intrusions.* Princeton: Princeton University Press.

Rossabi, Morris. 1970. "The Tea and Horse Trade with Inner Asia During the Ming." *Journal of Asian History* 4 (2):136–167.

————. 1975. *China and Inner Asia: From 1368 to the Present Day.* New York: Pica Books.

————. 1988. *Khubilai Khan: His Life and Times.* Berkeley: University of California Press.

————, ed. 1983. *China among Equals: The Middle Kingdom and Its Neighbors, 10th–14th Centuries.* Berkeley: University of California Press.

Rowe, William. 1993. "State and Market in Mid-Qing Economic Thought: The Case of Chen Hongmou." *Études Chinoises* 12 (1):7–39.

Rozman, Gilbert, ed. 1981. *The Modernization of China.* New York: Free Press.

Ruegg, D. Seyfort. 1991. "*Mchod yon, yon mchod,* and *mchod gnas/yon gnas:* On the Historiography and Semantics of a Tibetan Religio-Social and Religio-Political Concept." In Ernst Steinkellner, ed., *Tibetan History and Language,* 441–453. Vienna: Arbeitskreis für Tibetische und Buddhistische Studien Universität Wien.

Russell, Bertrand. 1922. *The Problem of China.* London: George Allen & Unwin.

Ryan, Michael. 1982. *Marxism and Deconstruction: A Critical Articulation.* Baltimore and London: Johns Hopkins University Press.

Rydell, Robert. 1984. *All the World's a Fair.* Chicago: University of Chicago Press.

Said, Edward. 1978. *Orientalism.* New York: Vintage Books.

Sakai, Robert K. 1968. "The Ryukyu (Liu-ch'iu) Islands as a Fief of Satsuma." In Fairbank, ed. 1968:112–134.

Serruys, Henry. 1960. "Four Documents Relating to the Sino-Mongol Peace of 1570–1571." *Monumenta Serica* 19:1–66.

———. 1967. *Sino-Mongol Relations During the Ming II: The Tribute System and Diplomatic Missions (1400–1600).* Melanges Chinois et Boddiques, vol. 14. Brussels: Institut Belge Des Hautes Etudes Chinoises.

Singer, Aubrey. 1992. *The Lion and the Dragon: The Story of the First British Embassy to the Court of the Emperor Qianlong in Peking 1792–1794.* London: Barrie & Jenkins.

Sinor, Denis. 1972. "Horse and Pasture in Inner Asian History." *Oriens Extremus* 19 (1–2):171–183.

Skocpol, Theda. 1985. "Bringing the State Back In: Strategies of Analysis in Current Research." In P. B. Evans, D. Rueschemeyer, and T. Skocpol, eds., *Bringing the State Back In*, 3–37. Cambridge: Cambridge University Press.

Smith, Adam. 1976. *An Inquiry into the Nature and Causes of the Wealth of Nations.* 2 vols. Ed. R. H. Cambell, A. S. Skinner, and W. B. Todd. Reprint, Indianapolis: Liberty Press, 1981.

———. 1978. *Lectures on Jurisprudence.* Ed. R. L. Meek, D. D. Raphael, and P. G. Stein. Reprint, Indianapolis: Liberty Press, 1982.

Smith, Anthony D. 1973. *The Concept of Social Change: A Critique of the Functionalist Theory of Social Change.* London: Routledge & Kegan Paul.

Smith, Arthur [1894] 1970. *Chinese Characteristics.* Reprint, Port Washington, N.Y.: Kennikat Press.

Smith, Richard J. 1993. "Divination in Ch'ing Dynasty China." In R. J. Smith and D.W.Y. Kwok, eds., *Cosmology, Ontology, and Human Efficacy*, 141–178. Honolulu: University of Hawaii Press.

Snellgrove, David L. 1959. "The Notion of Divine Kingship in Tantric Buddhism." In *The Sacral Kingship*, 204–218. Leiden: E. J. Brill.

———. 1987. *Indo-Tibetan Buddhism.* 2 vols. Boston: Shambala.

Spence, Jonathan. 1966. *Ts'ao Yin and the K'ang-hsi Emperor: Bondservant and Master.* New Haven: Yale University Press.

———. 1992. *Chinese Roundabout.* New York: W. W. Norton & Co.

———. 1990. *In Search of Modern China.* New York: W. W. Norton.

Spence, Jonathan, and John E. Wills, Jr., eds. 1979. *From Ming to Qing: Conquest, Region, and Continuity in Seventeenth-Century China.* New Haven and London: Yale University Press.

Sperling, Elliot. 1983. *Early Ming Policy toward Tibet.* Ph.D. diss., University of Indiana.

Spivak, Gayatri S. 1987. *In Other Worlds.* New York: Methuen.

————. 1990. *The Post-Colonial Critic.* New York: Routledge.

Stallybrass, Peter, and A. White. 1986. *The Politics and Poetics of Transgression.* Ithaca: Cornell University Press.

Staunton, George L. 1797. *An Authentic Account of an Embassy from the King of Great Britain to the Emperor of China.* 3 vols. London: G. Nichol.

Stearns, Peter, M. Adas, and S. B. Schwartz. 1992. *World Civilizations.* New York: Harper-Collins.

Steegmann, J. 1936. *The Rule of Taste, from George I to George IV.* London: Macmillan.

Steele, John. 1917. *Book of Etiquette and Ceremony.* London: Probsthain & Co.

Steuart, James. 1966. *An Inquiry into the Principles of Political Economy.* 2 vols. Ed. A. S. Skinner. Edinburgh: Oliver & Boyd.

Stewart, Susan. 1994. *Crimes of Writing: Problems in the Containment of Representation.* Durham: Duke University Press.

Stokes, Eric. 1959. *The English Utilitarians and India.* Oxford: Oxford University Press.

Stoler, Ann. 1989. "Making Empire Respectable: The Politics of Race and Sexual Morality in 20th-Century Colonial Cultures." *American Ethnologist* 16 (4):634–660.

Tambiah, S. J. 1976. *World Conqueror and World Renouncer.* London, New York, Melbourne: Cambridge University Press.

Taussig, Michael. 1987. *Shamanism, Colonialism, and the Wild Man.* Chicago: University of Chicago Press.

Teignmouth, John Shore, ed. 1807. *Memoirs of the Life, Writings, and Correspondence of Sir William Jones.* 13 vols. London: J. Hatchard.

Teng, Ssu-yu, and J. K. Fairbank. [1954] 1975. *China's Response to the West: A Documentary Survey 1839–1923.* Cambridge, Mass.: Harvard University Press.

Thackeray, W. 1991. *The History of Henry Edmonds, Esq.* Oxford: Oxford University Press.

Thomas, Mathias. 1794. *The Imperial Epistle from Kien Long Emperor of China to George the Third King of Great Britain in the year 1794.* London: R. White.

Thomas, N. Forthcoming. "Liscensed Curiosities: Ethnographic Collecting and the Politics of Science in Eighteenth Century Britain." In R. Cardinal and J. Elsner, eds., *The Cultures of Collecting.* London: Reaktion Books.

Torbert, Preston M. 1977. *The Ch'ing Imperial Household Department: A Study of Its Organization and Principal Functions, 1662–1796*. Cambridge, Mass.: Harvard University Press.

Tribe, Keith. 1978. *Land, Labour and Economic Discourse*. London: Routledge & Kegan Paul.

Tsiang, T'ing-fu. 1936. "China and European Expansion." *Politica* 2:1–18.

Turner, Ernest S. 1959. *The Court of St. James*. London: Michael Joseph Ltd.

Turner, Graeme. 1990. *British Cultural Studies: An Introduction*. Boston: Unwin Hyman.

Turner, Victor. 1969. *The Ritual Process*. Ithaca: Cornell University Press.

Van Gennep, Arnold. [1909] 1960. *Rites of Passage*. Chicago: University of Chicago Press.

Vattel, Emmerich de. 1916. *The Law of Nations or the Principles of Natural Law Applied to the Conduct and to the Affairs of Nations and of Sovereigns*. 3 vols. Trans. Charles G. Fenwick. Washington: Carnegie Institution.

Viraphol, Sarasin. 1977. *Tribute and Profit: Sino-Siamese Trade, 1652–1853*. Cambridge, Mass.: Harvard University Press.

Viswanathan, Gauri. 1989. *Masks of Conquest: Literary Study and British Rule in India*. New York: Columbia University Press.

Wakeman, Frederic. 1970. "High Ch'ing: 1683–1839." In J. B. Crowley, ed., *Modern East Asia: Essays in Interpretation*, 1–28. New York: Harcourt Brace.

———. 1975. "Introduction." In F. Wakeman and C. Grant, eds., *Conflict and Control in Late Imperial China*, 1–25. Berkeley: University of California Press.

Waley, Arthur. 1958. *The Way and Its Power*. New York: Grove Press.

Waley-Cohen, Joanna. 1993. "China and Western Technology in the Late Eighteenth Century." *American Historical Review* 98 (5):1525–1544.

Wang, Tseng-Tsai. 1971. "The Audience Question: Foreign Representatives and the Emperor of China, 1858–1873." *Historical Journal* 14 (3):617–633.

———. 1993. "The Macartney Mission: A Bicentennial Review." In Bickers 1993a: 43–56.

Wang, Y. C. 1966. *Chinese Intellectuals and the West, 1872–1949*. Chapel Hill: University of North Carolina Press.

Watson, J. Steven. 1960. *The Reign of George III, 1760–1815*. Oxford: Clarendon Press.

Wechsler, Howard. 1985. *Offerings of Jade and Silk.* New Haven: Yale University Press.

White, Hayden. 1978. *Tropics of Discourse.* Baltimore: Johns Hopkins University Press.

Williams, S. Wells. [1895] 1966. *The Middle Kingdom.* Reprint, New York: Paragon Books Reprint Corp.

Wills, John E., Jr. 1968. "Ch'ing Relations with the Dutch, 1662–1690." 225–256. In Fairbank, ed. 1968: 225–256.

———. 1974. *Pepper, Guds and Parleys: The Dutch East India Company and China 1622–1681.* Cambridge, Mass.: Harvard University Press.

———. 1979a. "Maritime China from Wang Chih to Shih Lang: Themes in Peripheral History." In Spence and Wills 1979: 201–238.

———. 1979b. "State Ceremony in Late Imperial China: Notes for a Framework for Discussion." *Bulletin of the Society for the Study of Chinese Religions* 7: 46–57.

———. 1984. *Embassies and Illusions: Dutch and Portuguese Envoys to Kang-hsi, 1666–1687.* Cambridge, Mass.: Harvard University Press.

———. 1988. "Tribute, Defensiveness, and Dependency: Uses and Limits of Some Basic Ideas about Mid-Ch'ing Foreign Relations." *American Neptune* 48: 225–229.

———. 1993. "Maritime Asia, 1500–1800: The Interactive Emergence of European Domination." *American Historical Review* 98 (1):83–105.

Willson, Beckles. 1903. *Ledger and Sword.* 2 vols. London: Longmans, Green, and Co.

Woodside, Alexander. 1971. *Vietnam and the Chinese Model: A Comparative Study of Nguyen and Ch'ing Civil Government in the First Half of the Nineteenth Century.* Cambridge, Mass.: Harvard University Press.

Wu, Silas. 1970. *Communication and Imperial Control in China.* Cambridge, Mass.: Harvard University Press.

Wylie, Turrell V. 1978. "Reincarnation: A Political Innovation in Tibetan Buddhism." In Louis Ligeti, ed., *Proceedings of the Csoma De Korös Memorial Symposium,* 579–586. Budapest: Académiai Kiadó.

———. 1980. "Lama Tribute in the Ming Dynasty." In Michael Aris and Aung San Suu Kyi, eds., *Tibetan Studies in Honour of Hugh Richardson,* 335–340. Warminster, England: Aris & Phillips Ltd.

Young, Marilyn. 1973. "Letter to the Editors." *Bulletin of Concerned Asian Scholars* 5 (2):34–35.

Young, Robert. 1990. *White Mythologies: Writing History and the West.* New York: Routledge.

Zelin, Madeleine. 1984. *The Magistrate's Tael.* Berkeley: University of California Press.

Zhang Shunhong. 1993. "Historical Anachronism: The Qing Court's Perception of and Reaction to the Macartney Embassy." In Bickers 1993a: 31–42.

Zito, Angela. 1984. "Re-presenting Sacrifice: Cosmology and the Editing of Texts." *Ch'ing-shih wen-t'i* 5 (2):47–78.

———. 1987. "City Gods, Filiality, and Hegemony in Late Imperial China." *Modern China* 13 (3):333–371.

———. 1989. *Grand Sacrifice as Text/Performance: Ritual and Writing in Eighteenth Century China.* Ph.D. diss., University of Chicago.

———. 1993. "Ritualizing *Li*: Implications for Studying Power and Gender." *positions* 1 (2):321–348.

———. Forthcoming. *The Editor's Gaze and the Emperor's Body: Grand Sacrifice as Text/Performance in Eighteenth Century China.* Chicago: University of Chicago Press.

Sources in Chinese

Chen Qingying and Ma Lianlong. 1988. *Zhangjia guoshi Robidoji zhuan* (Biography of National Perceptor Zhangjia). Peking: Minzu Chubanshe.

Da Qing huidian (Assembled canon of the Great Qing). 1904. Peking: Palace Edition.

Da Qing huidian shili (Precedents of the assembled canon of the Great Qing). 1899. Peking: Palace Edition.

Da Qing huidian tu (Illustrations of the assembled canon of the Great Qing). 1818. Peking: Palace Edition.

Da Qing tongli (Comprehensive rites of the Great Qing). 1756. Reprinted in *SKQS*, series 8, vols. 125–130.

Da Qing tongli (Comprehensive rites of the Great Qing) (*DQTL*). [1824] 1883. Peking: Palace Edition.

Da Tang Kaiyuan li (Rites of the Emperor Kaiyuan of the Great Tang). ca 732. Reprinted in *SKQS*, series 8, vols. 99–108.

Dai Yi. 1992. *Qianlong di jiqi shidai* (The Qianlong emperor and his times). Peking: People's University Press.

Du Jiang. 1993. "Yingshi Chengde zhi xing de huigu" (Recalling the British mission in Chengde). Paper presented at the SMFBM.

Gaozong Chun huangdi shilu (Veritable records of the Qianlong emperor). 1964. Taipei: Huawen Shuju.

Guo Chengkang. 1993. "Qianlong huangdi de xiyang guan" (The Qianlong emperor's view of the West). Paper presented at the SMFBM.

Guo Yunjing. 1991. "Shilun Qingdai bingfei biguan suoguo" (Discussion on why the Qing was not a "closed-door" period). In Association for the History of Sino-Foreign Relations, ed., *Zhongwai guanxishi luncong* (Collection of papers on Sino-foreign relations) 3:182–195. Peking: World Knowledge Press.

Hu Sheng. 1981. *Cong Yapian zhanzhen dao Wusi yundong* (From the Opium War to the May Fourth Movement). Peking: People's Press.

Huang Qing zhigong tu (The August Qing's illustrated accounts of tribute-bearing domains). [1761] 1796. In SKQS, series 3, vols. 170–171.

Huangchao tongdian (Comprehensive canon of the August Court). 1785. Peking: Palace Edition.

Huangchao tongzhi (Comprehensive annals of the August Court). 1785. Peking: Palace Edition.

Huangchao wenxian tongkao (Comprehensive examination of writings offered up to the August Court). 1785. Peking: Palace Edition.

Kuoerke jilue (Record of the Gurkha wars). 1793. Peking: Palace edition.

Libu zeli (Precedents of the Board of Rites). 1820. Peking: Palace Edition.

Liu Fengyun. 1993. "Lun shiba shiji Zhong Ying tongshi de lijie chongtu (A discussion of the ceremonial controversy during the British embassy to eighteenth-century China). Paper presented at the SMFBM.

Liu Yuwen. 1993. "Qianlong chao waishi ji dui wai zhengce chuyi" (A view of the Qianlong court's diplomacy and foreign policy). Paper presented at the SMFBM.

Ming jili (Collected rites of the Ming dynasty). 1530. Reprinted in SKQS, series 8, vols. 113–124.

Qinding Da Qing huidian (Collected statutes of the Qianlong reign). 1761. Peking: Woodblock Palace Edition.

Qing Jiaqingchao waijiao shiliao (Historical sources on the foreign relations of the Jiaqing Court). 1932. Peking.

Qing shigao (Draft history of the Qing dynasty). 1928. Peking: Peking Historical Association.

Rehe zhi (Gazetteer of Rehe). [1781] 1934. Reprint, Dalian, Liaodong: Leihai Shushe.

Shengzu Ren huangdi shilu (Veritable records of the Kangxi emperor). 1964. Taipei: Huawen Shuju.

Shiwen Shiquanji (Poems and Prose of the Ten Great Campaigns of the Qianlong Reign). 1962. Taiwan: Geda shuju.

Shizu Zhang huangdi shilu (Veritable records of the Shunzhi emperor). 1964. Taipei: Huawen Shuju.

Siku quanshu (Complete library of the Four Treasuries). [1970] 1982. Comp. Ji Yun. Original preface dated 1779. Reprint, Taipei: Shangwu Yinshuguan.

Tsiang T'ing-fu. [1934] 1965. "Zhongguo yu jindai shijie de dabianju" (China and the great transformation of the modern world). In *Tsiang T'ing-fu xuanji* (Selected works of Tsiang T'ing-fu), 3:519–569. Reprint, Taipei: Book World Co.

Wang Jiapeng. 1990. "Gugong Yuhua ge tan yuan." *Gugong bowuyuan yuankan* 1:50–62.

Wang Zhichun. [1879] 1989. *Qingchao rouyuan ji* (Records of the Qing Court's cherishing men from afar). Reprint, Peking: Zhonghua Shuju Chuban.

Weizang tongzhi (Gazetteer of Tibet). 1937. Shanghai: Shengyu Yinshuguan.

Wenxian congbian (Reprints of writings offered up to the Qing Court). 1930–1937. Peking: Palace Museum.

Wuli tongkao (Comprehensive examination of the Five Kingly Rites). 1761. Qin Huitian.

Ye Fengmei. 1993. "Mage'erni shi tuan dui Zhong-Ying guanxi de yingxiang" (The effect of the Macartney embassy on Sino-British relations). Paper presented at the SMFBM.

Zhang gu congbian (Collected historical documents). 1928–1930. Peking: Palace Museum.

Zhang Jiqian. 1993. "Lishi de mihuo—Cong Mage'erni xunjue shituan fang hua kan shiba shiji de Zhong-Ying guanxi" (The puzzles of history—eighteenth-century Sino-British relations from the viewpoint of the Lord Macartney embassy). Paper presented at the SMFBM.

Zhu Jieqing. 1984. "Yingguo diyici shituan laihua de mudi he yaoqiu" (The purpose and demands of the first British embassy to China). In *Zhongwai guanxishi lunwenji* (Collected articles on the history of Sino-foreign relations), 548–562. Henan: Henan People's Press.

Zhu Yong. 1989. *Buyuan dakaide zhongguo damen* (China's closed-door policy). Nanchang: Jiangxi People's Press.

INDEX

Abdel-Malek, Anwar, 5
Adams, John, 75
Adams, John Quincy, 232–33
Agui, 36, 136, 164
Aisin Gioro, 32, 35 n.15, 36
Althusser, Louis, 3
Amherst embassy, 214–16, 228; Macart-
    ney embassy as precedent for, 214
Amiot, Joseph-Maria, 96, 112
Anderson, Aeneas, 105 n.16, 218 n.9
Annam: and Qing imperium, 32, 51, 198
Annual Register, 71 n.17, 218 n.9
appearances and reality, 18–19, 70–71;
    Macartney on, 59
Attiret, Jean-Denis, 69, 108
audience with emperor: analysis of,
    170–76, 212–13; Boxer Protocol and,
    228; lamas and, 44–48; Macartney
    and, 105–108; negotiations of 1873,
    227–28; at Rehe, 1–2. *See also* Guest
    Ritual

Backhouse, Edmund, 238
Baker, Keith, 63
Barthes, Roland, 3
Bartlett, Beatrice, 35–36, 43 n.37
Barrow, John, 104
Batavia, Dutch establishment in, 96
Bawden, Charles, 39
Bell, Catherine, 21
Belsey, Catherine, 6 n.10
Benjamin, Walter, 5
bestowals: at British audience, 1, 178;
    centering and, 150; Portuguese prece-
    dent and, 151–52; supreme lord-lesser
    lord relations and, 129–30. *See also*
    Qianlong emperor
Bland, J. O. P., 238

Bloch, Maurice, 21
Blue, Gregory, 72
Board of Astronomy, 151, 154 n.28
Board of Revenue, 139
Board of Rites, 139, 172; presentation of
    local products at, 172
Board of Works, 139
bodhisattva, emperor as, 40
Bonaparte, Napoleon, 27
Boxer Protocol, 228, 236
British embassy: as British precedent,
    229–32; Chinese assessments of in
    twentieth century, 239–44; critics of,
    218 n.9; division of, 147, 152; epigram
    and, 229; Grand Council assessment
    of, 209; knowledge produced by,
    200–202, 205, 218–20; post-Opium
    War assessments of, 229–31; Qian-
    long's assessment of, 184–85, 190–91;
    as Qing precedent, 213–15, 226–28;
    time constraints regarding, 144, 146.
    See also Macartney, George Lord
British empire, 221
Browne, Henry, 82, 103, 135
Burke, Edmond, 64, 71, 74, 107

Cannadine, David, 234
Carl, Catherine, 236
centering (*fengjian shi zhong*), 123;
    altering imperial bestowals and,
    164, 202; departure of British em-
    bassy and, 196; distinguished from
    British ceremony and business,
    223–24; greeting and, 155–58; treat-
    ment of guests and, 143, 185. *See also*
    bestowals
ceremony and business. *See* Macartney,
    George Lord

ceremony and diplomacy, 74–76, 75
n.19, 234–35; Adams, John on, 75;
denegration of, 234; Macartney
invested as ambassador, 82
Certeau, Michel de, 244
Chambers, William, 69, 108
Changchun (Eternal Spring) Garden,
32, 171
Changlin, 162, 182, 207; announces
emperor's invitation for another
embassy, 205; appointed governor-
general of Liangguang, 185; care of
British fleet at Ningbo and Chusan, 162; concessions to British, 207;
emperor's instructions to, 186; Ma
Yu affair and, 140–41; rewarded by
court, 141; tea plants and, 204. *See
also* Macartney, George Lord
cherishing men from afar (*huairou
yuanren*), xi, 46, 135, 147, 193, 209
China: in British imaginary, 68, 72–
74; feminization of, 73, 78; in French
imaginary, 68
China-centered history, 8, 20
Chinoiserie, 68–70; taste and, 68–69
classification (*shu*), 123; British embassy
as meritorious undertaking and, 140;
and squaring with (*fangwei*), 145 n.14
closed-door policy, 242–43
Cohen, Paul, 7–8, 240 n.2
Co-hong (*gonghang*). See *hang*
Comaroff, Jean, 20
Comprehensive Rites of the Great Qing,
16, 116, 173–74; and Amherst embassy,
214 n.5
Confucius, 68
Congress of Vienna, 235
Cook, James: voyages of, 60
Cox's Museum, 103 n.15
Cranmer-Byng, J. L., 146 n.17

curiosities, 85 n.3
Curtis, Lewis, 64

Dai, Yi, 199
Dalai Lama, 39, 43–45
D'Almeida, Joseph-Bernard, 97, 146 n.17
Daoguang emperor, 244
Der Ling, Princess, 236
despotism: Chinese, 79, 94–95
Dinwiddie, James, 104; on emperor's re-
action to British gifts, 110; tea plants
and, 204 n.11
diplomacy and trade. See trade
discourse, 6
Donghua lu, 232
Dundas, Henry, 57 n.1, 58, 80, 218
Durand, Pierre-Henri, 199 n.4
Dutch embassy of 1795, 213–14

Eagleton, Terry, 73
East India Company, 57–58, 82, 134. *See
also* Macartney, George Lord
embassies: Qing understanding of,
52–53
envoy (*qincha*), misapplied to Macartney, 157 n.29
epigram on Macartney embassy, 229,
231

Fairbank, John K., 9–12, 237
Fanglue guan. *See* Office of Military
Archives
Five Imperial Rites, 22
Fletcher, Joseph, 12
Foucault, Michel: and enunciative
function, 6
Four Treasuries of the Emperor's Library,
35
French Revolution, 112, 208 n.15
Fuchang'an, 101, 111, 197

Fukang'an, 109, 111, 113 n.18, 162, 197. *See also* Macartney, George Lord

Garden of Ten-thousand Trees (Wanshu yuan), 1, 167
gender: British masculinity, 71; China as feminine, 78, 79; Chinese emperor as masculine, 78; public sphere, 64
gentlemen, 64–65
Gentleman's Magazine, 64, 218 n.9
George III, 1; letter to Qianlong emperor 59, 60–62; portrait of displayed by Macartney, 99
gifts for Qianlong emperor, 77–78, 92, 135; correlation with human attributes, 149–50; division of, 150–51; displayed at Yuanming Gardens, 104–105, 110, 152–54; distinguished from trade items, 77–79, 102; emperor's reported reaction to, 110; list of, 91, 135, 147–48; list of Macartney's retinue and, 144; looted in 1860, 225; Macartney shown ones similar to British gifts, 179; Qing court reaction to, 102. *See also* Qianlong emperor
Gillan, Hugh, 87
gonghang. See hang
Gower, Erasmus, 83, 111, 161, 163 n.35
grace, of the emperor (*en*), 47, 127, 162
Grammont, Jean-Joseph de, 96–97
Gramsci, Antonio, 5, 27
Grand Council (*Junji chu*), 35–36, 209; and announcement phase of embassy, 136; assessment of Macartney's requests, 181–82; bestowal and, 151
Grand Sacrifice, 18, 124
Great Transition, 7
Great Unity (*datong*), 32 n.8
Great Wall, 87–88
Grupper, Samuel, 40

Guang Hui, 227
guest, definitions of, 117
Guest Ritual (*Binli*): alteration of audience procedure, 168–69; announcement phase, 134–38; audience for British, 175–76; audience protocol for British, 163; defined, 118–21; departure ceremonies, 192–93, 197; feasts and, 179; and higher order rites, 116, 121–22, 124; human agency and, 216–17; imperial bestowal and, 129; local products and, 119, 121, 172; lordship or rulership and, 31, 125–30; and lower order rites, 118 n.5; one of five imperial rites, 22–23; precedents and, 139, 213; preparation phase of, 138–40, 165–67; sequence of, 132–33; West Ocean precedents and, 170–72
Guo Shixun, 135–37, 141–42, 207
Guo, Yunjing, 243–44
Gurkha Wars, 31, 113

Habermas, Jürgen, 3, 63 n.10
Hall, Stuart, 3
hang, 53–54, 193–96
Hansen, Valerie, 22 n.38
Haraway, Donna, 27
Hay, John, 21–22, 122 n.14
hegemony, 25–26
Heshen, 136 n.4, 141, 179, 190, 192, 197; announcement of embassy and, 136; audience for British and, 106. *See also* Macartney, George Lord
hierarchy, 24; contrast between Qing and British views of, 221–24; Qing imperial ritual and, 128–30; Qing notion of submission and, 48
Hindess, Barry, 3
Hirst, Paul, 3, 16 n.28
Hocart, A. M., 117 n.3

hong. See *hang*

Hongli. *See* Qianlong emperor

Hsü, Immanuel, 143 n.12

Hume, David, 71 n.17, 72; on British and Chinese national character, 66–67

Hung Taiji, 32, 41, 177

Hunt, Michael, 12

Hu Sheng, 241

imperial formations, 25; Qing and British empires as, 25–28. *See also* Qing imperium

Imperial Household Department (*Neiwufu*), 33 n.11, 36; criticized by emperor, 160–62

imperialism and colonialism, 2–7, 13 n.24; British in nineteenth century, 221

Inden, Ronald, 6 n.11, 25 n.41

instruction (*shangyu*), 36 n.19, 138

interdomainal relations, 27–28

international relations, 27–28

Irwin, Eyles, 82

Izmaylov, Leon (Russian envoy), 171 n.5

Jackson, William, 82

Jebtsundamba Khutukhtu, 39, 45–46

Jiangnan, 33–34, 34 n.12

Jiaqing emperor, 214–16, 226–27

Jin Jian, 94 n.10, 104, 150, 152–53, 160–62, 163 n.33

Jiqing, 137 n.5, 139, 141, 147 n.19, 151 n.25

Johnson, Samuel, 69, 71, 106–107; on ideal observer, 85

Johnston Reginald, 236

Jones, William, 64; and China, 71–72

Junji chu. See Grand Council

Kangxi emperor, 32, 45, 171, 199 n.6, 206

Kant, Immanuel, 78

Keshi'na, 140–41

Korea and Qing imperium, 50

koutou (kowtow), 1, 175, 221; Adams, John Quincy on, 233; as fetish, 232; as object of struggle, 232–237; Qianlong on, 157–58; as three kneelings and nine bows (*sangui jiukou*), 45, 158

lama-patron relations, 38–39; supreme lord-lesser lord relations and, 47–49

Latour, Bruno, 27, 246

Lattimore, Owen, 31 n.6

Law of Nations, 24–25, 74–75, 235

Lcang-skya Khutukhtu, 41–42

lesser lord (*fanwang*): attributes of, 126, 137; Guest Ritual and, 117, 125–28; sincerity of, 126

Liang Kentang, 106, 137 n.5, 140–43, 198; responsibilities in Guest Ritual, 144. *See also* Macartney, George Lord

Lifan yuan. See Ministry of Outer Dependencies

Ligdan Khan, 37 n.20

limited contact policy, 241

Literary Club, 64–65, 67; as intellectual aristocracy, 65; Macartney and, 64

Liuqiu and Qing imperium, 51

local products (*fangwu*), 44, 119, 172, 211; as offering, 128. *See also* tribute

Louis XIV, 199

Macartney, George Lord: Amiot interview, 112; arrives in China, 84; audience negotiations, 97–102; audience with Qianlong emperor and, 1–2, 105–108, 175–76, 221–24; British national character and, 58, 207; on Buddhism and Roman Catholicism, 108; business phase of embassy and, 108–14, 181–84, 197–209; career of, 26; on ceremony and business, 59,

91; Changlin and, 203–207; China, views on, 58, 58 n.4, 59; on Chinese behavior toward visitors, 92, 94; on Chinese character, 92–94, 93 n.9, 99; on Chinese ceremony as tricks of behavior, 221; on Chinese despotism, 79, 94–95; concessions on trade and, 207; confusion over treatment by Qing court, 114; as cousin of King George, 76; distinguishes allies and enemies, 93–94, 96–97; East India Company report, 208–209; embassy, assessment of, 112–13, 205, 206–209; embassy, epigram on, 229, 231; fleet to Chusan and, 91; Fukang'an and, 109, 113; genuflections and prostrations, 79–80 (*See also* koutou); gift list, 147; gifts for Qianlong emperor, *see* gifts for Qianlong emperor; Great Wall and, 87–88; Heshen and, 100–101, 109–11, 164, 179; on immutable laws of China, 102; invested as British ambassador, 82; Literary Club and, 64; Liang Kentang and, 91–92, 164; library of, 59 n.4; meeting with court officials in Yuanming Gardens, 111, 190; military strength of Qing assessed by, 112–13, 201–202; missionaries and embassy, 96–97, 112; naturalist's gaze and, 84–90, 95–96; observations on Qing officials, 91, 93–94; oriental customs and ideas and, 59, 106; as pedagogue, 103, 206; planning of embassy and, 58–59; portraits of British King and Queen displayed by, 99; proclamation to embassy, 83; Qianlong emperor and, 105–107, 109; on Qing military capabilities, 200–202; rank of Qing officials and, 90–91; reaction to European mechanical devices at

Rehe, 90–91; requests of Qing court, 109, 181, 193; requests to Changlin, 203; 1795 communication to Qing court and, 218–20; Songyun and, 108, 114, 197–202; strategies for approaching Qing court, 76–80; styles emperor King Solomon, 107; styles emperor Nebuchadnezzer, 108; on Tartars, 92, 207; tea plants and, 204; *Tianjin Gazette* and, 90; Zhengrui and, 92–93, 95, 98–101, 109

Mackintosh, William, 83, 109, 181
Mancall, Mark, 18
Marshall, Peter, 220
Martin, Dan, 38
masculinity, 73–74
Ma Yu incident, 140–42
Meadows, Thomas, 228
meritorious undertaking (*haoshi*), 140, 142, 162, 166
Mill, James, 13 n.24
Millward, James, 31 n.6
Ministry of Outer Dependencies (*Lifan yuan*), 34
Mongol lords: Qing imperium and, 31–32; as rivals of Qing emperors, 38–39; rotational attendance and, 37
Montesquieu, Charles, 66
morals and manners, 66–67
More, Thomas, 68
Mountain Retreat for Avoiding Summer Heat at Rehe (Bishu shanz huang), 1
multitude of lords, 30
Muteng'e, 137 n.5, 139, 151 n.24

Napier, Lord, 230
Naquin, Susan, 22 n.38
national character, 58, 66–68
naturalist's gaze, 84–86
Nurhaci, 32, 41, 177

ocular faculties, 5
Office of Banqueting (*Guanglu si*), 139
Office of Guest Ceremony (*Honglu si*),
    139, 171–72
Office of Military Archives (*Fanglue
    guan*), 36
orientalism, 5–7, 18, 19–20

palace memorials, vermilion rescripted
    (*zhupi zoushe*), 36; contrasted to
    other forms of communication, 36
    n.19
Panchen Lama, 46–47
Parish, Henry, 87–88
Parker, E. H., 232, 238
Parsons, Talcott, 11 n.20
patterning discourse, 122, 217, 248;
    rulership and, 122
Pavilion of Purple Brightness (*Zeguang
    ge*), 44 n.38
Peyrefitte, Alain, 57 n.1, 242
Pileng, 113 n.18
poem, by Qianlong emperor on em-
    bassy, 177–78; on tapestry, 177 n.13
Poirot, Louis de, 96–97
Polachek, James, 12
Portuguese precedent. *See* precedents
postcolonial criticism, 2–7
precedents: Portuguese, 139, 144, 151,
    164, 170–71, 213; West Ocean, 171–72
Pritchard, E. H., 236–37, 241
Proctor, Captain, 140–42
Pronouncements on Lamas (*Lama
    shuo*), 38
protocols of rites (*lijie*), 132, 155
public sphere, 60, 62–63; Macartney
    and, 97–102; naturalist's gaze and, 85

Qianlong emperor (Hongli): audience
    with Lord Macartney, 1–2, 105–108,
    175–76, 221–24; bestowals to British,

178, 200 n.7; on British gifts, 149, 188;
    as cakravartin king, 30; on centering,
    143, 155, 185; classification of embassy,
    140; Guest Ritual, evaluation of, 185;
    on *hangs*, 193–96; initial response
    to embassy, 136–38; instructions to
    George III, *see* Qianlong letter to
    George III; instructions to officials
    on treatment of British, 138, 143,
    185–86, 205; intervention in ritual
    process, 162, 216–17; Macartney,
    evaluation of, 159, 163–64, 170, 186,
    190, 197; on Macartney's six requests,
    193–97; as Mañjuśrī, 39; poem on
    embassy, 177–78; reprimands offi-
    cials, 140–41, 160–62; on resident
    ministers, *see* resident minister issue;
    rewards officials, 141; Tibetan Bud-
    dhism and, 38, 40–42, 48; titles and,
    30; on Zhengrui and Macartney, 145
    n.15, 146 n.16, 154, 156–57
Qianlong letter to George III, 187–89;
    history of, 238–39
Qiao Renjie, 90–91, 97–101, 105, 111, 147,
    198
Qing imperium: extent of, 29, 37; geo-
    political strategies of in China and
    Inner Asia, 31–36; knowledge of
    England, 113 n.18; observations on,
    247; palace building and, 32; Tibetan
    Buddhism and, 38–42

Raux, Nicolas, 96–97
Rawski, Evelyn, 31 n.6
reciprocal advantages, 62, 74, 102
Rehe, 1–2, 32; other events during
    British embassy, 249–51
Reiss, Timothy, 122 n.14
representationalism, 4–5, 211
resident minister issue, 61, 184–85, 187,
    189

rites controversy, 199 n.6
Rites of Zhou, 118–19
ritual: as artifice, 221; and bodily practice and, 45–47, 221, 223–24; and
centering, 123, 212–13; and classification, 123; and editing, 213 n.2;
functionalism and, 17; as historical
action, 130–33; and hierarchy, 24; and
homology, 22, 24; and lordship, 122;
and Macartney, 221; metaphysics of
Qing rites, 121–25; and microcosm-
macrocosm relations, 22; and Orientalism, 17–18; and patterning
discourse, 122; and Qing sovereignty,
217; and representation, 221; and
symbolism, 17; and synecdoche, 22–
24; theories of, 15–16; and Tibetan
initiations, 41; and transformation,
126, 137
Royal Sovereign (model of), 78, 211
rulership. *See* Guest Ritual: lordship or
rulership and
Russell, Bertrand, 238

Said, Edward, 5–7; critique of, 5 n.9
Secret and Superintending Committee,
82, 134–35
1795 communication to Qing court,
218–20
Shengzhu, 135
Shenyang (Mukden), 32
Shore, John, 208 n.15
Shunzhi emperor, 43–44, 213 n.2
sincerity (*cheng*), 48, 138; and Guest
Ritual, 160, 170; of facing toward
transformation (*xiang hua zhi
cheng*), 126, 137, 145
Skinner, G. William, 8
Snellgrove, David, 40
sociocultural theory, 7–8
Songyun: appointed envoy, 197; re-

port on Macartney, 203. *See also*
Macartney, George Lord
Southeast Asian kingdoms: and Qing
imperium, 50–52
sovereignty, 74–75; British notions of,
74–76, 74 n.18; ceremony and, 75–76;
and European diplomatic practices,
233; and Qing rulership, 123–24, 170,
217
Stallybrass, Peter, 63, 73, 234
Staunton, George L., 62, 87 n.5, 91, 205
n.12; on audience with Qianlong
emperor, 168; on cause of Chinese
attitudes towards British, 76; on
Chinese tea, 72; gifts for Qianlong
emperor and, 77; Heshen, meeting
with, 100; proposed to lead second
embassy, 218
Staunton, George T., 99, 168 n.2, 178,
214 n.5, 227 n.1
Suleng'e, 207, 215 n.7, 227
supreme lord-lesser lord relations,
32, 120–21; as superior and inferior
relations, 123–25

Tartars. *See* Macartney, George Lord
taste, 69–70; as value of the gentleman,
64
Taussig, Michael, 21, 27
Thomas, Nicholas, 85 n.3
Thompson, E. P., 3
Tianjin: ceremony at, 155–60, 164
Tibet, 198; British and, 93, 113
Tibetan Buddhism: Sa-skya-pa sect, 38,
41; Yellow (dGe-lugs-pa) Sect, 39, 41,
48
trade: British with China, 57–58; diplomacy and, 59, 80–82; as imperial
bestowal, 53–54; nations and, 80;
nature and, 80; as obligation of
nations, 80 n.25; Qianlong emperor

trade (*continued*)
    on, 193–95; Qing management of, 49;
    sovereign and, 61, 80–81
tradition and modernity, 2, 7 n.13;
    Sino-Western conflict as clash of, 240
tribute (*gong*), 9; local products, 121; as
    offering, 128; as precious things, 118.
    See also gifts for Qianlong emperor
tribute system, 9–15, 238–39, 240; and
    appearances, 14, 18; dualism of, 14;
    and Macartney, 11; and symbolism,
    17
Tsiang, T'ing-fu, 239–40
Turks, 199

usages (customs or habits) and national
    character, 66

Vattel, Emmerich de, 75, 80
Vietnam. *See* Annam
virtue (*de*), 119

Wade, Thomas, 227–28
Waley, Arthur, 119
Wang, Wenxiong, 90–91, 97–101, 105,
    111, 147, 198
Wang Zhichun, 227
West Ocean kingdoms (Europe), 52–55

White, Allon. *See* Stallybrass, Peter
Whitehead, William, 70
Williams, Raymond, 3
Williams, S. Wells, 229
Wills, John E., 13–14, 18, 169 n.3
Wooley, Penny. *See* Hirst, Paul

Yiling'a, 150, 152–53, 160–62
Yongzheng emperor, 171, 199 n.6
Yuanming (Encompassing Illumina-
    tion) Garden, 32, 104–105, 111, 151–54,
    177 n.13, 190; looted by British in
    1860, 225

Zhang Shunhong, 241–42
Zhengrui, 92; appointed imperial envoy
    (*qincha*), 139; audience negotiations
    and, 98–102; and British gifts, 92;
    relieved of duties, 197; reports British
    practicing koutou, 159; reprimanded
    by emperor, 161–62; responsibilities
    in Guest Ritual, 139, 141, 142. *See also*
    Macartney, George Lord
Zhu, Jieqing, 241
Zhu, Yong, 241–42
zhupi zouzhe. *See* palace memorials
Zito, Angela, 23–24
Zongli Yamen, 227

James L. Hevia is Assistant Professor of History at North
Carolina A & T University. He is Associate Editor of
positions: east asia cultures critique.

Library of Congress Cataloging-in-Publication Data
Hevia, James Louis
    Cherishing men from afar : Qing guest ritual and the Macartney
Embassy of 1793 / James L. Hevia.
        p.   cm.
    Includes bibliographical references and index.
    ISBN 0-8223-1625-0.   ISBN 0-8223-1637-4 (pbk.)
    1. China — Foreign relations — Great Britain.   2. Great Britain —
Foreign relations — China.   3. China — Foreign relations — 1644-
1912.   4. Diplomatic etiquette — China.   5. Macartney, George
Macartney, Earl, 1737–1806.   I. Title.
DS740.5.G5H48   1995
327.51041'09'033 — dc20
                                                        94-43610
                                                          CIP